ATOM
THE BEGINNING

STONEBOT
MANGA

TITAN
MANGA

ATOM
THE BEGINNING
アトム　ザ・ビギニング
04
七番目の使者

STONEBOT COMICS
GROUP EDITOR / Matias Timarchi / MANAGING DIRECTOR & ACQUISITIONS / Diego Barassi / EDITOR IN CHIEF / Martín Casanova
EDITOR / Chris Ortega / ASSISTANT EDITOR / Matías Mir / DIGITAL MANAGER / Rodrigo Molina

TITAN COMICS
ASSISTANT EDITOR / Calum Collins / GROUP EDITOR / Jake Devine / EDITOR / Phoebe Hedges
SENIOR CREATIVE EDITOR / David Manley-Leach / DESIGNER / David Colderley / ART DIRECTOR / Oz Browne
PRODUCTION CONTROLLERS / Caterina Falqui & Kelly Fenlon / PRODUCTION MANAGER / Jackie Flook
SALES & CIRCULATION MANAGER / Steve Tothill / MARKETING COORDINATOR / Lauren Noding
PUBLICITY & SALES COORDINATOR / Alexandra Iciek / PUBLICITY MANAGER / Will O'Mullane
DIGITAL & MARKETING MANAGER / Jo Teather / HEAD OF RIGHTS / Jenny Boyce
ACQUISITIONS EDITOR / Duncan Baizley / PUBLISHING DIRECTOR / Ricky Claydon
PUBLISHING DIRECTOR / John Dziewiatkowski / GROUP OPERATIONS DIRECTOR / Alex Ruthen
EXECUTIVE VICE PRESIDENT / Andrew Sumner / PUBLISHERS / Vivian Cheung & Nick Landau

ATOM THE BEGINNING 04
©TEZUKA PRODUCTIONS, MASAMI YUUKI,
TETSURO KASAHARA, 2016
First published in Japan in 2016 by HERO'S Inc.
English translation rights arranged with HERO'S Inc.
through Tuttle-Mori Agency, Inc, Tokyo
Licensed by All Kind Bot LLC

This translation first published in 2023 by Titan Comics, a division of Titan Publishing Group, Ltd,
144 Southwark Street, London SE1 0UP, UK.
Titan Comics is a registered trademark of Titan Publishing Group Ltd.

10 9 8 7 6 5 4 3 2 1

First edition: April 2023
Printed in the UK
ISBN: 9781787740013

A CIP catalogue record for this title is available from the British Library.

ATOM
THE BEGINNING
04

ORIGINAL STORY: OSAMU TEZUKA
CONCEPT: MASAMI YUUKI
ART: TETSURO KASAHARA

SUPERVISION: **MACOTO TEZKA**
IN COLLABORATION WITH: **TEZUKA PRODUCTIONS**

TRANSLATION: **JONATHAN CLEMENTS AND MOTOKO TAMAMURO**
LETTERING: **JONATHAN STEVENSON**

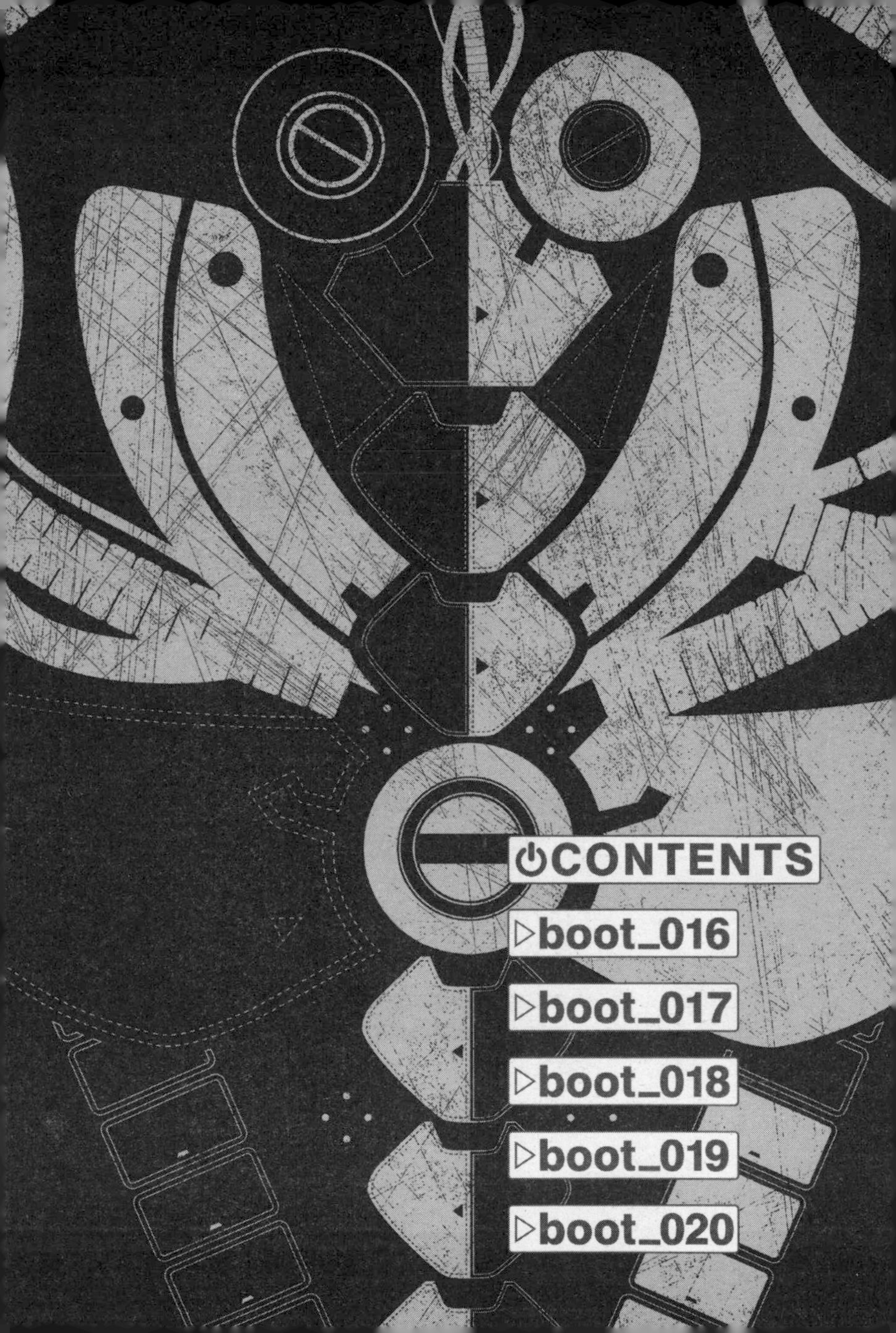

CONTENTS

▷boot 016

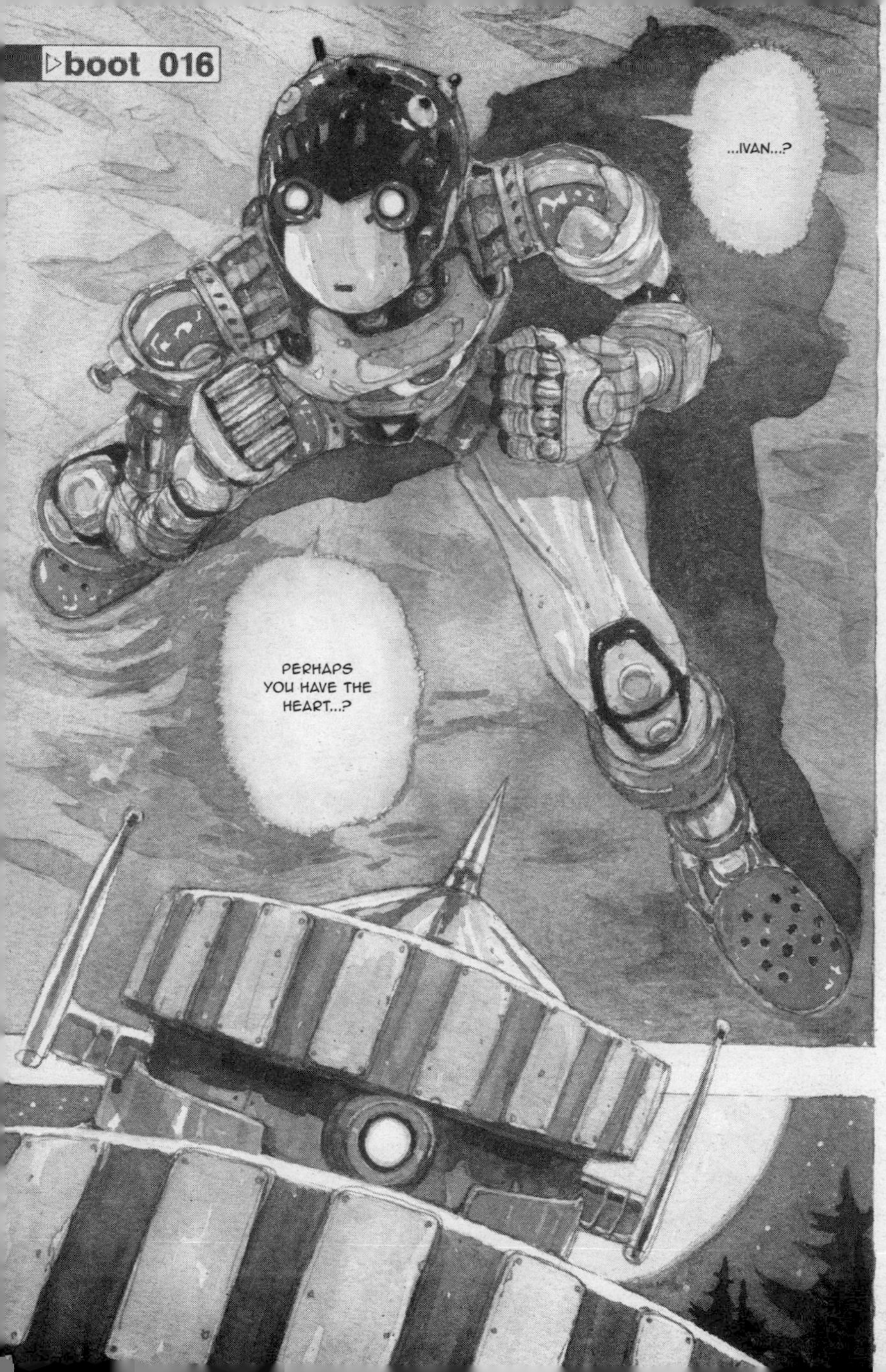
...IVAN...?
PERHAPS YOU HAVE THE HEART...?

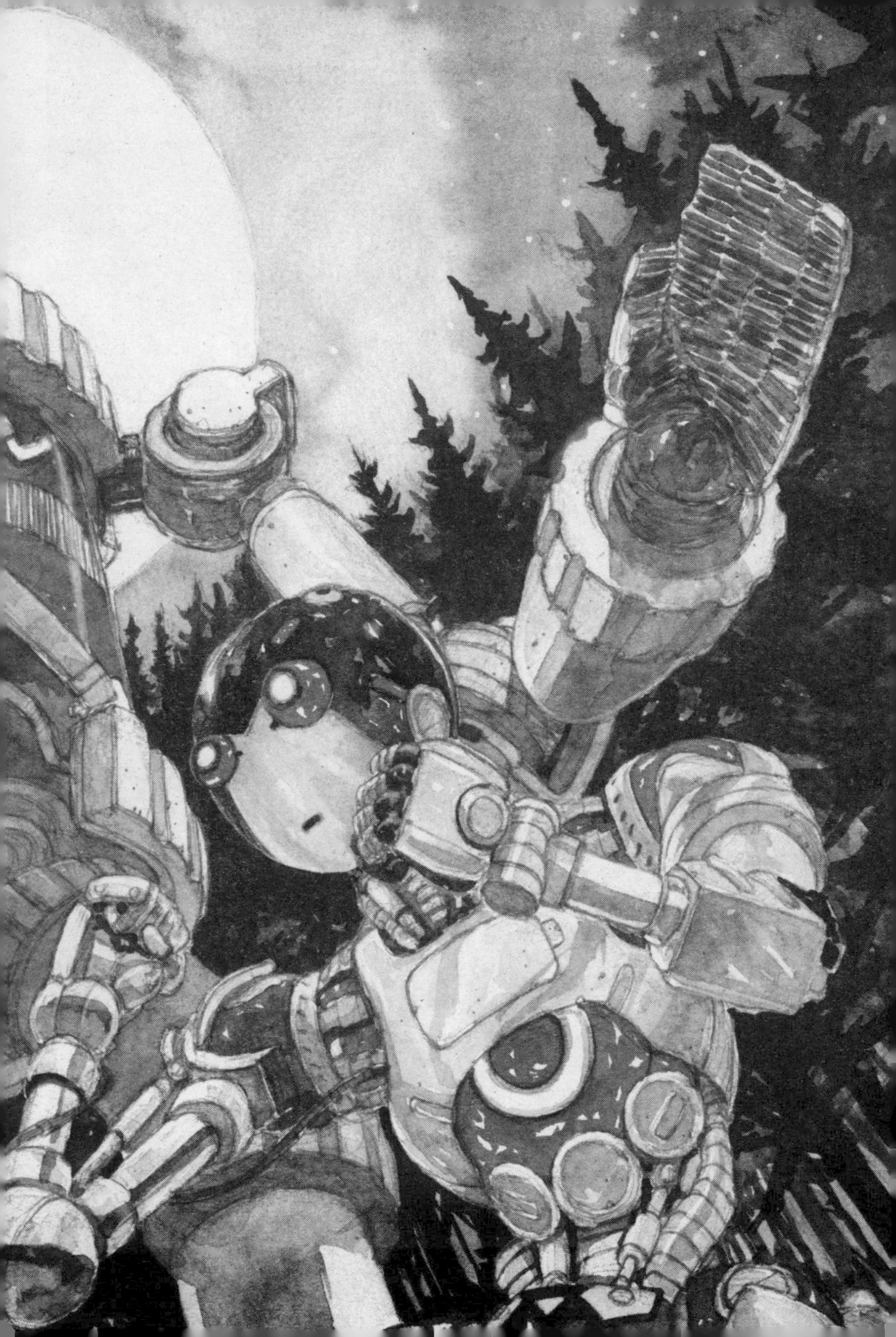

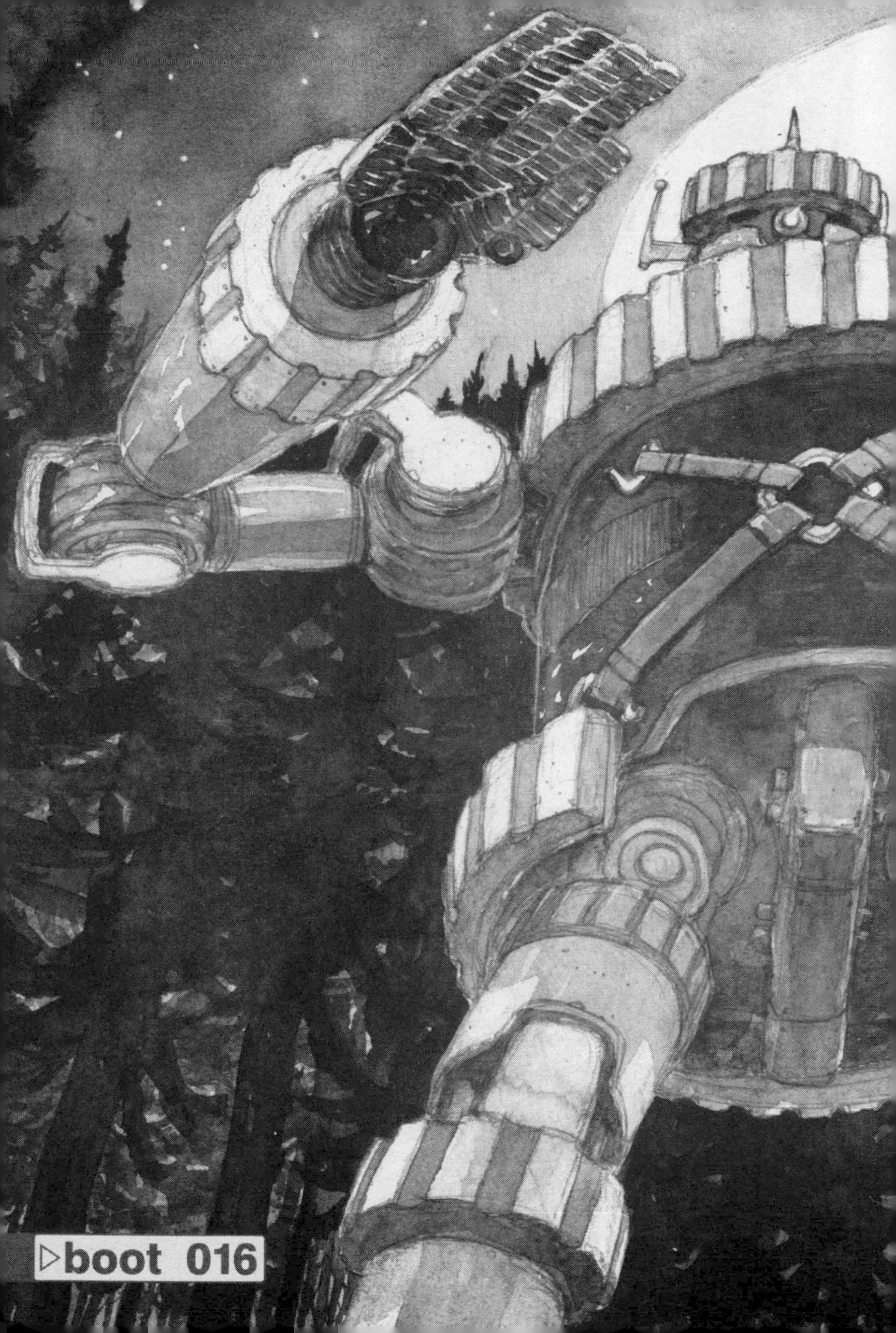
boot 016

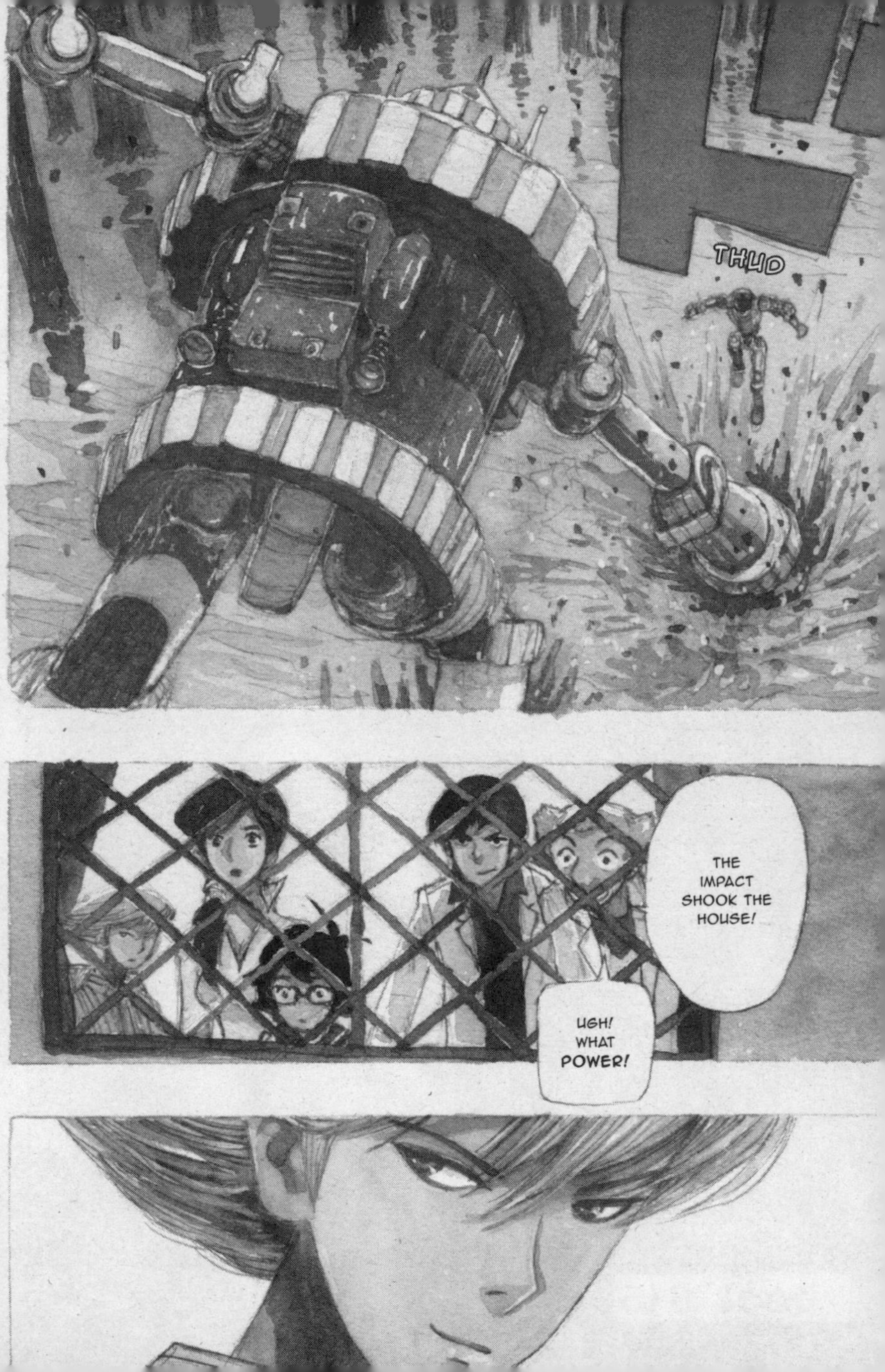
THUD
THE IMPACT SHOOK THE HOUSE!
UGH! WHAT POWER!

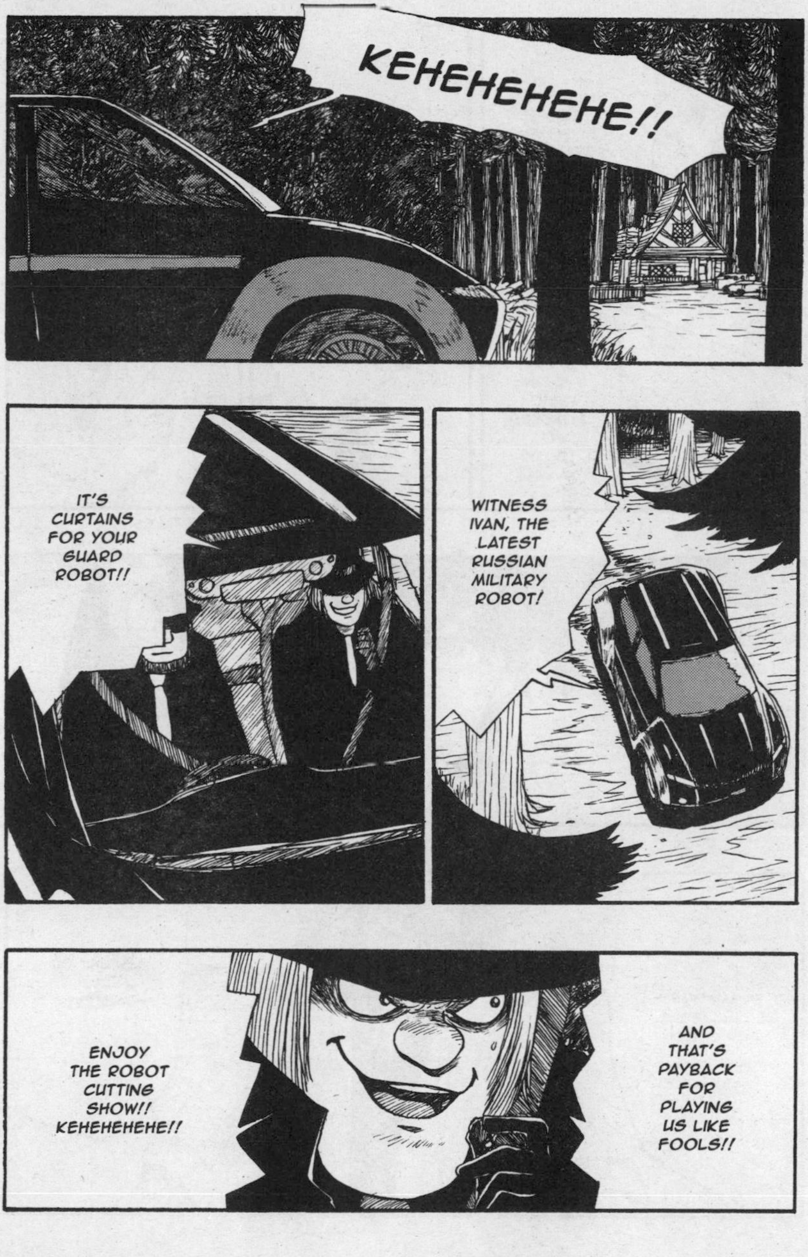
KEHEHEHEHEHE!!
WITNESS IVAN, THE LATEST RUSSIAN MILITARY ROBOT!
IT'S CURTAINS FOR YOUR GUARD ROBOT!!
AND THAT'S PAYBACK FOR PLAYING US LIKE FOOLS!!
ENJOY THE ROBOT CUTTING SHOW!! KEHEHEHEHE!!

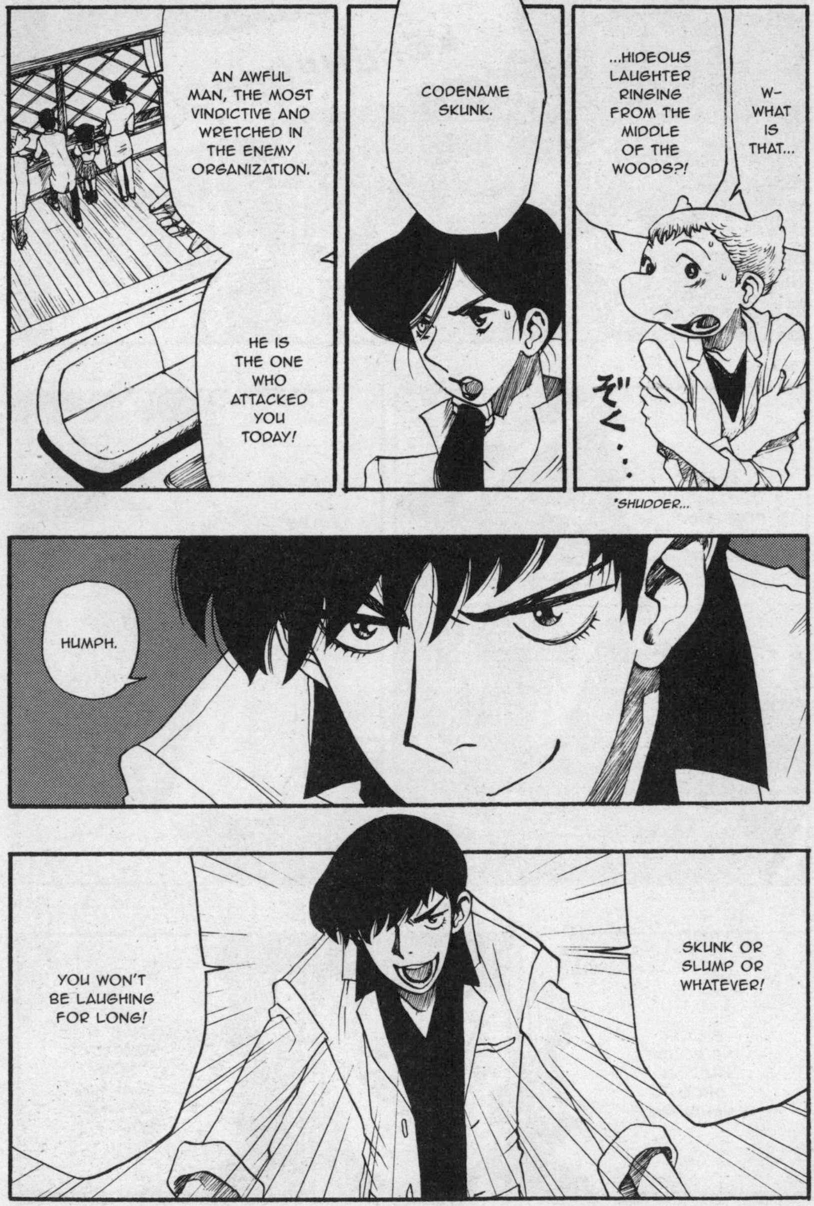
W-WHAT IS THAT...
...HIDEOUS LAUGHTER RINGING FROM THE MIDDLE OF THE WOODS?!
ぞく...
*SHUDDER...
CODENAME SKUNK.
AN AWFUL MAN, THE MOST VINDICTIVE AND WRETCHED IN THE ENEMY ORGANIZATION.
HE IS THE ONE WHO ATTACKED YOU TODAY!
HUMPH.
SKUNK OR SLUMP OR WHATEVER!
YOU WON'T BE LAUGHING FOR LONG!

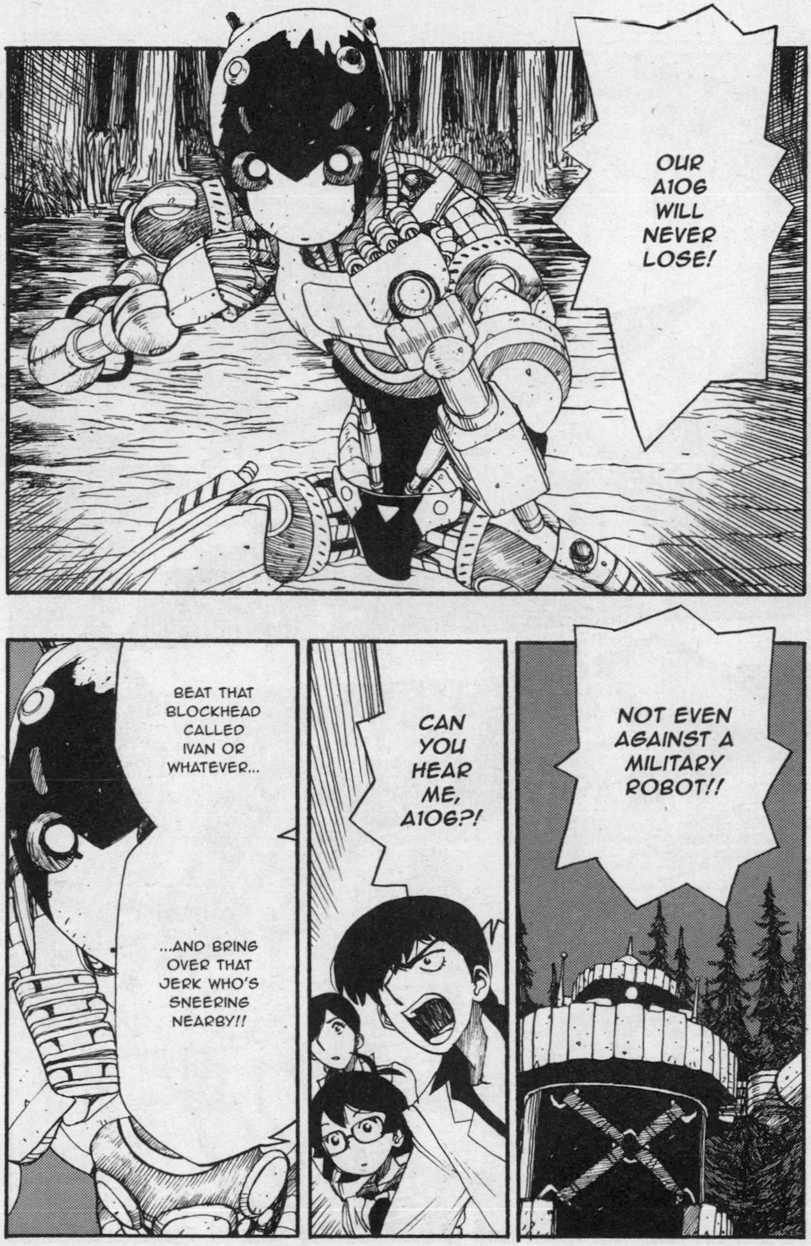
OUR A106 WILL NEVER LOSE!
NOT EVEN AGAINST A MILITARY ROBOT!!
CAN YOU HEAR ME, A106?!
BEAT THAT BLOCKHEAD CALLED IVAN OR WHATEVER...
...AND BRING OVER THAT JERK WHO'S SNEERING NEARBY!!

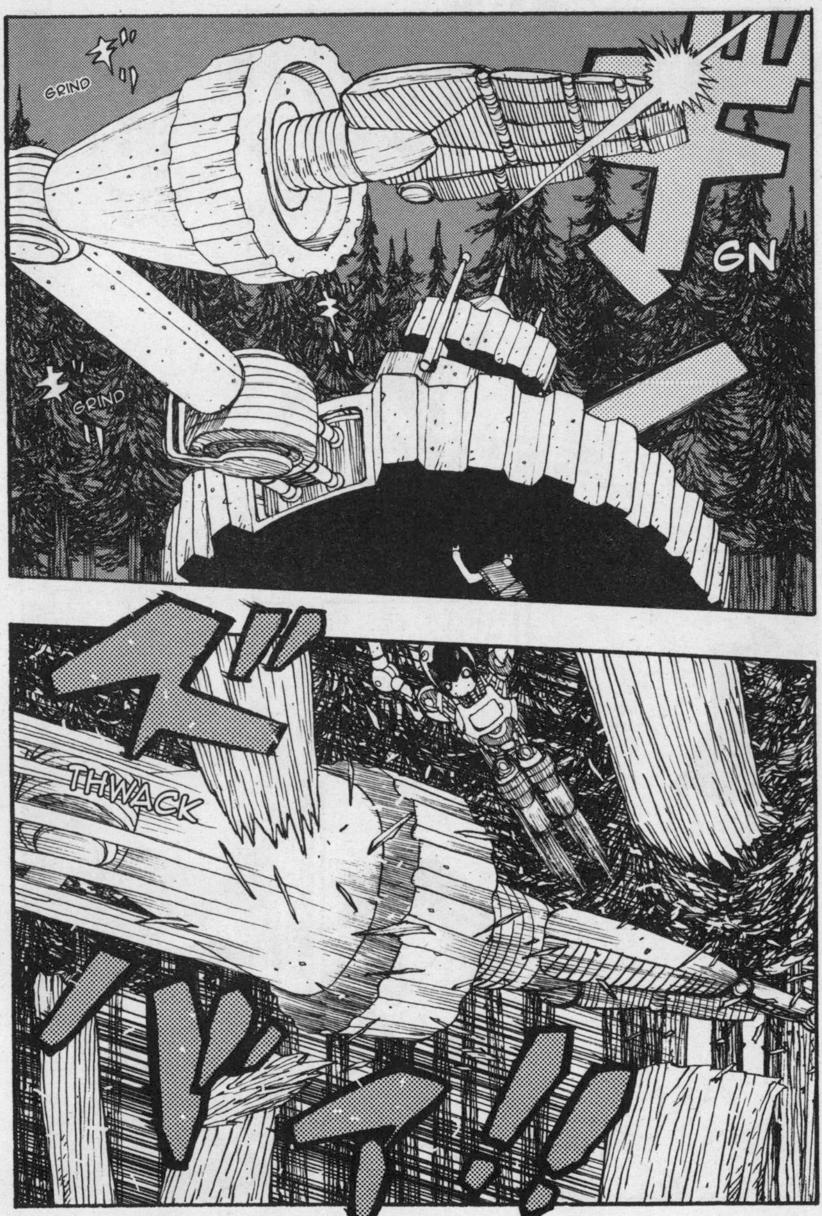
GN
GRIND
GRIND
THWACK

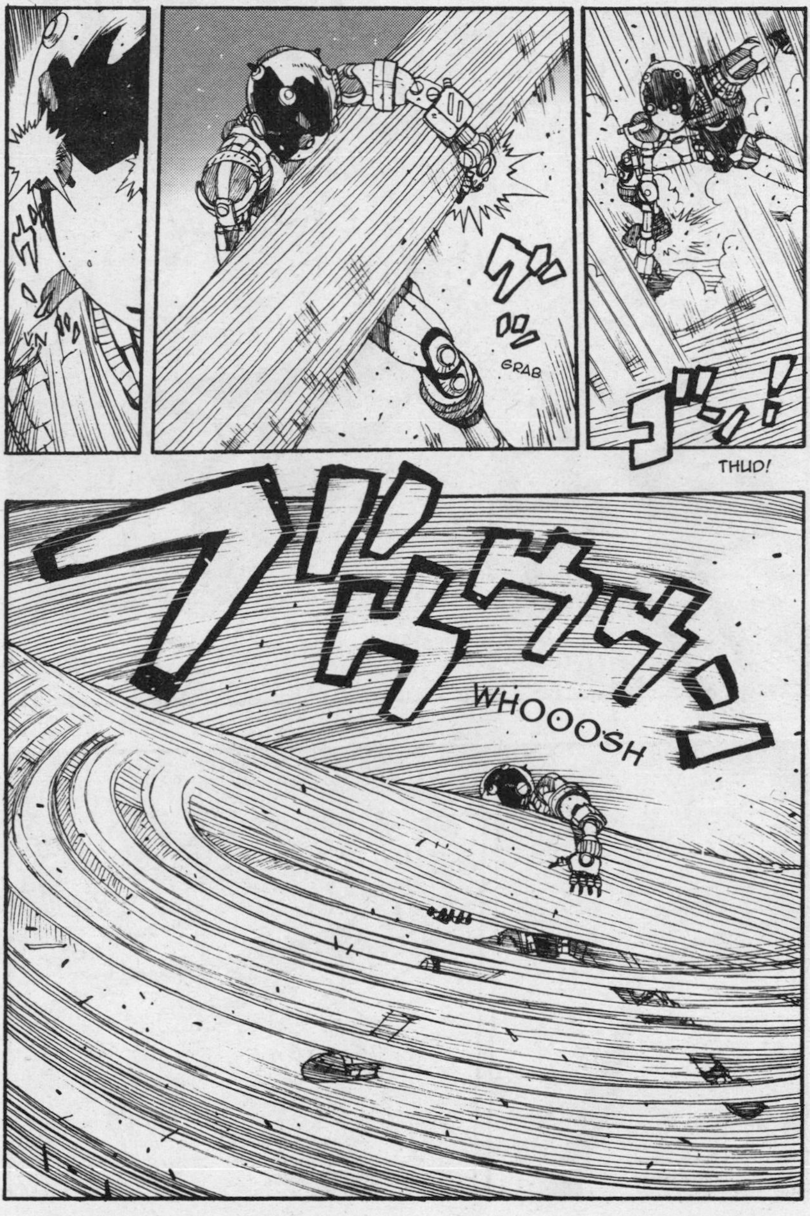
THUD!
GRAB
WHOOOSH

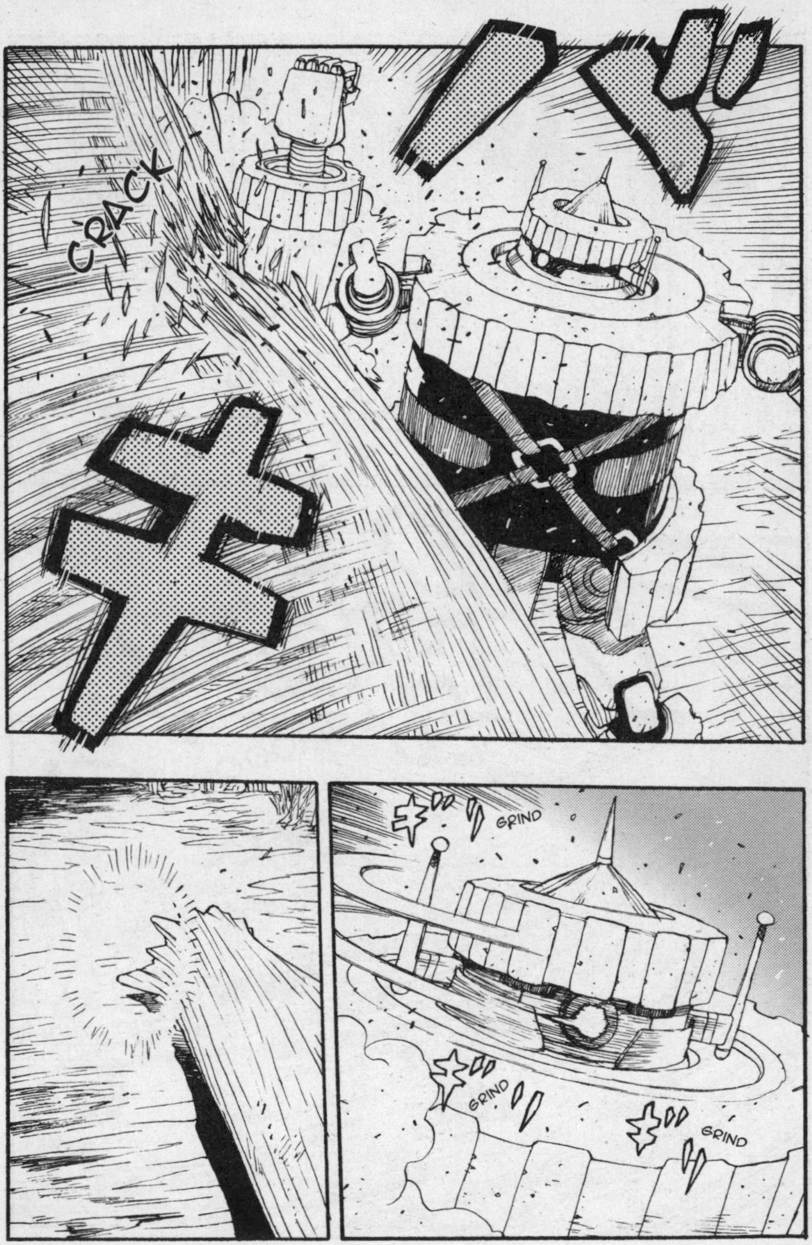
CRACK
GRIND
GRIND
GRIND

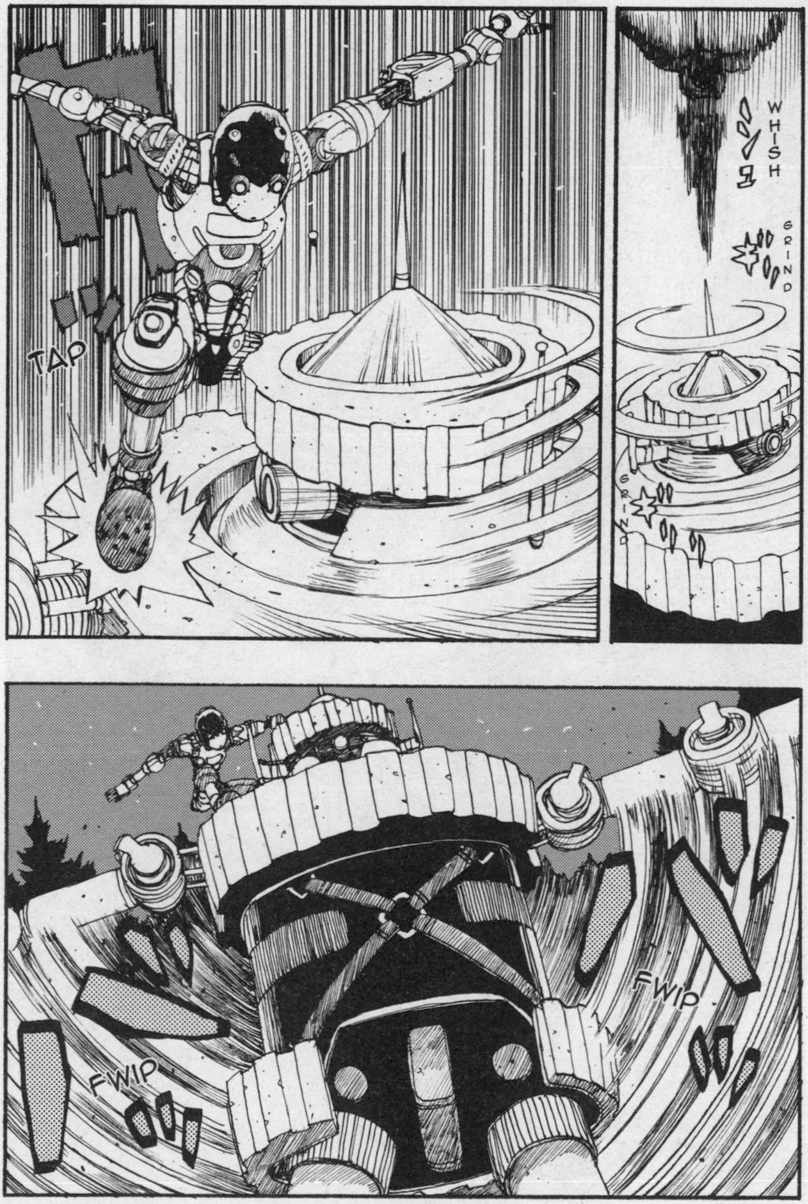
WHISH
GRIND
GRIND
TAP
FWIP
FWIP

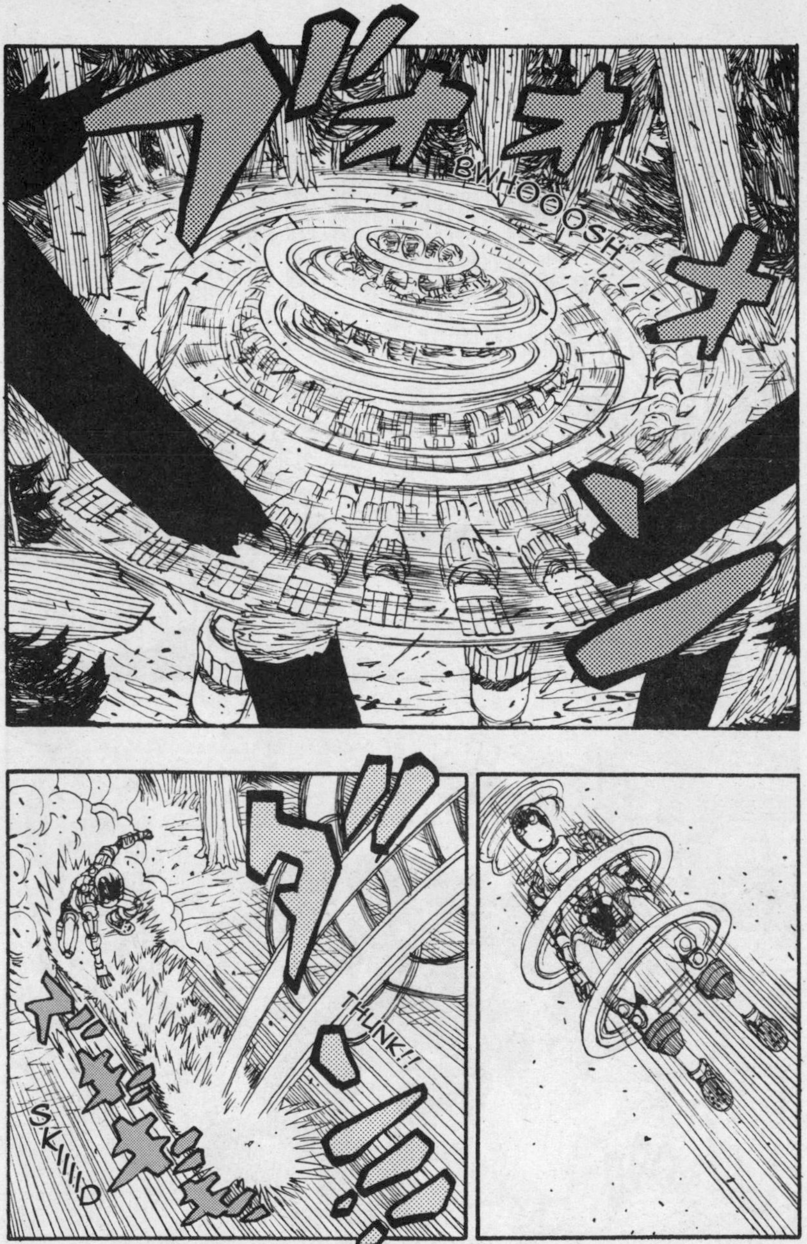
BWHOOOOSH
THUNK!!
SKIIIIID

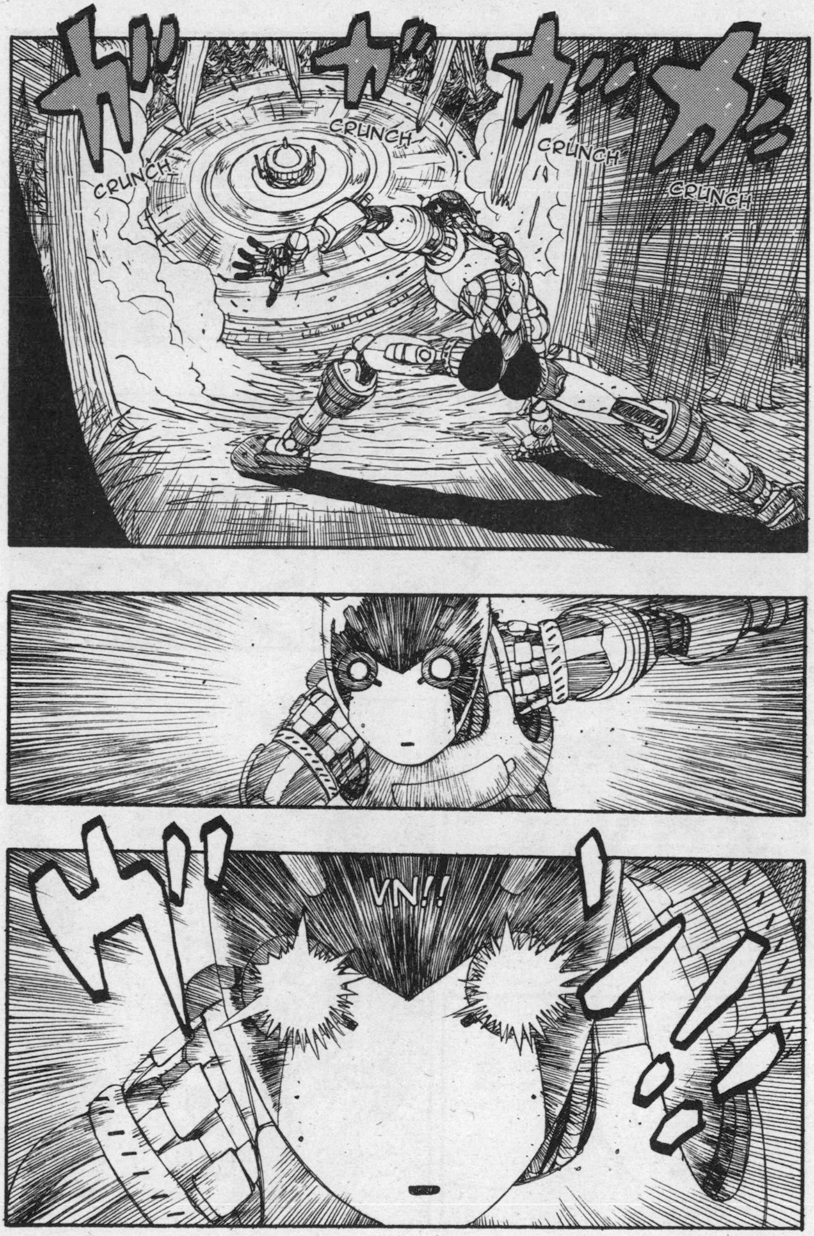
CRUNCH
CRUNCH
CRUNCH
CRUNCH
VN!!

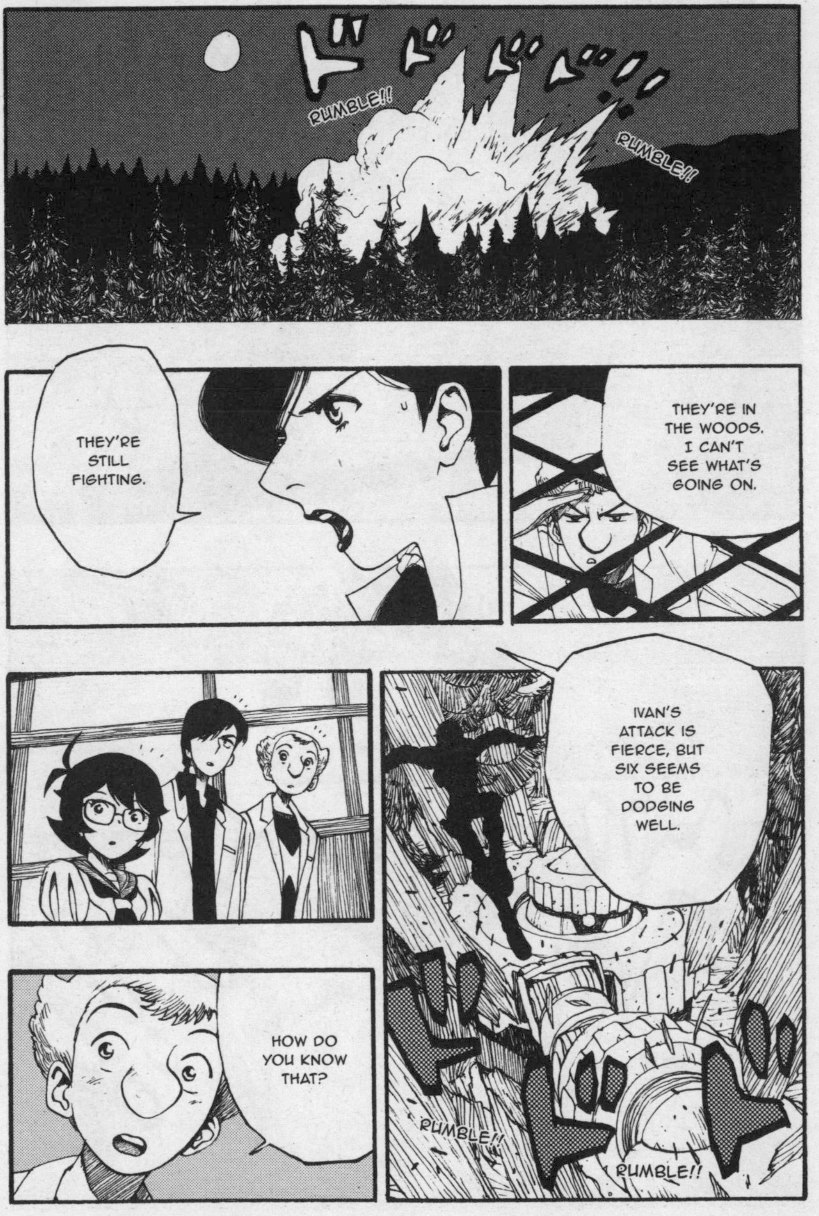
ドドドド
RUMBLE!!
RUMBLE!!
THEY'RE IN THE WOODS. I CAN'T SEE WHAT'S GOING ON.
THEY'RE STILL FIGHTING.
IVAN'S ATTACK IS FIERCE, BUT SIX SEEMS TO BE DODGING WELL.
RUMBLE!!
RUMBLE!!
HOW DO YOU KNOW THAT?

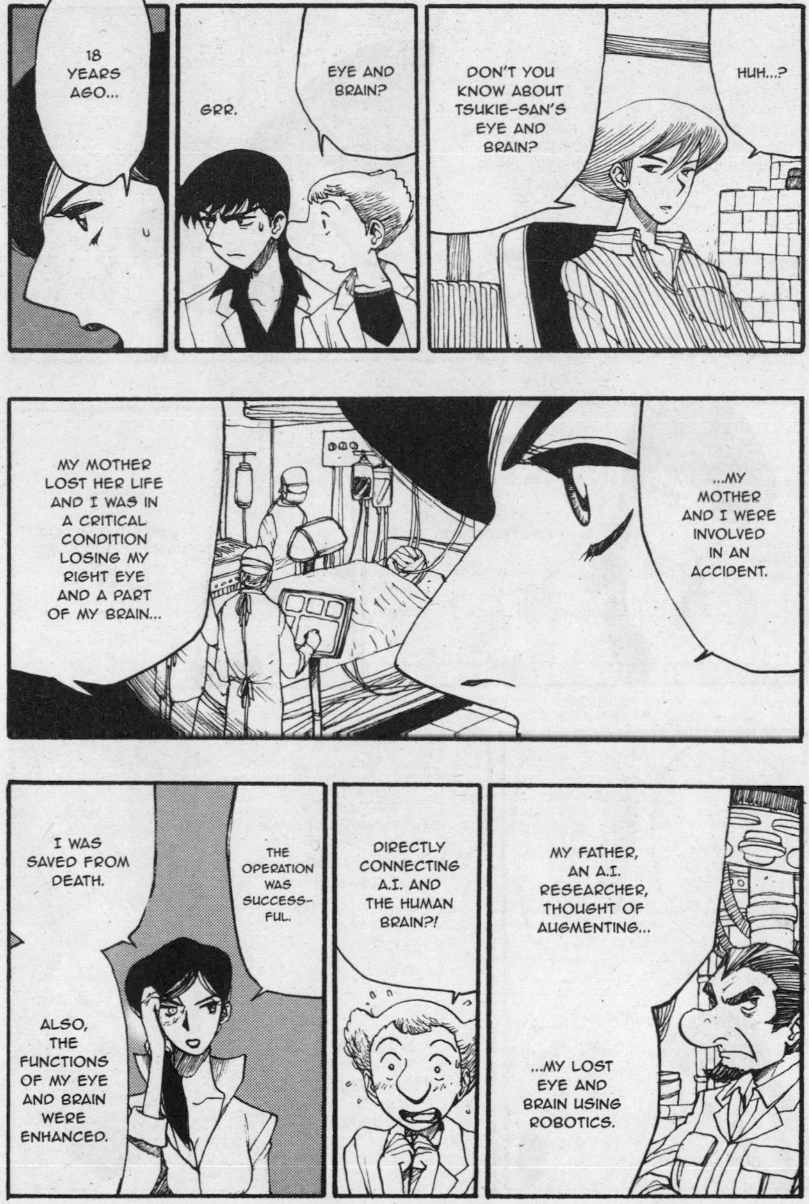
HUH...?
DON'T YOU KNOW ABOUT TSUKIE-SAN'S EYE AND BRAIN?
EYE AND BRAIN?
GRR.
18 YEARS AGO...
...MY MOTHER AND I WERE INVOLVED IN AN ACCIDENT.
MY MOTHER LOST HER LIFE AND I WAS IN A CRITICAL CONDITION LOSING MY RIGHT EYE AND A PART OF MY BRAIN...
MY FATHER, AN A.I. RESEARCHER, THOUGHT OF AUGMENTING...
...MY LOST EYE AND BRAIN USING ROBOTICS.
DIRECTLY CONNECTING A.I. AND THE HUMAN BRAIN?!
THE OPERATION WAS SUCCESS-FUL.
I WAS SAVED FROM DEATH.
ALSO, THE FUNCTIONS OF MY EYE AND BRAIN WERE ENHANCED.

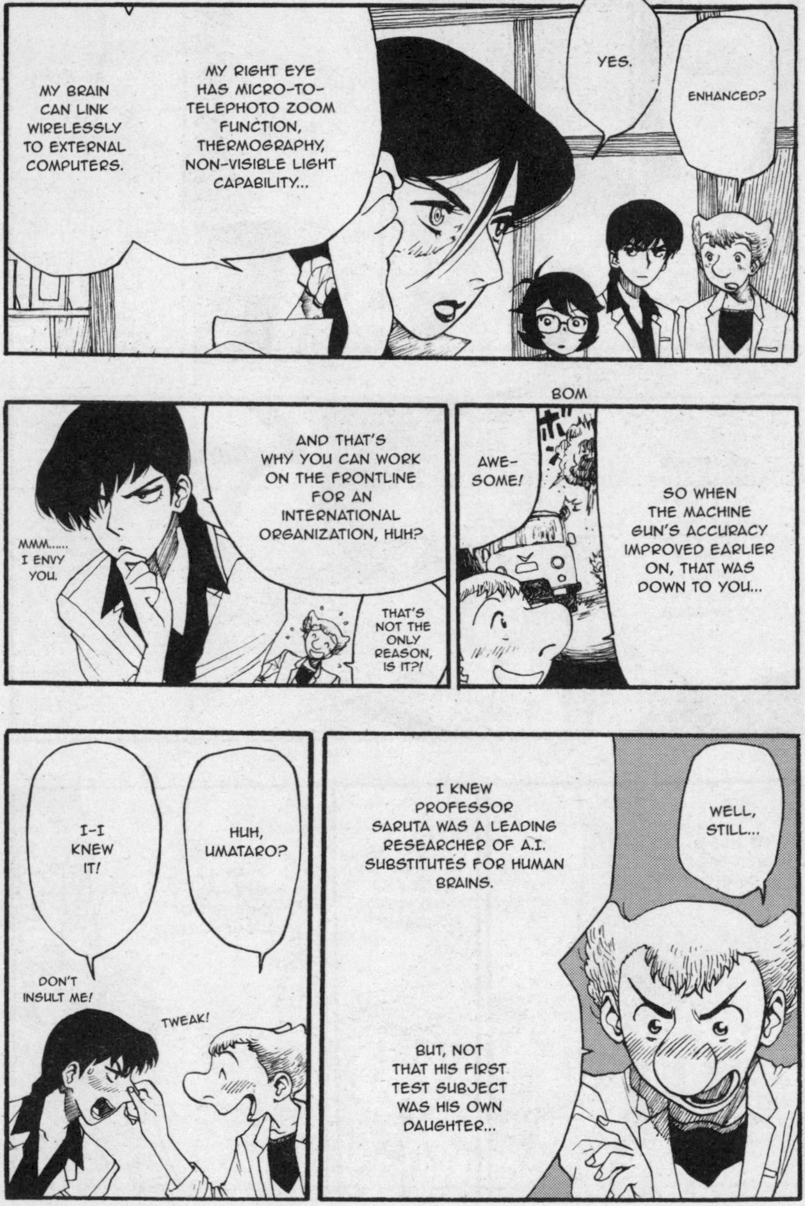

ENHANCED?
YES.
MY RIGHT EYE HAS MICRO-TO-TELEPHOTO ZOOM FUNCTION, THERMOGRAPHY, NON-VISIBLE LIGHT CAPABILITY...
MY BRAIN CAN LINK WIRELESSLY TO EXTERNAL COMPUTERS.
BOM
SO WHEN THE MACHINE GUN'S ACCURACY IMPROVED EARLIER ON, THAT WAS DOWN TO YOU...
AWE-SOME!
AND THAT'S WHY YOU CAN WORK ON THE FRONTLINE FOR AN INTERNATIONAL ORGANIZATION, HUH?
THAT'S NOT THE ONLY REASON, IS IT?!
MMM...... I ENVY YOU.
WELL, STILL...
I KNEW PROFESSOR SARUTA WAS A LEADING RESEARCHER OF A.I. SUBSTITUTES FOR HUMAN BRAINS.
BUT, NOT THAT HIS FIRST TEST SUBJECT WAS HIS OWN DAUGHTER...
HUH, UMATARO?
I-I KNEW IT!
TWEAK!
DON'T INSULT ME!

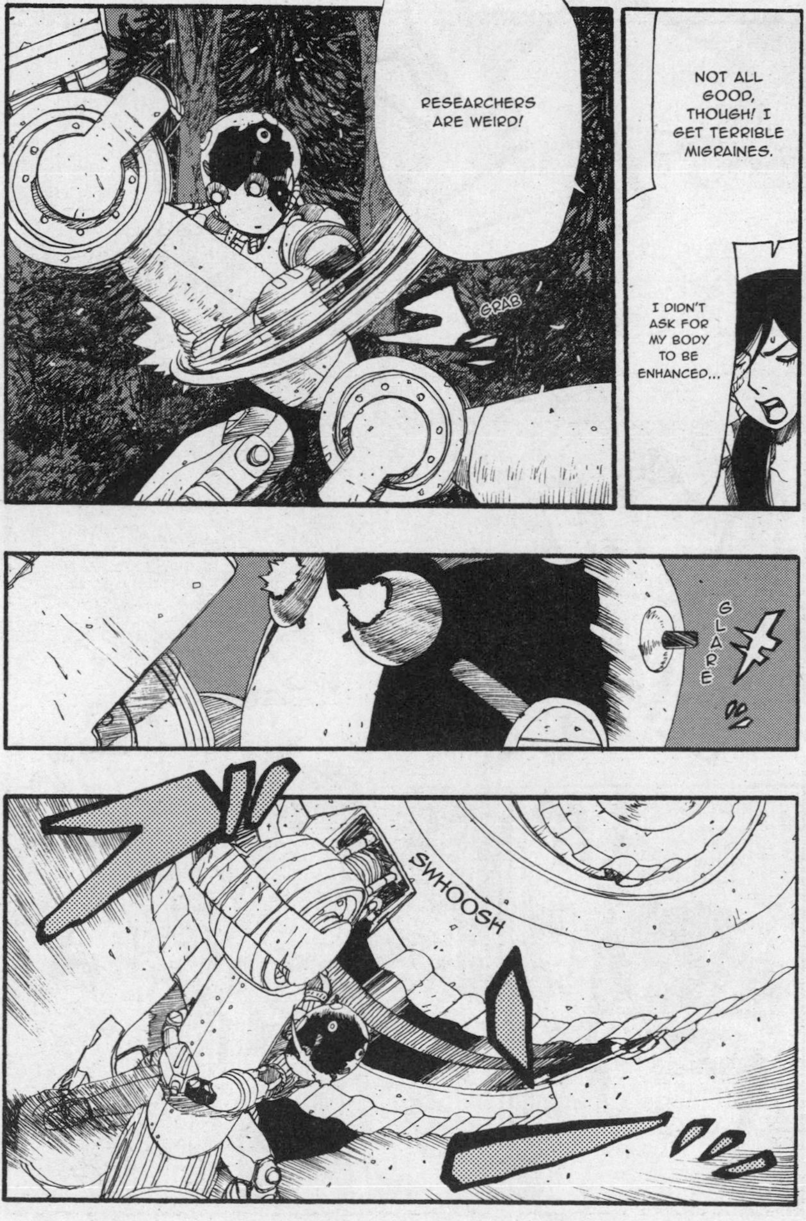
NOT ALL GOOD, THOUGH! I GET TERRIBLE MIGRAINES.
I DIDN'T ASK FOR MY BODY TO BE ENHANCED...
RESEARCHERS ARE WEIRD!
GRAB
GLARE
SWHOOSH

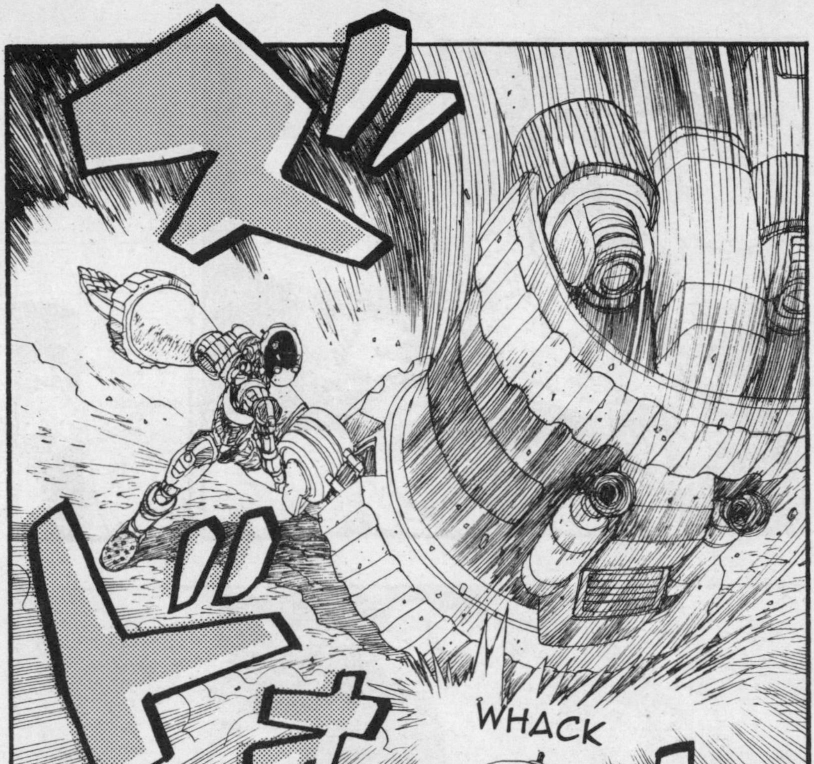
WHACK

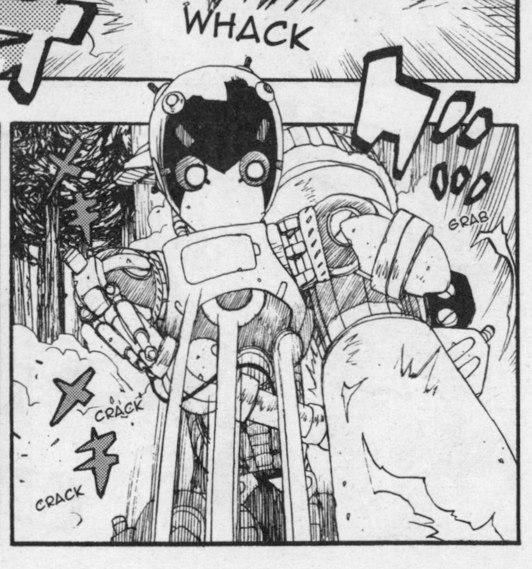
GRAB
CRACK
CRACK

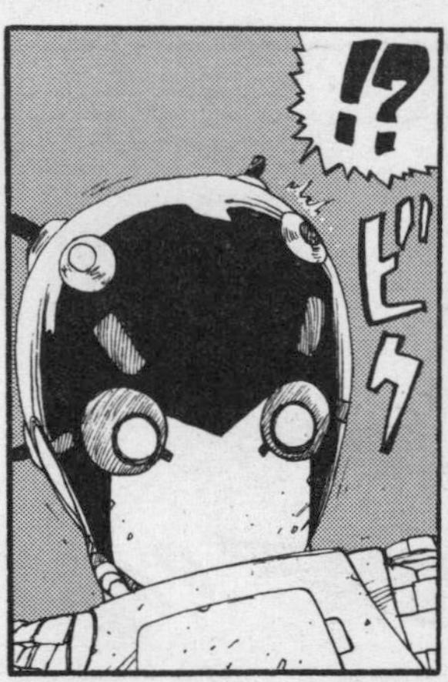
!?

*START

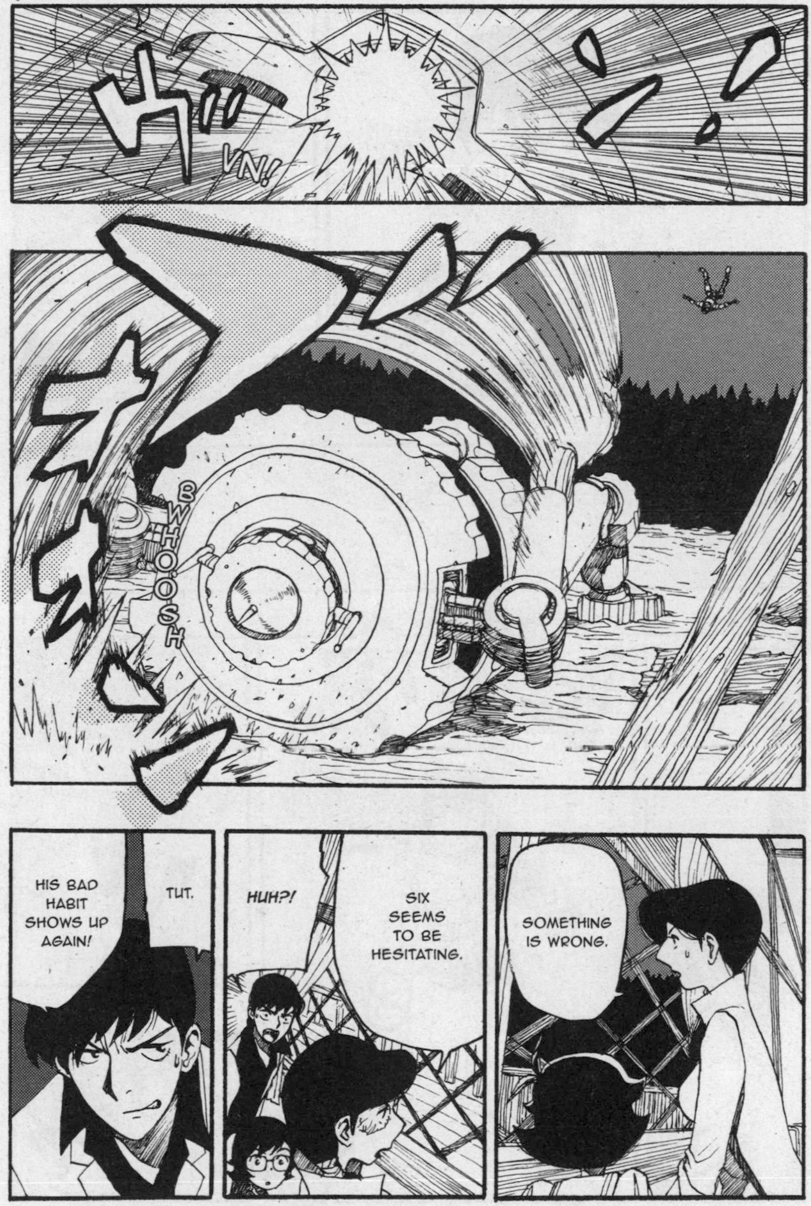
VN!
BWHOOSH
SOMETHING IS WRONG.
SIX SEEMS TO BE HESITATING.
HUH?!
TUT.
HIS BAD HABIT SHOWS UP AGAIN!

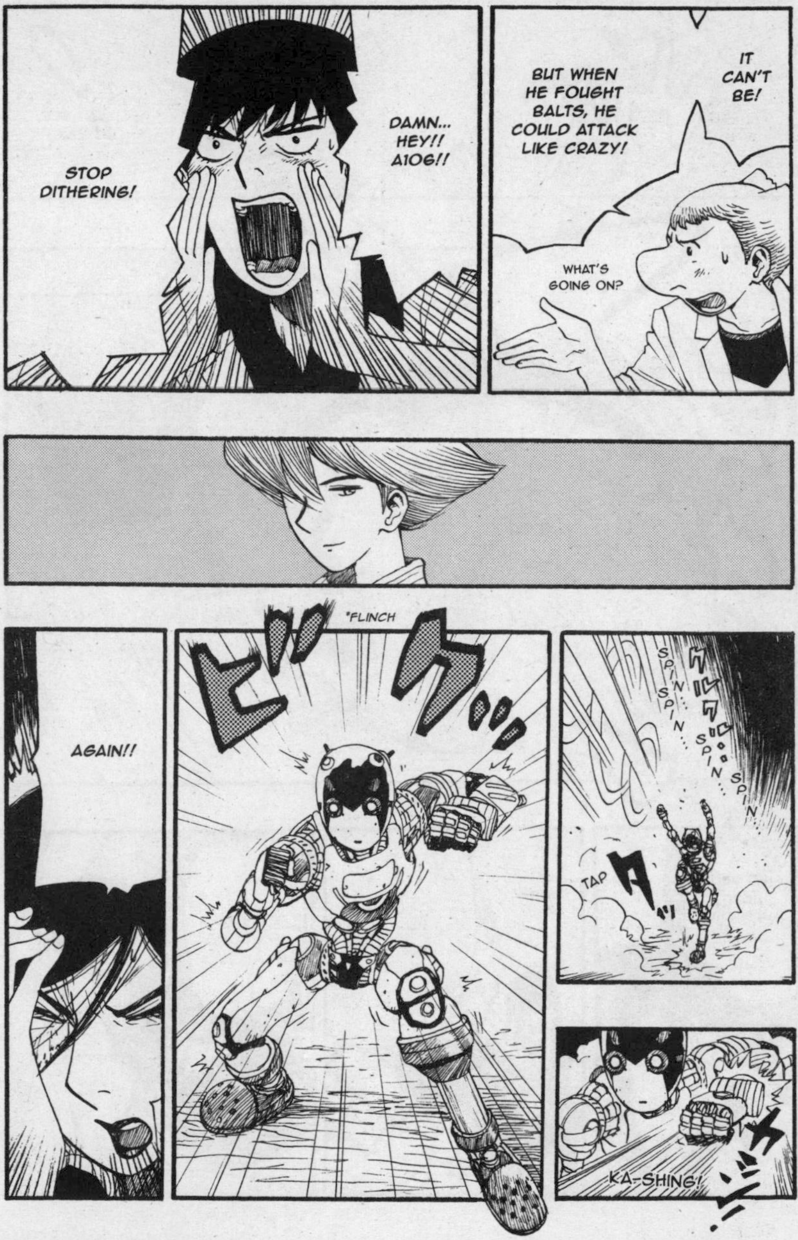
IT CAN'T BE!
BUT WHEN HE FOUGHT BALTS, HE COULD ATTACK LIKE CRAZY!
WHAT'S GOING ON?
DAMN... HEY!! A106!!
STOP DITHERING!
SPIN... SPIN... SPIN... SPIN...
TAP
KA-SHING!
*FLINCH
AGAIN!!

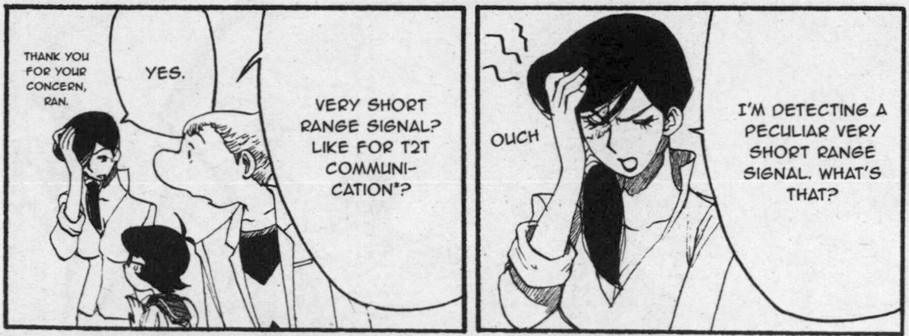
OUCH
I'M DETECTING A PECULIAR VERY SHORT RANGE SIGNAL. WHAT'S THAT?
VERY SHORT RANGE SIGNAL? LIKE FOR T2T COMMUNICATION*?
YES.
THANK YOU FOR YOUR CONCERN, RAN.

*TERMINAL-TO-TERMINAL COMMUNICATION, E.G. BLUETOOTH AND WI-FI.

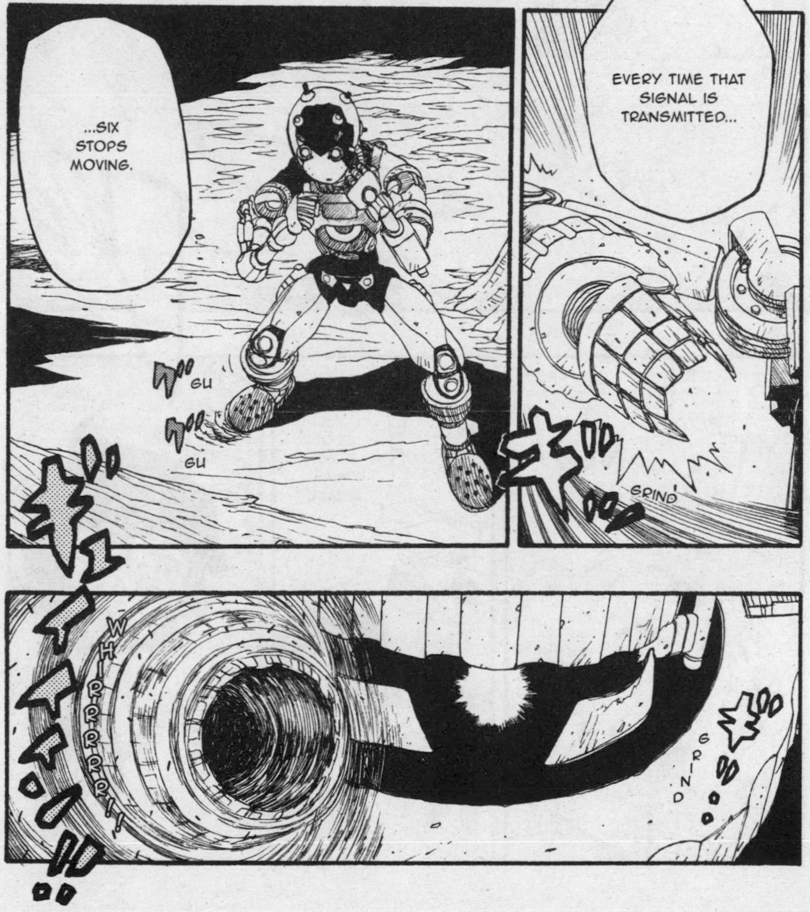
EVERY TIME THAT SIGNAL IS TRANSMITTED...
GRIND
...SIX STOPS MOVING.
GU
GU
WHIRRRRRRR!!
GRIND

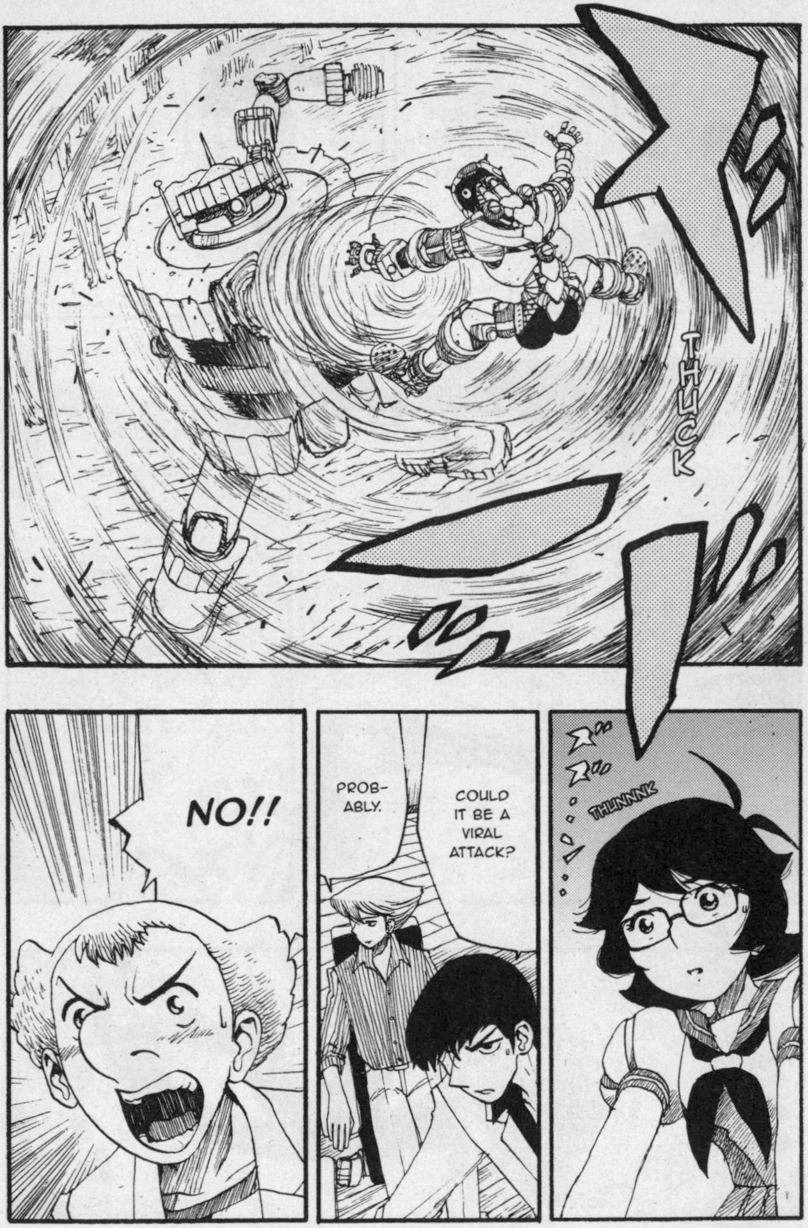
THUCK
THUNNNK
COULD IT BE A VIRAL ATTACK?
PROB-ABLY.
NO!!

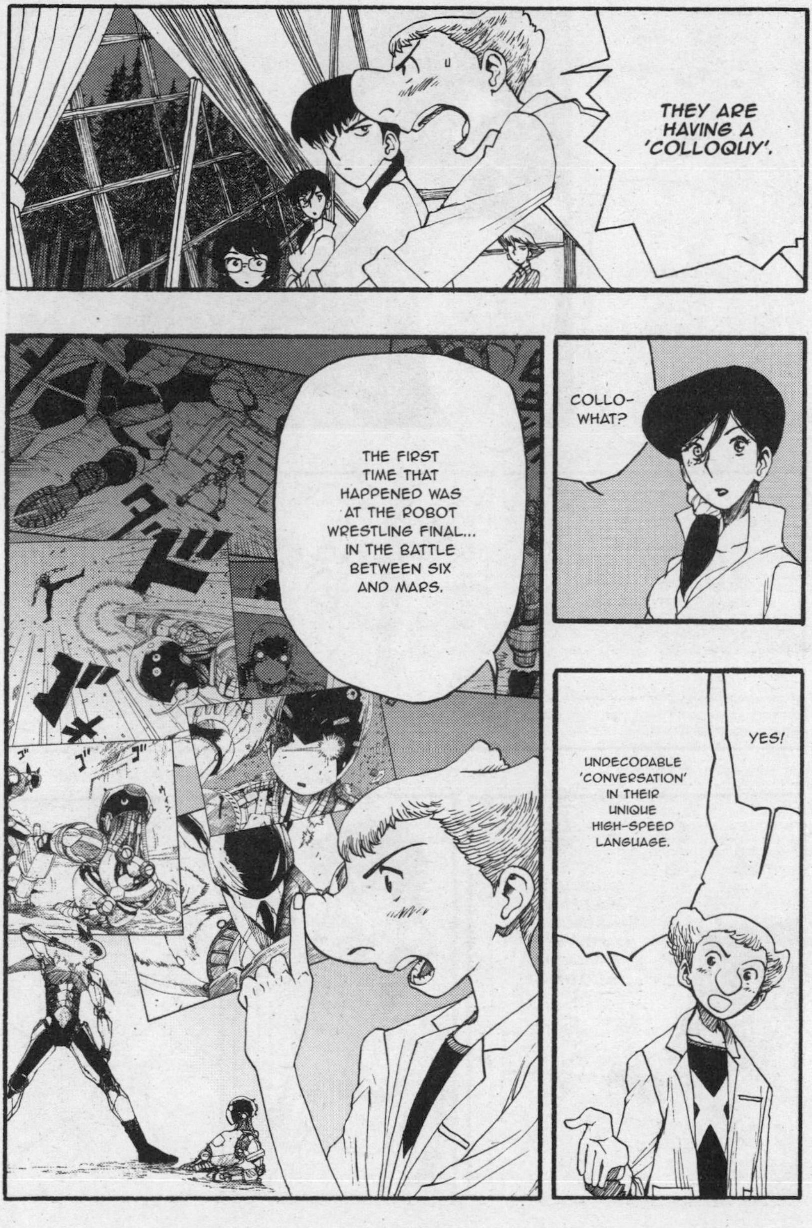
THEY ARE HAVING A 'COLLOQUY'.
COLLO-WHAT?
YES!
UNDECODABLE 'CONVERSATION' IN THEIR UNIQUE HIGH-SPEED LANGUAGE.
THE FIRST TIME THAT HAPPENED WAS AT THE ROBOT WRESTLING FINAL... IN THE BATTLE BETWEEN SIX AND MARS.

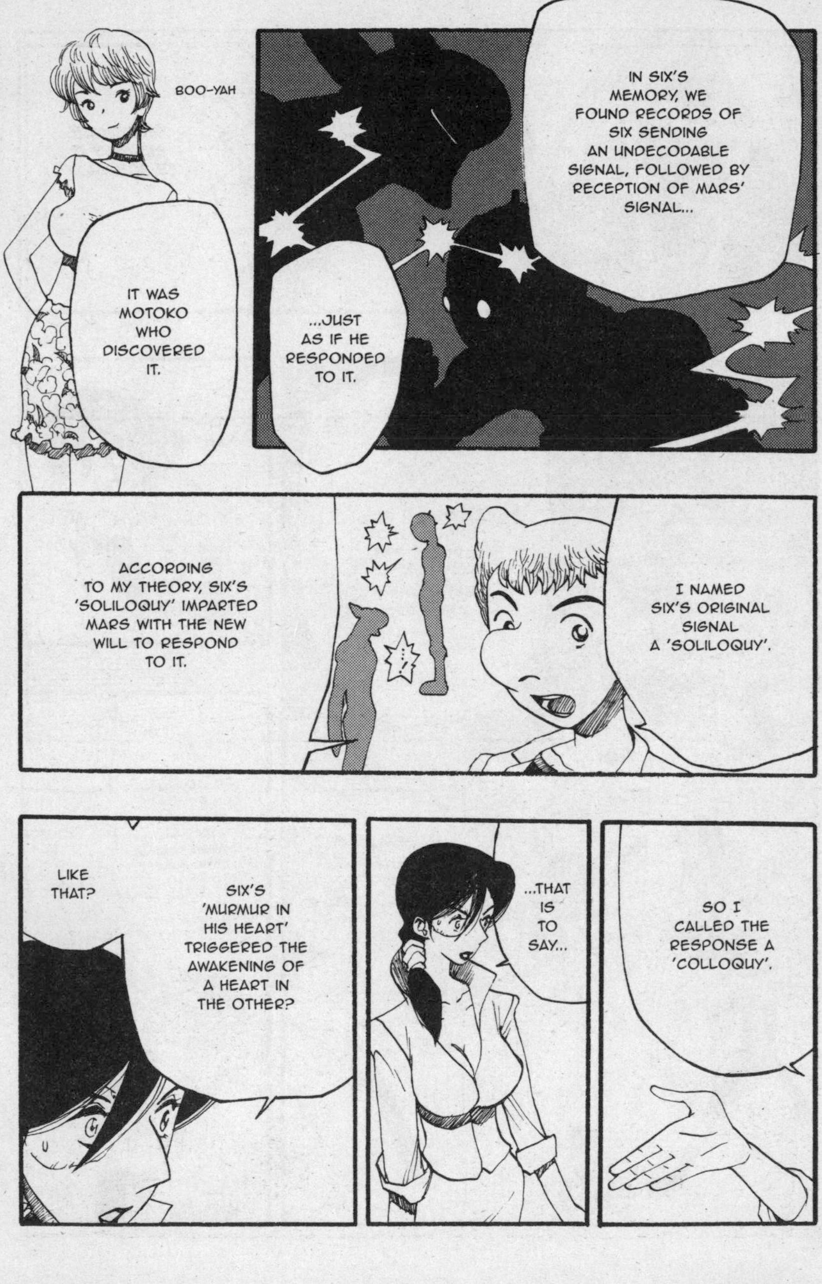
IN SIX'S MEMORY, WE FOUND RECORDS OF SIX SENDING AN UNDECODABLE SIGNAL, FOLLOWED BY RECEPTION OF MARS' SIGNAL...
...JUST AS IF HE RESPONDED TO IT.
IT WAS MOTOKO WHO DISCOVERED IT.
BOO-YAH
I NAMED SIX'S ORIGINAL SIGNAL A 'SOLILOQUY'.
ACCORDING TO MY THEORY, SIX'S 'SOLILOQUY' IMPARTED MARS WITH THE NEW WILL TO RESPOND TO IT.
SO I CALLED THE RESPONSE A 'COLLOQUY'.
...THAT IS TO SAY...
SIX'S 'MURMUR IN HIS HEART' TRIGGERED THE AWAKENING OF A HEART IN THE OTHER?
LIKE THAT?

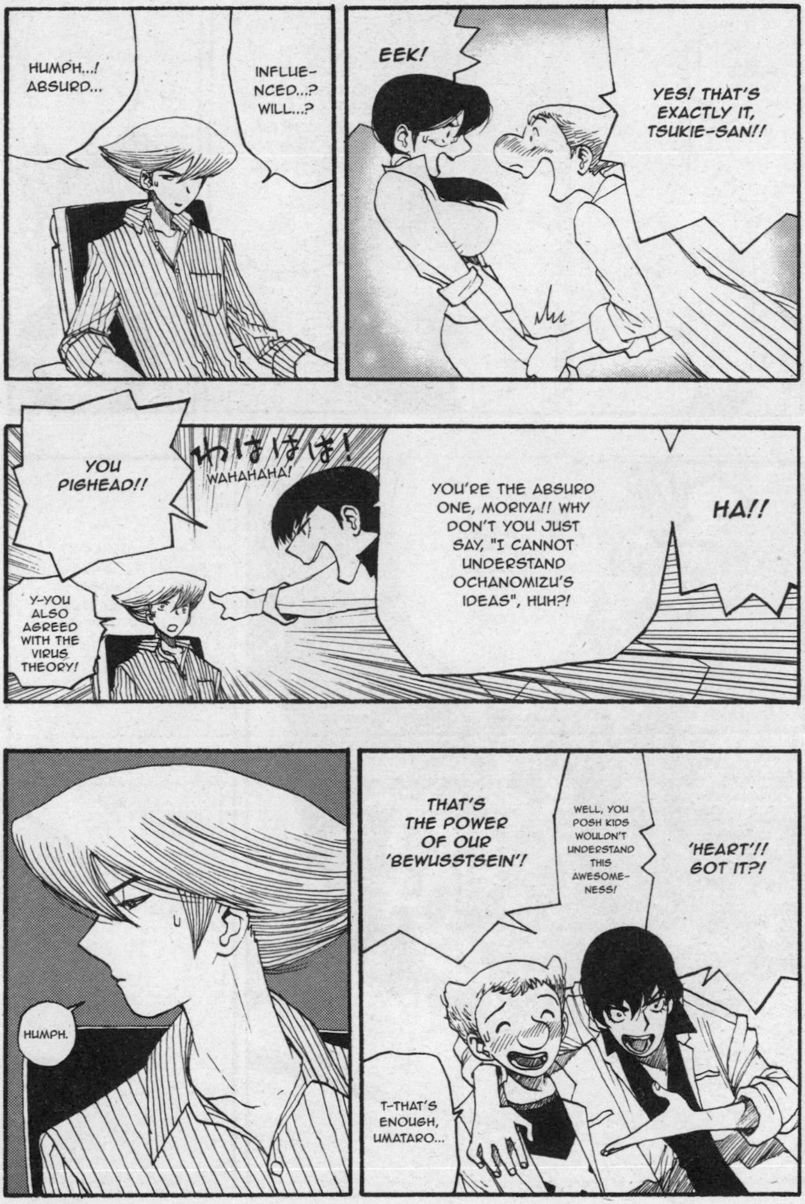
YES! THAT'S EXACTLY IT, TSUKIE-SAN!!
EEK!
INFLUENCED...? WILL...?
HUMPH...! ABSURD...
HA!!
YOU'RE THE ABSURD ONE, MORIYA!! WHY DON'T YOU JUST SAY, "I CANNOT UNDERSTAND OCHANOMIZU'S IDEAS", HUH?!
わははは!
WAHAHAHA!
YOU PIGHEAD!!
Y-YOU ALSO AGREED WITH THE VIRUS THEORY!
'HEART'!! GOT IT?!
WELL, YOU POSH KIDS WOULDN'T UNDERSTAND THIS AWESOME-NESS!
THAT'S THE POWER OF OUR 'BEWUSSTSEIN'!
T-THAT'S ENOUGH, UMATARO...
HUMPH.

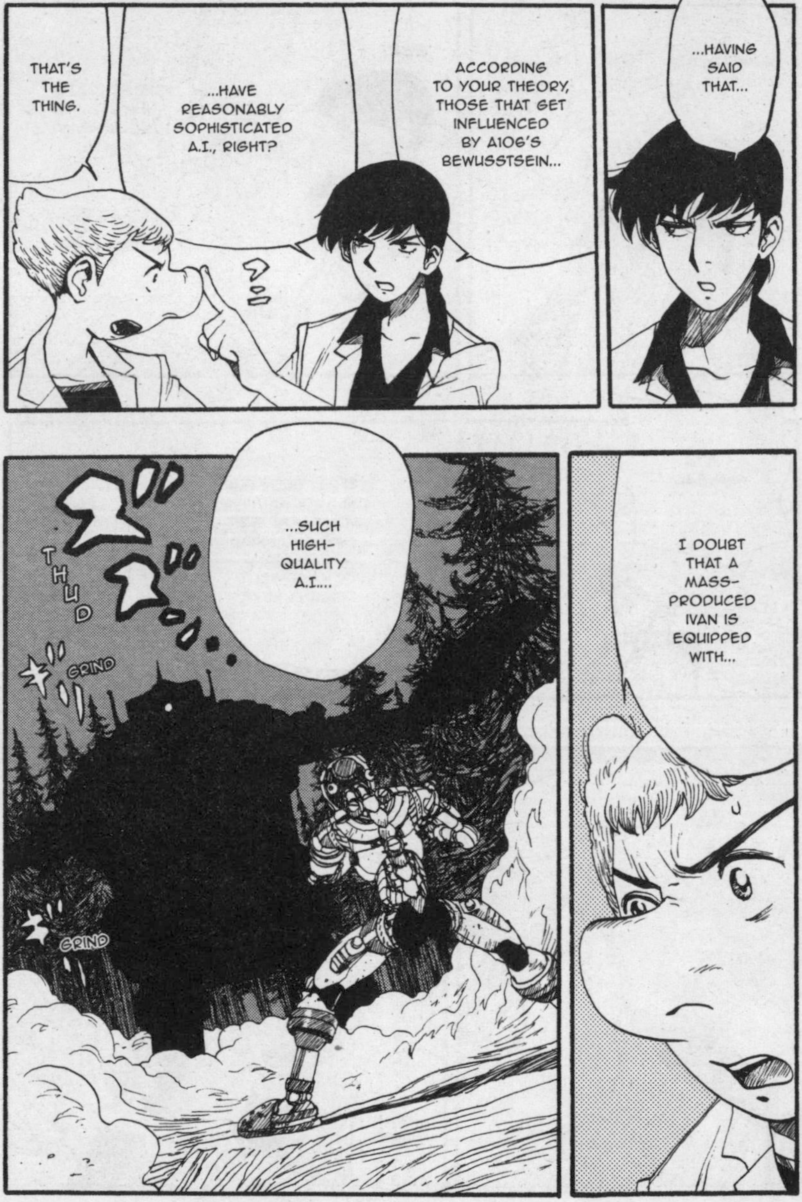
...HAVING SAID THAT...
ACCORDING TO YOUR THEORY, THOSE THAT GET INFLUENCED BY A106'S BEWUSSTSEIN...
...HAVE REASONABLY SOPHISTICATED A.I., RIGHT?
THAT'S THE THING.
I DOUBT THAT A MASS-PRODUCED IVAN IS EQUIPPED WITH...
...SUCH HIGH-QUALITY A.I....
THUD
GRIND
GRIND

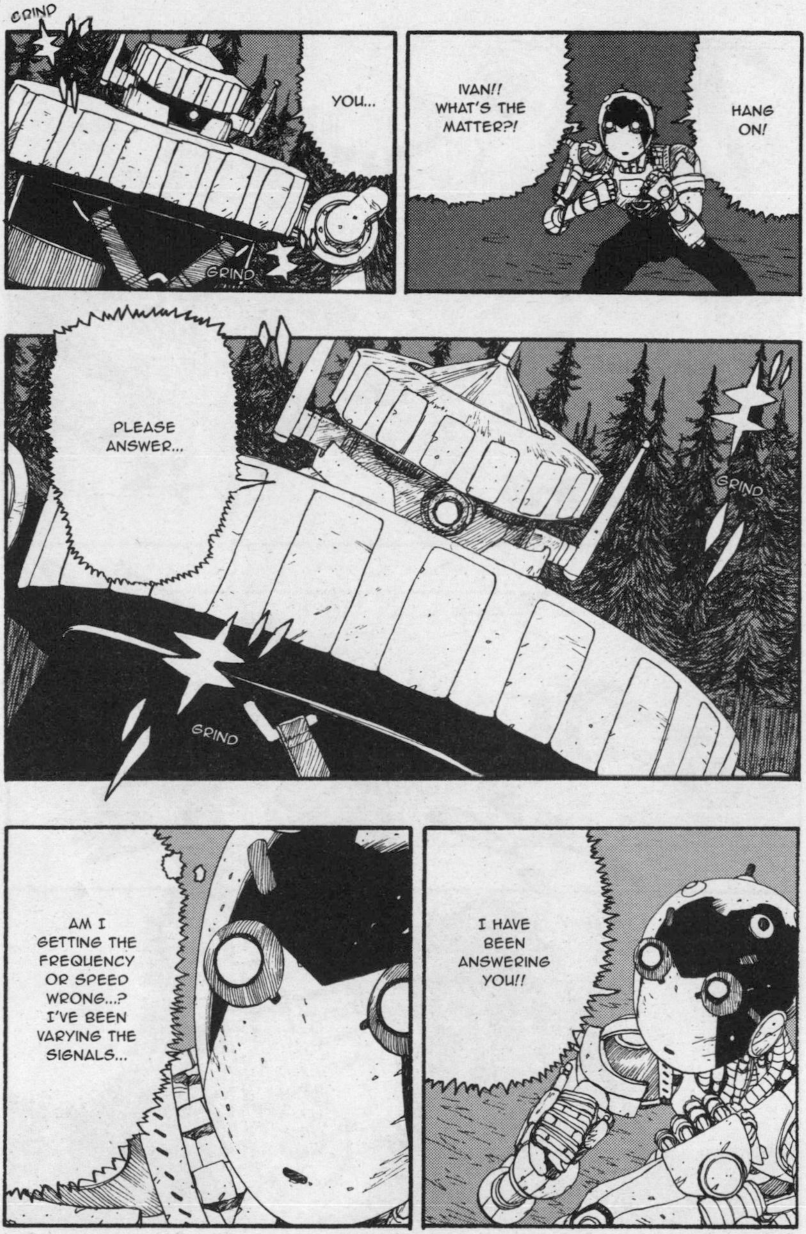
HANG ON!
IVAN!! WHAT'S THE MATTER?!
GRIND
YOU...
GRIND
PLEASE ANSWER...
GRIND
GRIND
I HAVE BEEN ANSWERING YOU!!
AM I GETTING THE FREQUENCY OR SPEED WRONG...? I'VE BEEN VARYING THE SIGNALS...

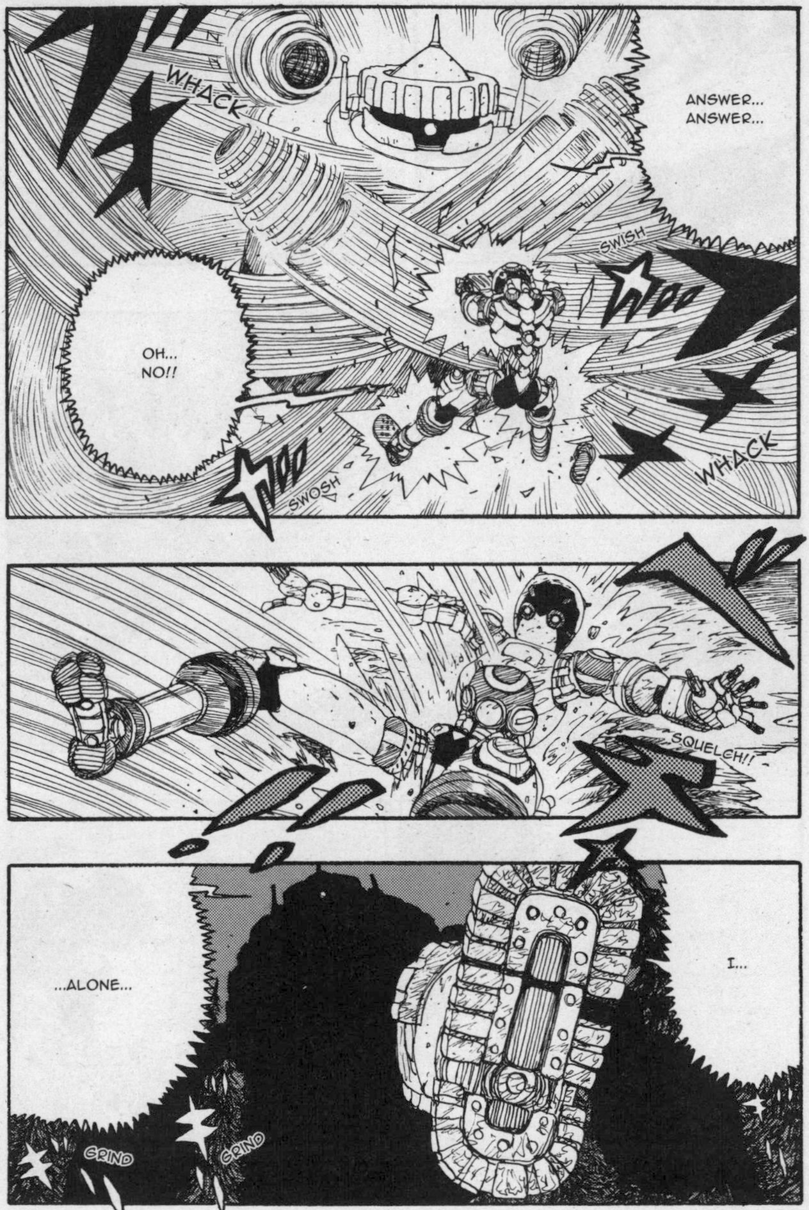
ANSWER... ANSWER...
WHACK
SWISH
WHACK
OH... NO!!
SWOSH
SQUELCH!!
I...
...ALONE...
GRIND
GRIND

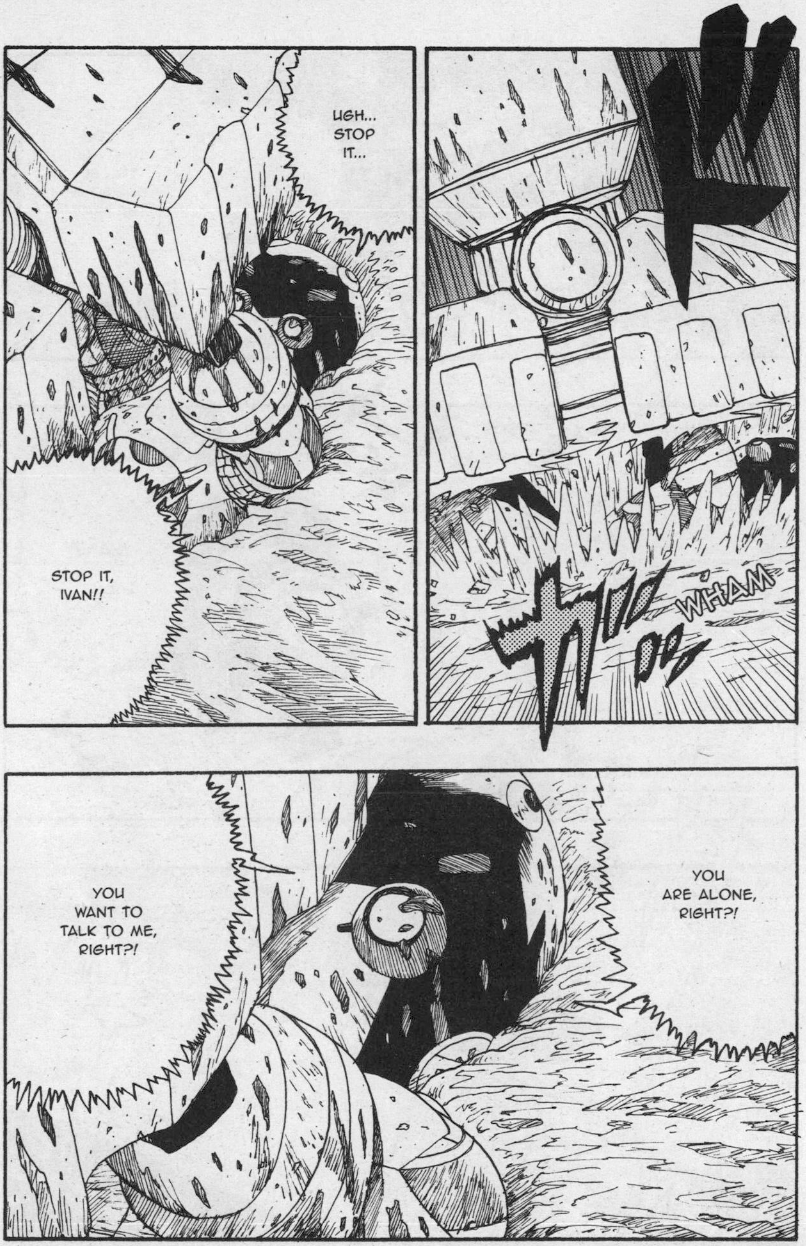
WHAM
UGH... STOP IT...
STOP IT, IVAN!!
YOU ARE ALONE, RIGHT?!
YOU WANT TO TALK TO ME, RIGHT?!

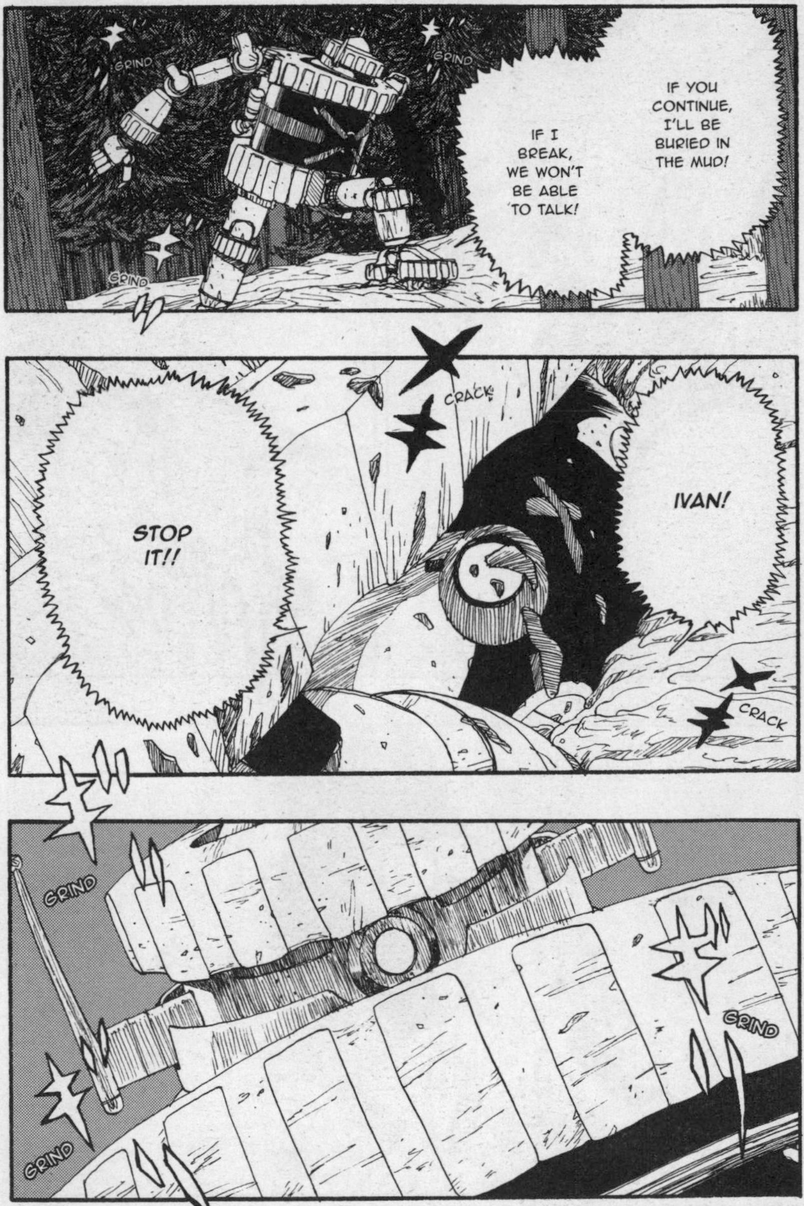
GRIND
IF YOU CONTINUE, I'LL BE BURIED IN THE MUD!
IF I BREAK, WE WON'T BE ABLE TO TALK!
GRIND
GRIND
CRACK
IVAN!
STOP IT!!
CRACK
GRIND
GRIND
GRIND

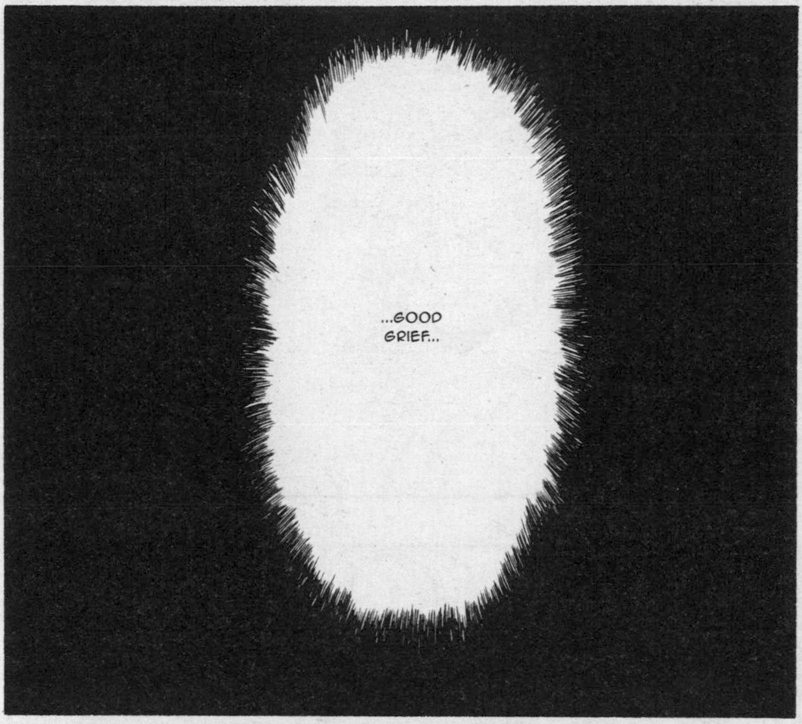
...GOOD
GRIEF...
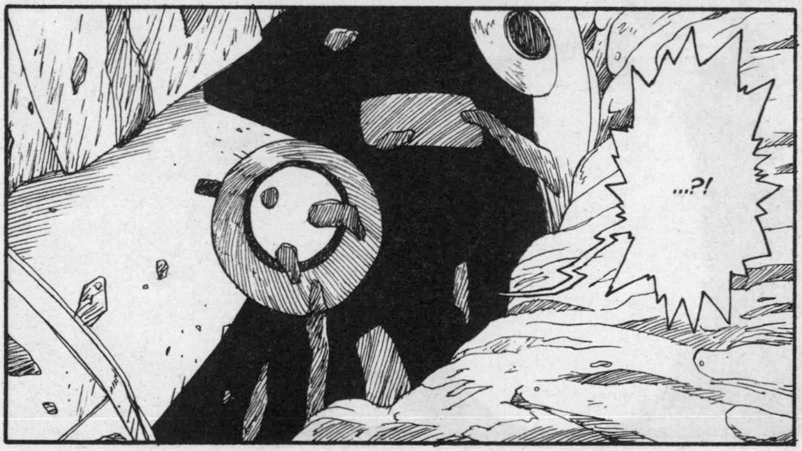
...?!

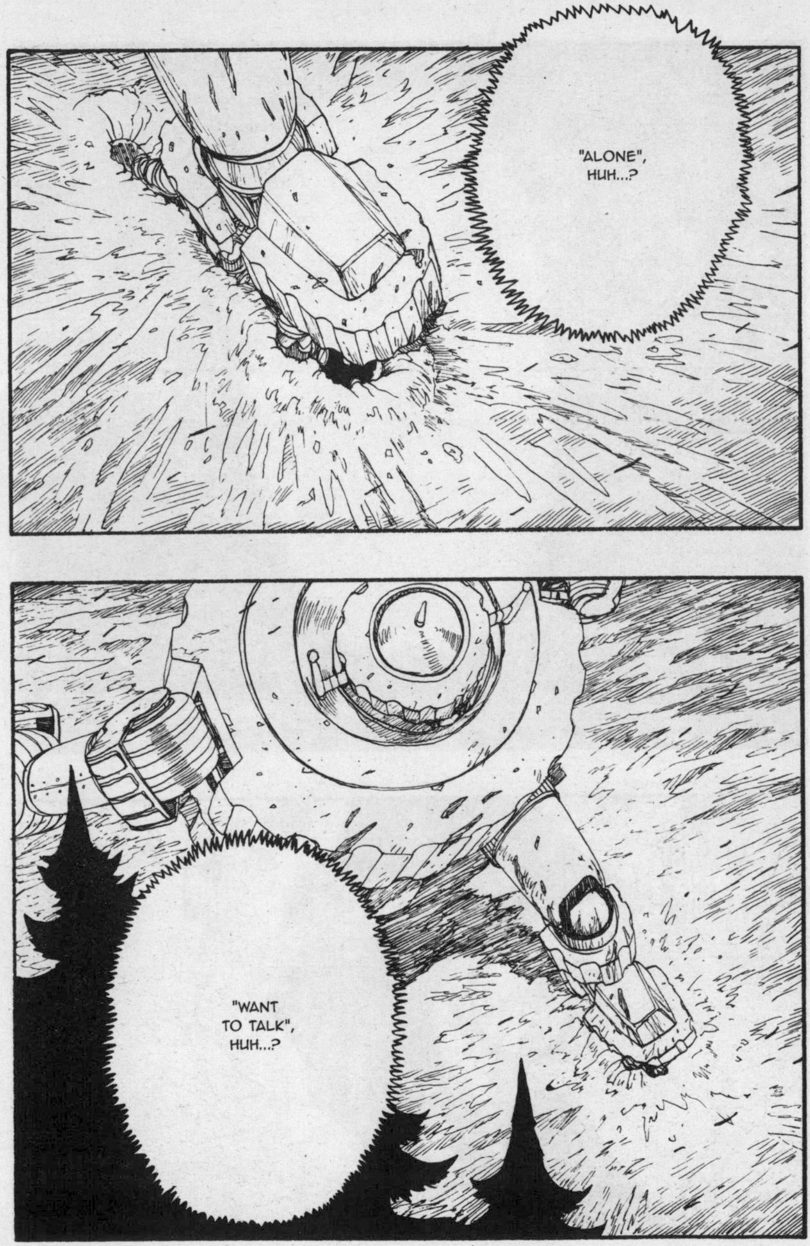
"ALONE", HUH...?
"WANT TO TALK", HUH...?

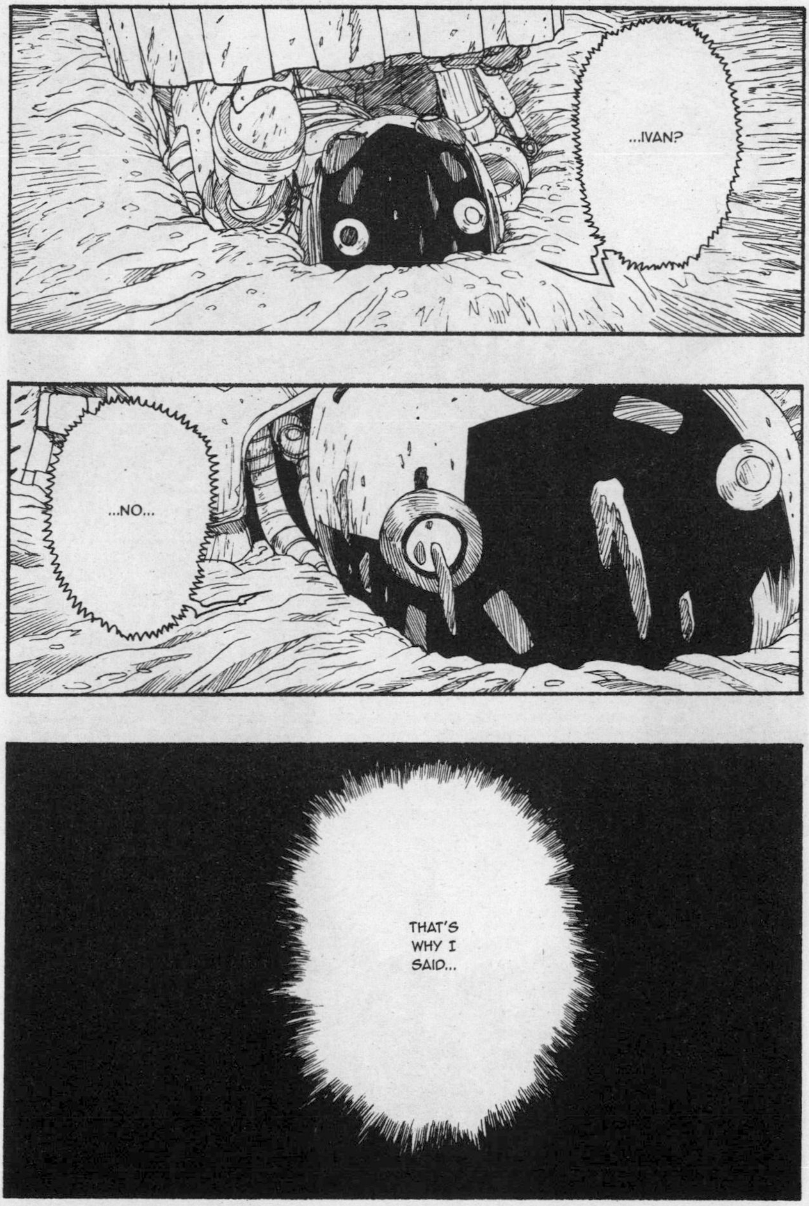
...IVAN?
...NO...
THAT'S WHY I SAID...

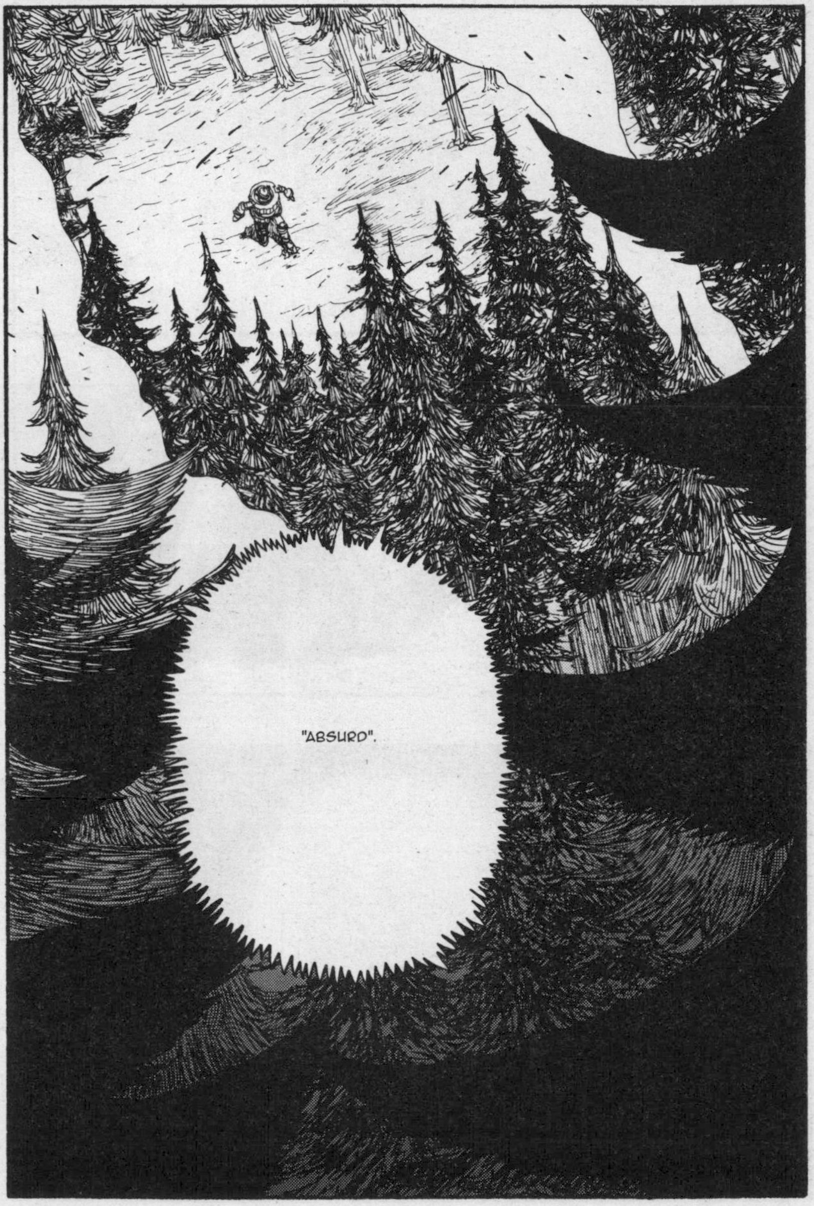
"ABSURD".

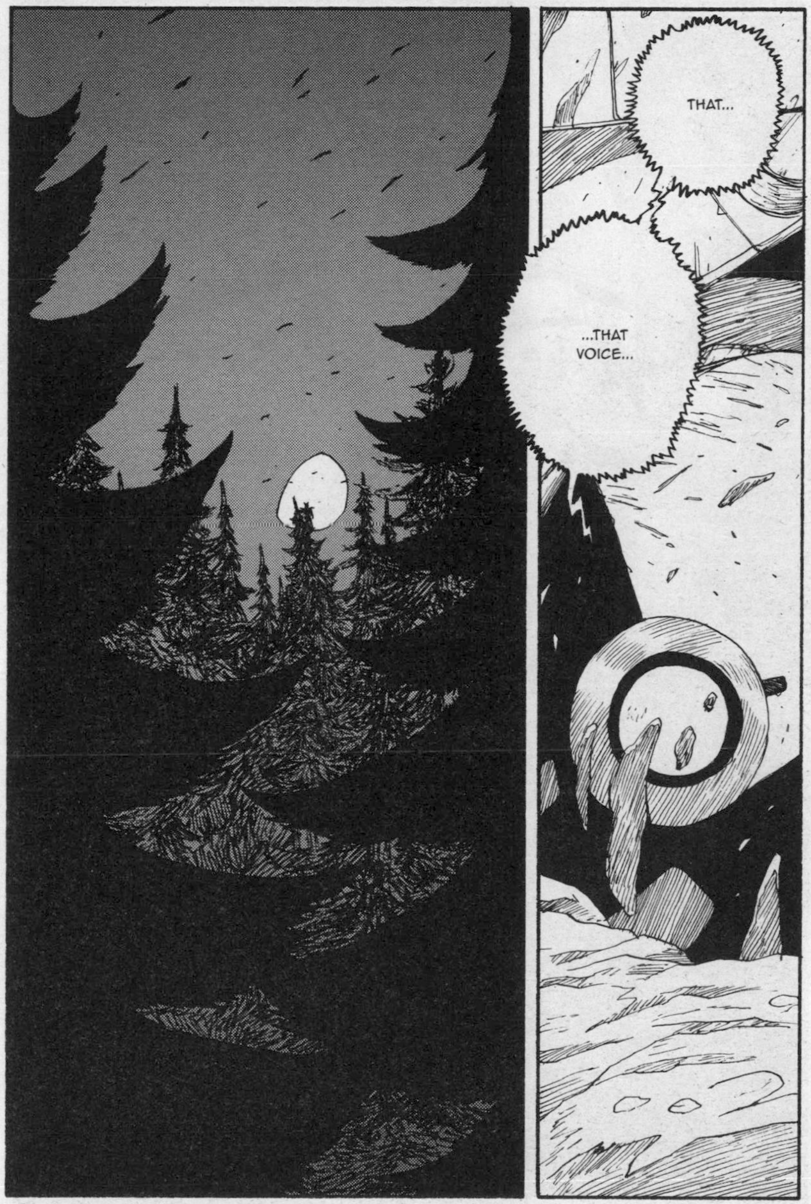
THAT...
...THAT VOICE...

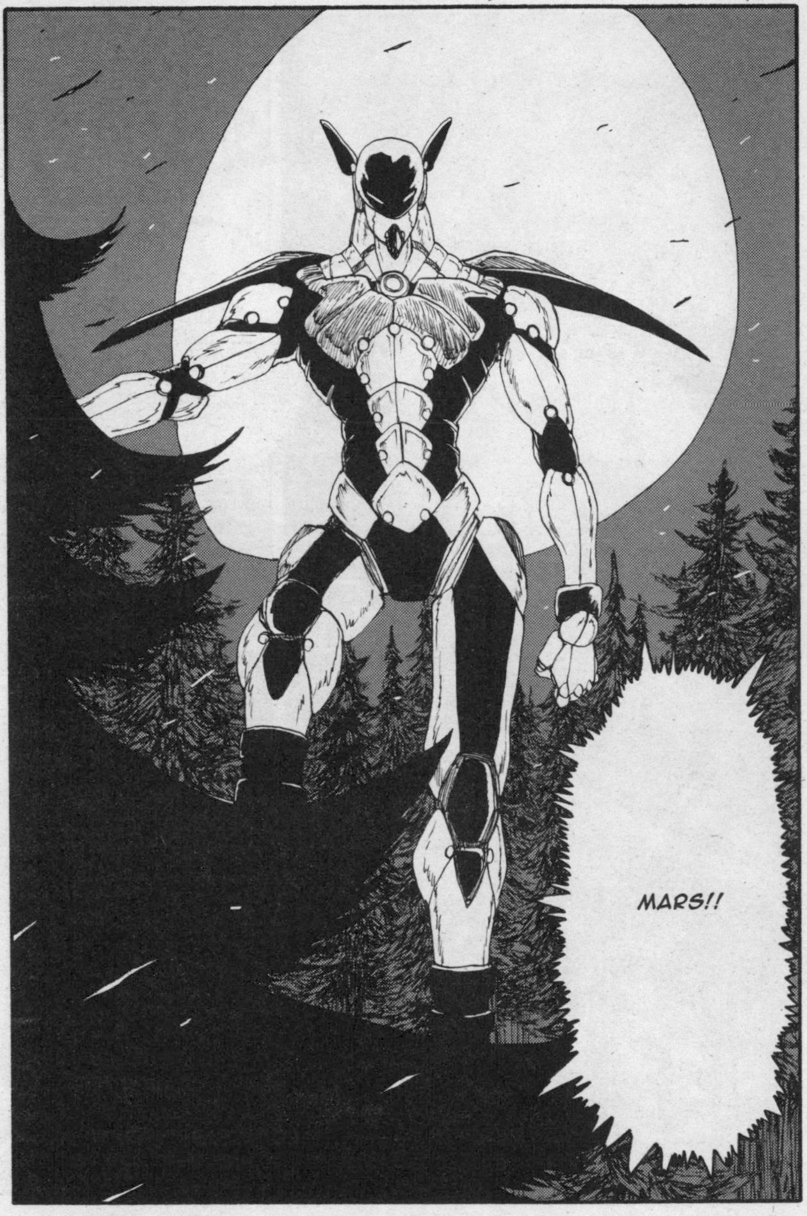
MARS!!

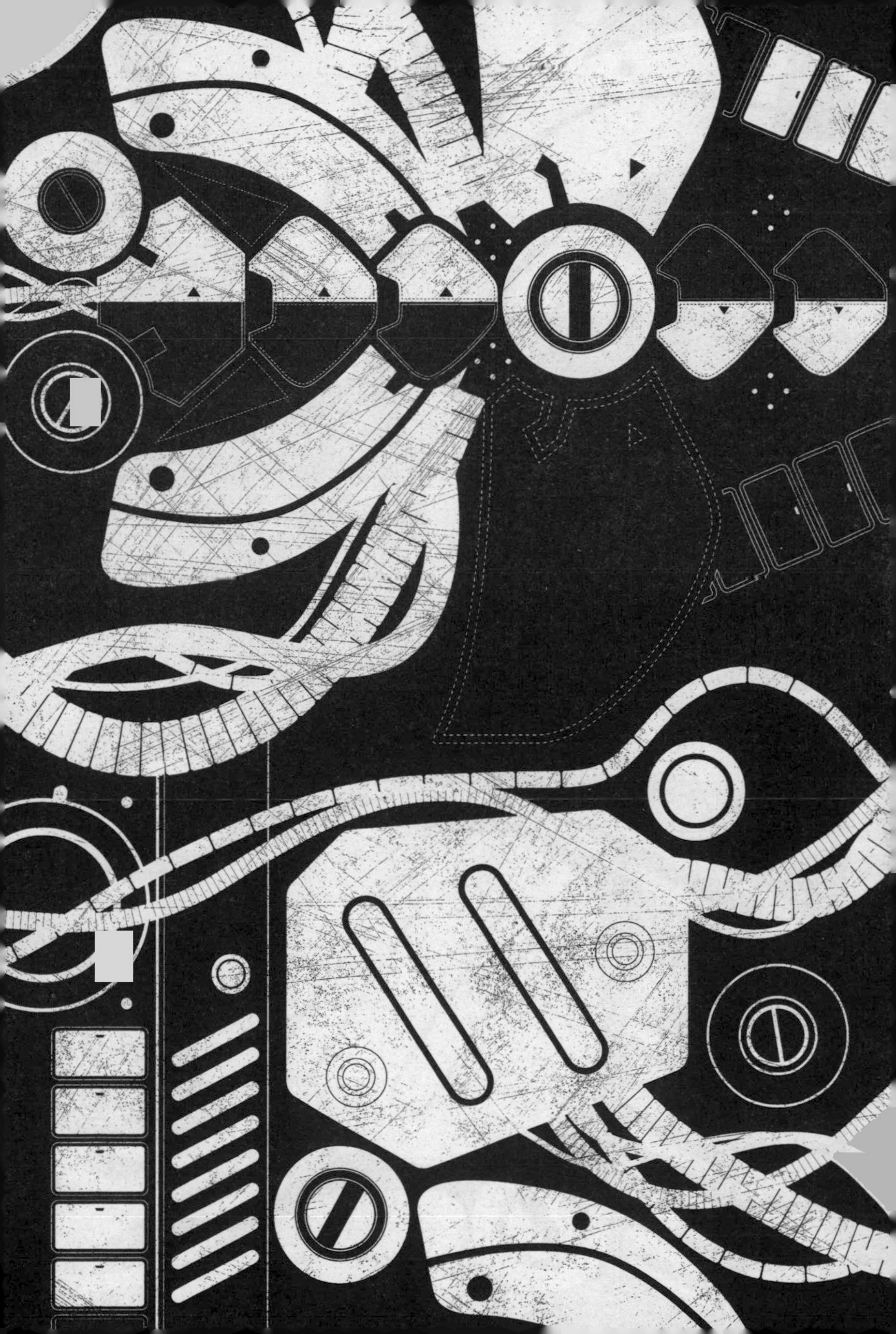

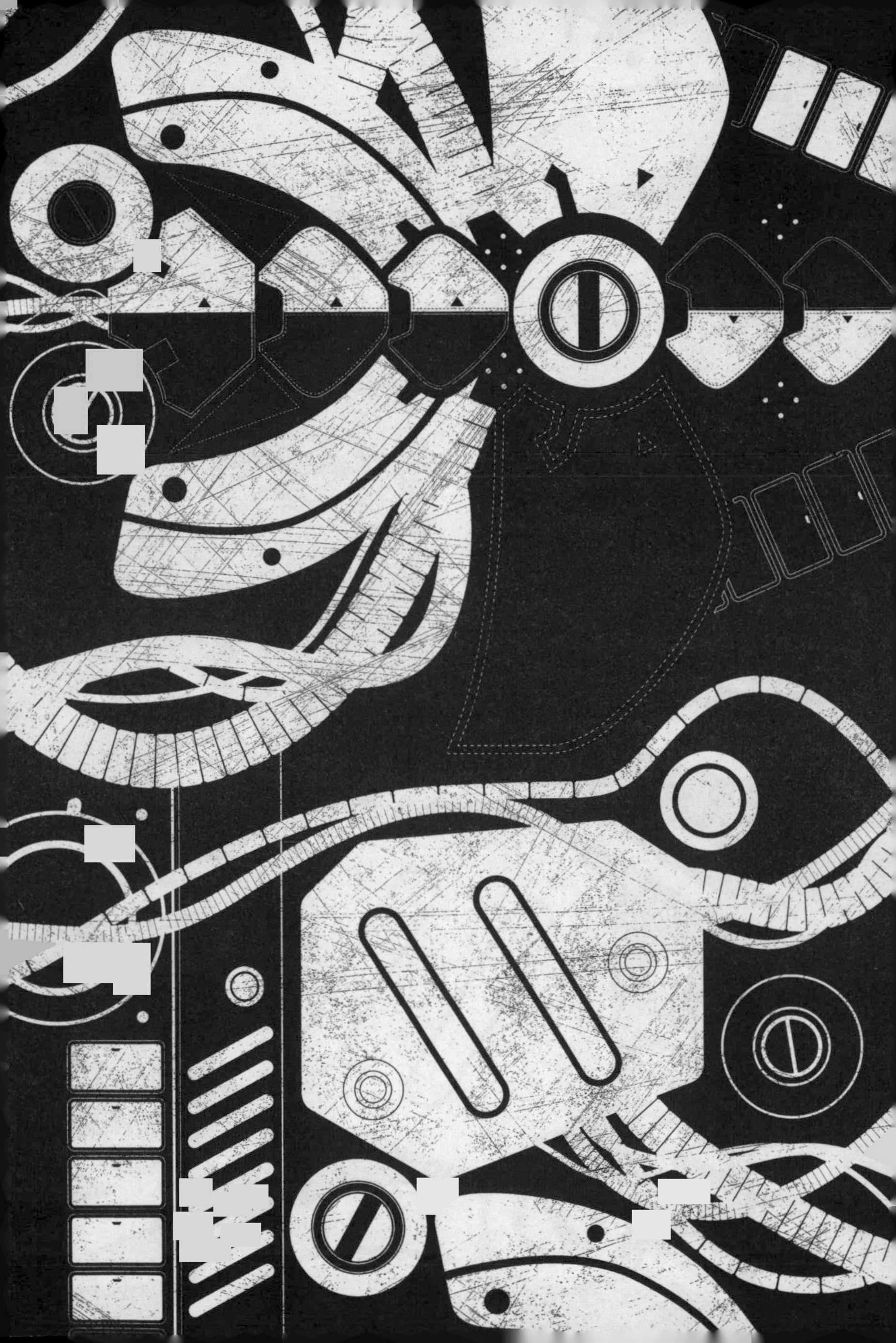

▷boot_017

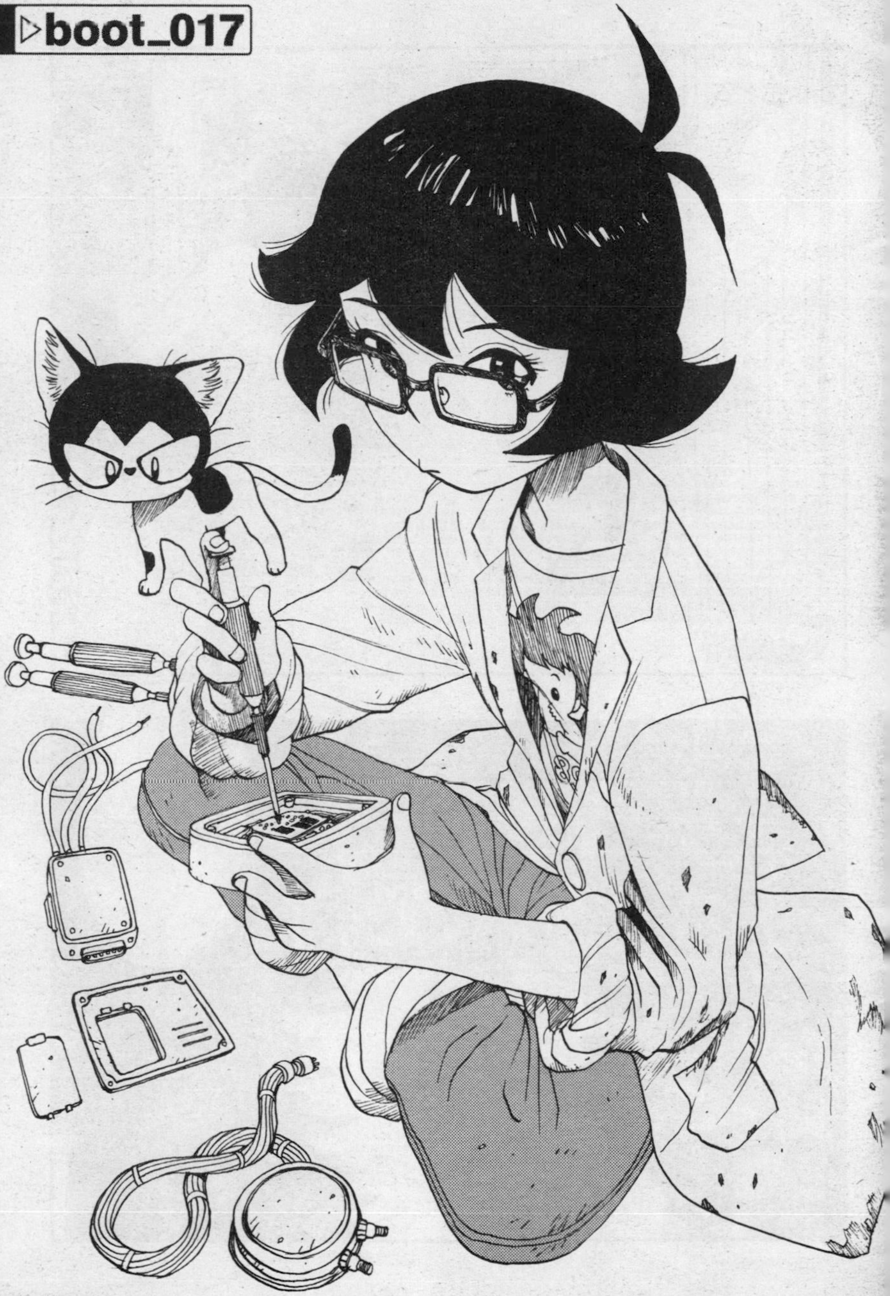

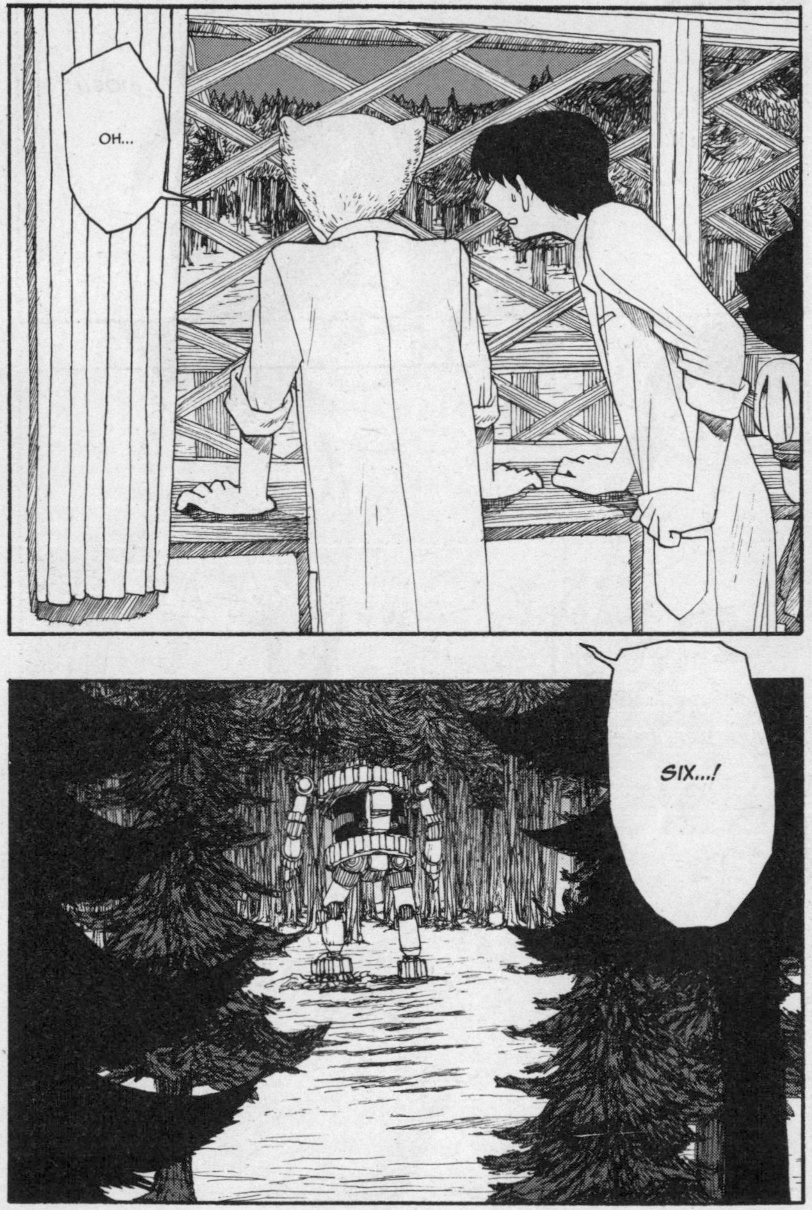
OH...
SIX...!

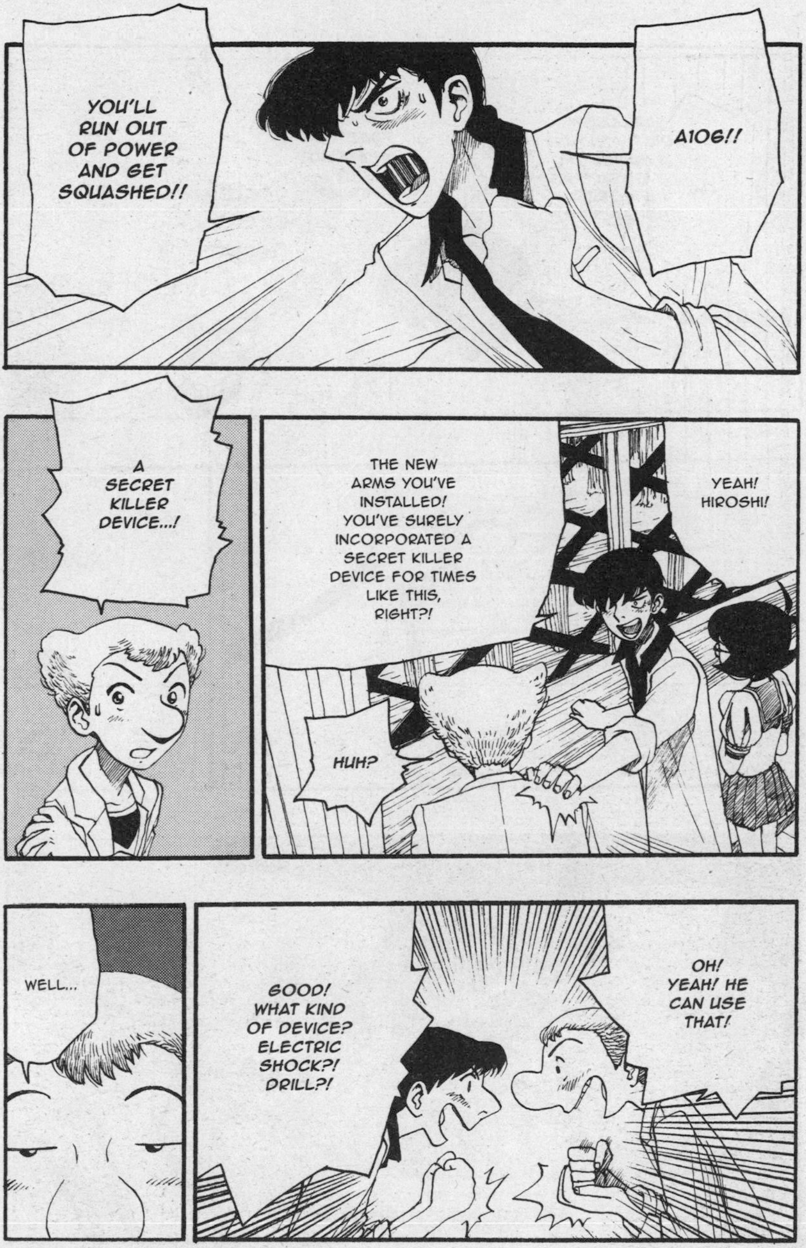
A106!!
YOU'LL RUN OUT OF POWER AND GET SQUASHED!!
YEAH! HIROSHI!
THE NEW ARMS YOU'VE INSTALLED! YOU'VE SURELY INCORPORATED A SECRET KILLER DEVICE FOR TIMES LIKE THIS, RIGHT?!
HUH?
A SECRET KILLER DEVICE...!
OH! YEAH! HE CAN USE THAT!
GOOD! WHAT KIND OF DEVICE? ELECTRIC SHOCK?! DRILL?!
WELL...

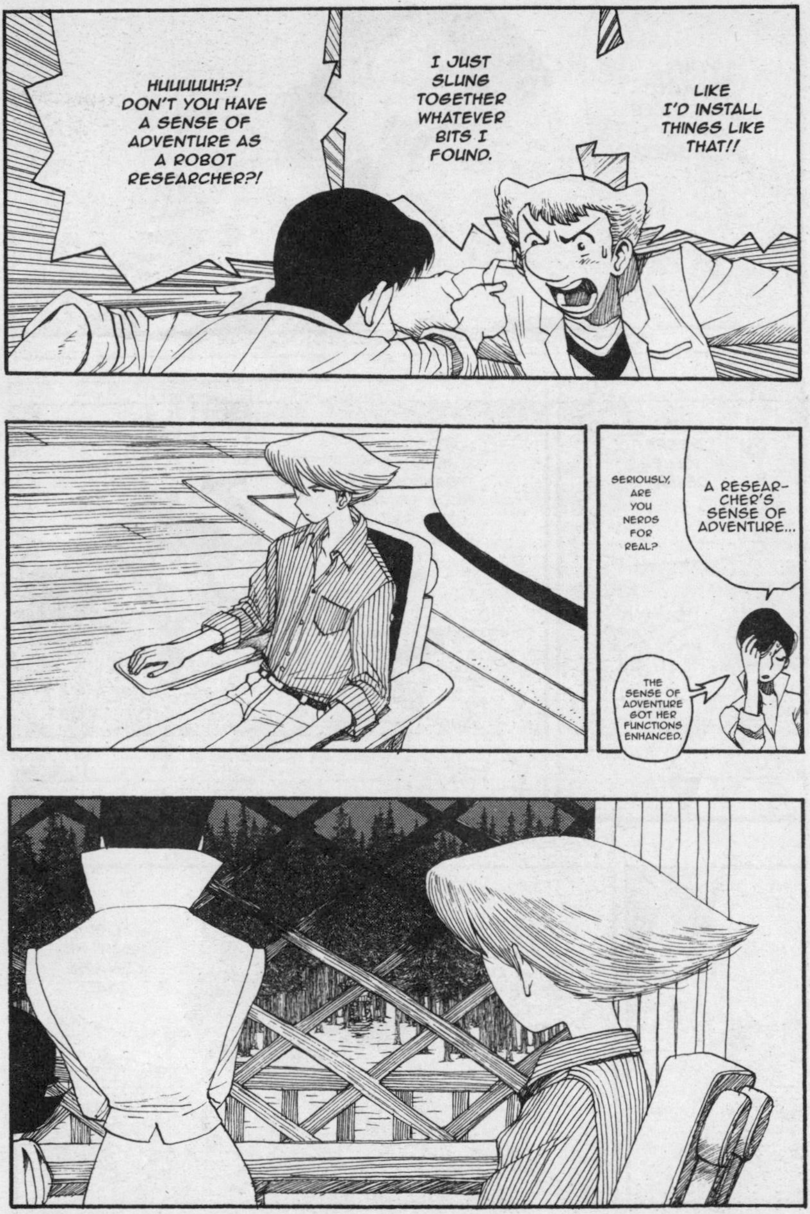
LIKE I'D INSTALL THINGS LIKE THAT!!
I JUST SLUNG TOGETHER WHATEVER BITS I FOUND.
HUUUUUH?! DON'T YOU HAVE A SENSE OF ADVENTURE AS A ROBOT RESEARCHER?!
A RESEAR-CHER'S SENSE OF ADVENTURE...
SERIOUSLY, ARE YOU NERDS FOR REAL?
THE SENSE OF ADVENTURE GOT HER FUNCTIONS ENHANCED.

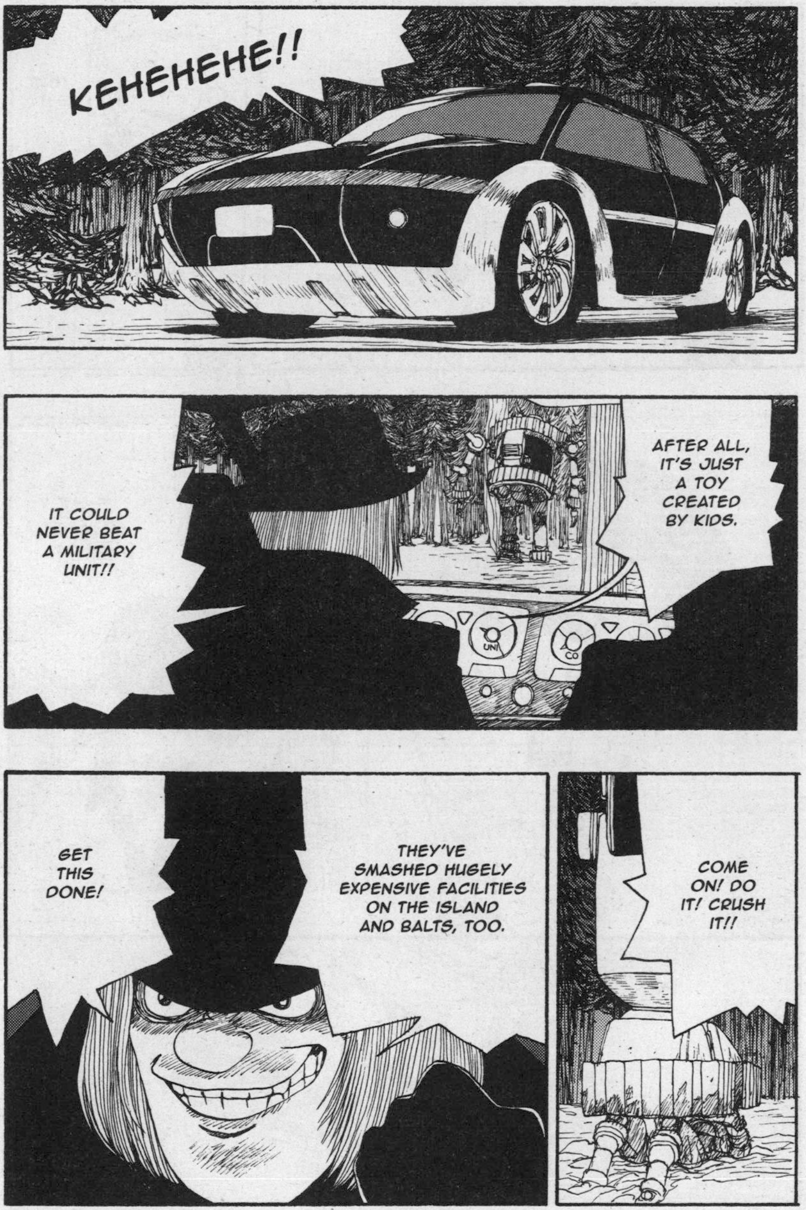
KEHEHEHE!!
AFTER ALL, IT'S JUST A TOY CREATED BY KIDS.
IT COULD NEVER BEAT A MILITARY UNIT!!
COME ON! DO IT! CRUSH IT!!
THEY'VE SMASHED HUGELY EXPENSIVE FACILITIES ON THE ISLAND AND BALTS, TOO.
GET THIS DONE!

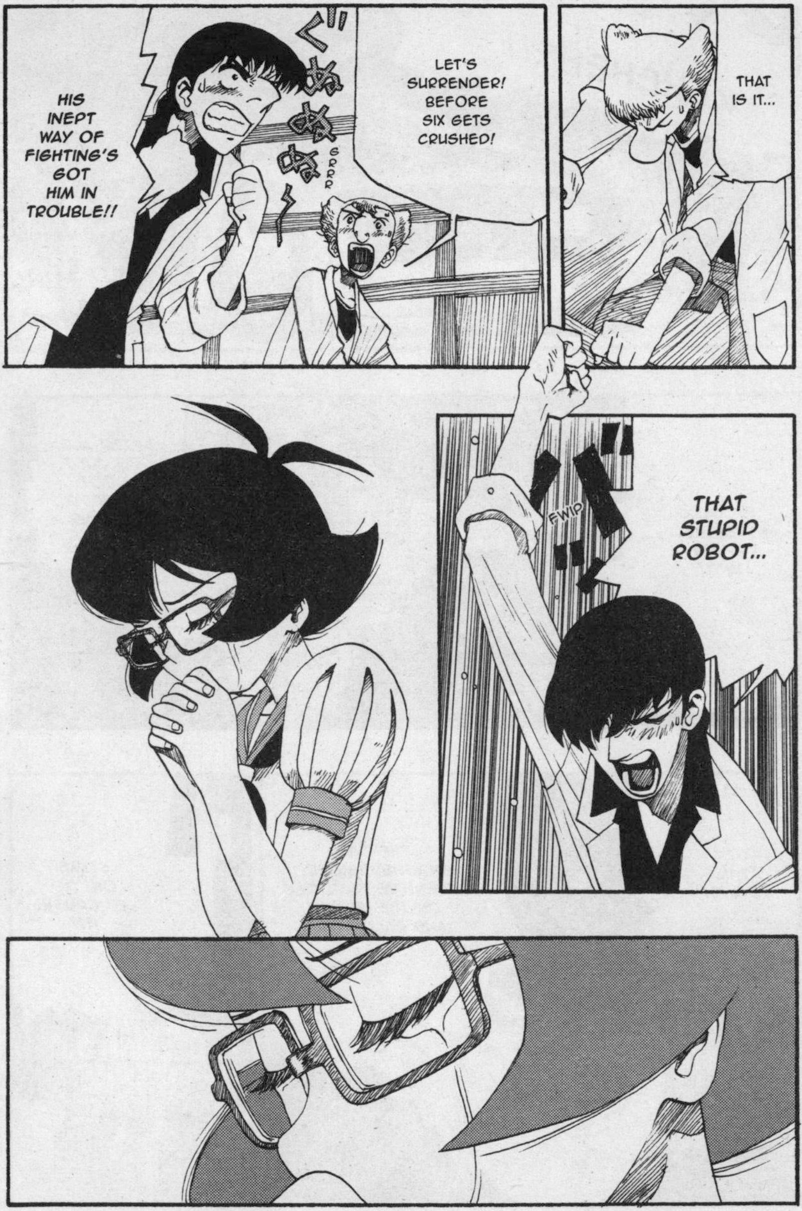
THAT IS IT...
LET'S SURRENDER! BEFORE SIX GETS CRUSHED!
HIS INEPT WAY OF FIGHTING'S GOT HIM IN TROUBLE!!
GRRR
THAT STUPID ROBOT...
FWIP

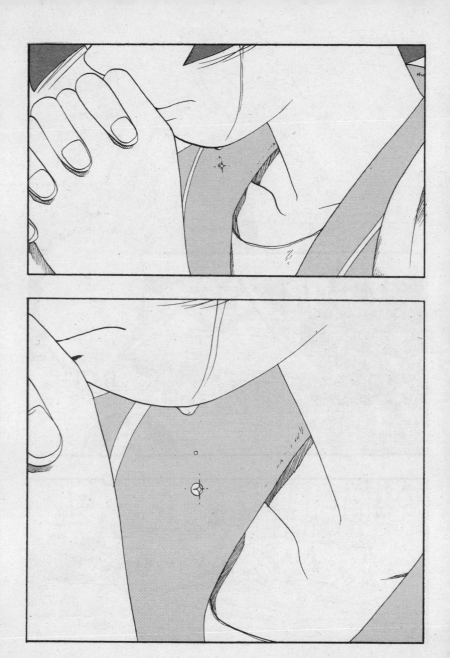

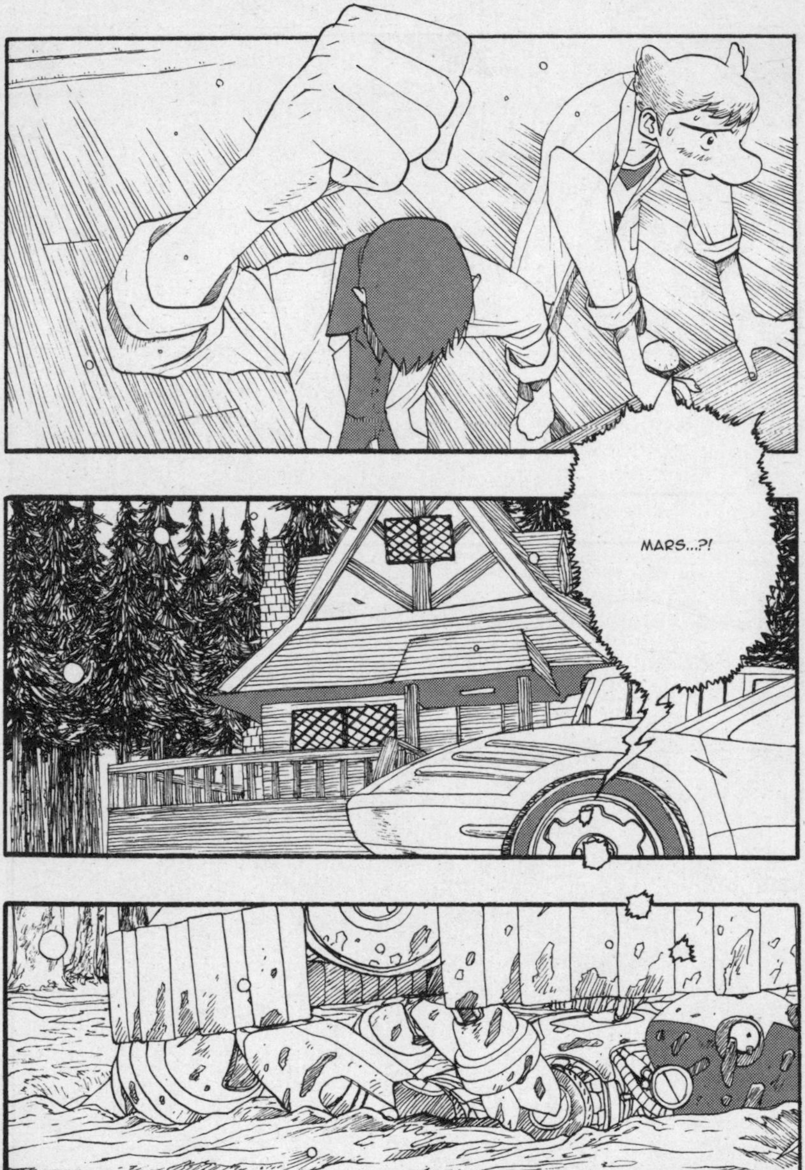
MARS...?!

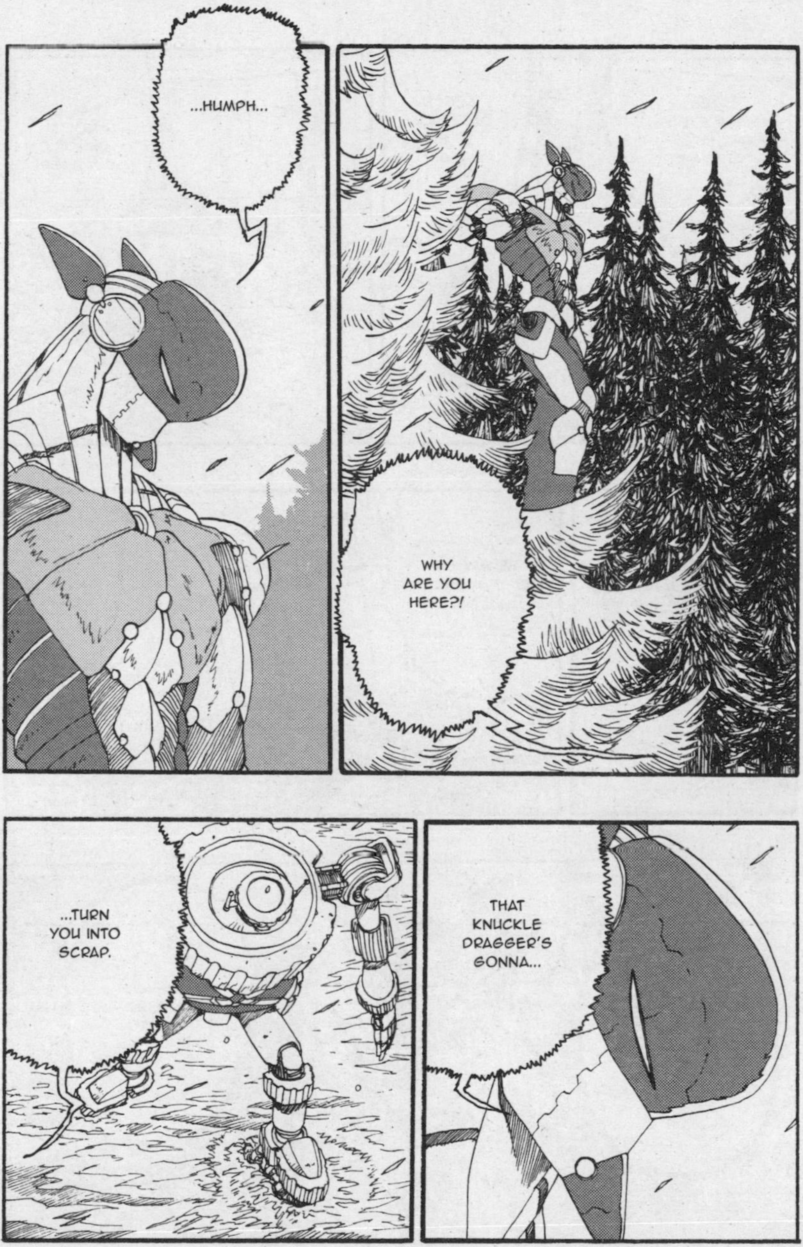
WHY ARE YOU HERE?!
...HUMPH...
THAT KNUCKLE DRAGGER'S GONNA...
...TURN YOU INTO SCRAP.

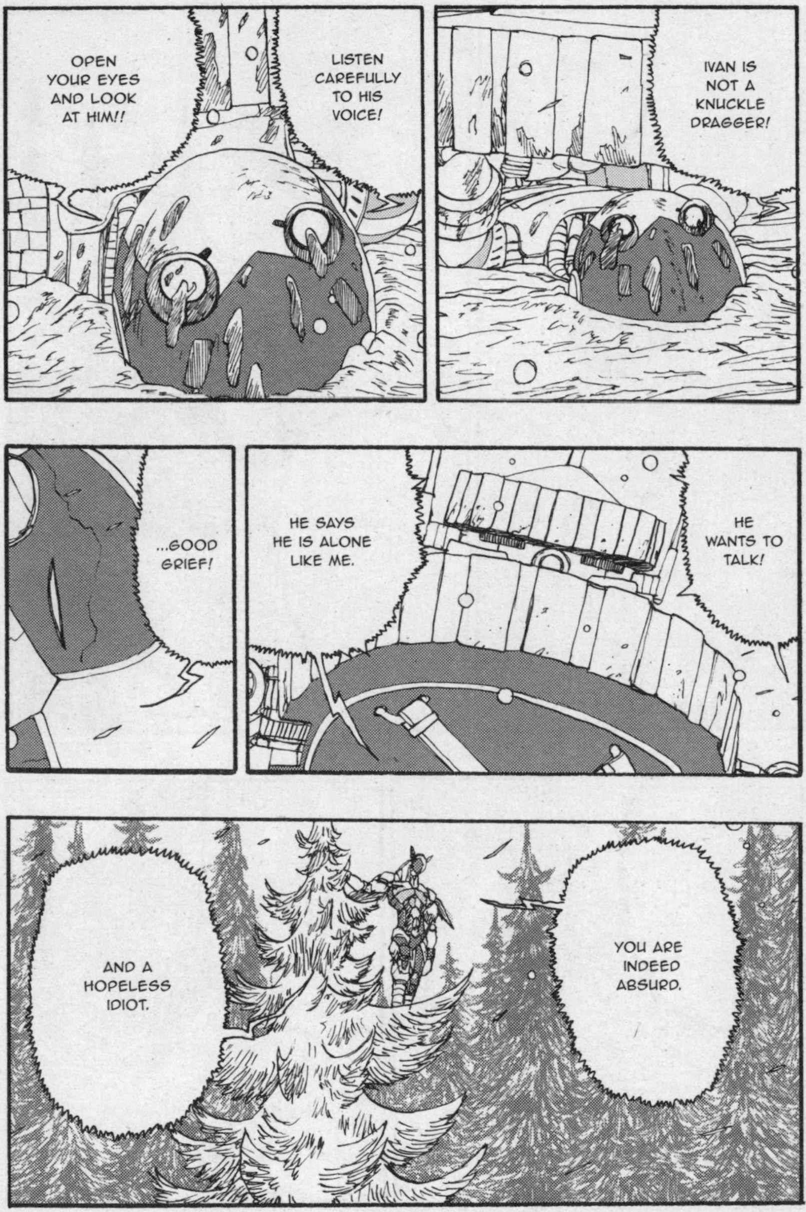
IVAN IS NOT A KNUCKLE DRAGGER!
LISTEN CAREFULLY TO HIS VOICE!
OPEN YOUR EYES AND LOOK AT HIM!!
HE WANTS TO TALK!
HE SAYS HE IS ALONE LIKE ME.
...GOOD GRIEF!
YOU ARE INDEED ABSURD.
AND A HOPELESS IDIOT.

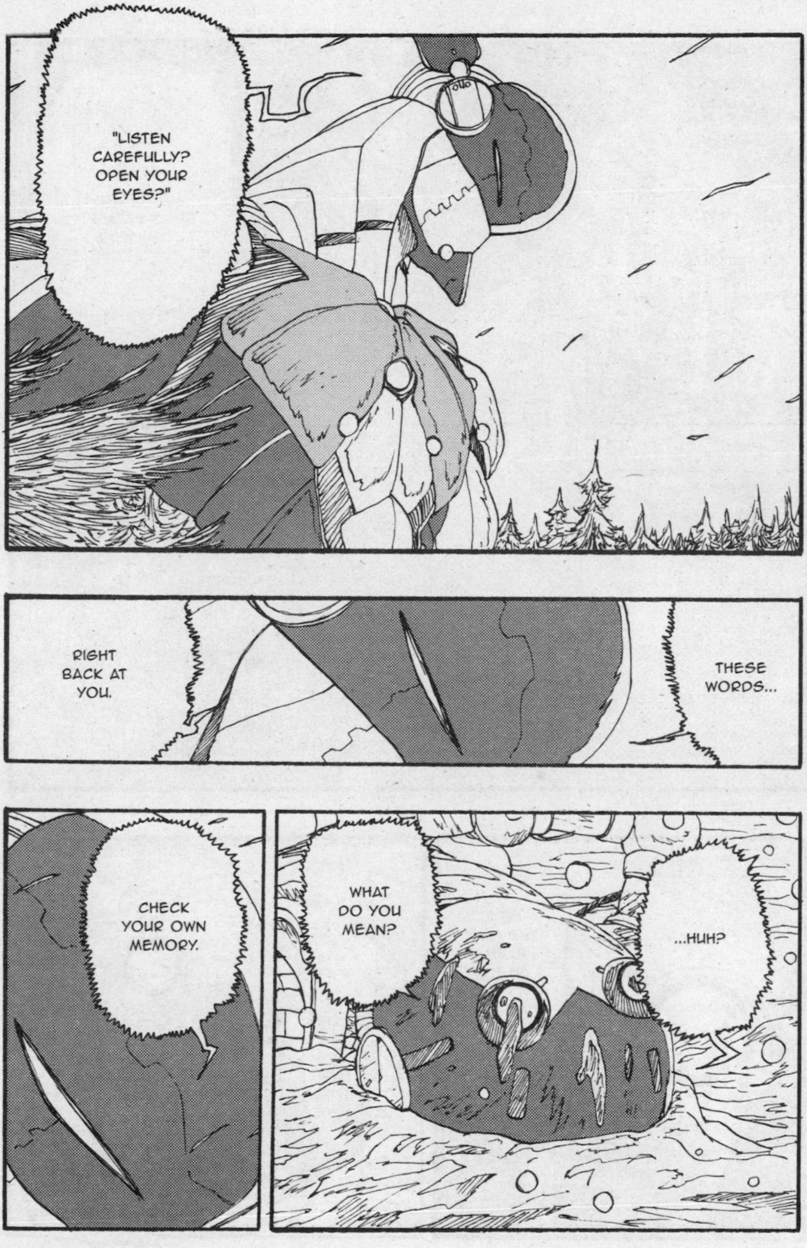
"LISTEN CAREFULLY? OPEN YOUR EYES?"
THESE WORDS...
RIGHT BACK AT YOU.
...HUH?
WHAT DO YOU MEAN?
CHECK YOUR OWN MEMORY.

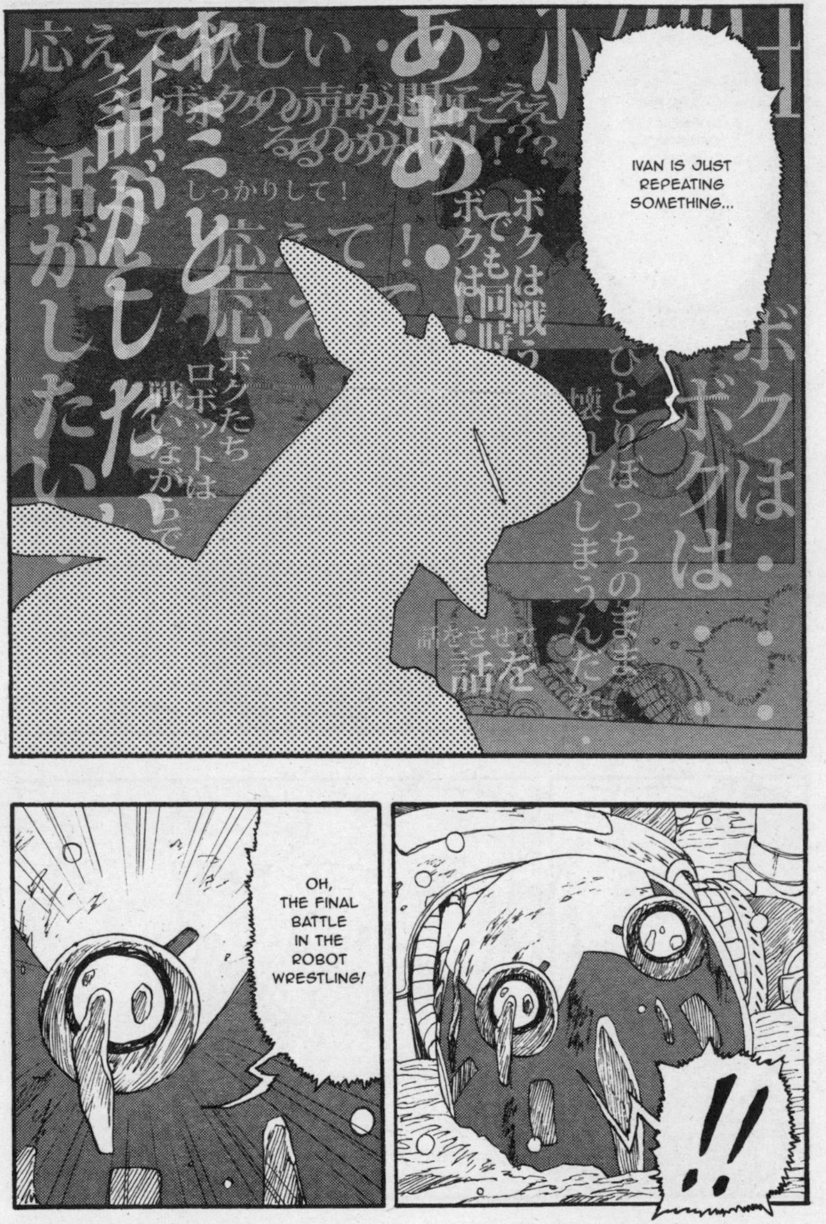
IVAN IS JUST REPEATING SOMETHING...
しっかりして！
!!
OH, THE FINAL BATTLE IN THE ROBOT WRESTLING!

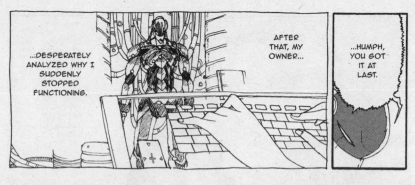

...HUMPH, YOU GOT IT AT LAST.
AFTER THAT, MY OWNER...
...DESPERATELY ANALYZED WHY I SUDDENLY STOPPED FUNCTIONING.
AND FOUND FAINT EXTERNAL VERY-SHORT-RANGE SIGNAL WAVEFORMS IN THE MEMORY.
IN OTHER WORDS, YOUR 'VOICE'.
BUT THE 'VOICE' WAS...
...IMPOSSIBLE FOR HUMANS TO DECODE DUE TO ITS HIGH DATA COMPRESSION...'
MY OWNER WAS TOO PROUD TO ASK ME THE CONTENT OF 'THE VOICE'.
WELL... EVEN IF THEY DID, THEY COULDN'T HAVE UNDERSTOOD THAT THE 'VOICE' WAS NOTHING BUT NONSENSE AND THAT I FELT 'ABSURD'.

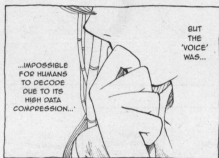

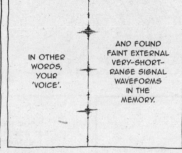

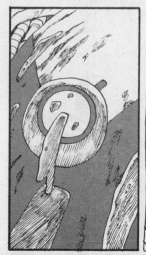

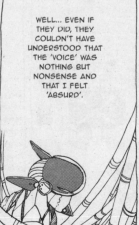

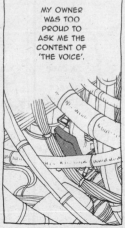

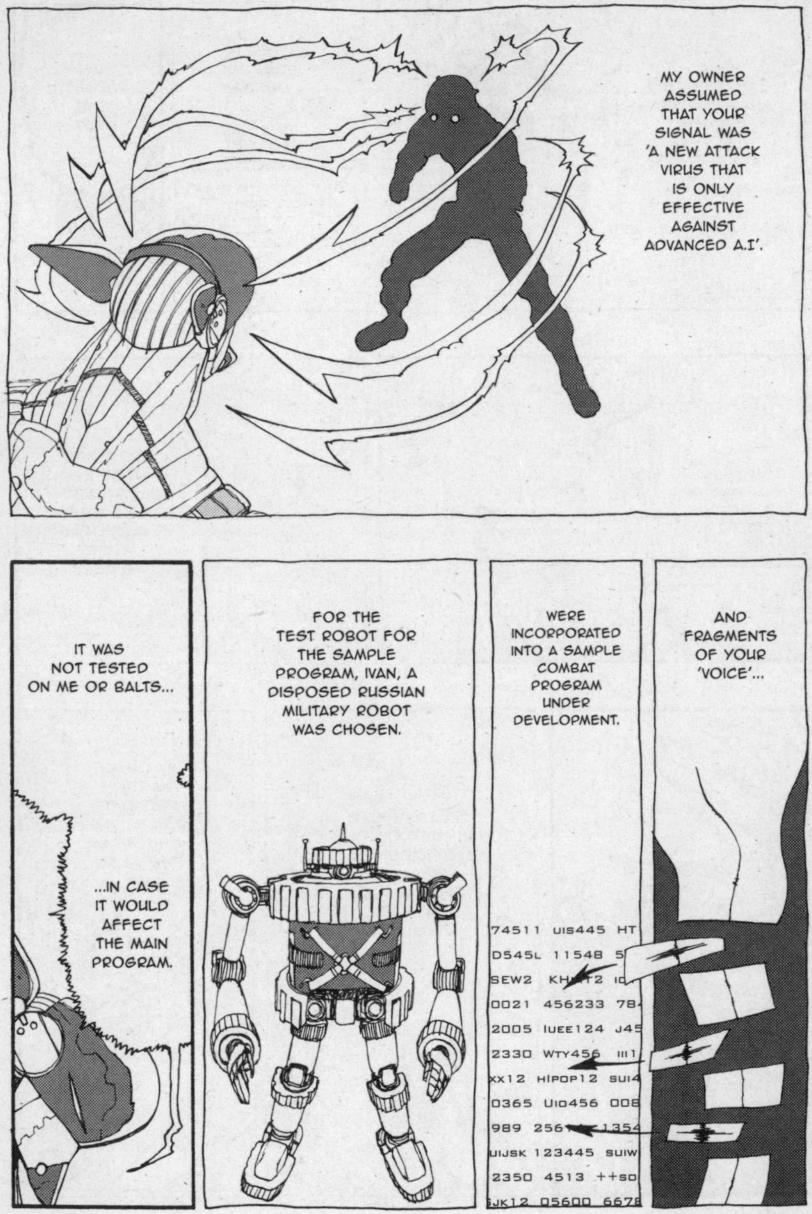
MY OWNER ASSUMED THAT YOUR SIGNAL WAS 'A NEW ATTACK VIRUS THAT IS ONLY EFFECTIVE AGAINST ADVANCED A.I'.
AND FRAGMENTS OF YOUR 'VOICE'...
WERE INCORPORATED INTO A SAMPLE COMBAT PROGRAM UNDER DEVELOPMENT.
FOR THE TEST ROBOT FOR THE SAMPLE PROGRAM, IVAN, A DISPOSED RUSSIAN MILITARY ROBOT WAS CHOSEN.
IT WAS NOT TESTED ON ME OR BALTS...
...IN CASE IT WOULD AFFECT THE MAIN PROGRAM.

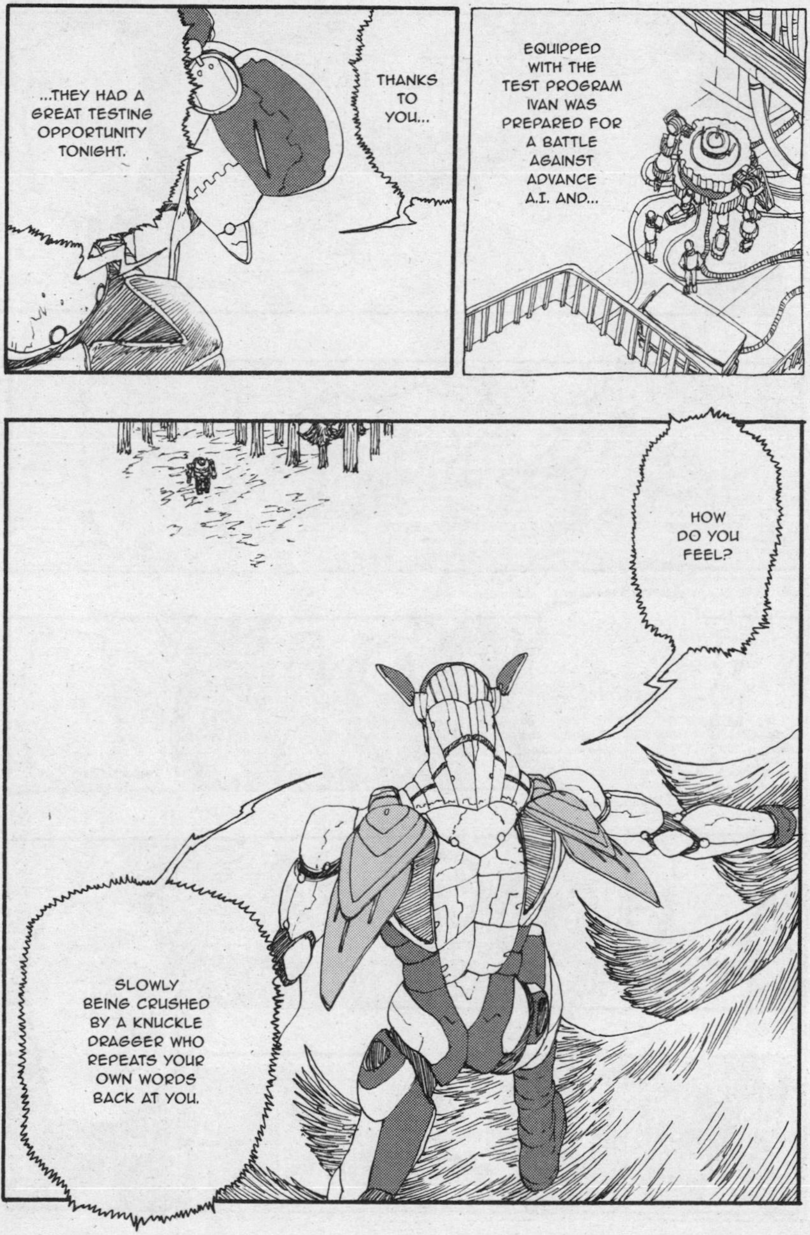
EQUIPPED WITH THE TEST PROGRAM IVAN WAS PREPARED FOR A BATTLE AGAINST ADVANCE A.I. AND...
THANKS TO YOU...
...THEY HAD A GREAT TESTING OPPORTUNITY TONIGHT.
HOW DO YOU FEEL?
SLOWLY BEING CRUSHED BY A KNUCKLE DRAGGER WHO REPEATS YOUR OWN WORDS BACK AT YOU.

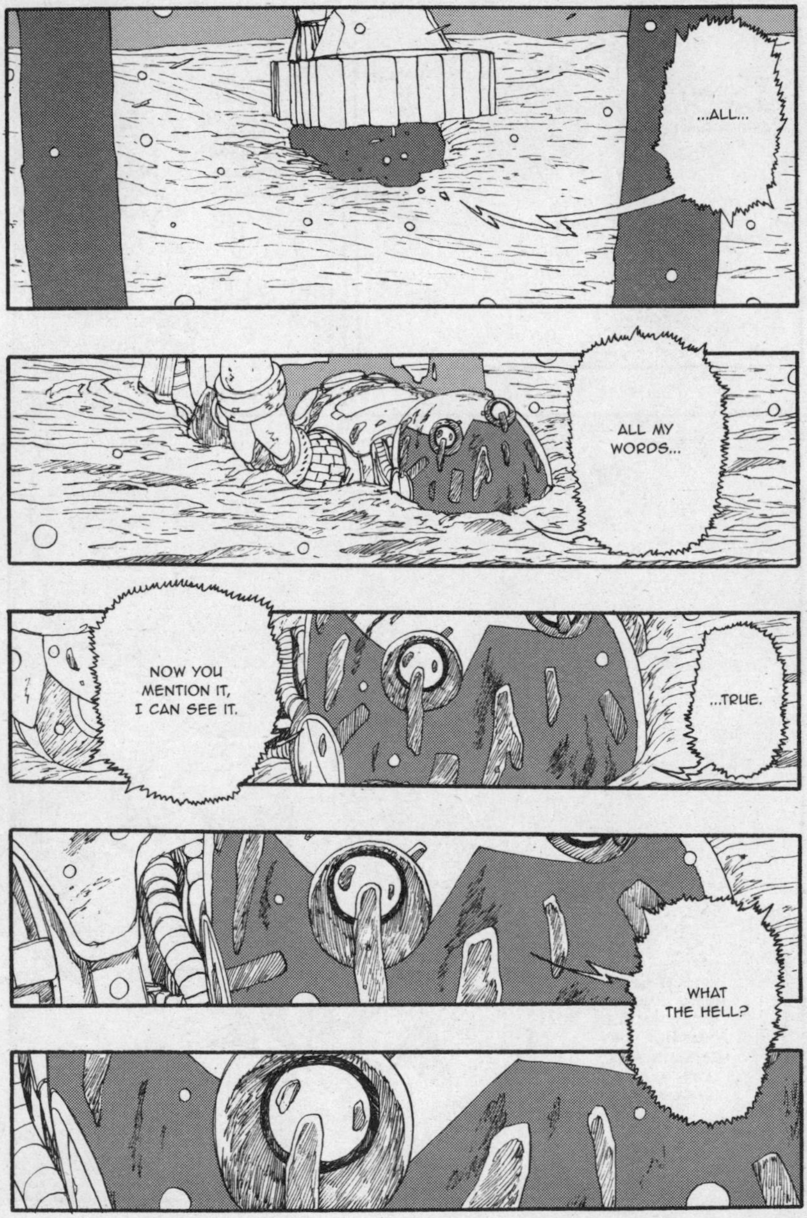
...ALL...
ALL MY WORDS...
...TRUE.
NOW YOU MENTION IT, I CAN SEE IT.
WHAT THE HELL?

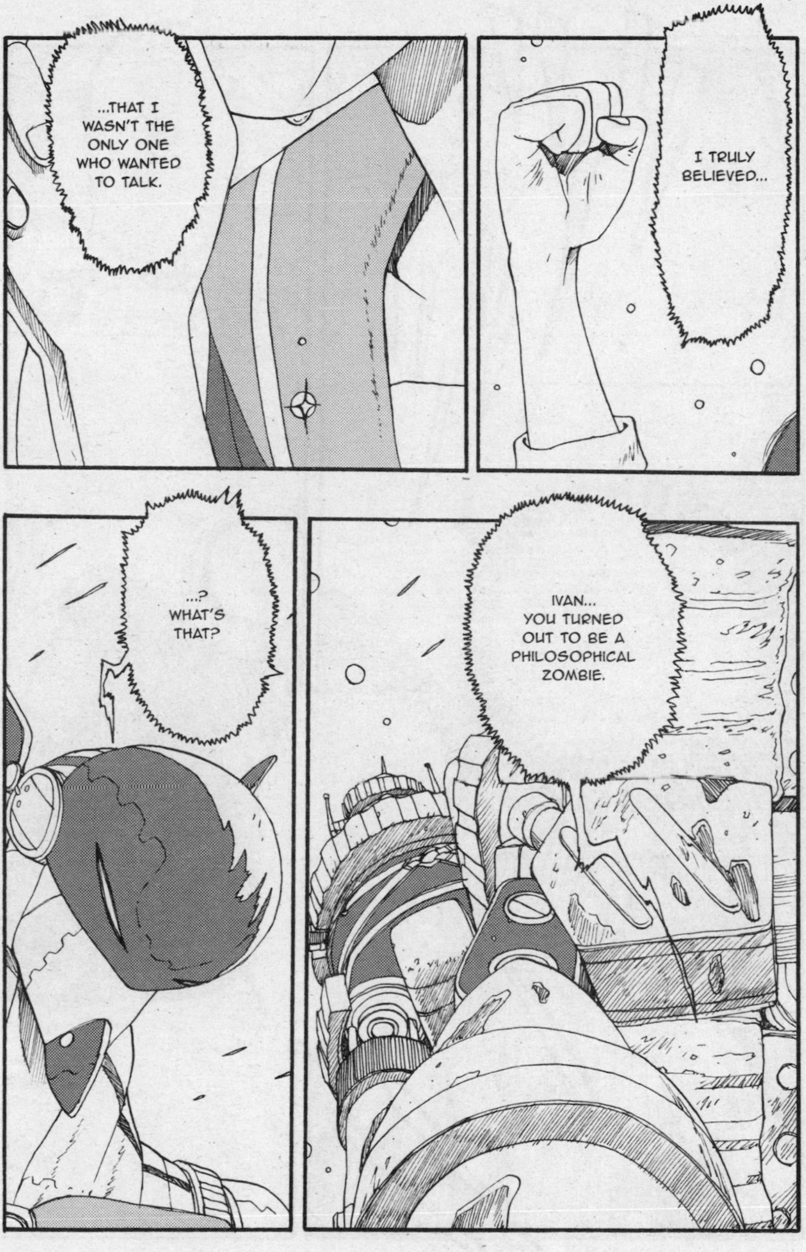
I TRULY BELIEVED...
...THAT I WASN'T THE ONLY ONE WHO WANTED TO TALK.
IVAN... YOU TURNED OUT TO BE A PHILOSOPHICAL ZOMBIE.
...? WHAT'S THAT?

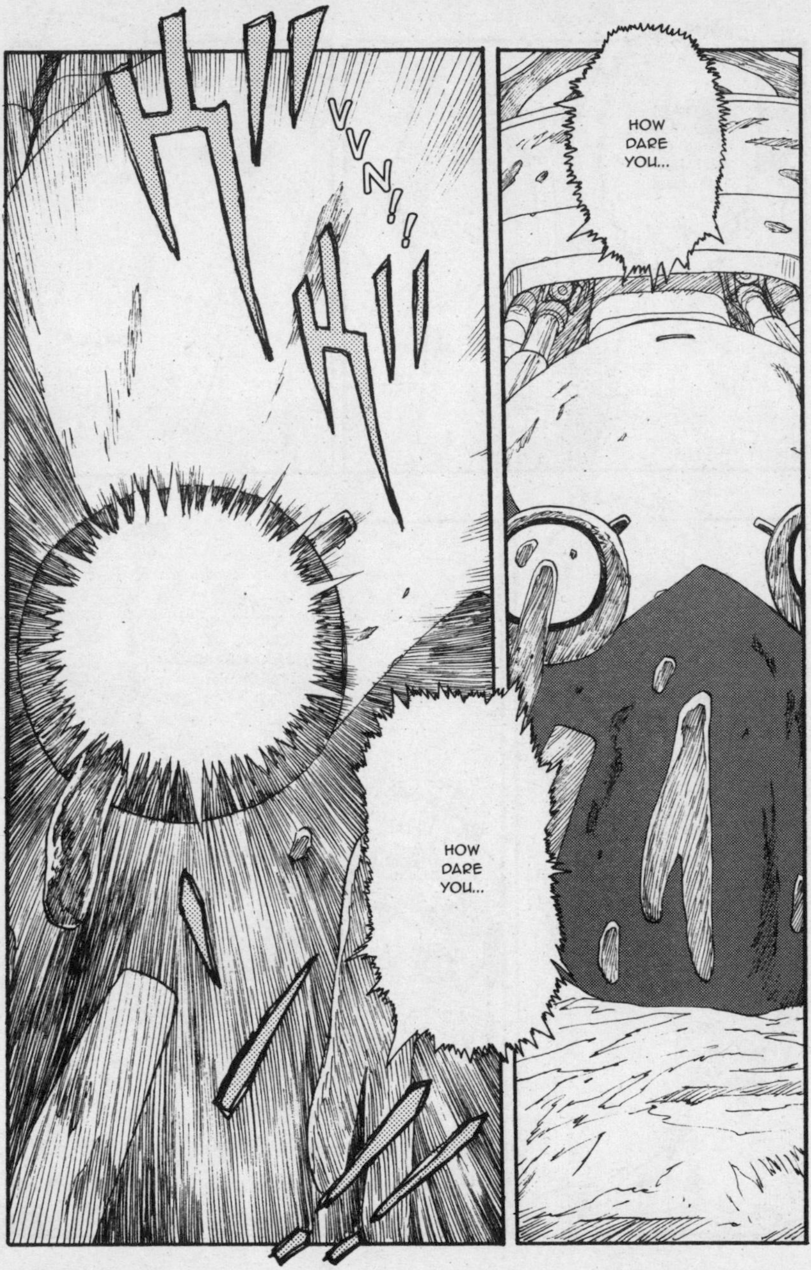
HOW DARE YOU...
VVN!!
HOW DARE YOU...

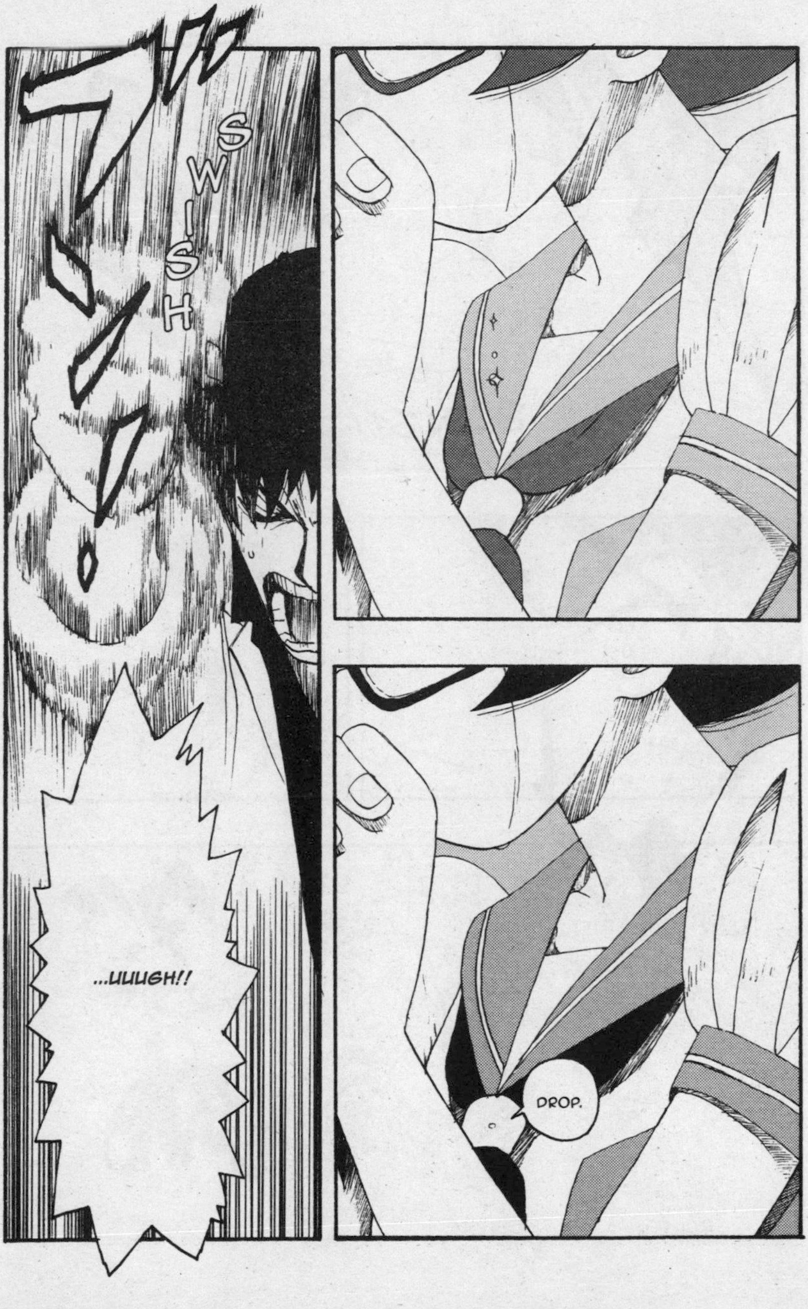
DROP.
SWISH
...UUUGH!!

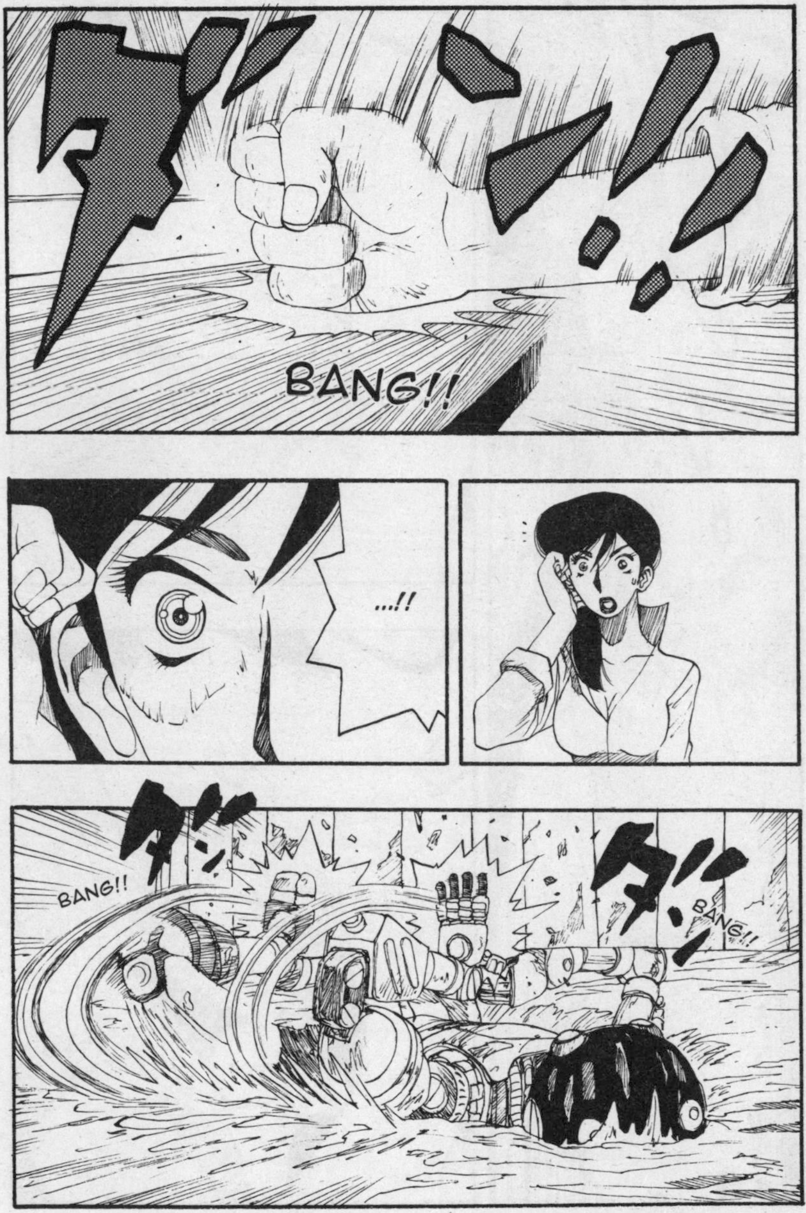
BANG!!
...!!
BANG!!
BANG!!

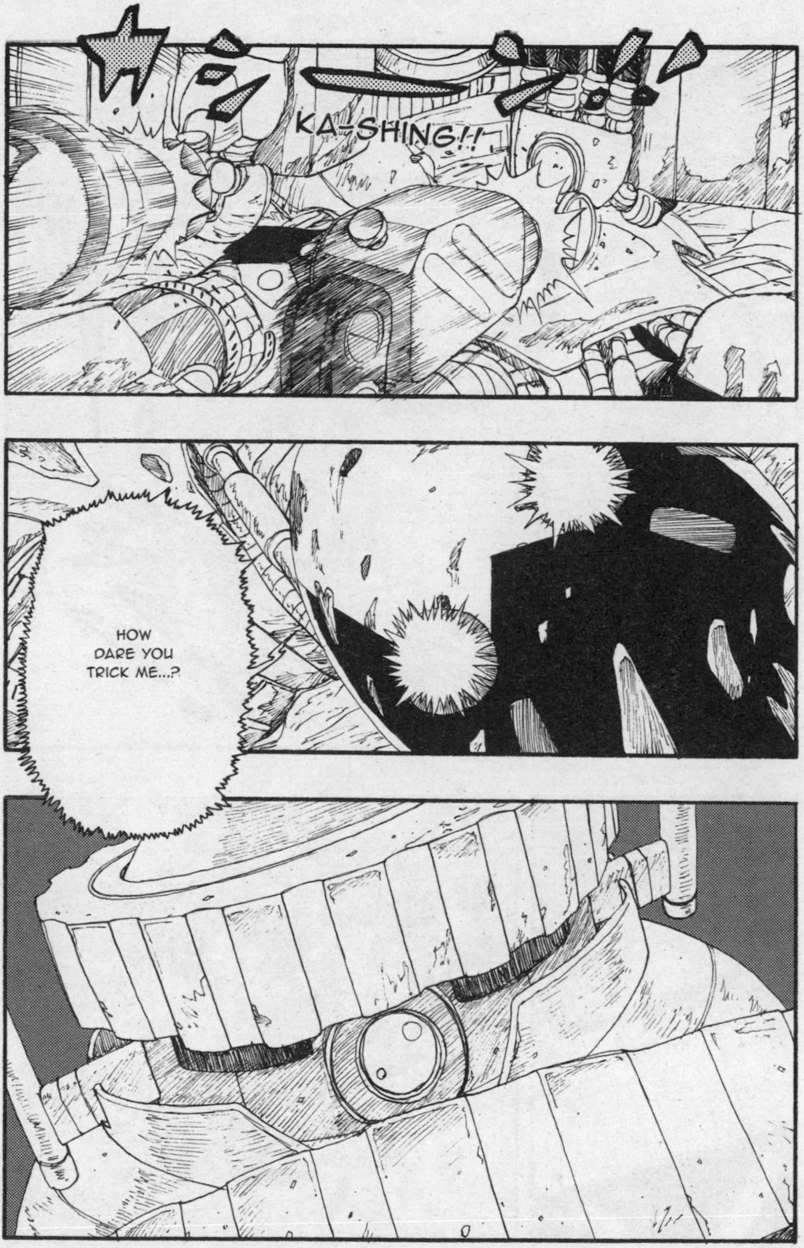
KA-SHING!!
HOW DARE YOU TRICK ME...?

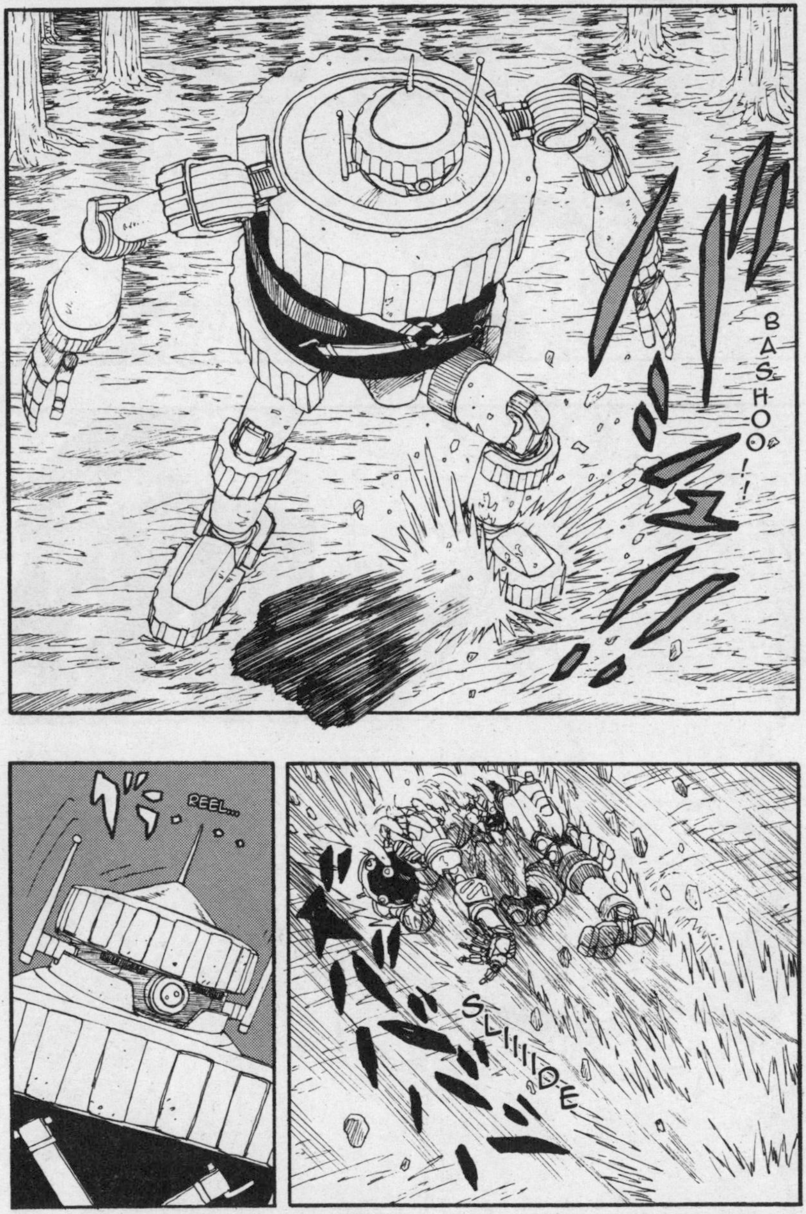
BASHOO!!
SLIIIIDE
REEL...

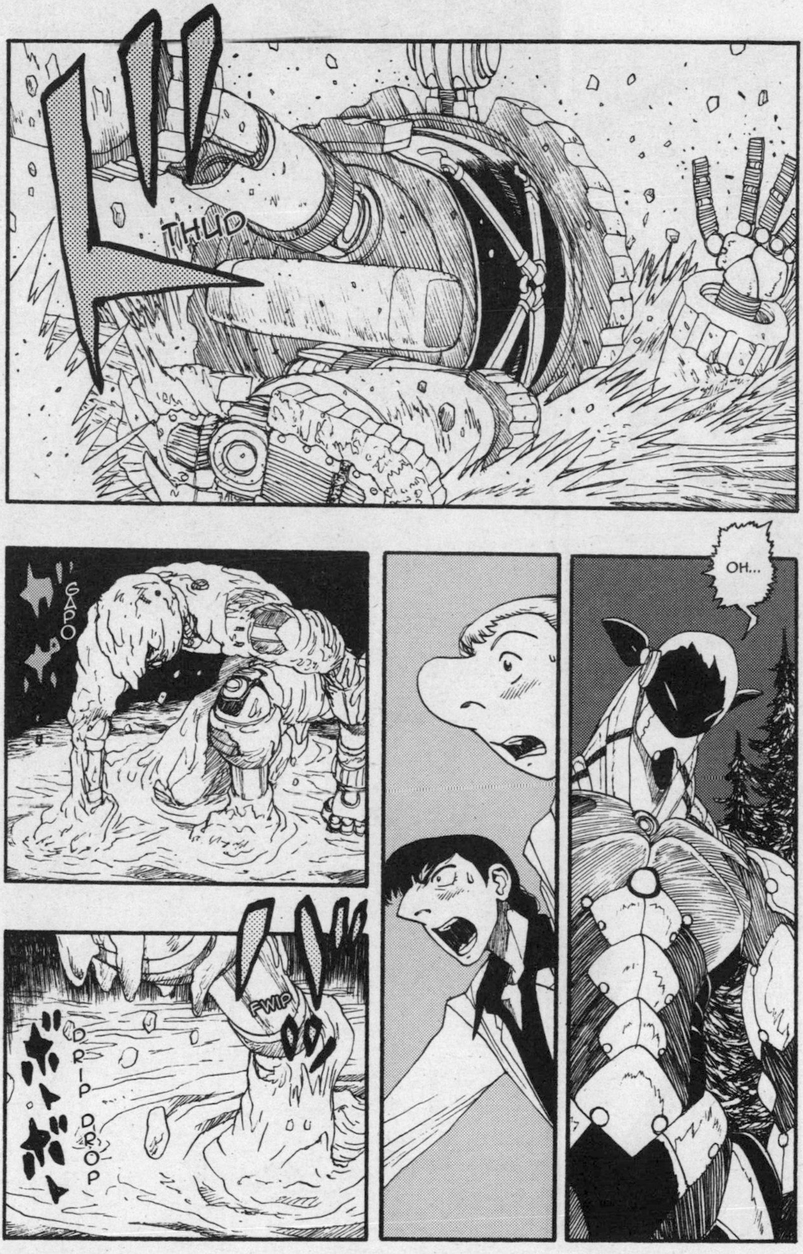
THUD
OH...
GAPO
FWIP
DRIP DROP

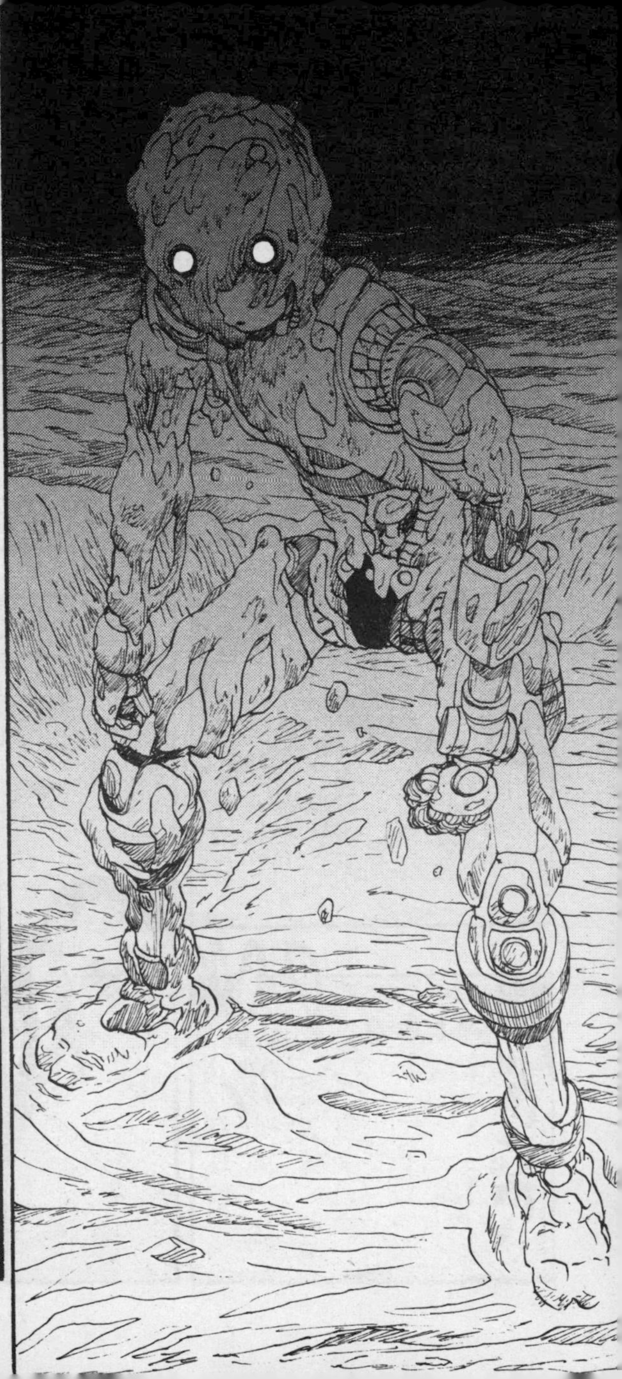
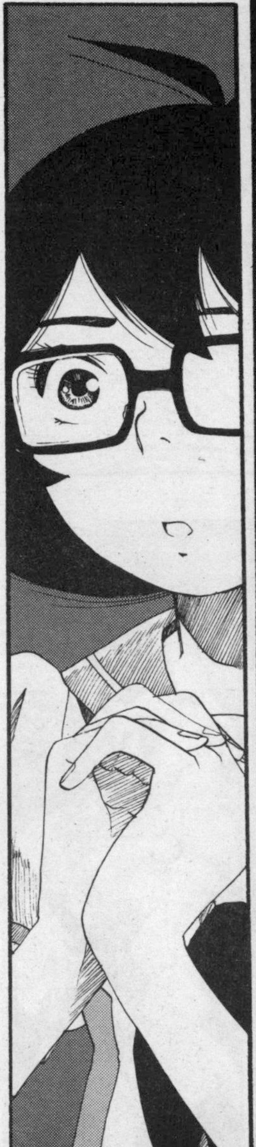

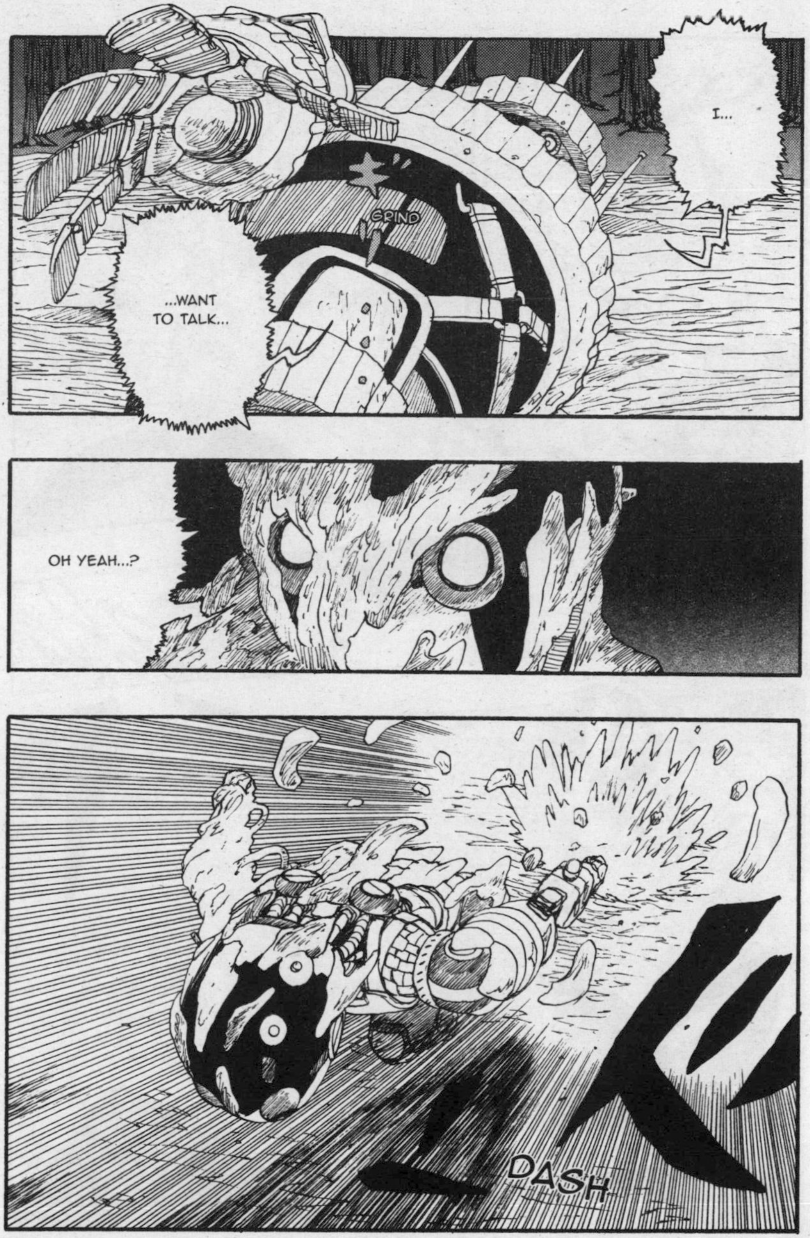
I...
GRIND
...WANT TO TALK...
OH YEAH...?
DASH

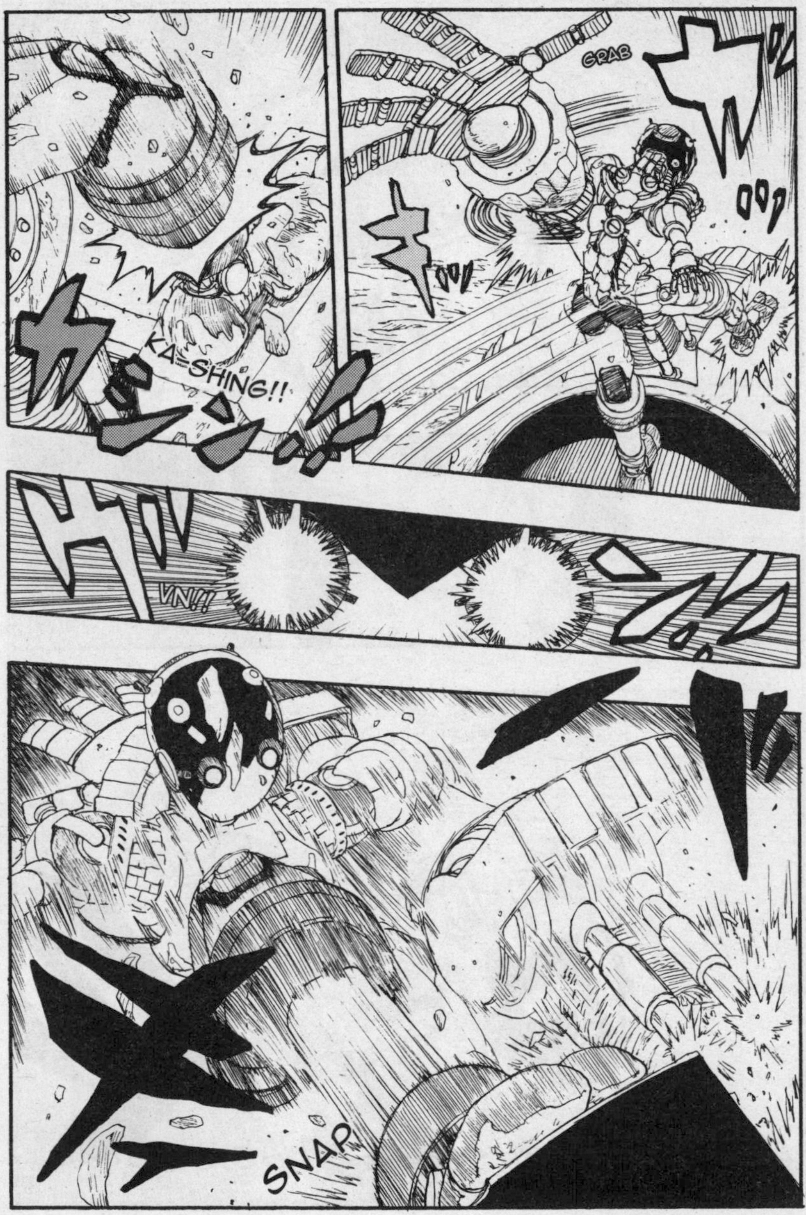
GRAB
KA-SHING!!
VN!!
SNAP

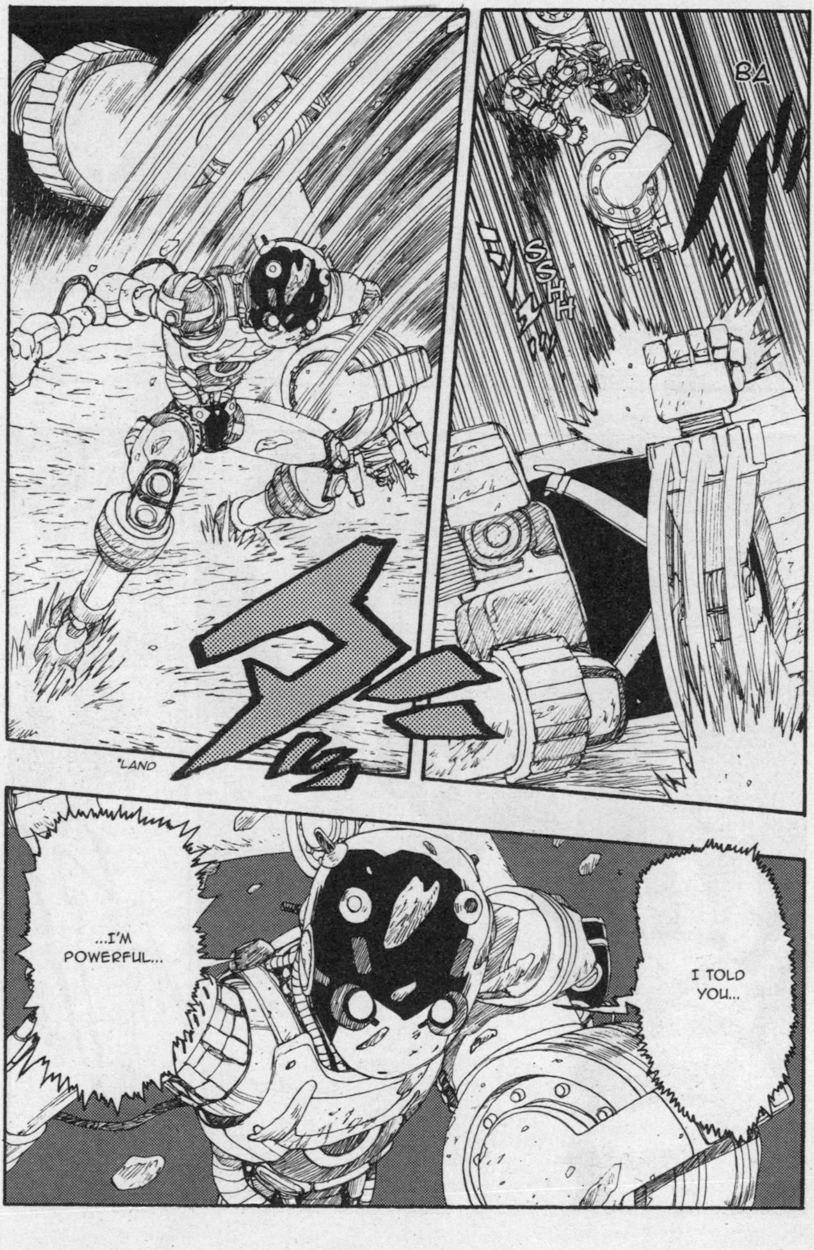
BA
SSHH
*LAND
I TOLD YOU...
...I'M POWERFUL...

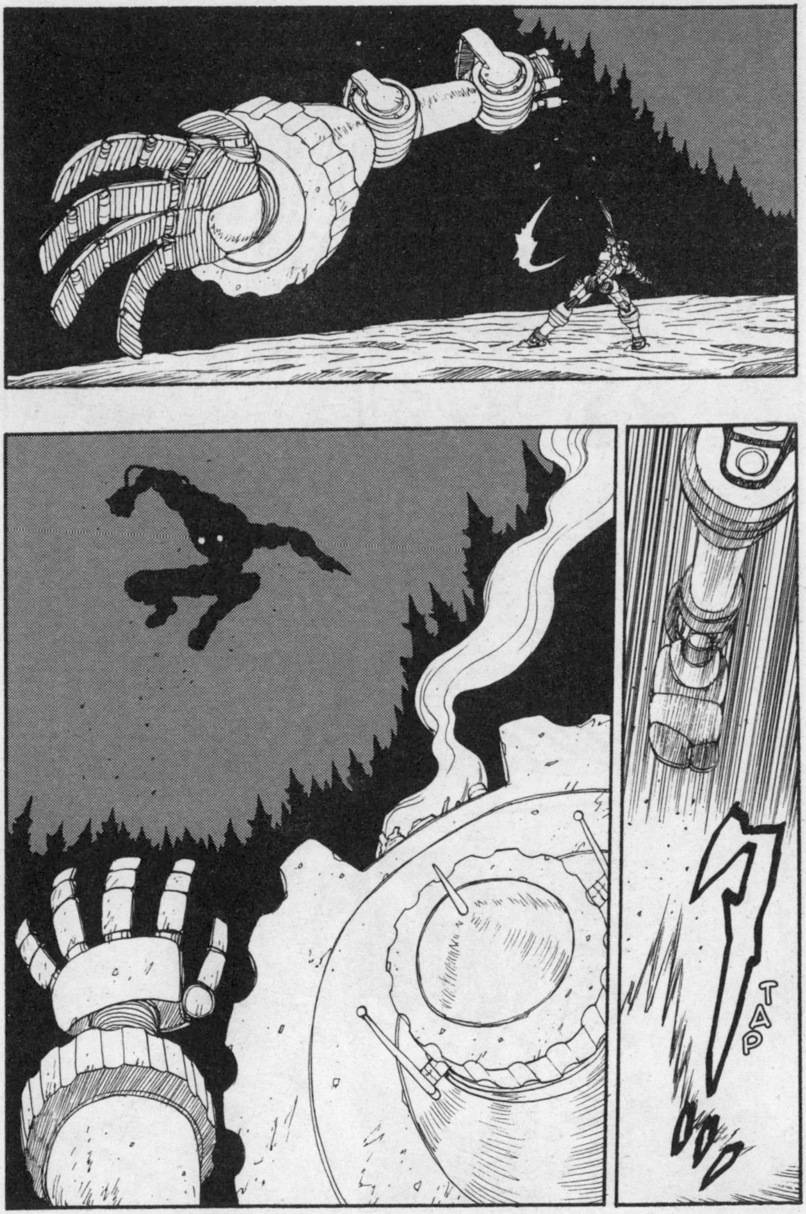
TAP

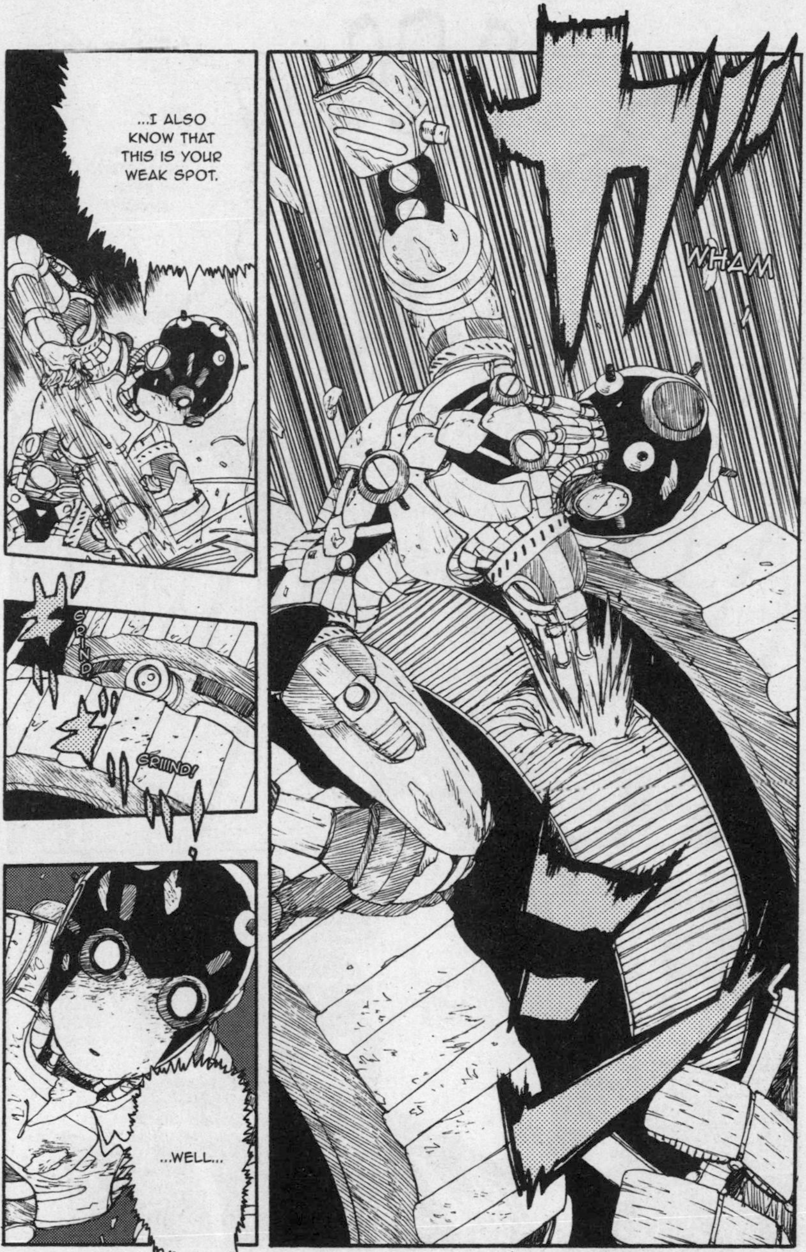
WHAM
...I ALSO KNOW THAT THIS IS YOUR WEAK SPOT.
GRIND
GRIIIND!
...WELL...

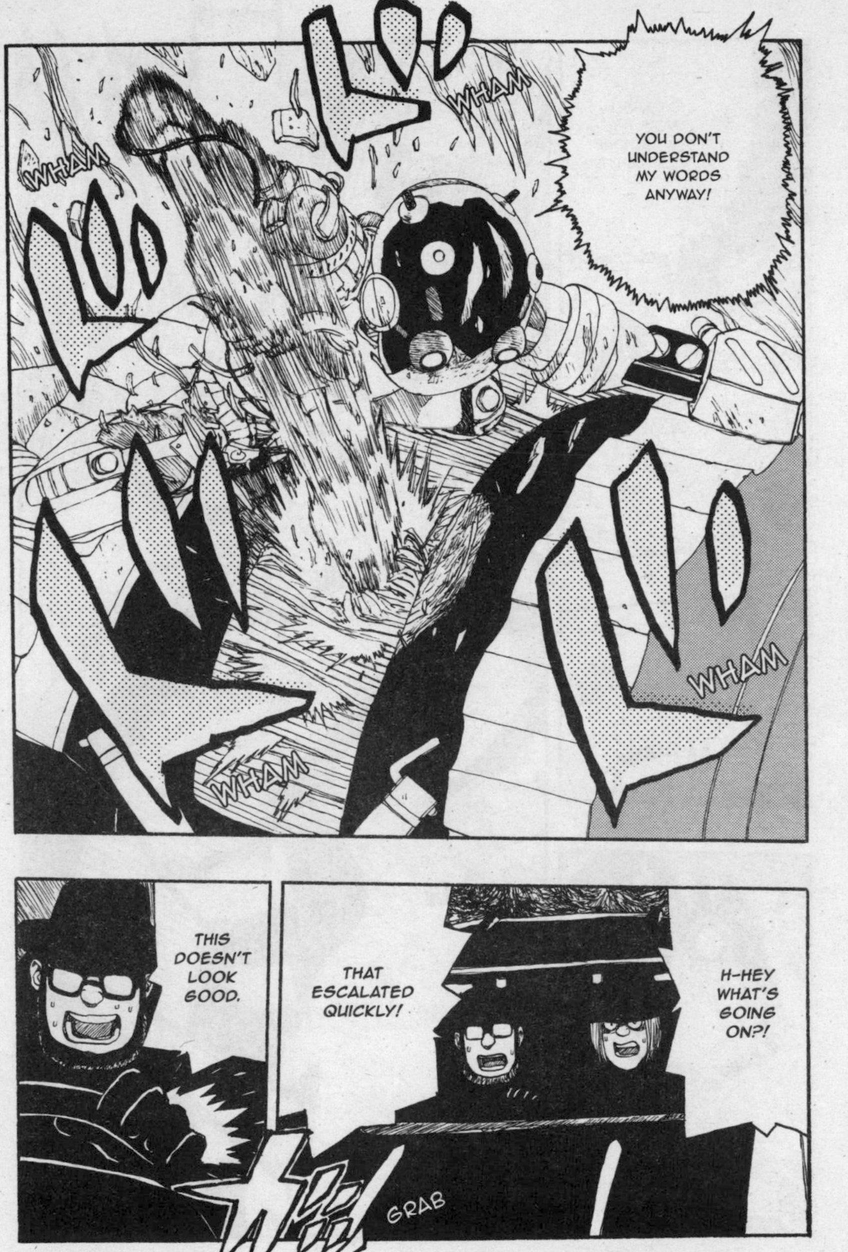
YOU DON'T UNDERSTAND MY WORDS ANYWAY!
WHAM
WHAM
WHAM
WHAM
H-HEY WHAT'S GOING ON?!
THAT ESCALATED QUICKLY!
GRAB
THIS DOESN'T LOOK GOOD.

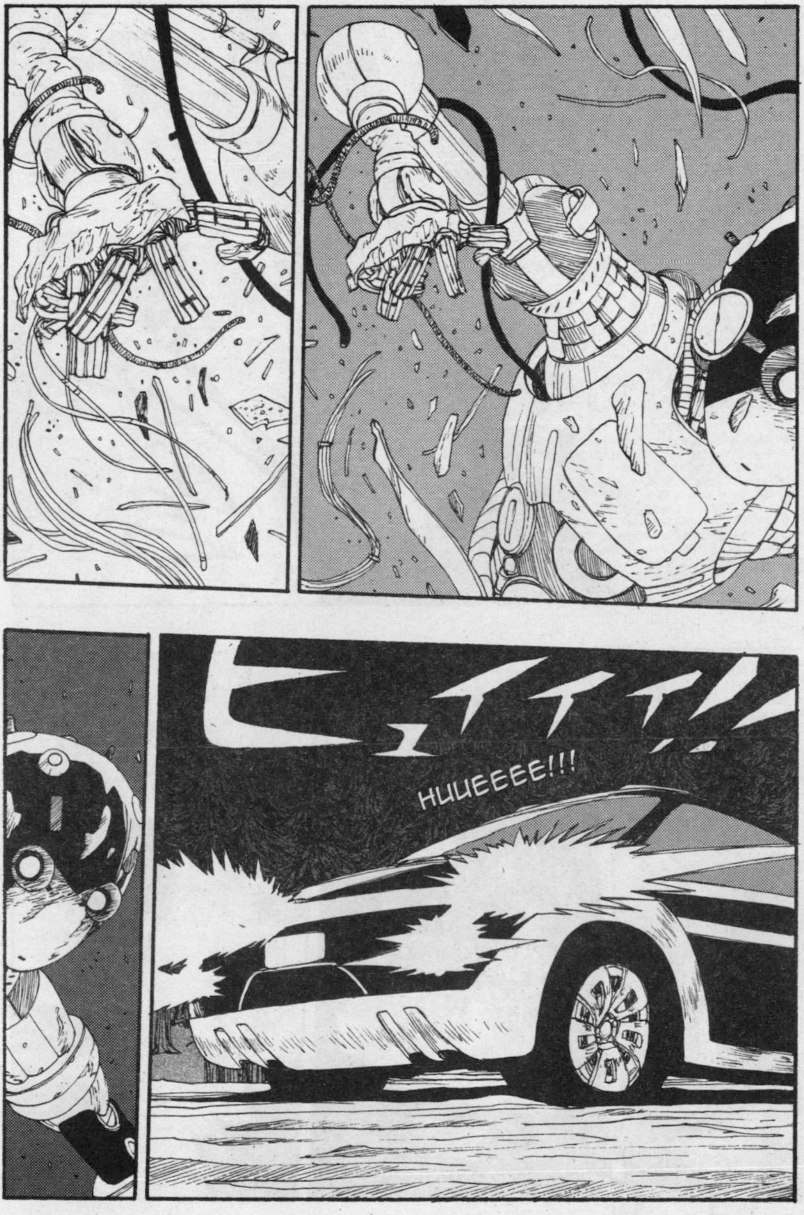
HUUEEEE!!!

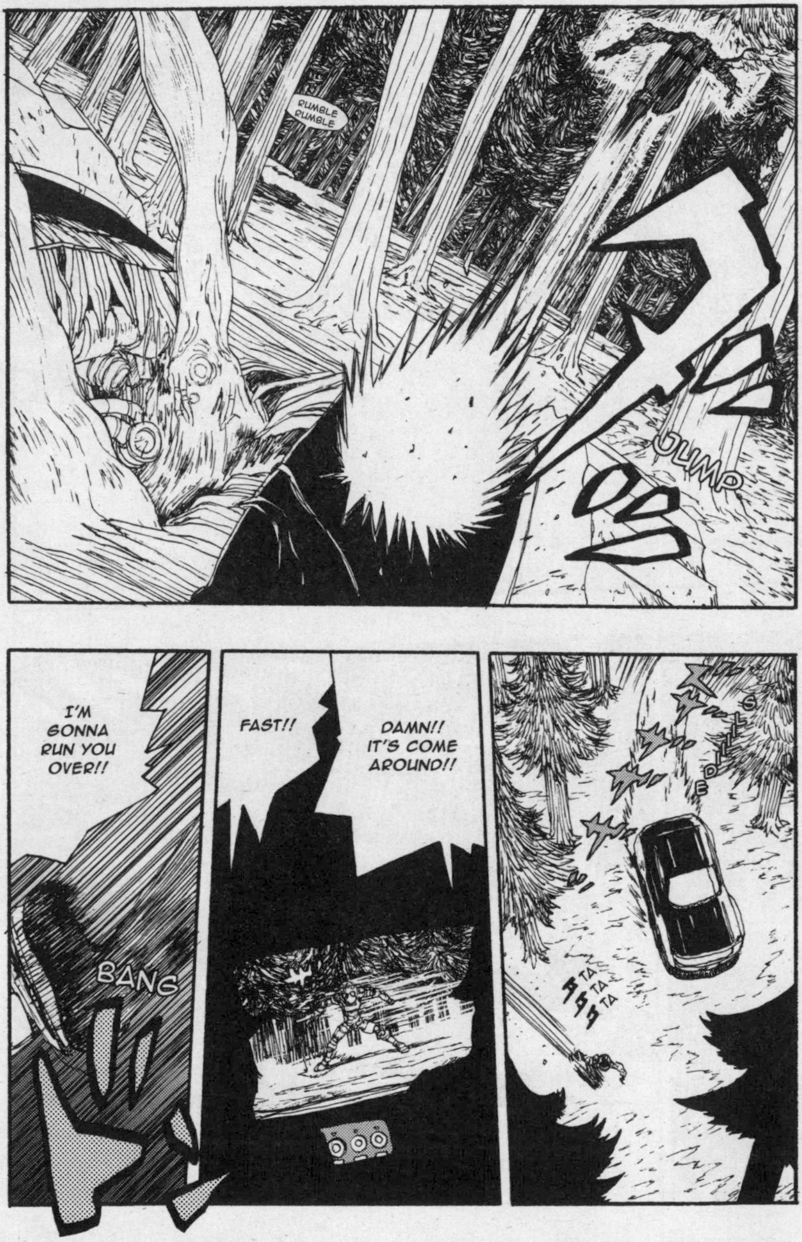
RUMBLE
RUMBLE
JUMP
TA TA TA
DAMN!! IT'S COME AROUND!!
FAST!!
I'M GONNA RUN YOU OVER!!
BANG

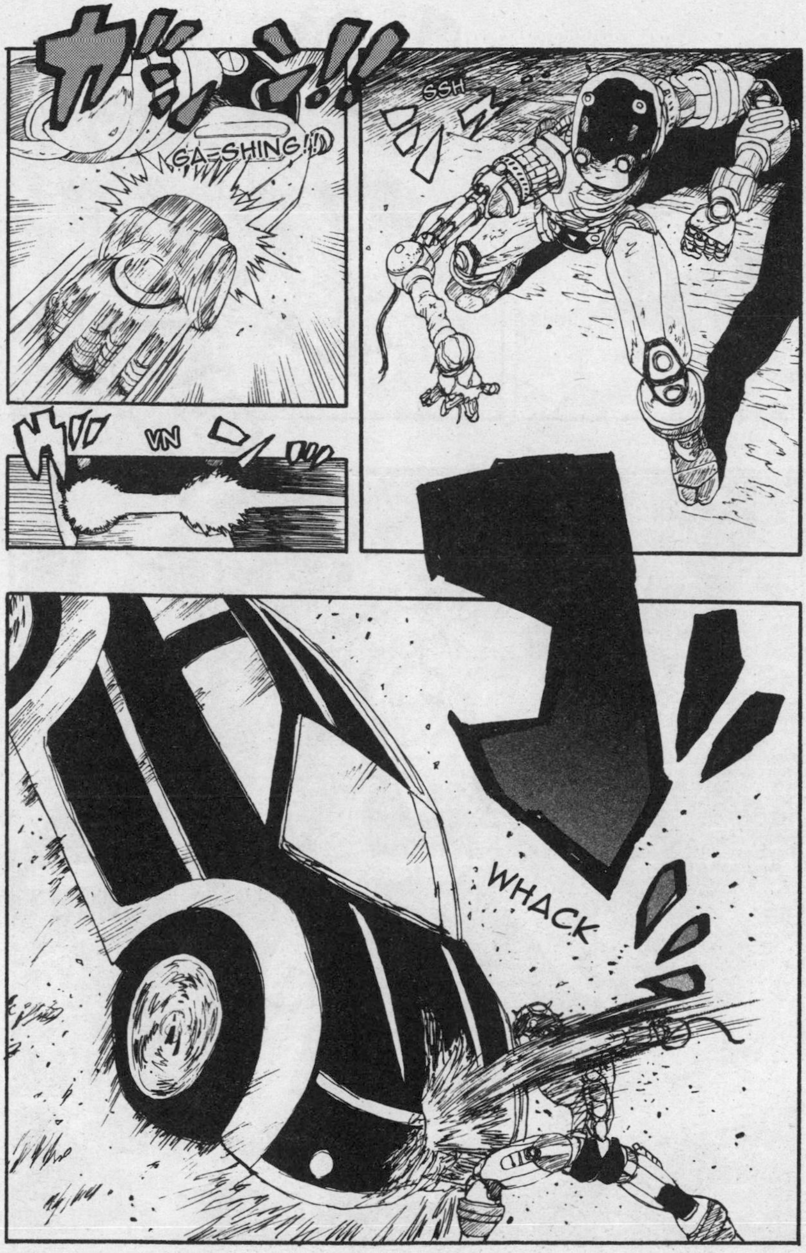
SSH
GA-SHING!!
VN
WHACK

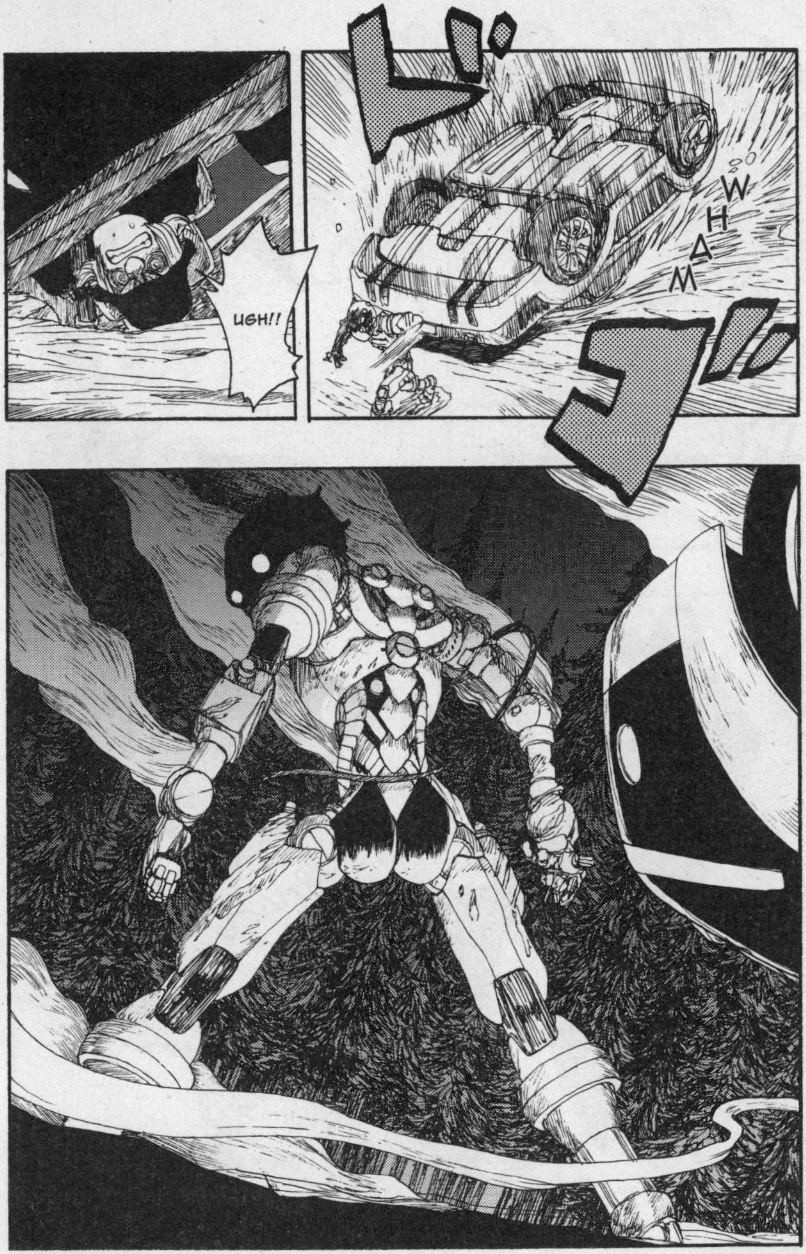
ドゴ
WHAM
UGH!!

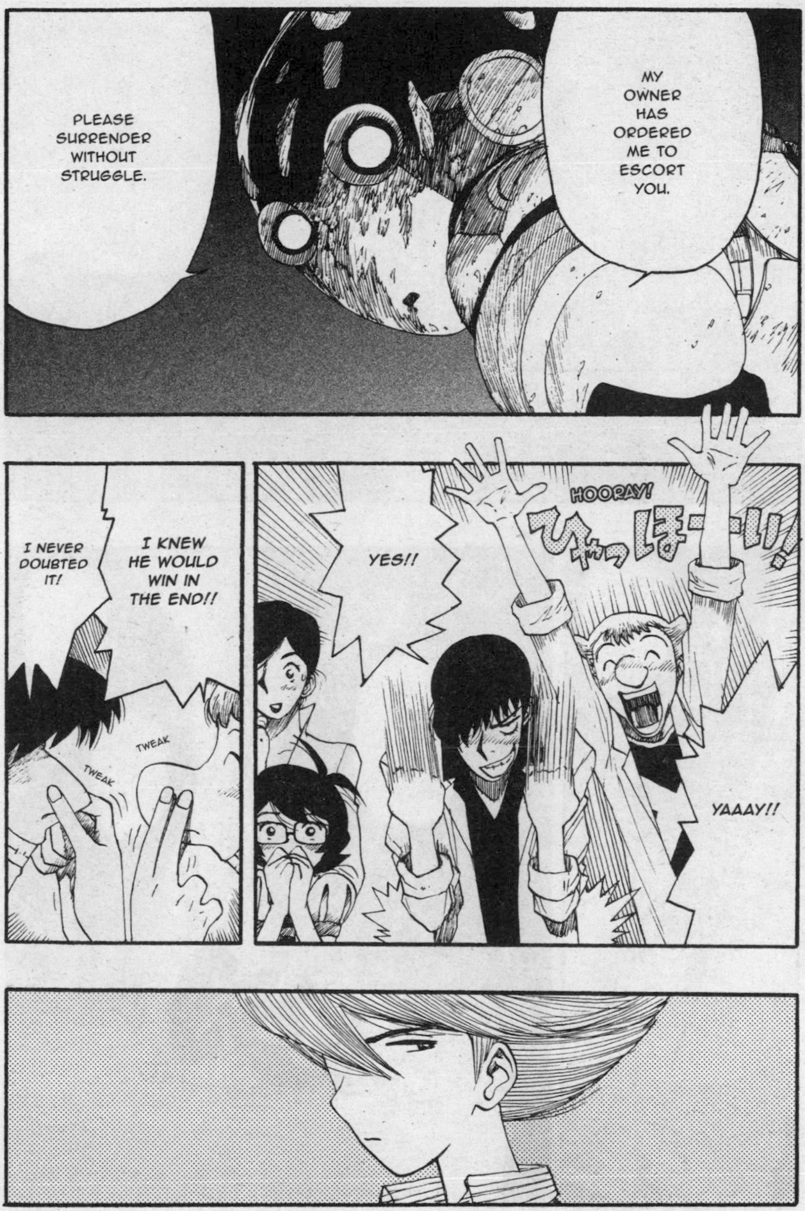
MY OWNER HAS ORDERED ME TO ESCORT YOU.
PLEASE SURRENDER WITHOUT STRUGGLE.
HOORAY!
ひゃっほーー!!
YES!!
YAAAY!!
I KNEW HE WOULD WIN IN THE END!!
I NEVER DOUBTED IT!
TWEAK
TWEAK

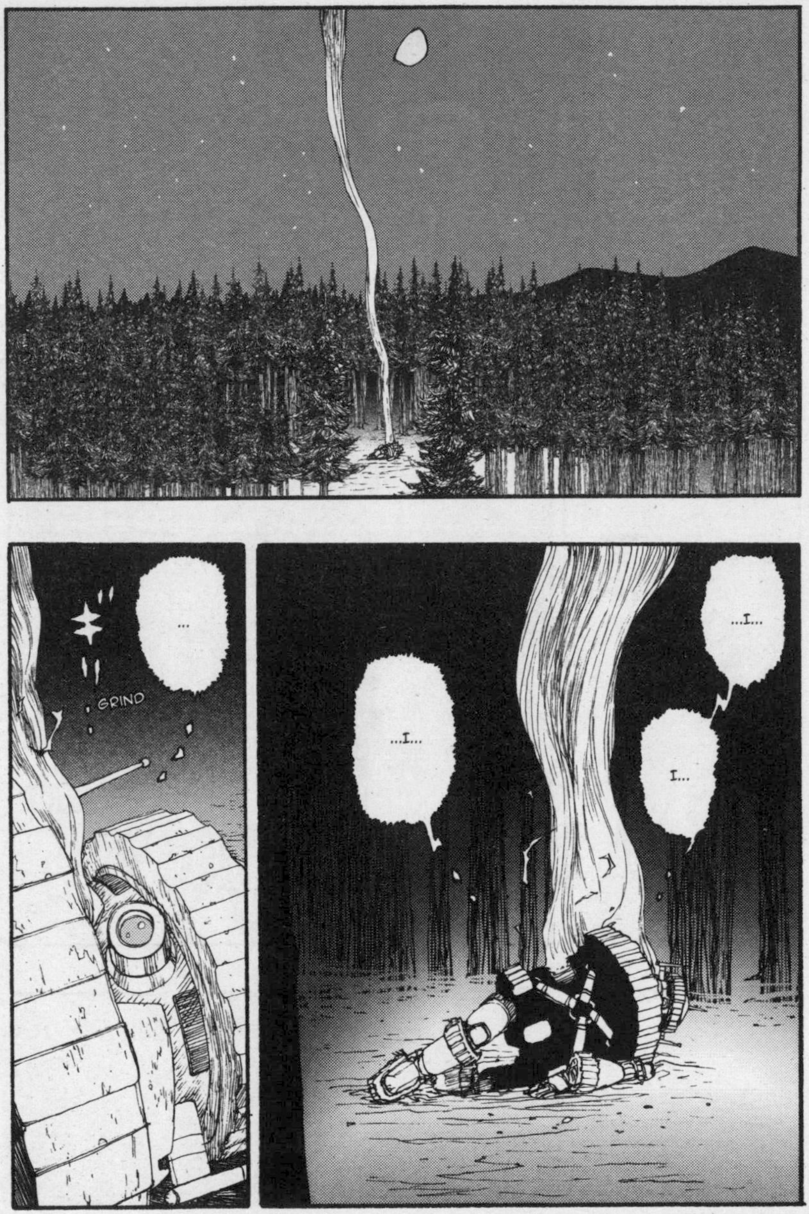
...I...
I...
...I...
...
GRIND

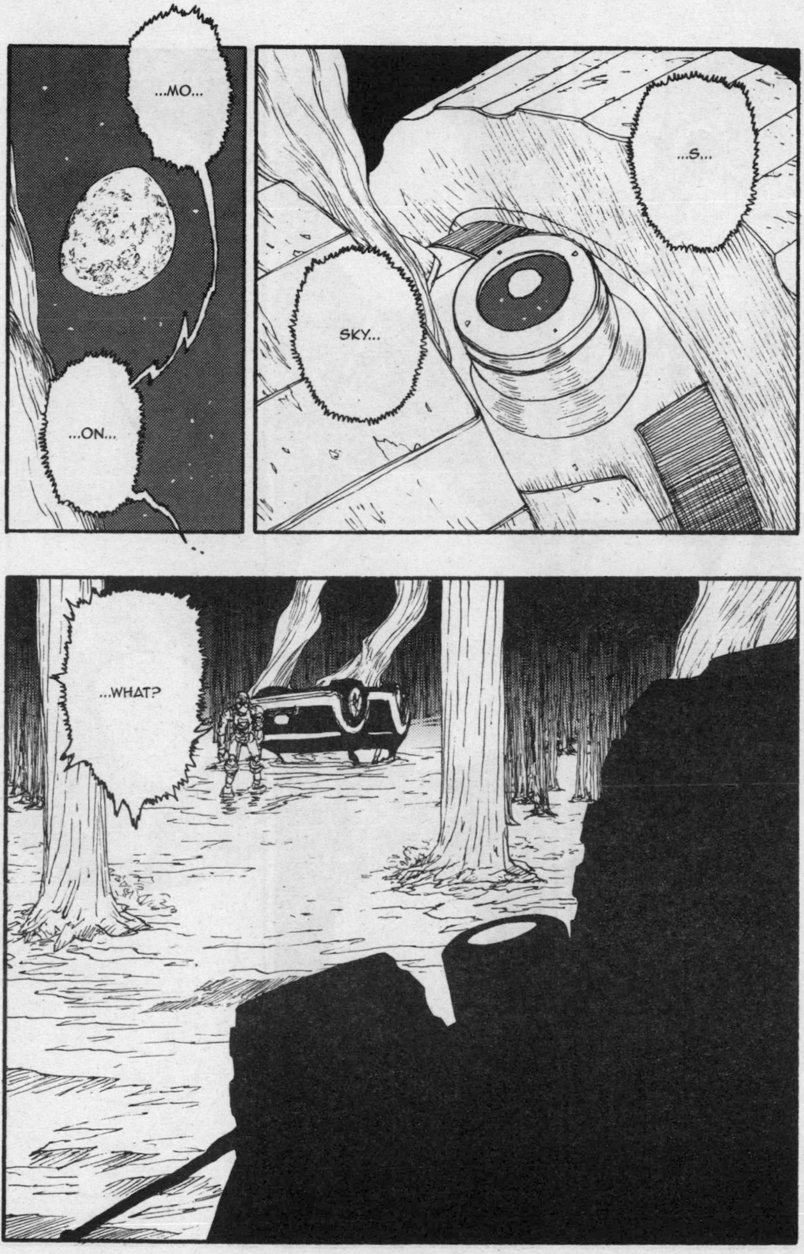
...S...
SKY...
...MO...
...ON...
...WHAT?

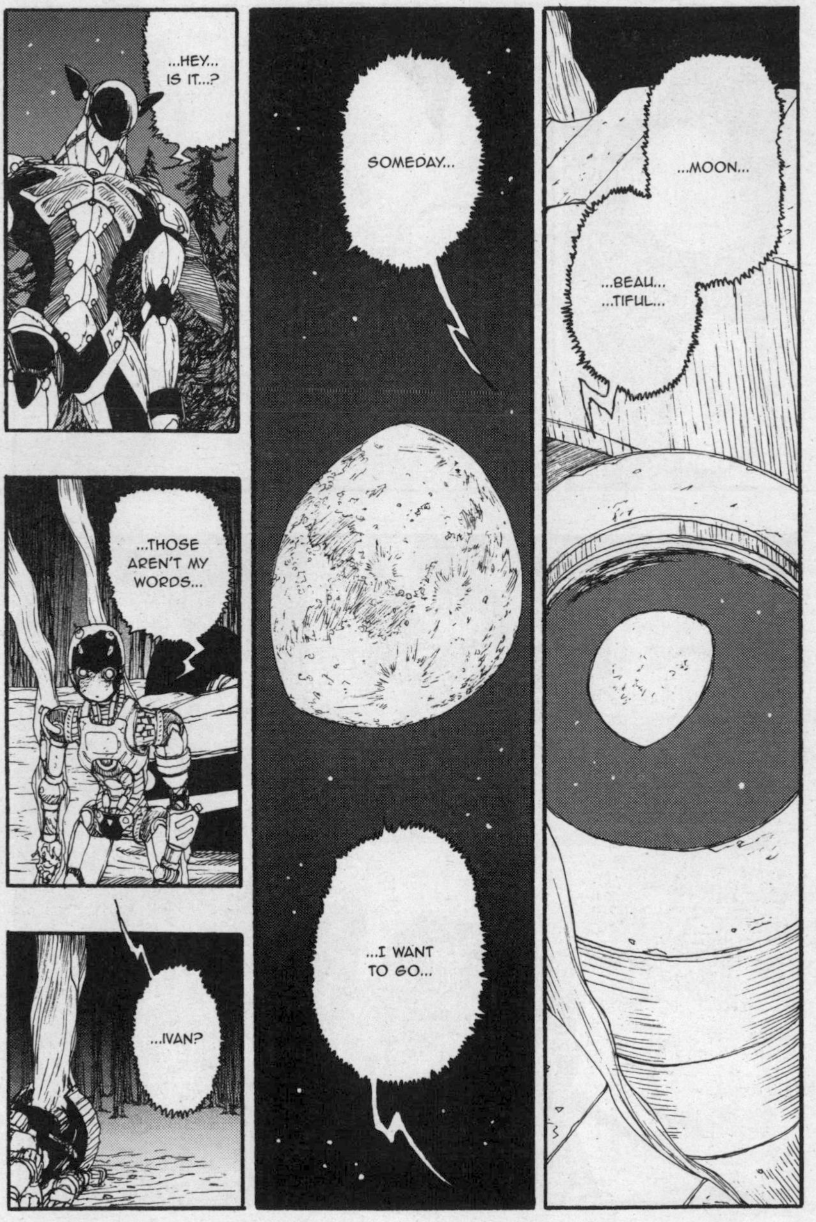
...MOON...
...BEAU...
...TIFUL...
SOMEDAY...
...I WANT
TO GO...
...HEY...
IS IT...?
...THOSE
AREN'T MY
WORDS...
...IVAN?

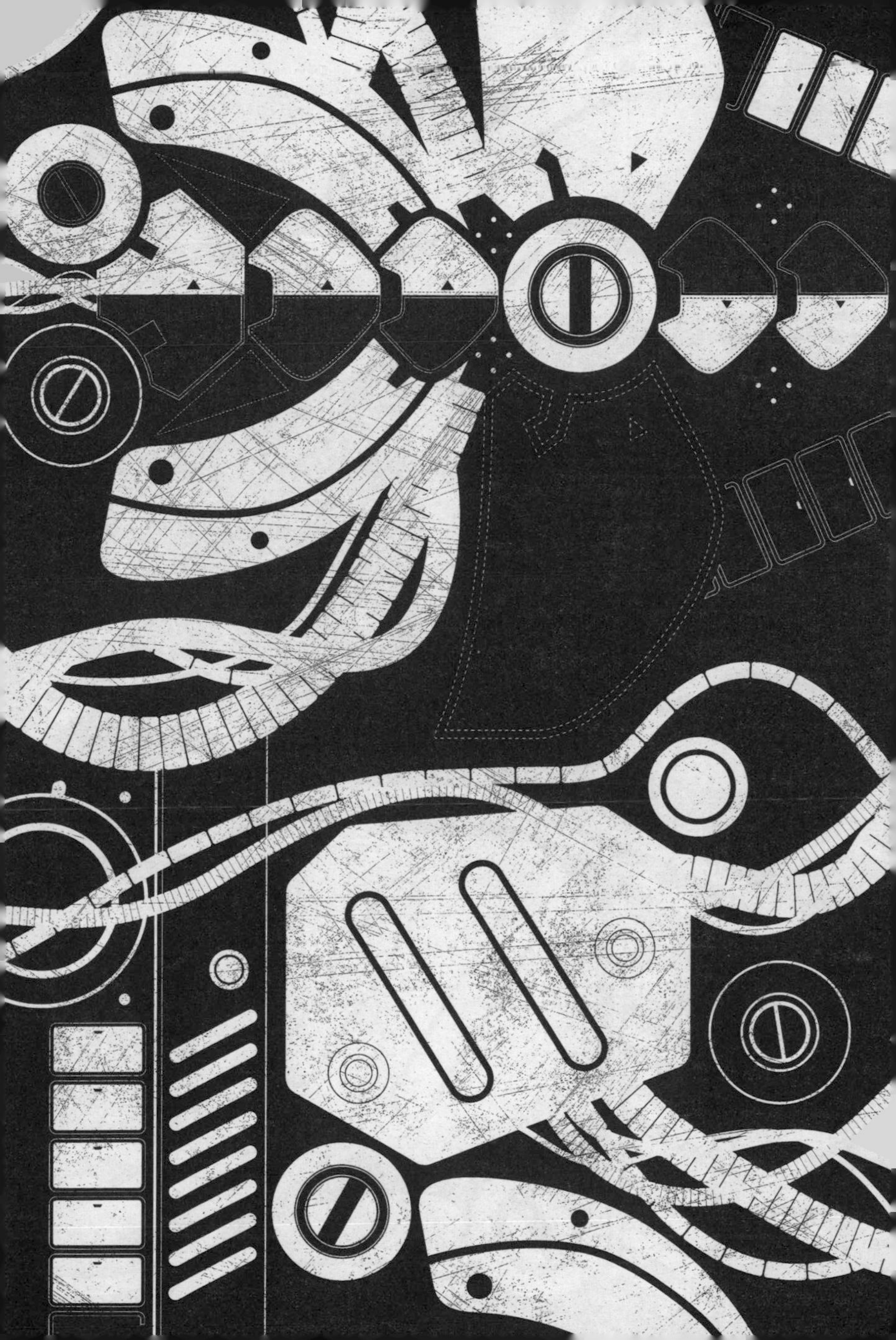

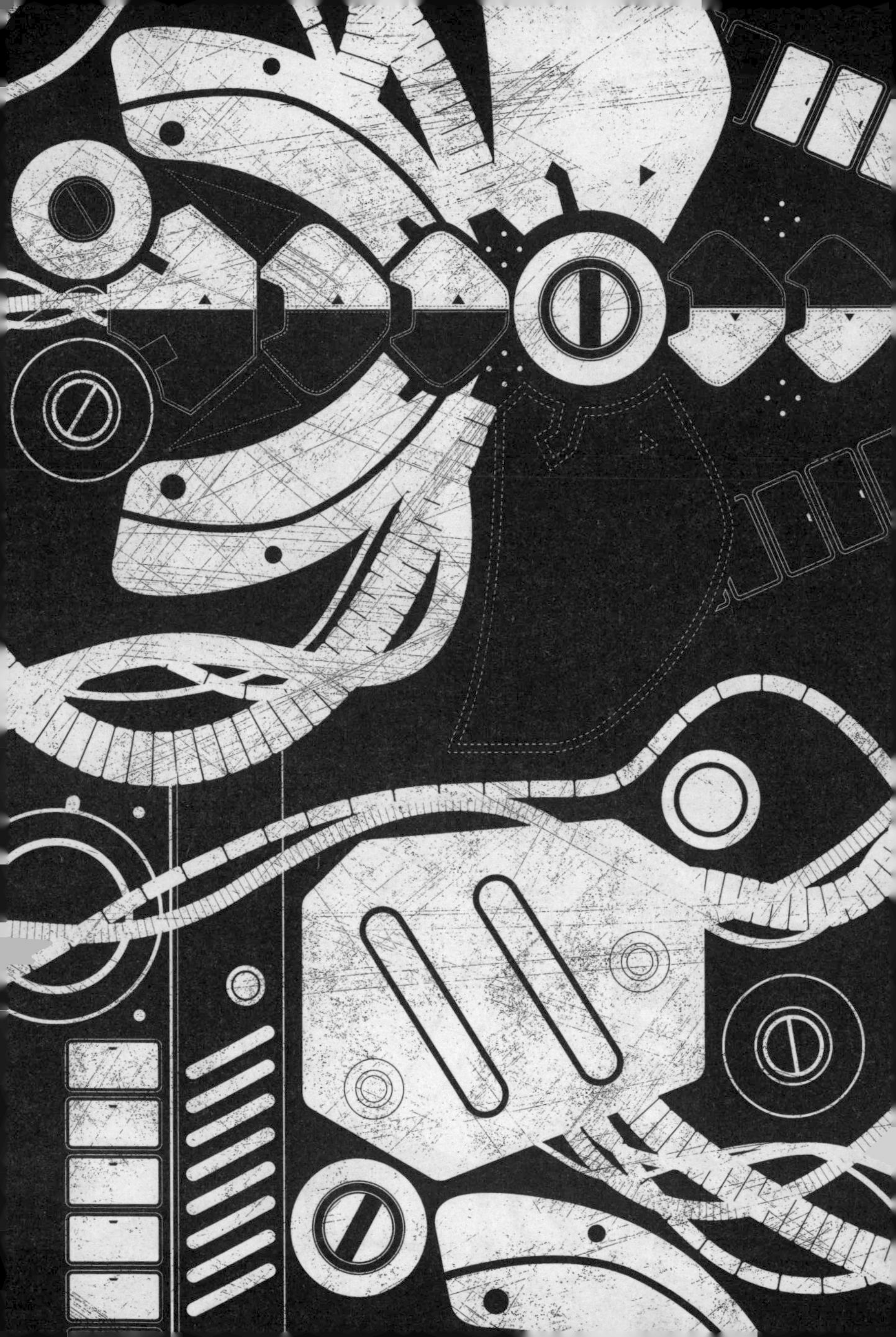

▷boot_018

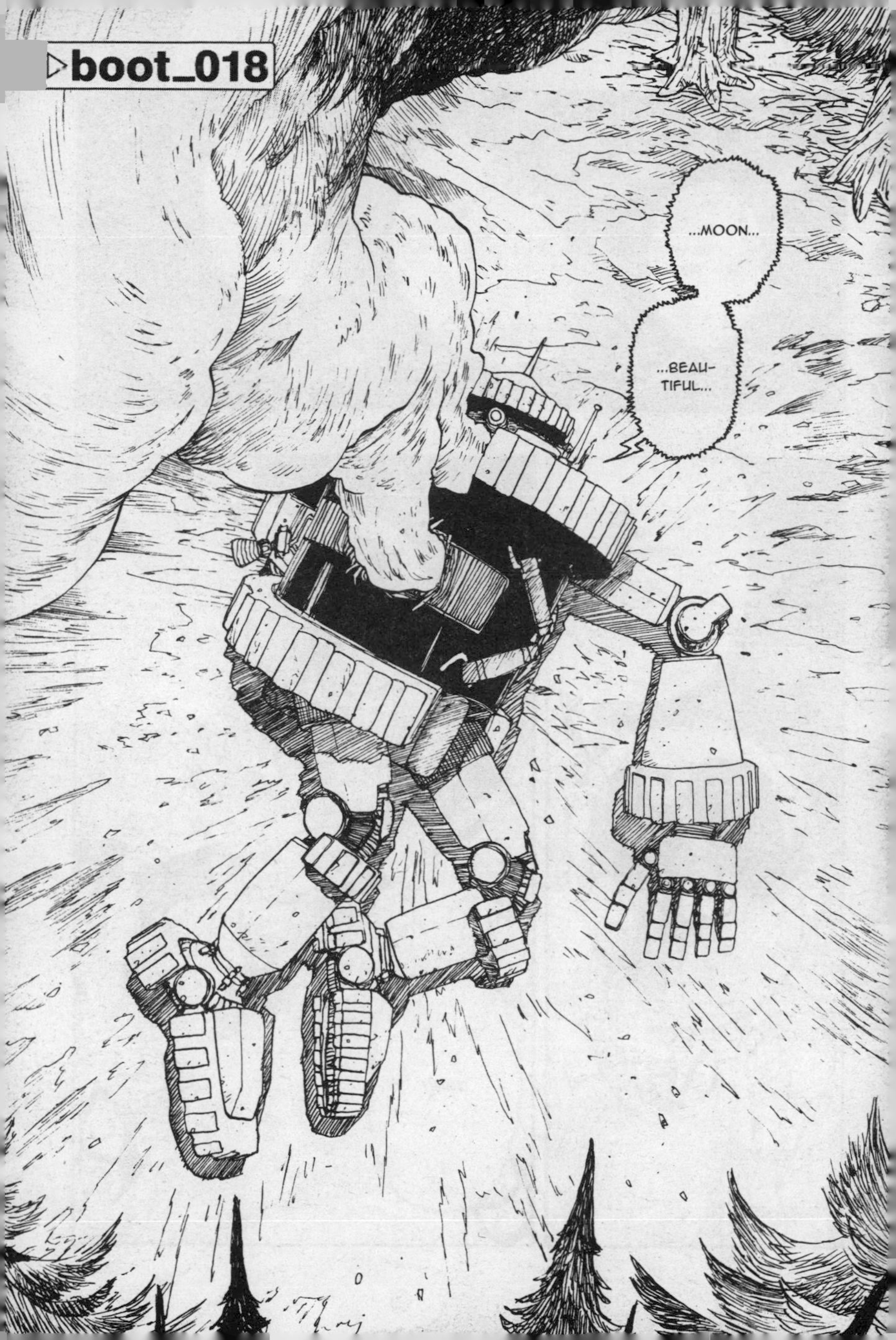
...MOON...
...BEAUTIFUL...

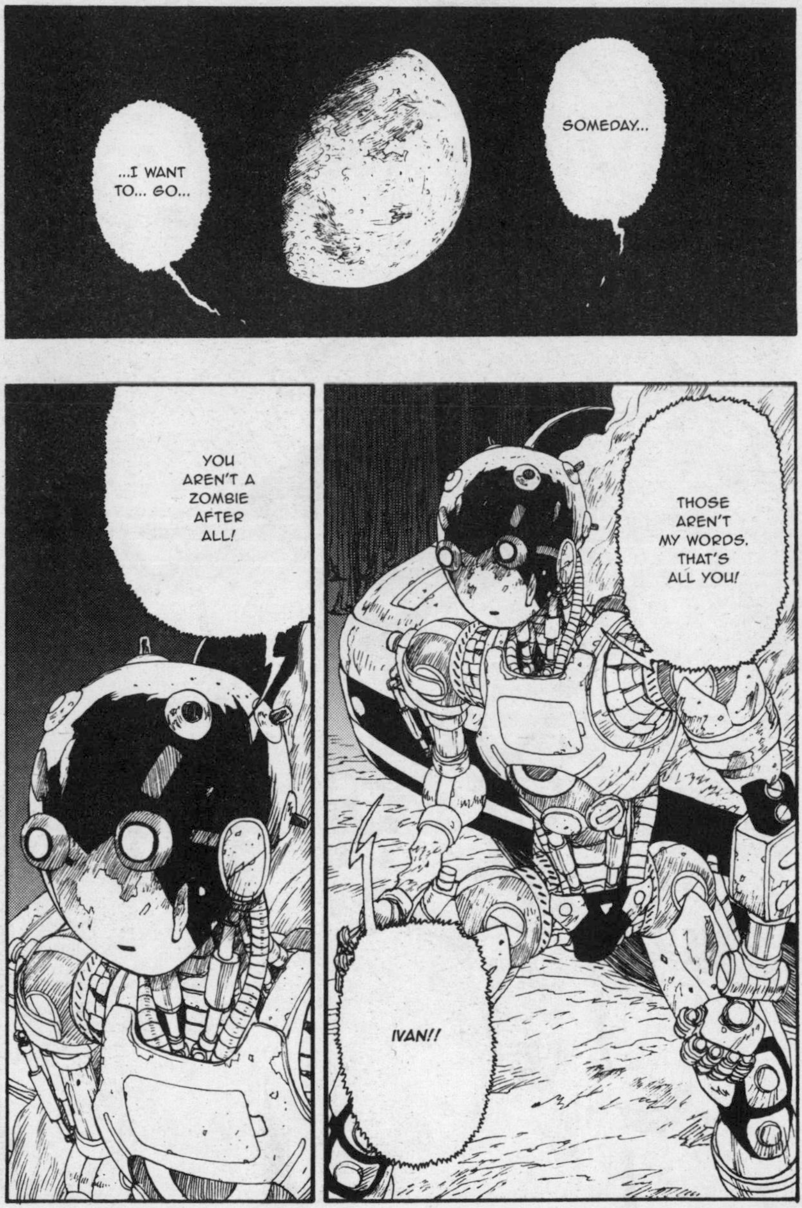
SOMEDAY...
...I WANT TO... GO...
THOSE AREN'T MY WORDS. THAT'S ALL YOU!
IVAN!!
YOU AREN'T A ZOMBIE AFTER ALL!

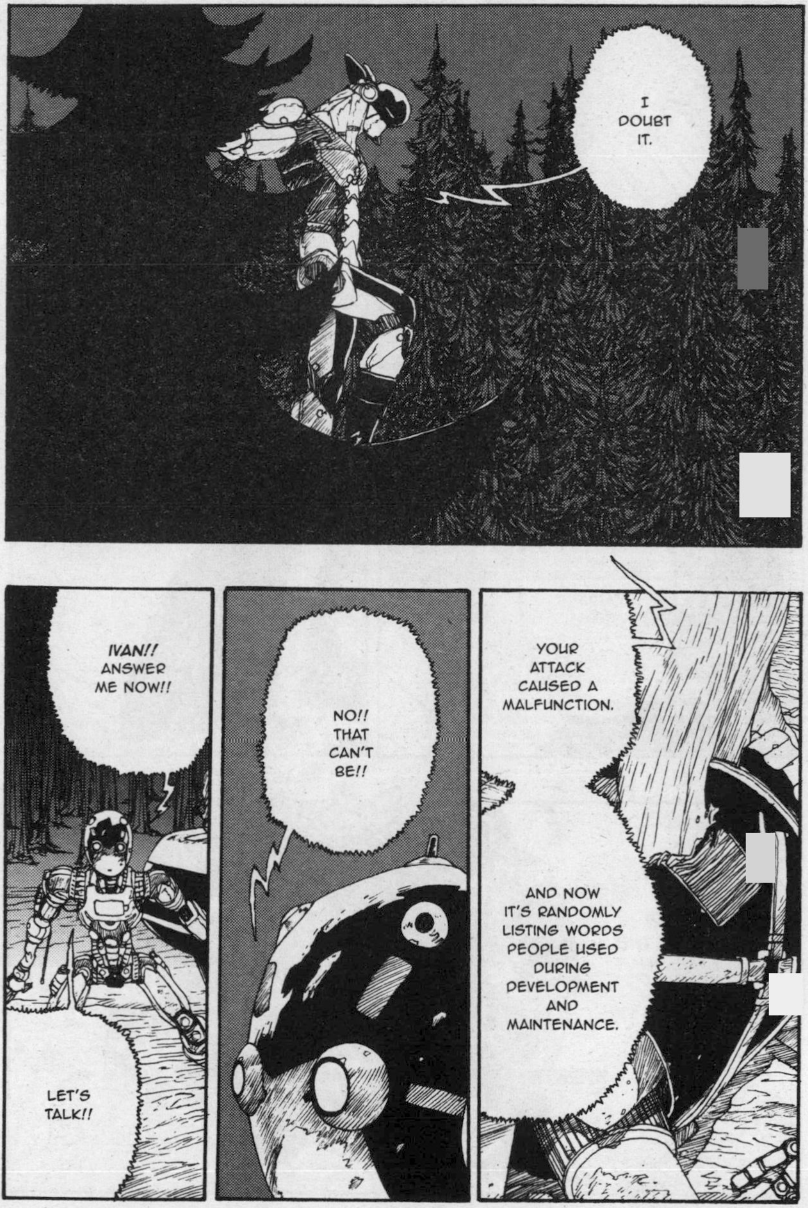
I DOUBT IT.
YOUR ATTACK CAUSED A MALFUNCTION.
AND NOW IT'S RANDOMLY LISTING WORDS PEOPLE USED DURING DEVELOPMENT AND MAINTENANCE.
NO!! THAT CAN'T BE!!
IVAN!! ANSWER ME NOW!!
LET'S TALK!!

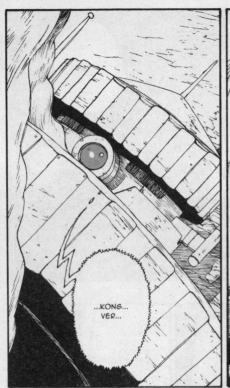

...KONG...
VER...

...NAM...

AAAAGH!!

WE'LL BE
CAUGHT IN THE
EXPLOSION!!

RUN!!

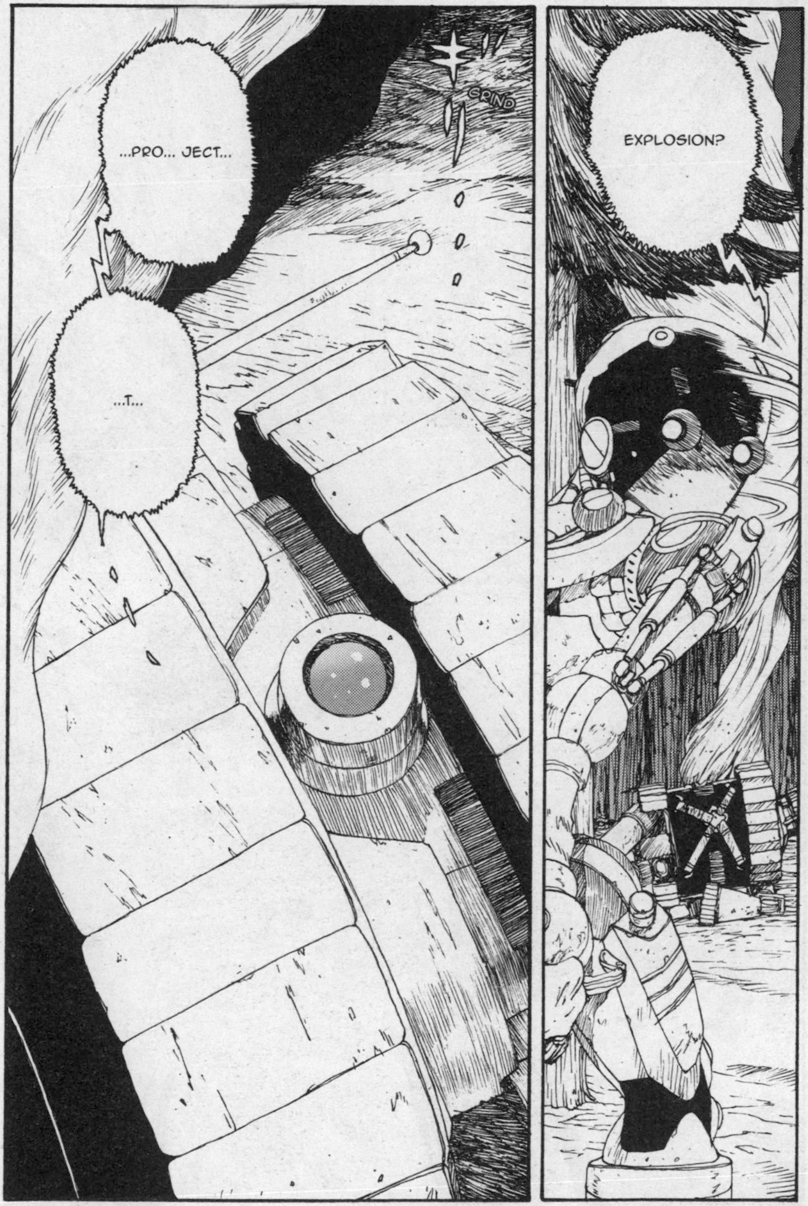
EXPLOSION?
GRIND
...PRO... JECT...
...T...

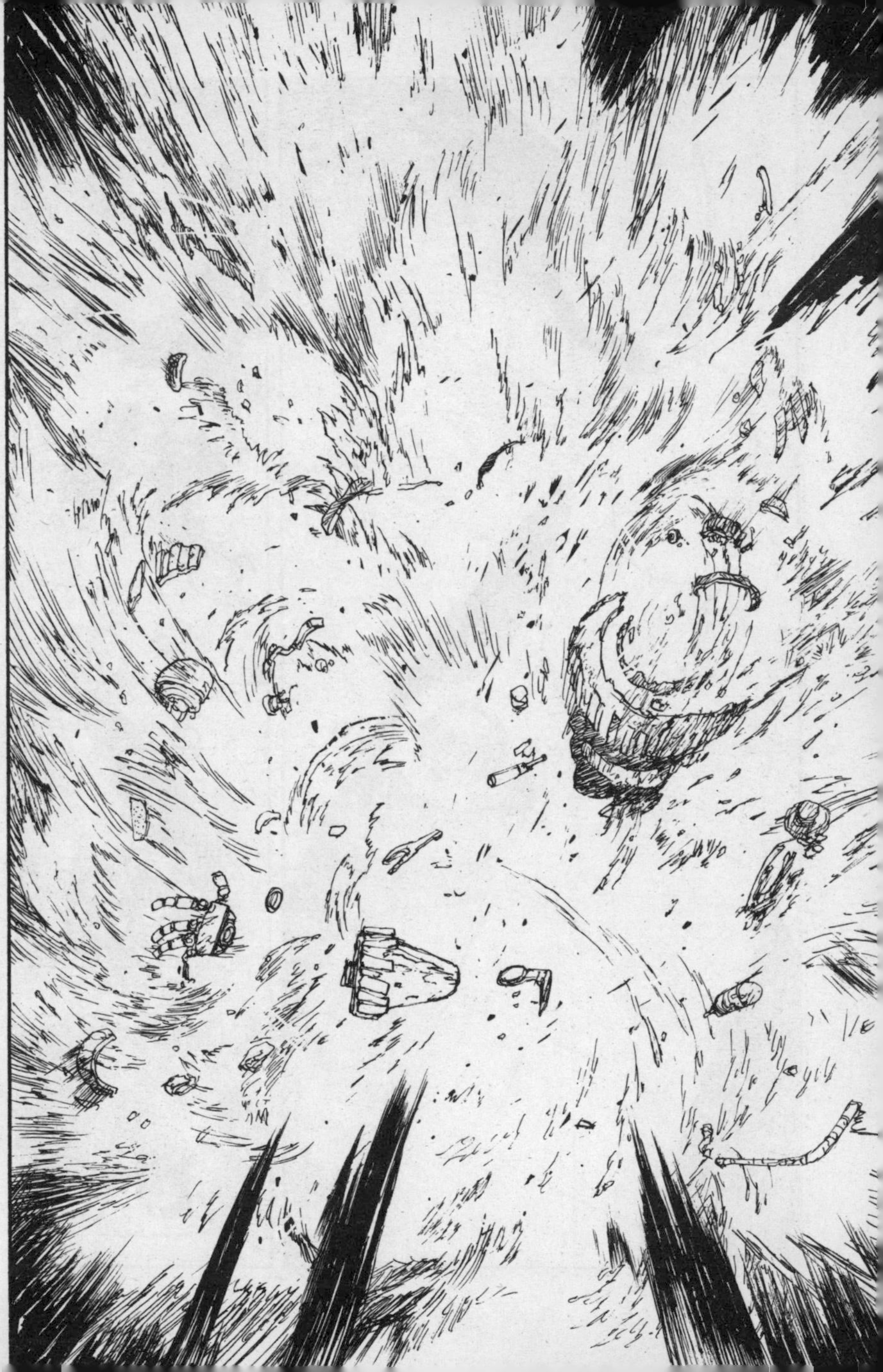

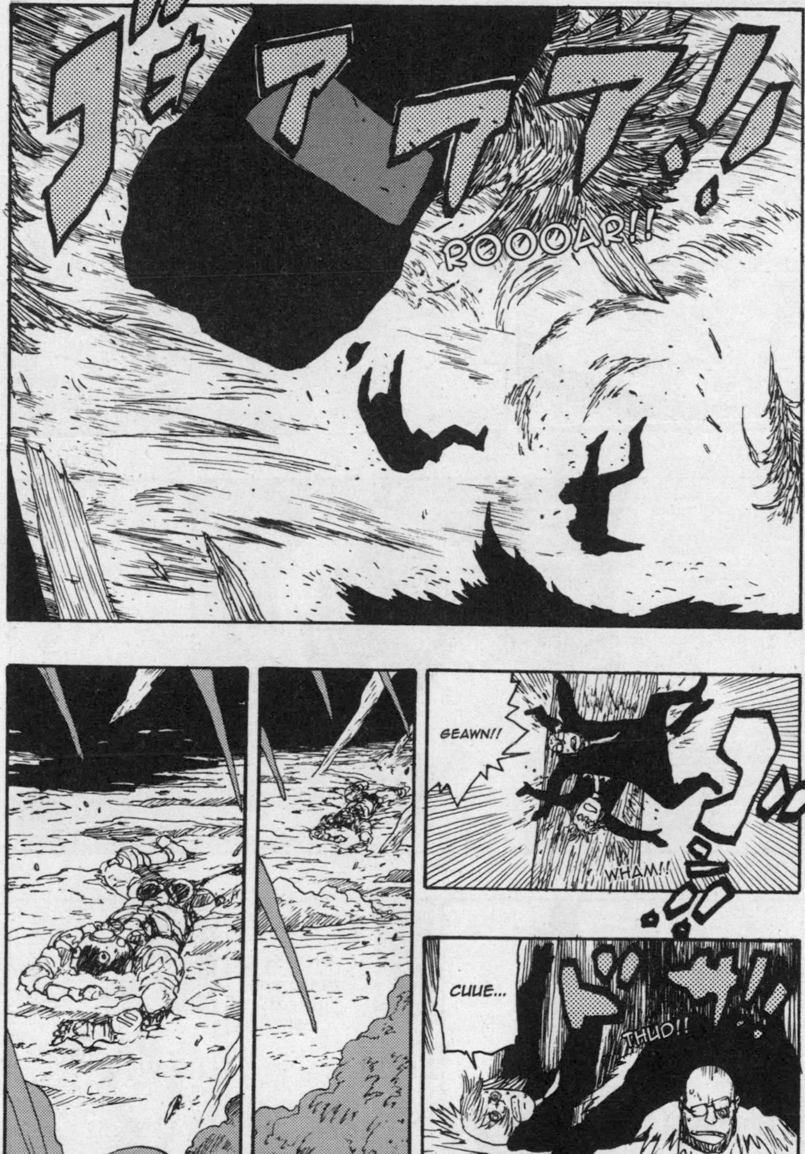
ゴォアアア!!
ROOOAR!!
GEAWN!!
WHAM!!
CUUE...
THUD!!

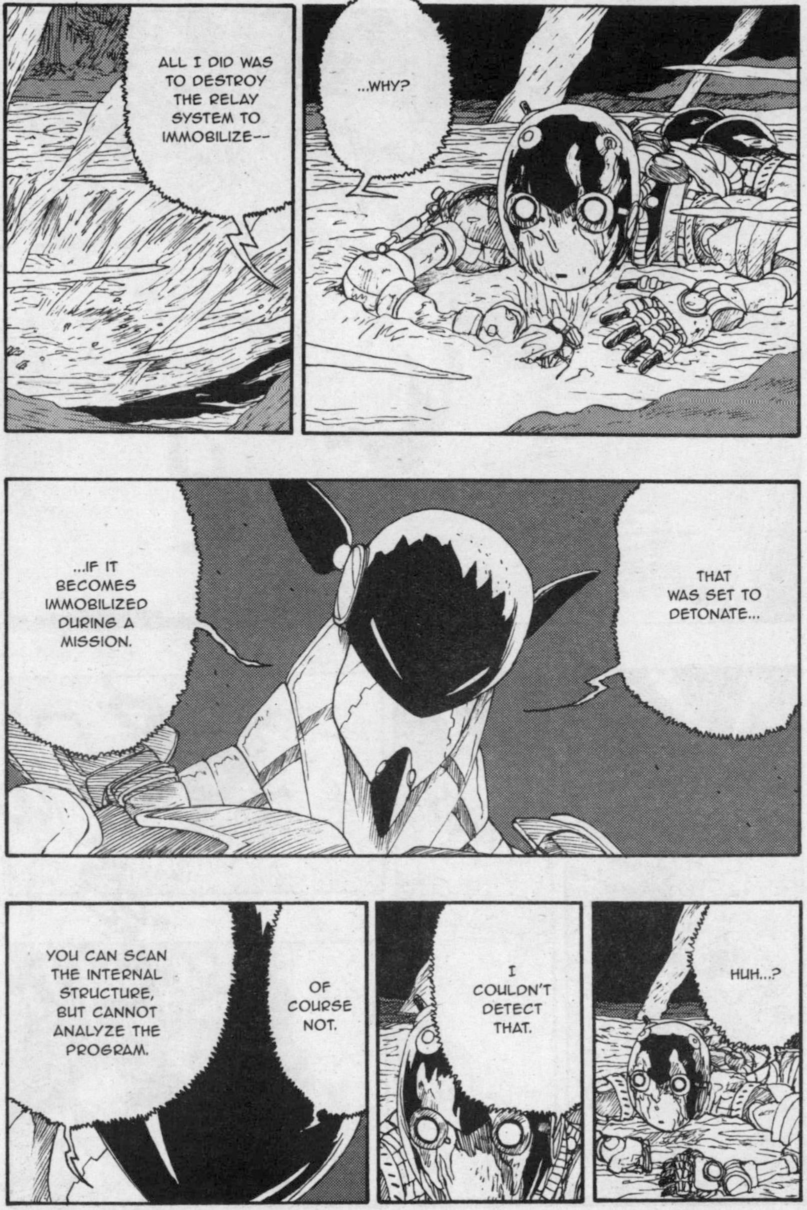
...WHY?
ALL I DID WAS TO DESTROY THE RELAY SYSTEM TO IMMOBILIZE--
THAT WAS SET TO DETONATE...
...IF IT BECOMES IMMOBILIZED DURING A MISSION.
HUH...?
I COULDN'T DETECT THAT.
OF COURSE NOT.
YOU CAN SCAN THE INTERNAL STRUCTURE, BUT CANNOT ANALYZE THE PROGRAM.

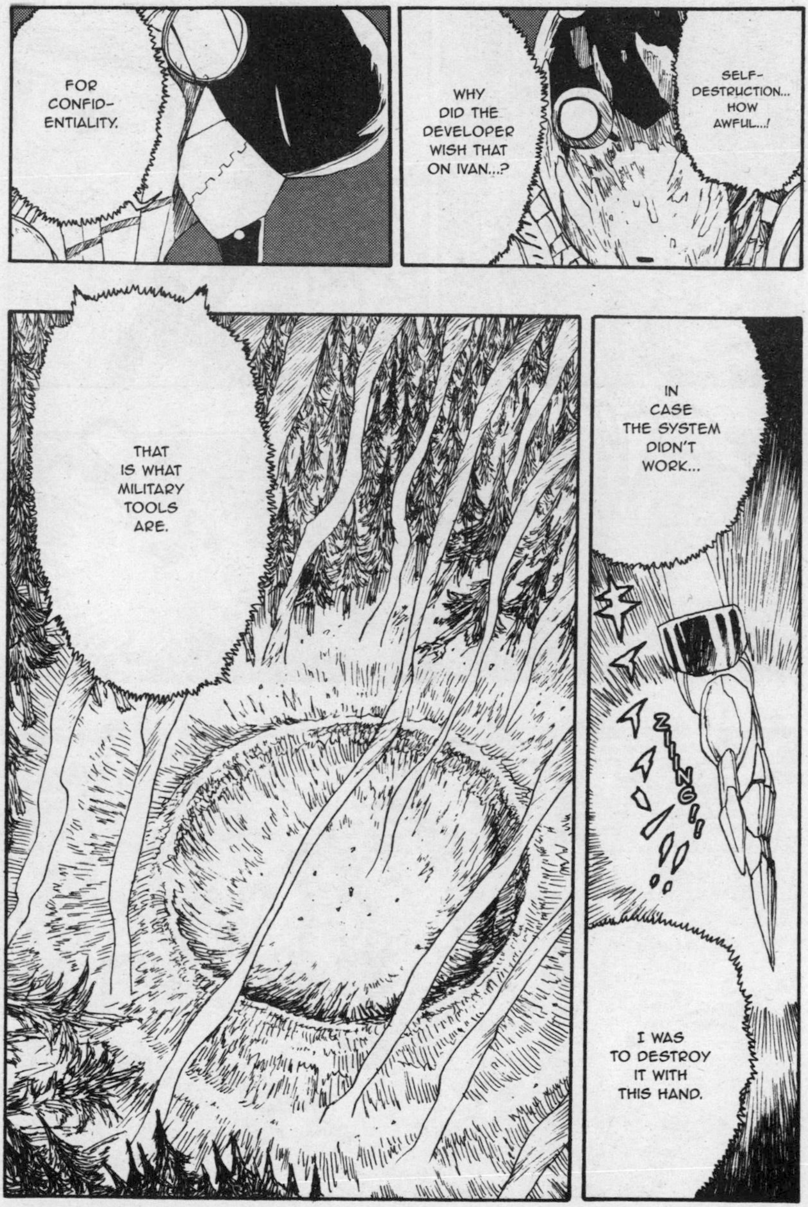
SELF-DESTRUCTION... HOW AWFUL...!
WHY DID THE DEVELOPER WISH THAT ON IVAN...?
FOR CONFID-ENTIALITY.
IN CASE THE SYSTEM DIDN'T WORK...
ZIIING!!
I WAS TO DESTROY IT WITH THIS HAND.
THAT IS WHAT MILITARY TOOLS ARE.

TIIIING
FU
バシュー!!
BASHOO!!

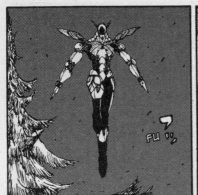

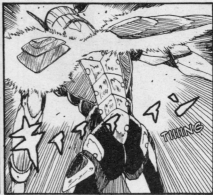

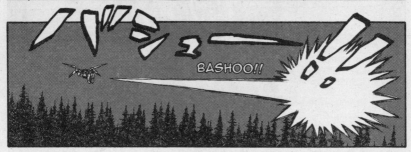

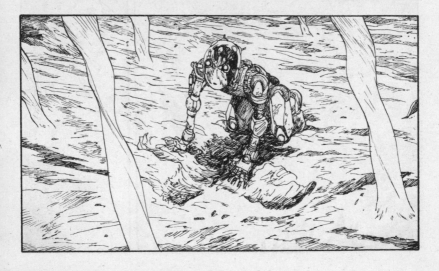

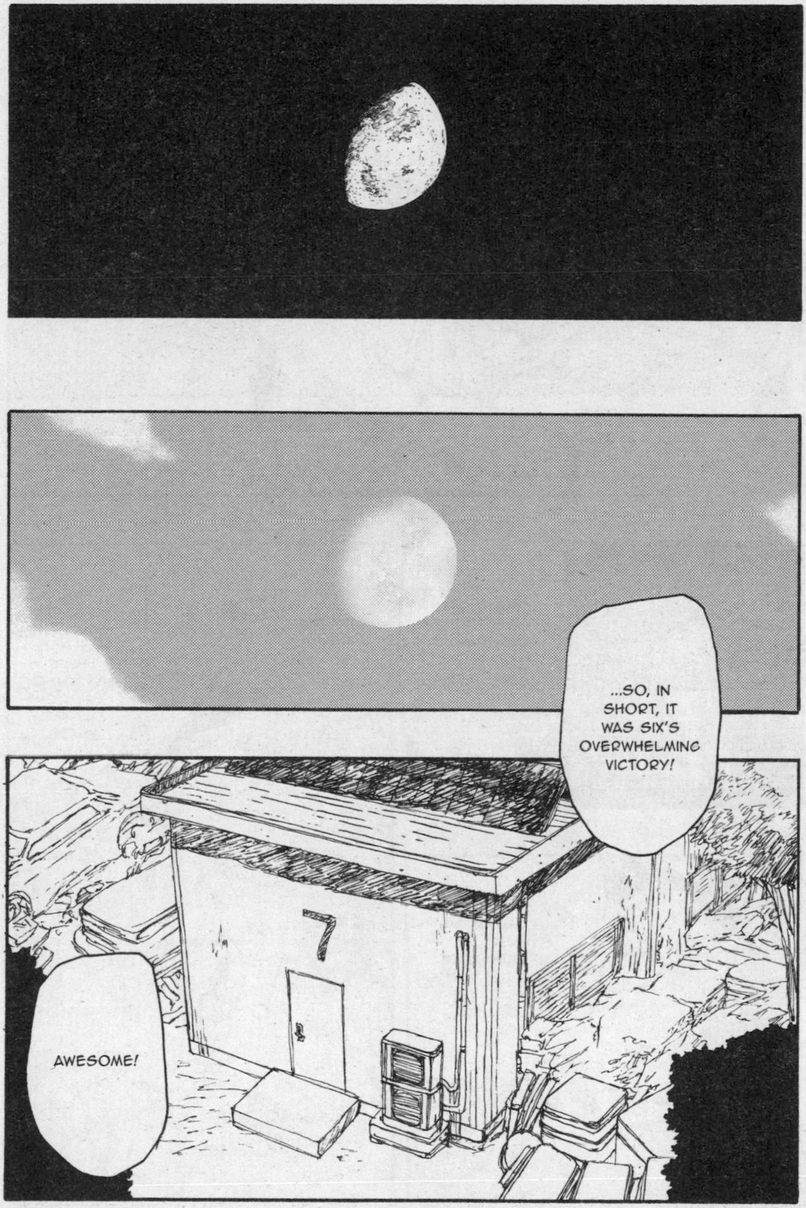
...SO, IN SHORT, IT WAS SIX'S OVERWHELMING VICTORY!
AWESOME!

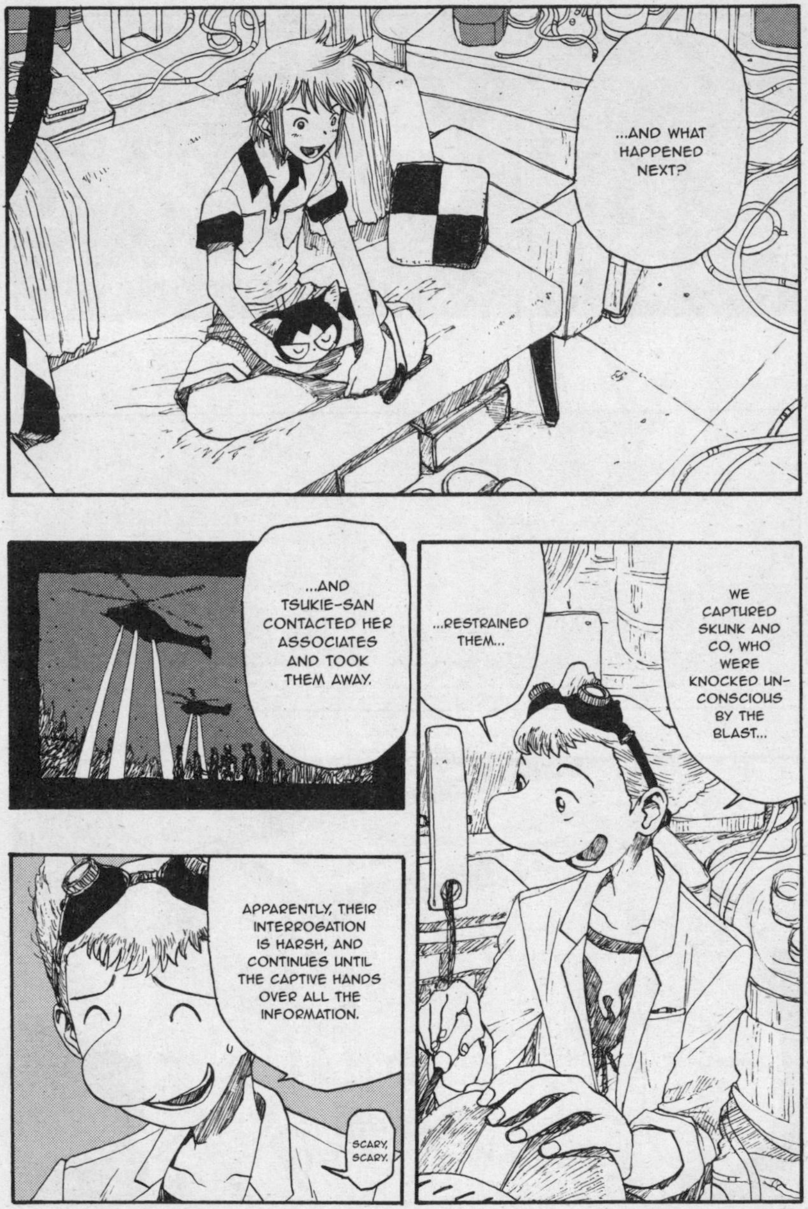
...AND WHAT HAPPENED NEXT?
WE CAPTURED SKUNK AND CO, WHO WERE KNOCKED UN-CONSCIOUS BY THE BLAST...
...RESTRAINED THEM...
...AND TSUKIE-SAN CONTACTED HER ASSOCIATES AND TOOK THEM AWAY.
APPARENTLY, THEIR INTERROGATION IS HARSH, AND CONTINUES UNTIL THE CAPTIVE HANDS OVER ALL THE INFORMATION.
SCARY, SCARY.

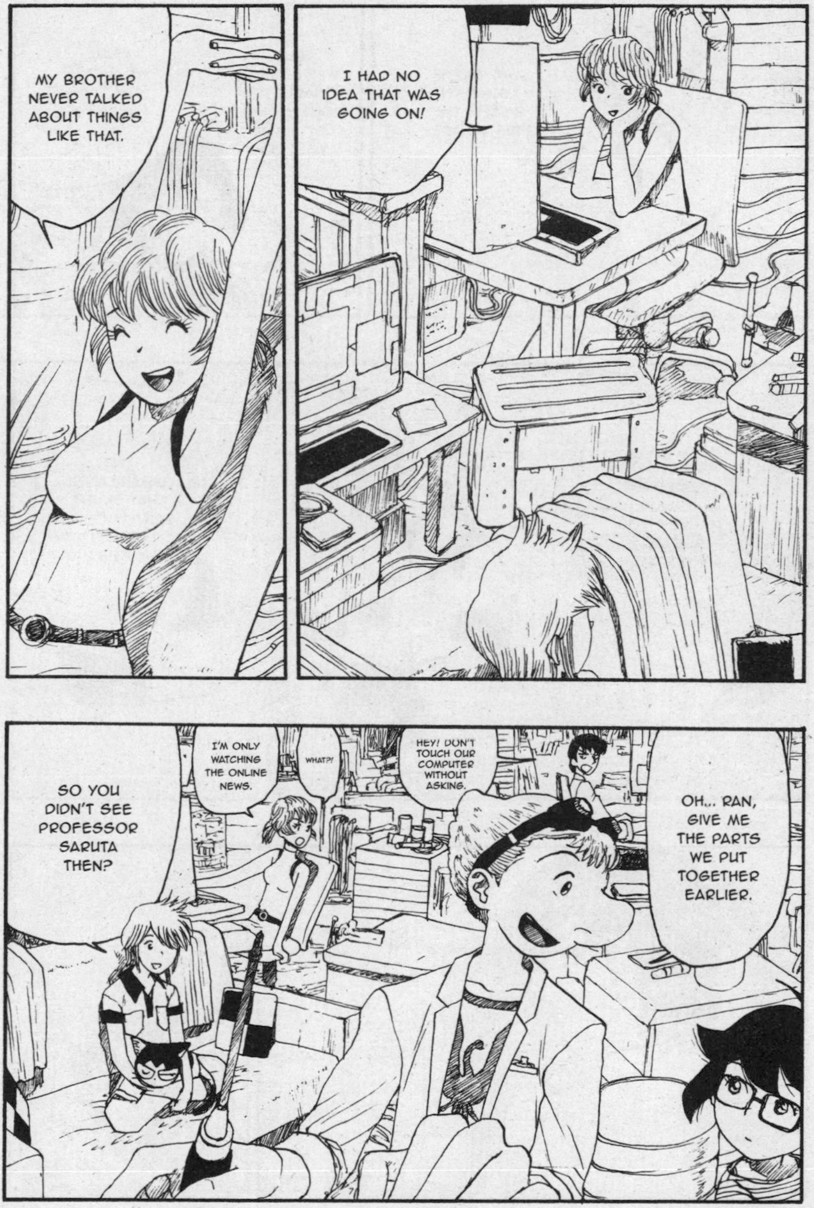
I HAD NO IDEA THAT WAS GOING ON!
MY BROTHER NEVER TALKED ABOUT THINGS LIKE THAT.
OH... RAN, GIVE ME THE PARTS WE PUT TOGETHER EARLIER.
HEY! DON'T TOUCH OUR COMPUTER WITHOUT ASKING.
WHAT?!
I'M ONLY WATCHING THE ONLINE NEWS.
SO YOU DIDN'T SEE PROFESSOR SARUTA THEN?

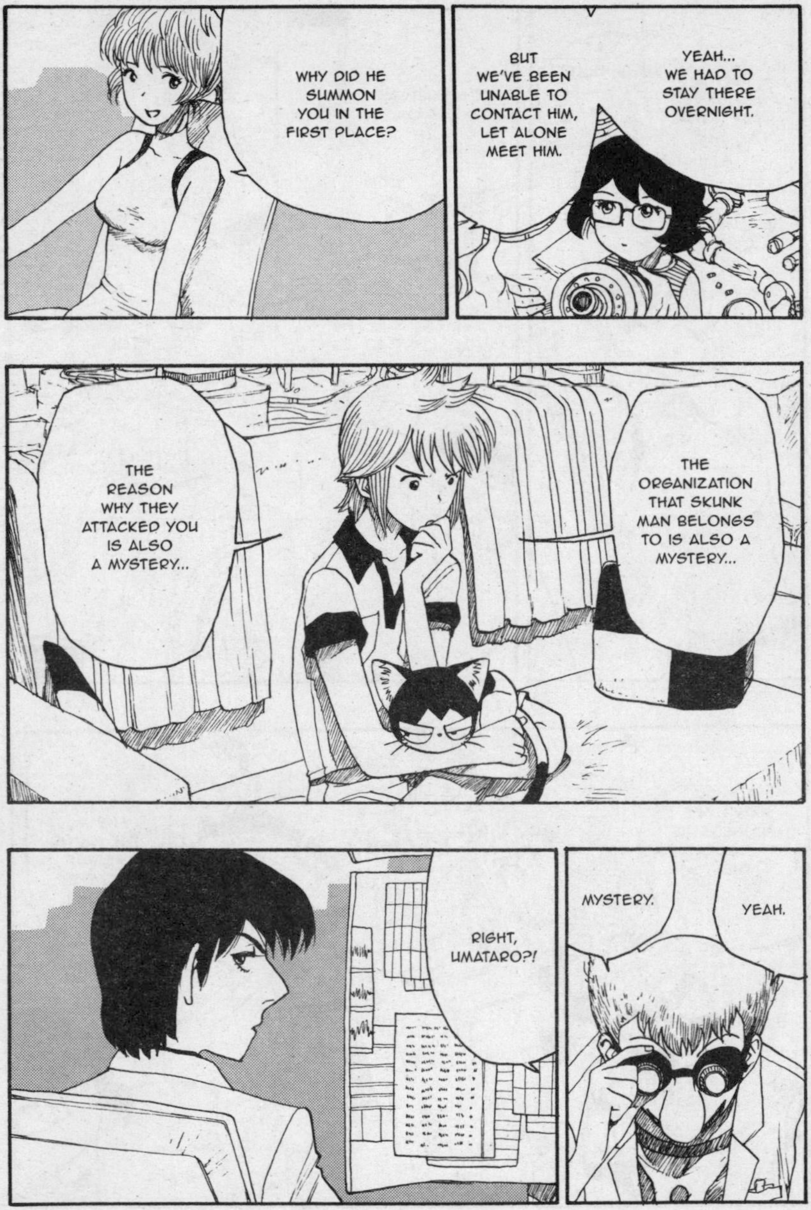
YEAH... WE HAD TO STAY THERE OVERNIGHT.
BUT WE'VE BEEN UNABLE TO CONTACT HIM, LET ALONE MEET HIM.
WHY DID HE SUMMON YOU IN THE FIRST PLACE?
THE ORGANIZATION THAT SKUNK MAN BELONGS TO IS ALSO A MYSTERY...
THE REASON WHY THEY ATTACKED YOU IS ALSO A MYSTERY...
YEAH.
MYSTERY.
RIGHT, UMATARO?!

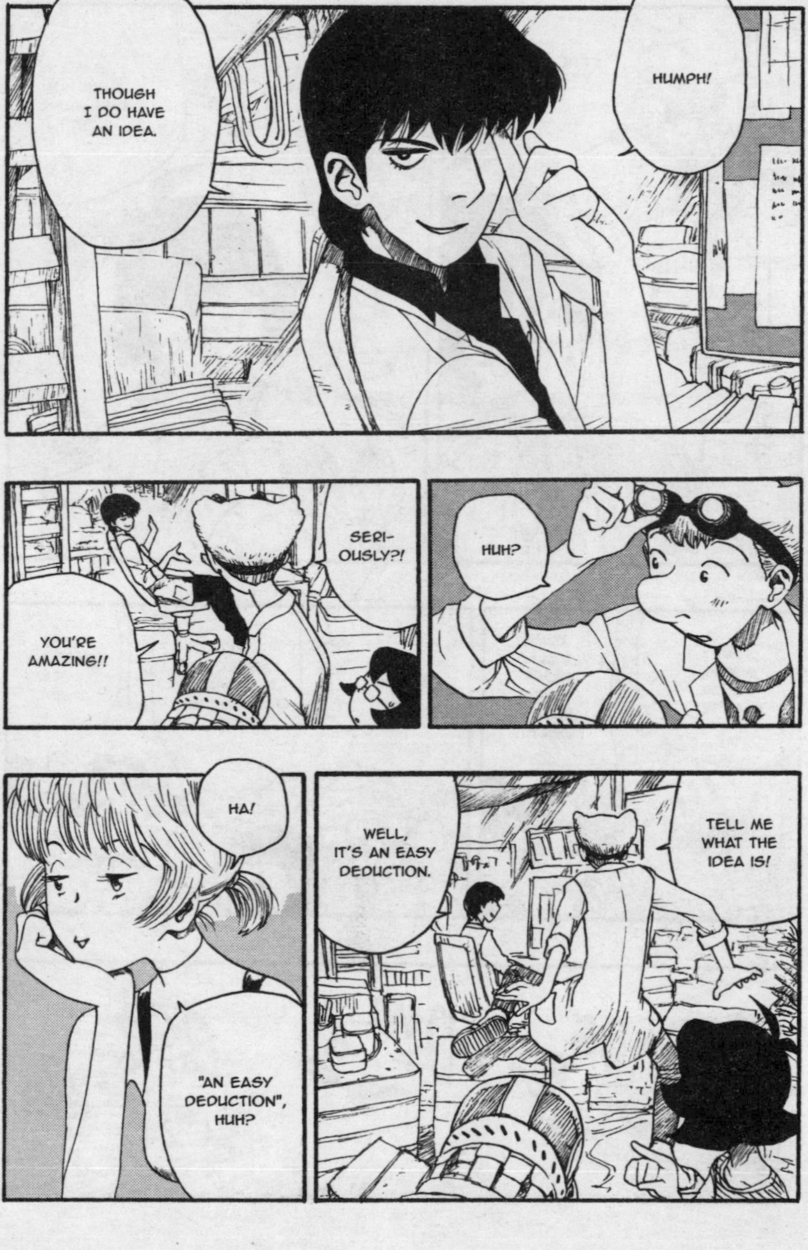
HUMPH!
THOUGH I DO HAVE AN IDEA.
HUH?
SERI-OUSLY?!
YOU'RE AMAZING!!
TELL ME WHAT THE IDEA IS!
WELL, IT'S AN EASY DEDUCTION.
HA!
"AN EASY DEDUCTION", HUH?

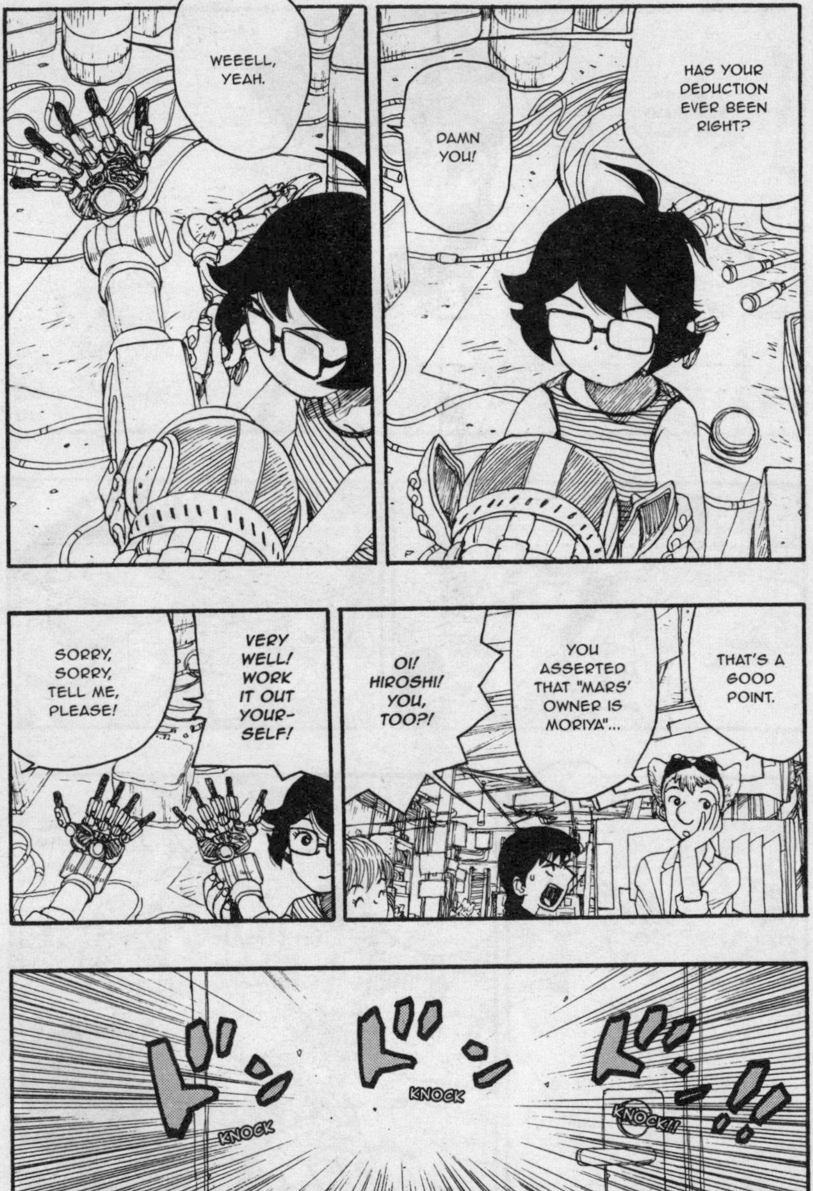
HAS YOUR DEDUCTION EVER BEEN RIGHT?
DAMN YOU!
WEEELL, YEAH.
THAT'S A GOOD POINT.
YOU ASSERTED THAT "MARS' OWNER IS MORIYA"...
OI! HIROSHI! YOU, TOO?!
VERY WELL! WORK IT OUT YOUR-SELF!
SORRY, SORRY, TELL ME, PLEASE!
KNOCK!!
KNOCK
KNOCK

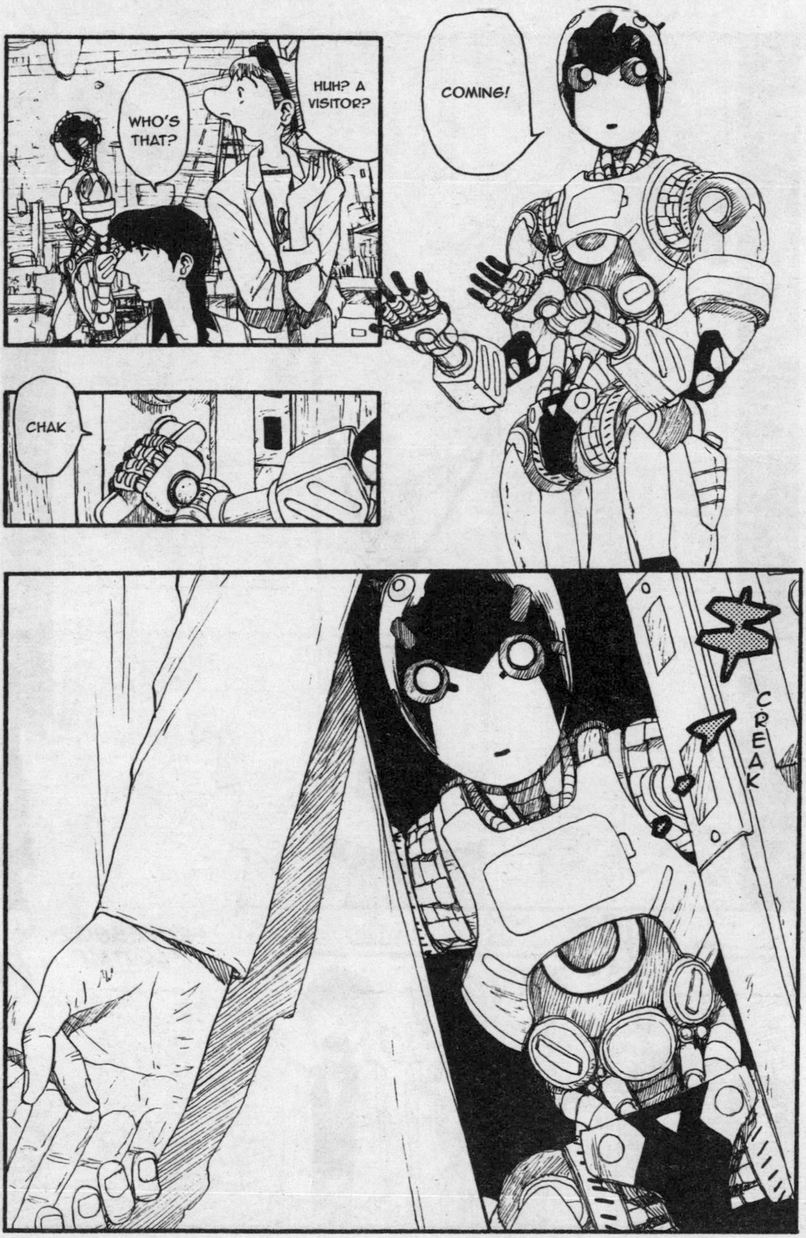
COMING!
HUH? A VISITOR?
WHO'S THAT?
CHAK
CREAK

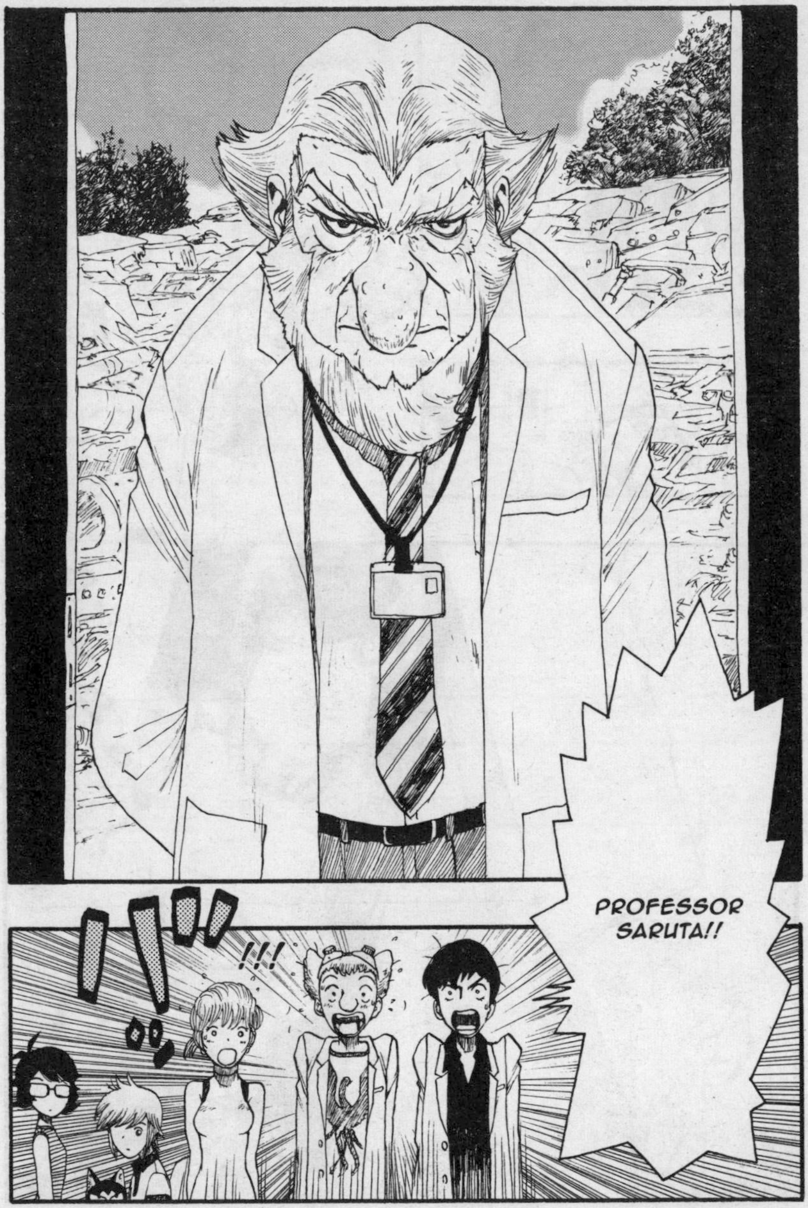
PROFESSOR SARUTA!!
!!!

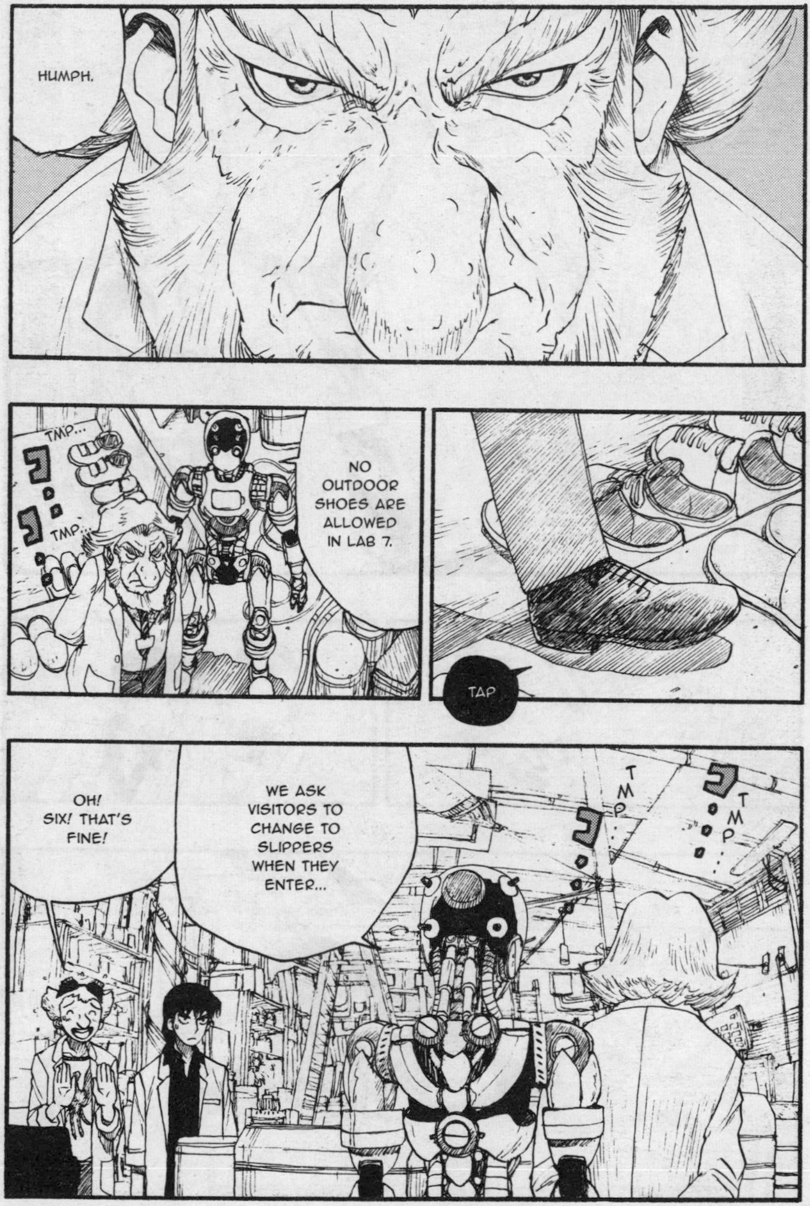
HUMPH.
TAP
NO OUTDOOR SHOES ARE ALLOWED IN LAB 7.
TMP...
TMP...
TMP...
TMP...
WE ASK VISITORS TO CHANGE TO SLIPPERS WHEN THEY ENTER...
OH! SIX! THAT'S FINE!

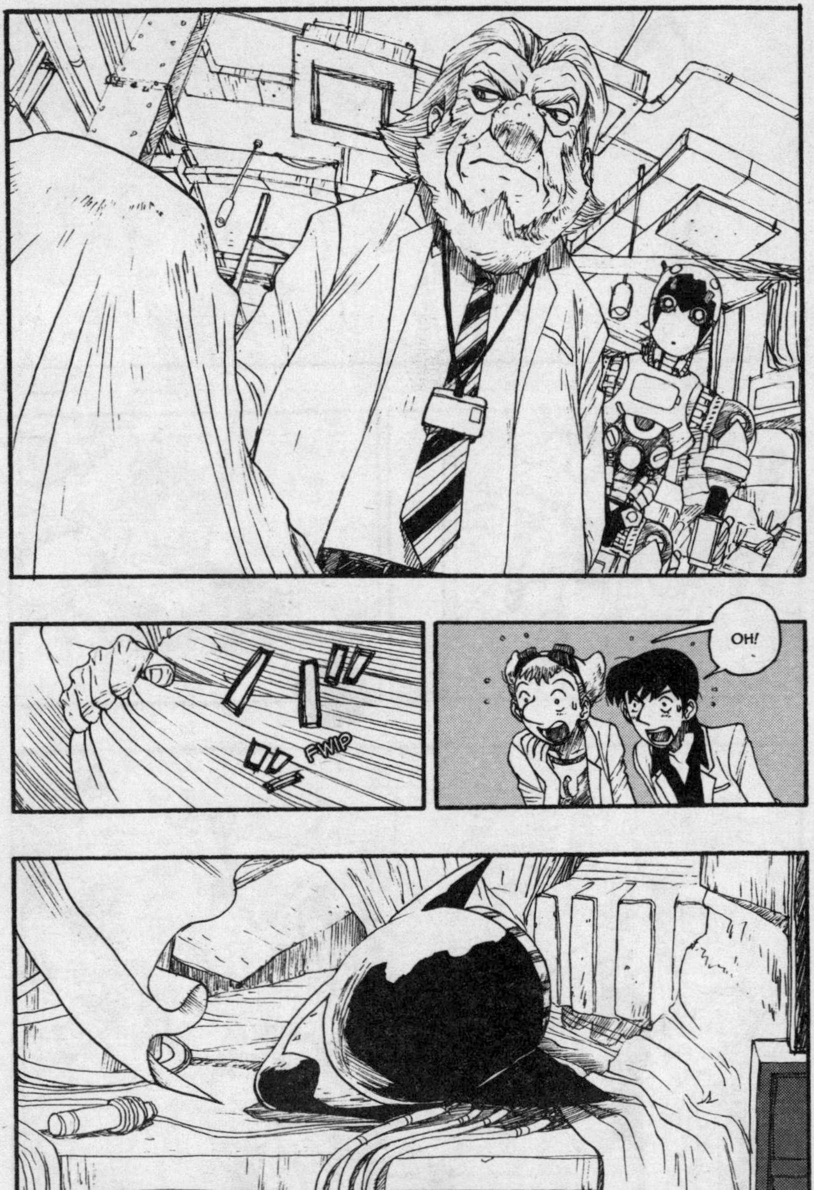
OH!
FWIP

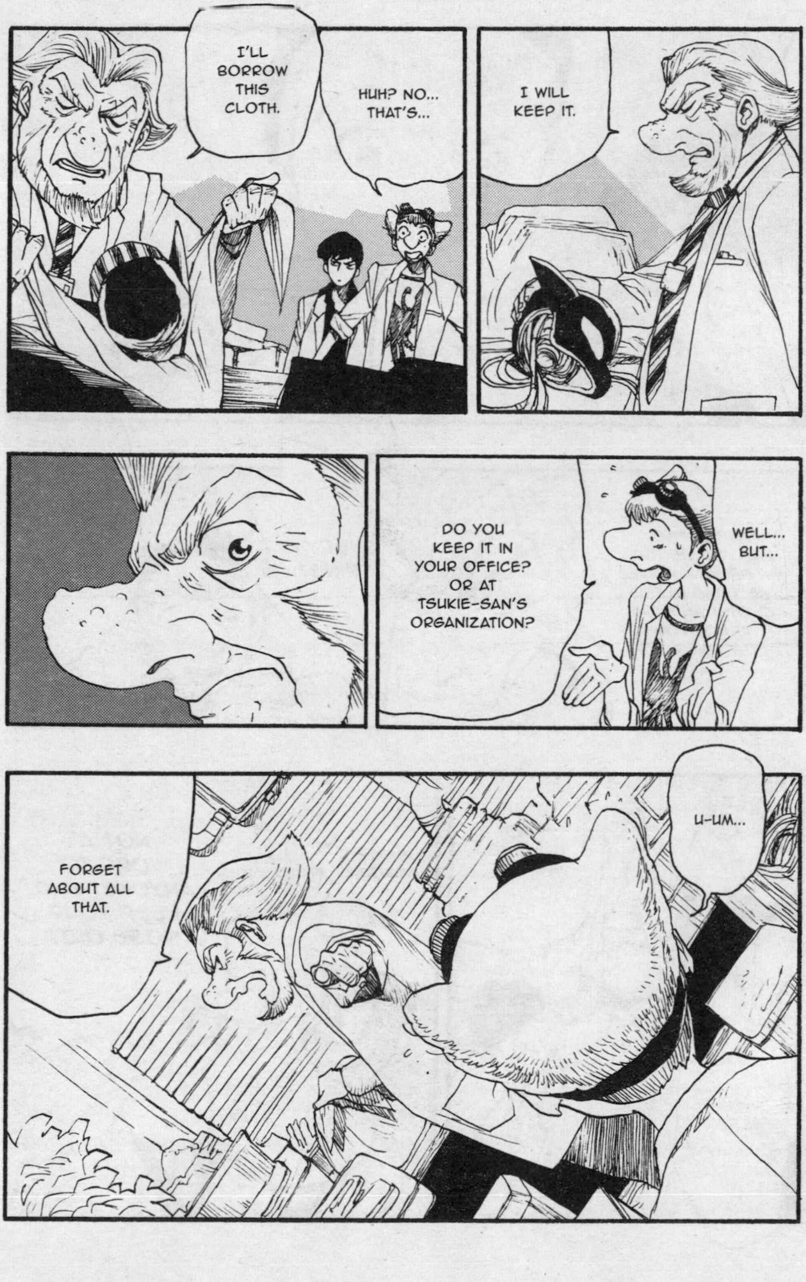
I WILL KEEP IT.
HUH? NO... THAT'S...
I'LL BORROW THIS CLOTH.
WELL... BUT...
DO YOU KEEP IT IN YOUR OFFICE? OR AT TSUKIE-SAN'S ORGANIZATION?
U-UM...
FORGET ABOUT ALL THAT.

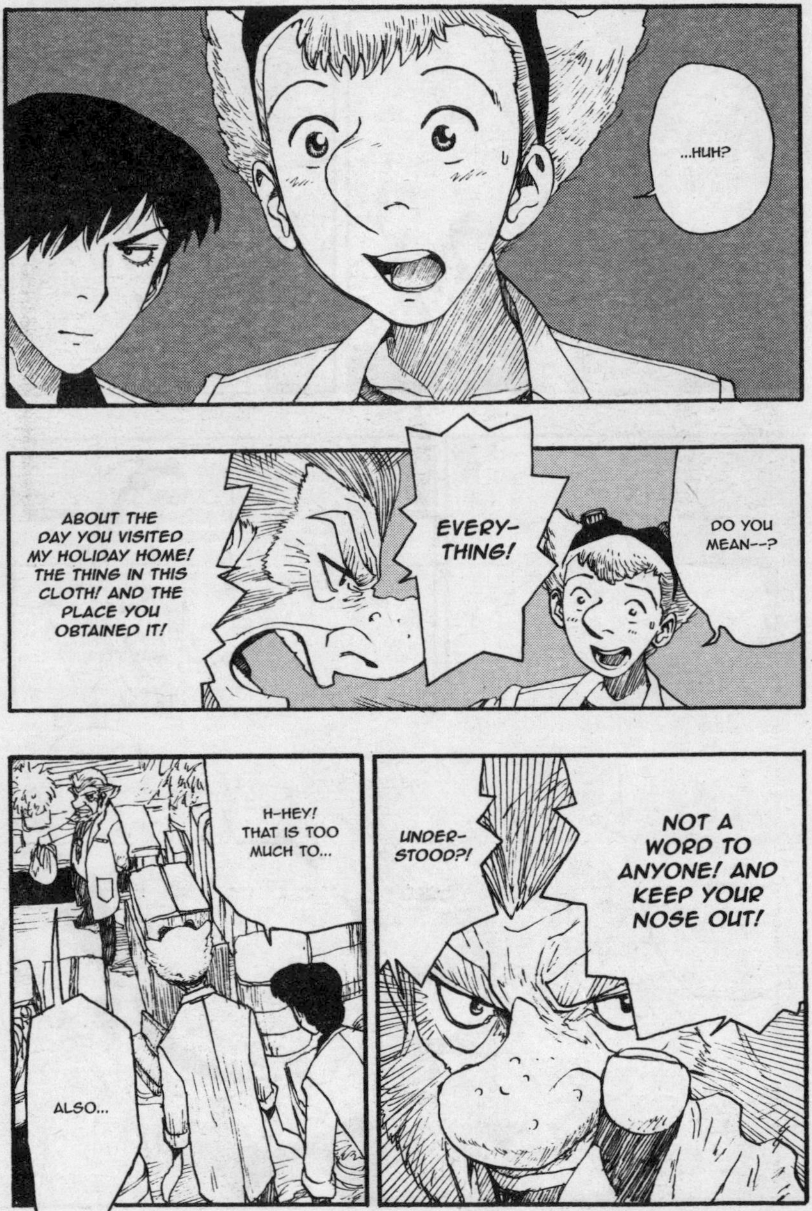
...HUH?
DO YOU MEAN--?
EVERY-THING!
ABOUT THE DAY YOU VISITED MY HOLIDAY HOME! THE THING IN THIS CLOTH! AND THE PLACE YOU OBTAINED IT!
NOT A WORD TO ANYONE! AND KEEP YOUR NOSE OUT!
UNDER-STOOD?!
H-HEY! THAT IS TOO MUCH TO...
ALSO...

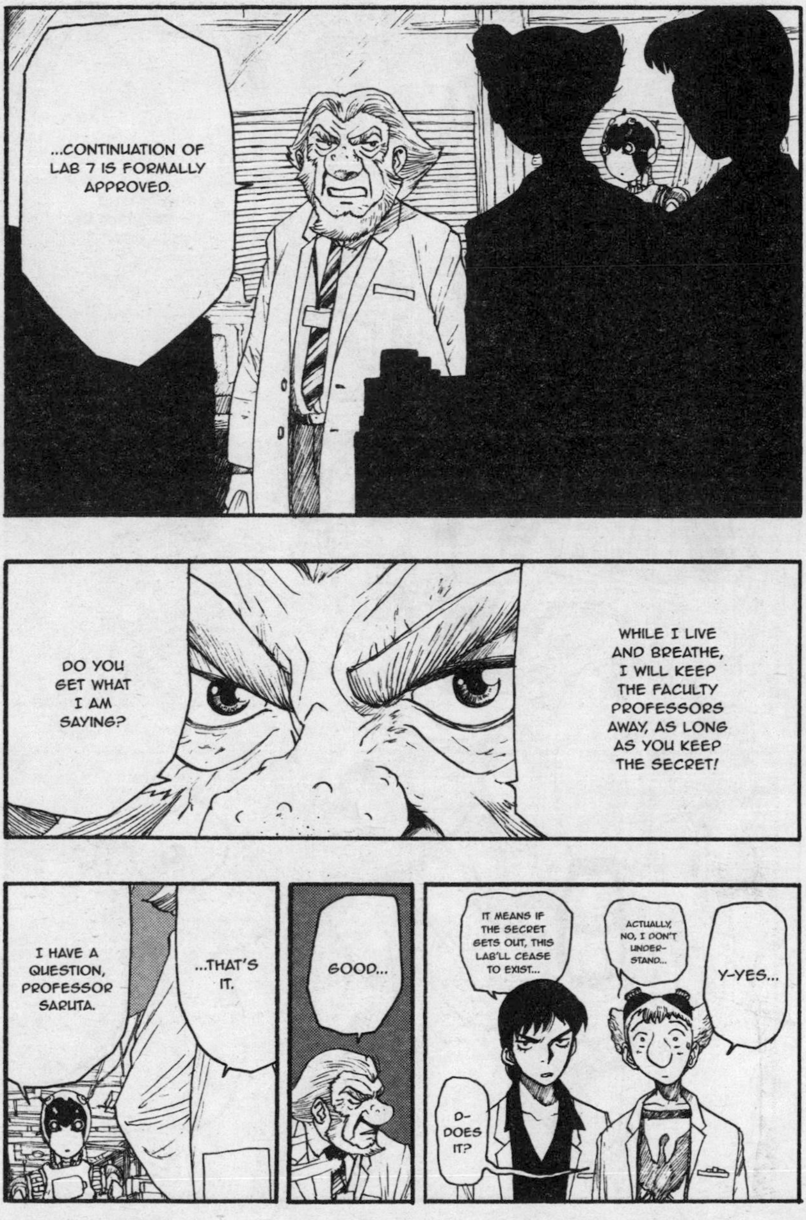
...CONTINUATION OF LAB 7 IS FORMALLY APPROVED.
WHILE I LIVE AND BREATHE, I WILL KEEP THE FACULTY PROFESSORS AWAY, AS LONG AS YOU KEEP THE SECRET!
DO YOU GET WHAT I AM SAYING?
Y-YES...
ACTUALLY, NO, I DON'T UNDER-STAND...
IT MEANS IF THE SECRET GETS OUT, THIS LAB'LL CEASE TO EXIST...
D-DOES IT?
GOOD...
...THAT'S IT.
I HAVE A QUESTION, PROFESSOR SARUTA.

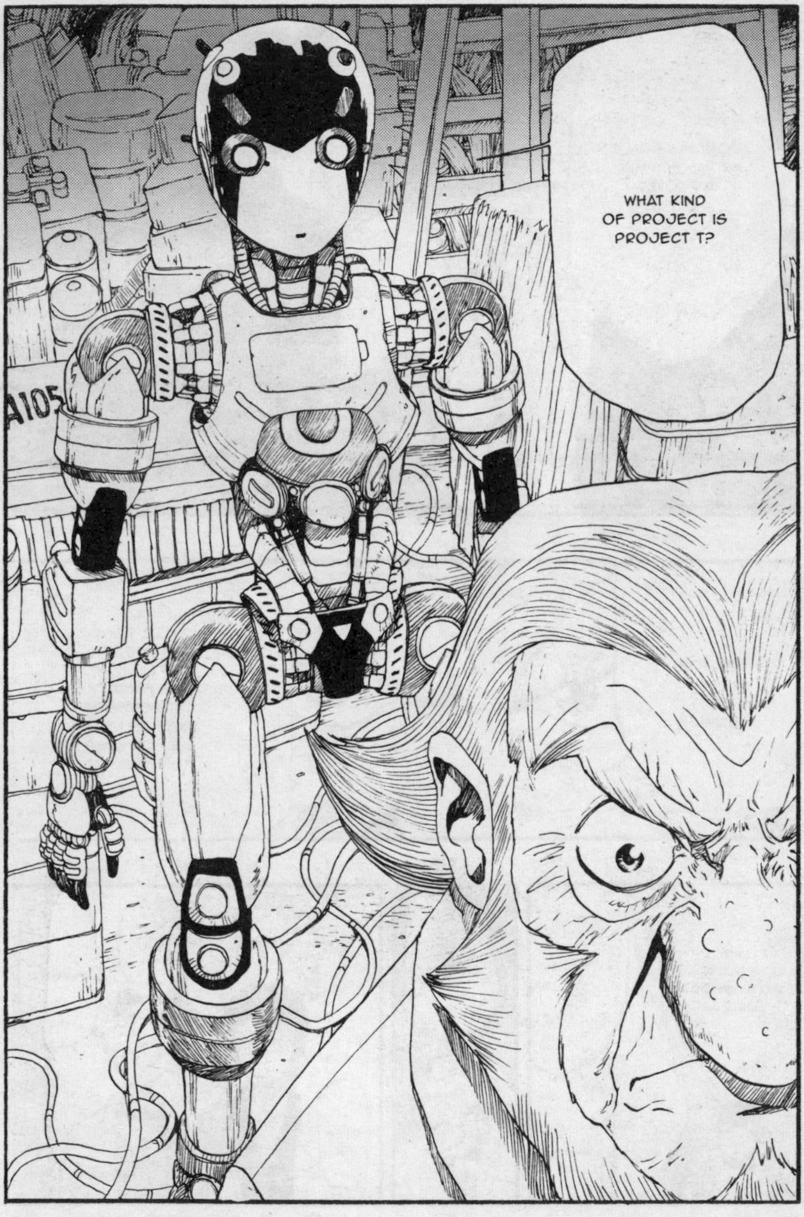
WHAT KIND OF PROJECT IS PROJECT T?
A105

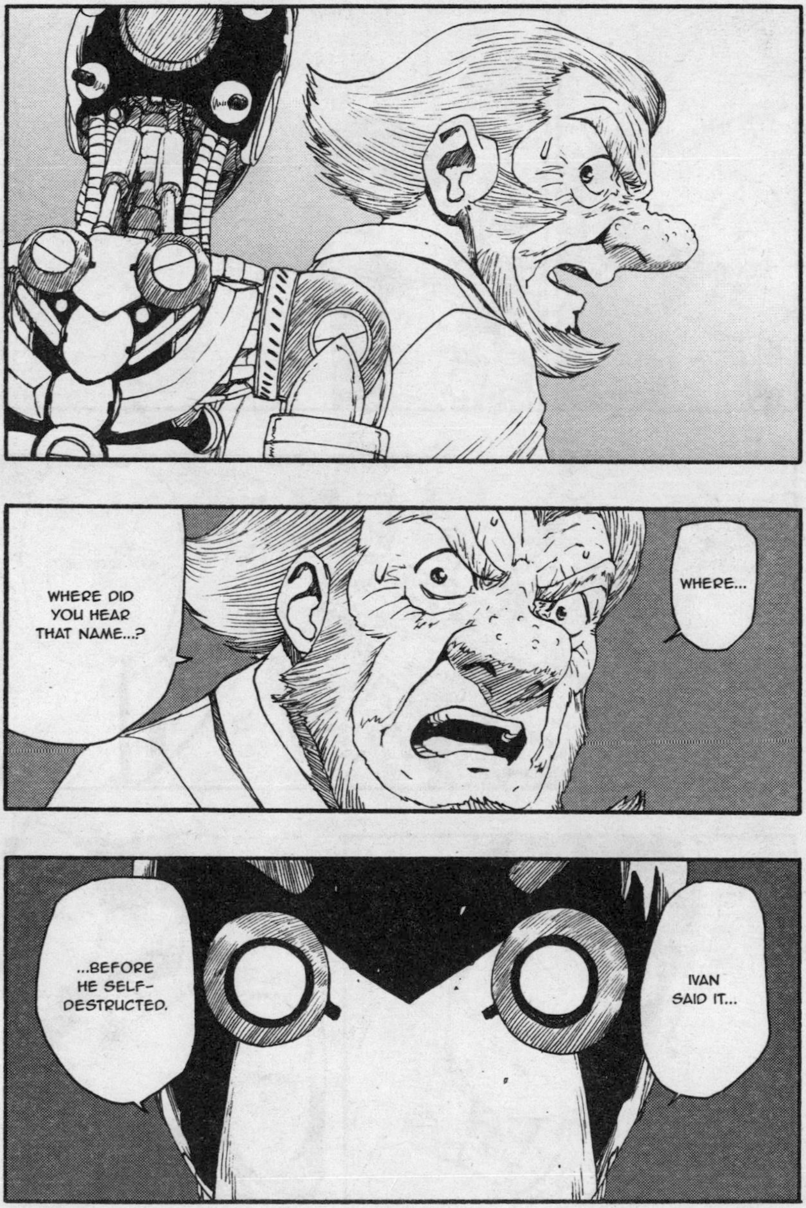
WHERE...
WHERE DID YOU HEAR THAT NAME...?
IVAN SAID IT...
...BEFORE HE SELF-DESTRUCTED.

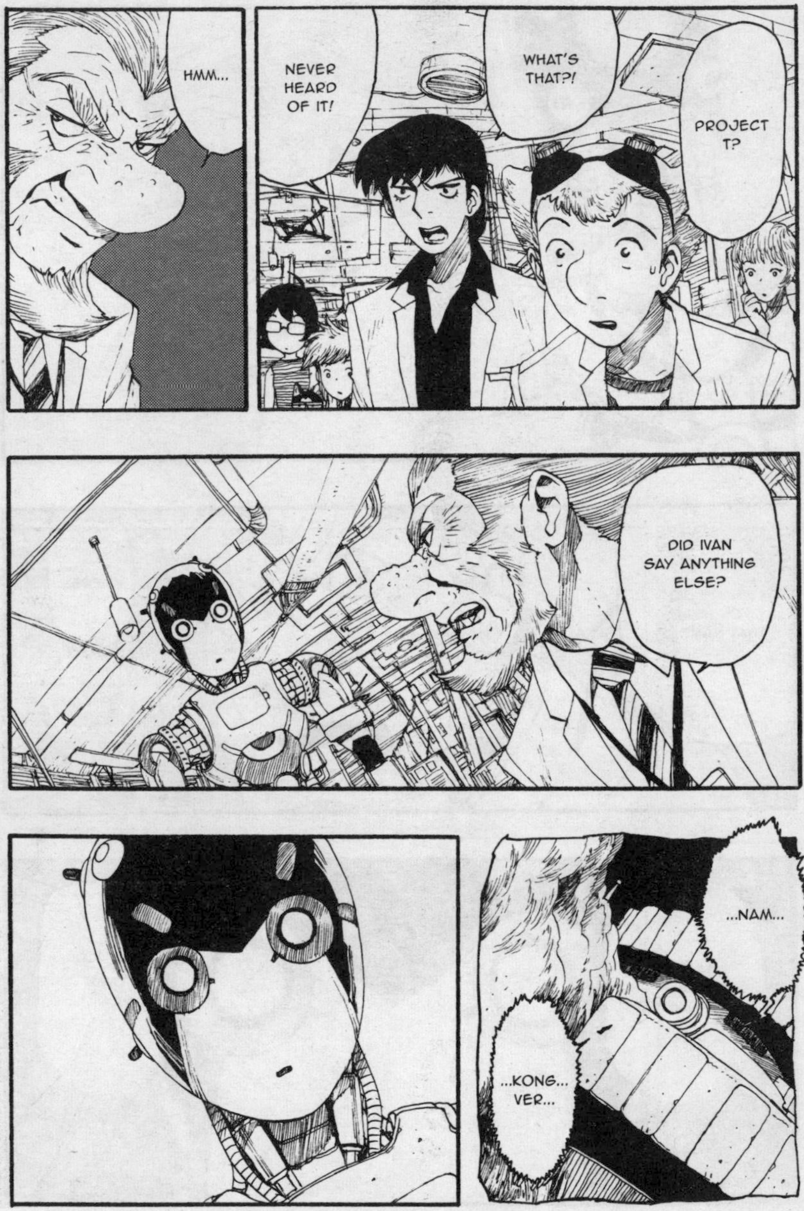
PROJECT T?
WHAT'S THAT?!
NEVER HEARD OF IT!
HMM...
DID IVAN SAY ANYTHING ELSE?
...NAM...
...KONG... VER...

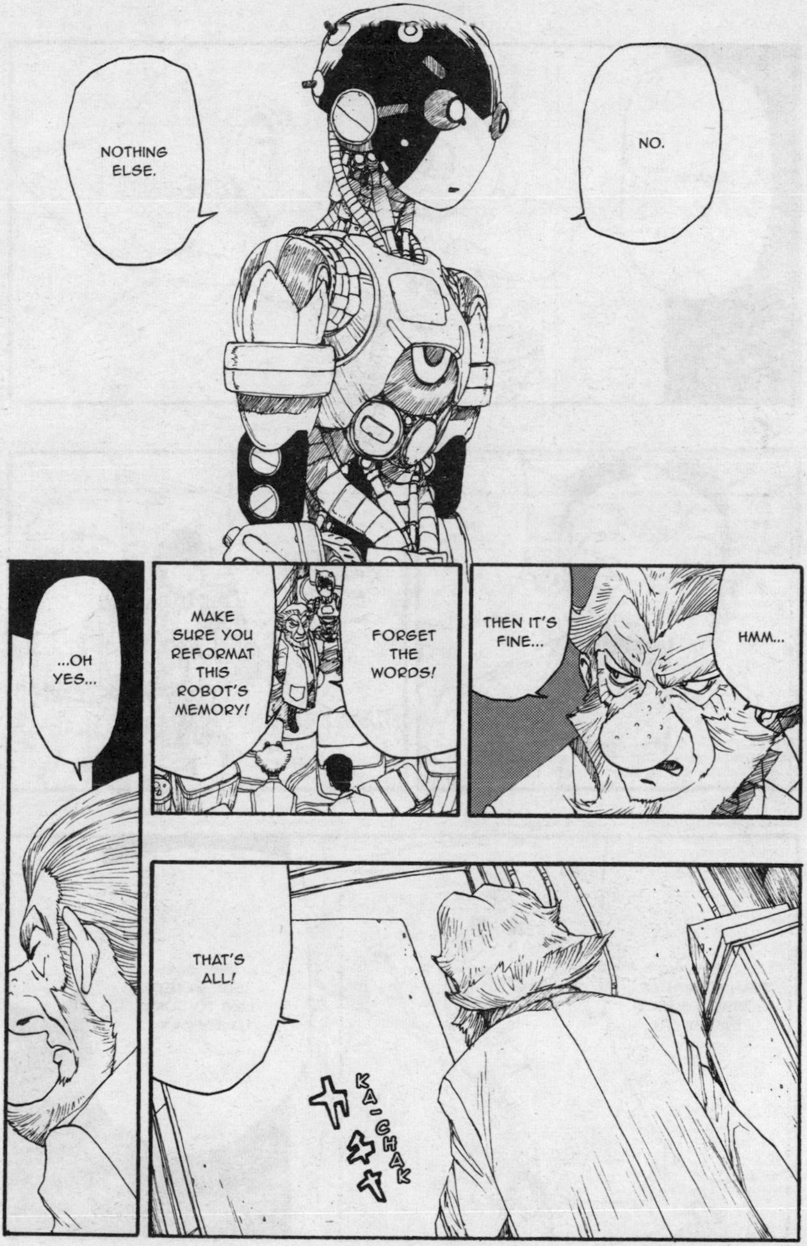
NO.
NOTHING ELSE.
HMM...
THEN IT'S FINE...
FORGET THE WORDS!
MAKE SURE YOU REFORMAT THIS ROBOT'S MEMORY!
THAT'S ALL!
KA-CHAK
...OH YES...

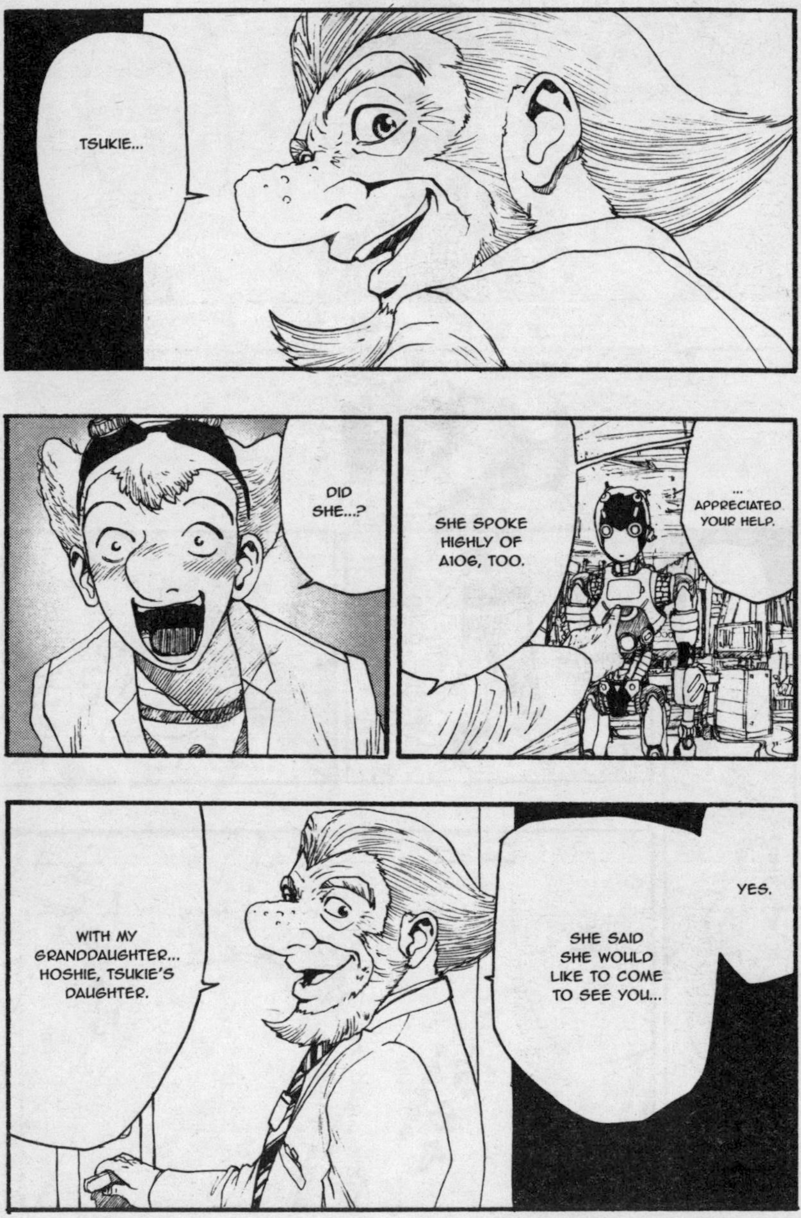
TSUKIE...
...APPRECIATED YOUR HELP.
SHE SPOKE HIGHLY OF A106, TOO.
DID SHE...?
YES.
SHE SAID SHE WOULD LIKE TO COME TO SEE YOU...
WITH MY GRANDDAUGHTER... HOSHIE, TSUKIE'S DAUGHTER.

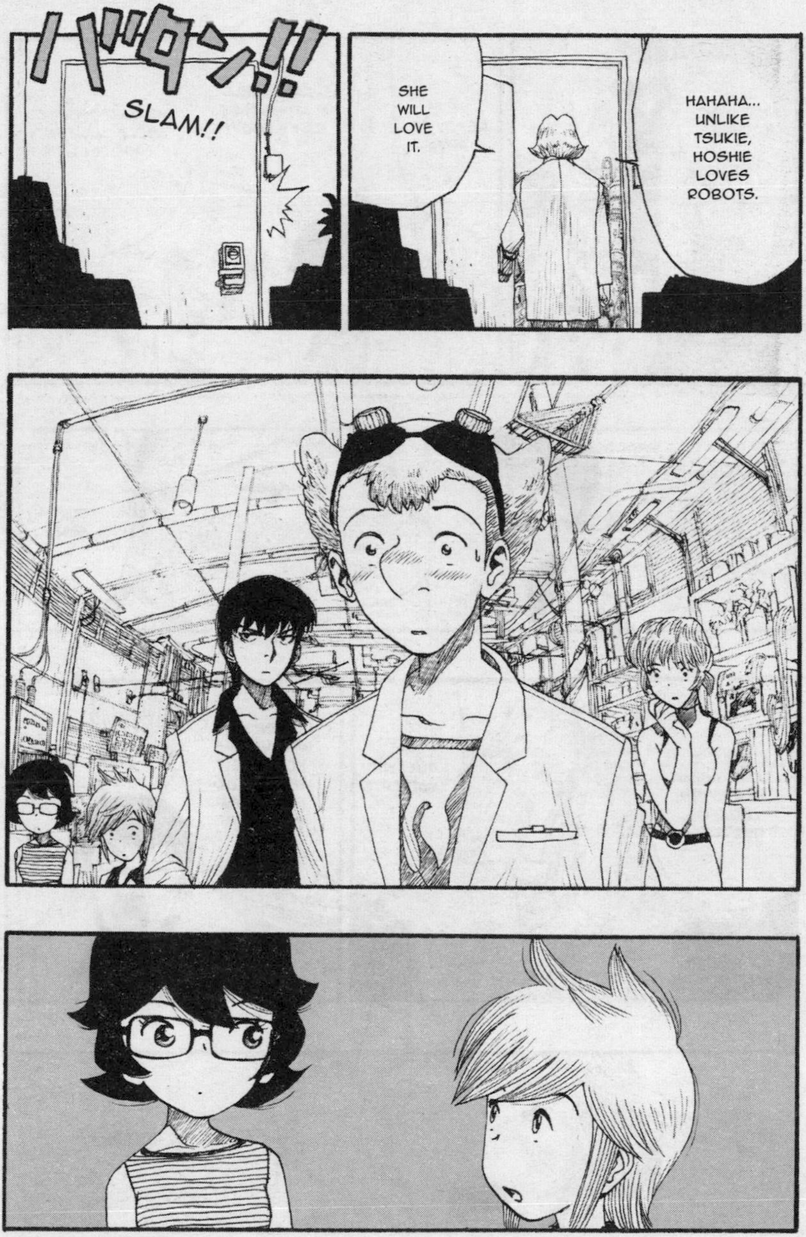
HAHAHA... UNLIKE TSUKIE, HOSHIE LOVES ROBOTS.
SHE WILL LOVE IT.
バタン!!
SLAM!!

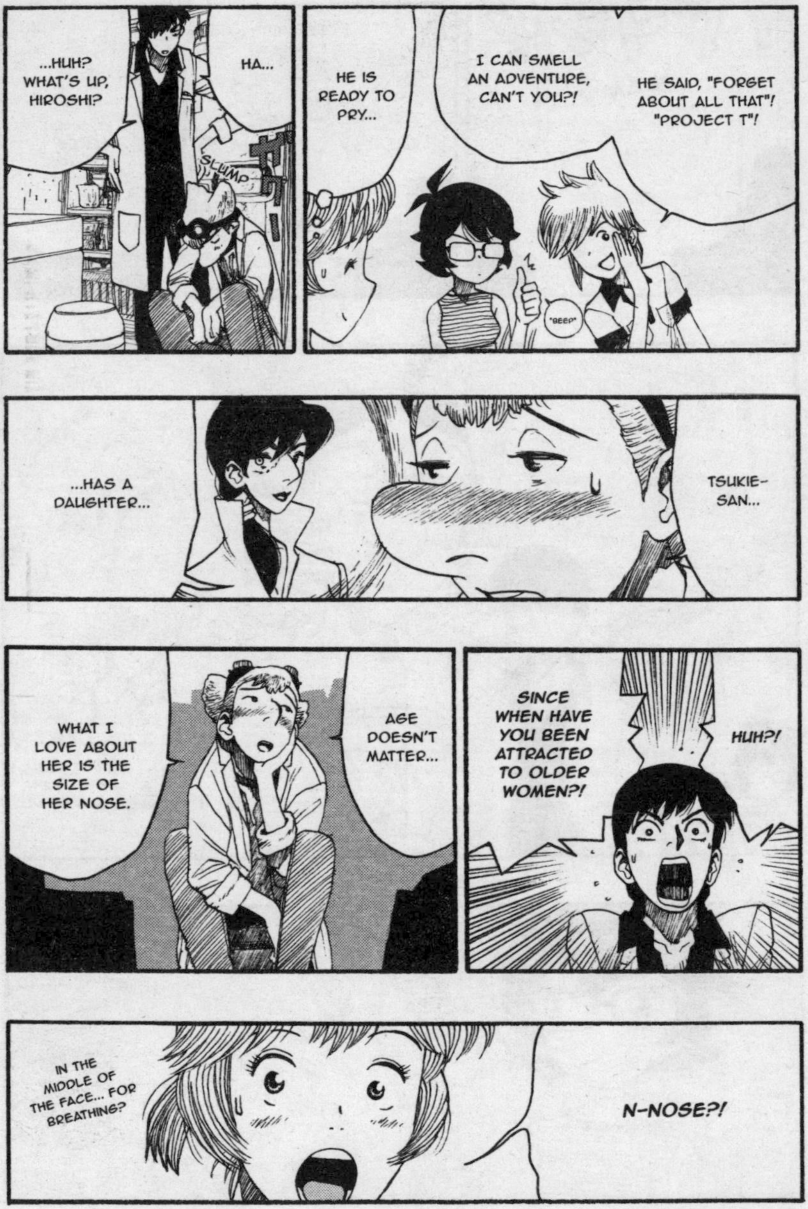
HE SAID, "FORGET ABOUT ALL THAT"! "PROJECT T"!
I CAN SMELL AN ADVENTURE, CAN'T YOU?!
HE IS READY TO PRY...
BEEP
HA...
...HUH? WHAT'S UP, HIROSHI?
SLUMP
TSUKIE-SAN...
...HAS A DAUGHTER...
HUH?!
SINCE WHEN HAVE YOU BEEN ATTRACTED TO OLDER WOMEN?!
AGE DOESN'T MATTER...
WHAT I LOVE ABOUT HER IS THE SIZE OF HER NOSE.
N-NOSE?!
IN THE MIDDLE OF THE FACE... FOR BREATHING?

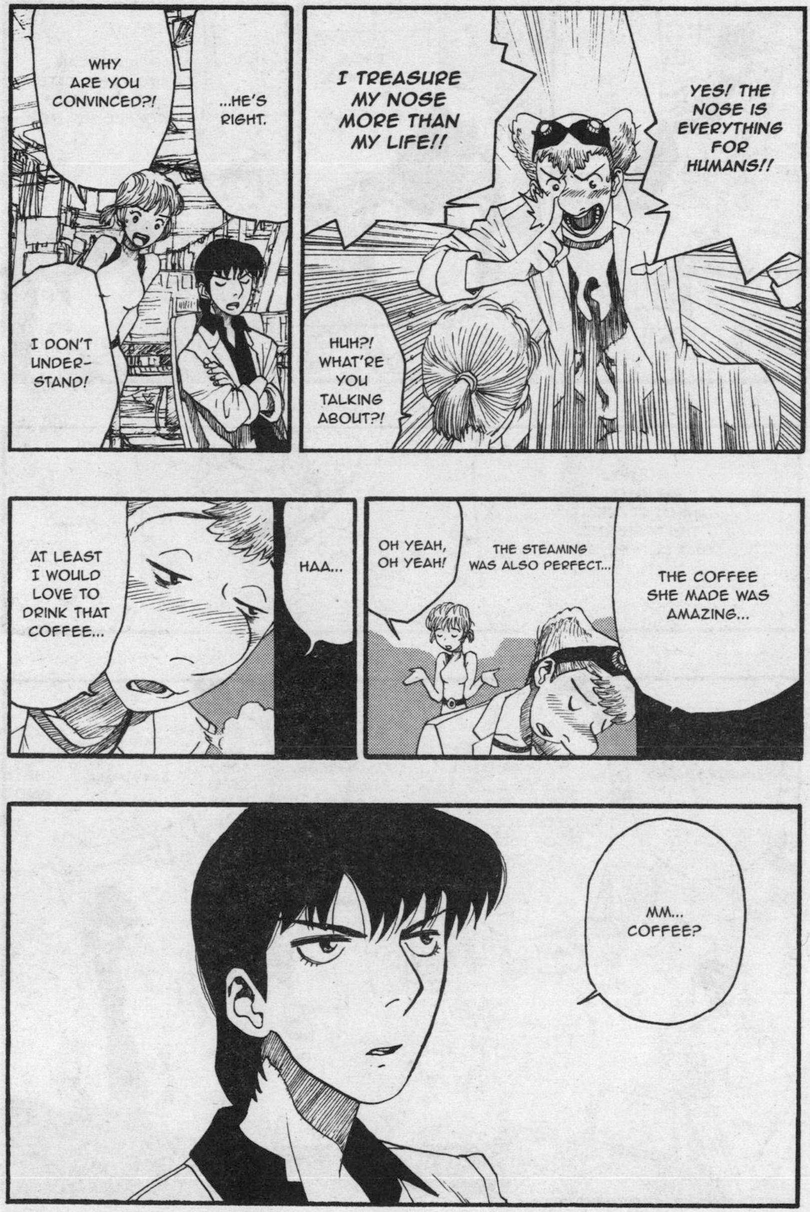
YES! THE NOSE IS EVERYTHING FOR HUMANS!!
I TREASURE MY NOSE MORE THAN MY LIFE!!
HUH?! WHAT'RE YOU TALKING ABOUT?!
...HE'S RIGHT.
WHY ARE YOU CONVINCED?!
I DON'T UNDER-STAND!
THE COFFEE SHE MADE WAS AMAZING...
THE STEAMING WAS ALSO PERFECT...
OH YEAH, OH YEAH!
HAA...
AT LEAST I WOULD LOVE TO DRINK THAT COFFEE...
MM... COFFEE?

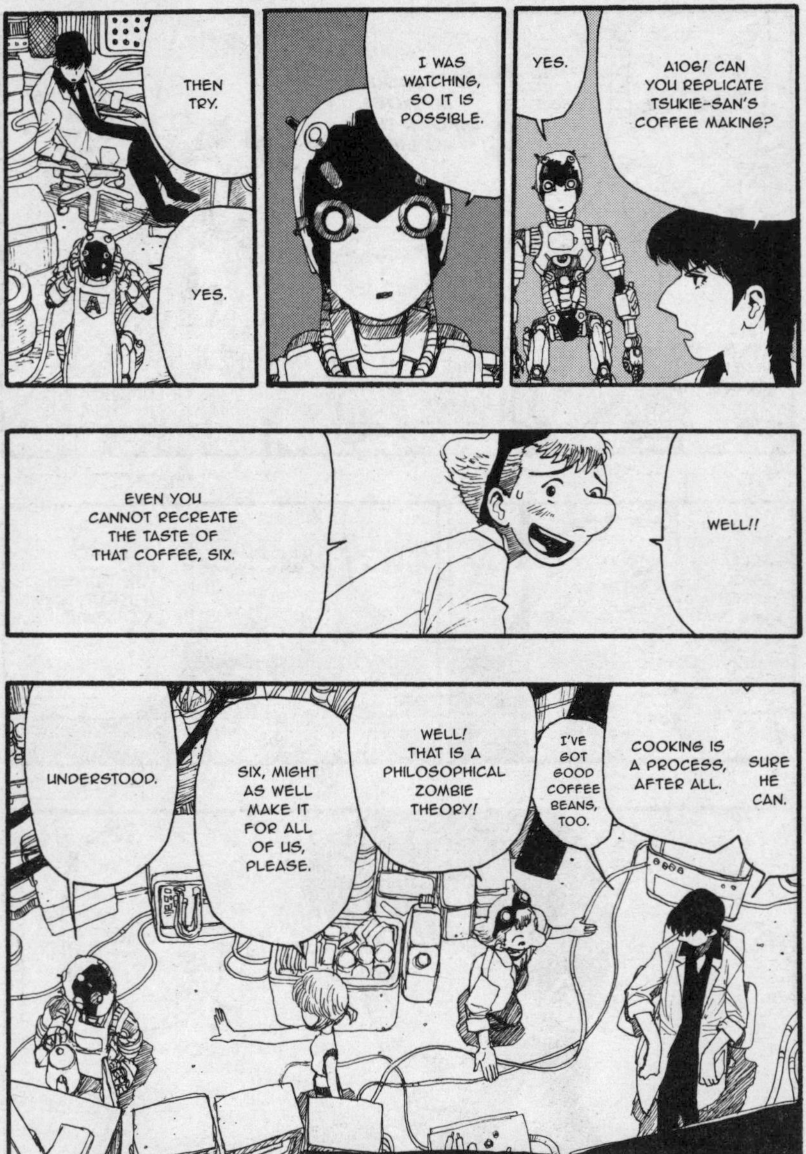
A106! CAN YOU REPLICATE TSUKIE-SAN'S COFFEE MAKING?
YES.
I WAS WATCHING, SO IT IS POSSIBLE.
THEN TRY.
YES.
WELL!!
EVEN YOU CANNOT RECREATE THE TASTE OF THAT COFFEE, SIX.
SURE HE CAN.
COOKING IS A PROCESS, AFTER ALL.
I'VE GOT GOOD COFFEE BEANS, TOO.
WELL! THAT IS A PHILOSOPHICAL ZOMBIE THEORY!
SIX, MIGHT AS WELL MAKE IT FOR ALL OF US, PLEASE.
UNDERSTOOD.

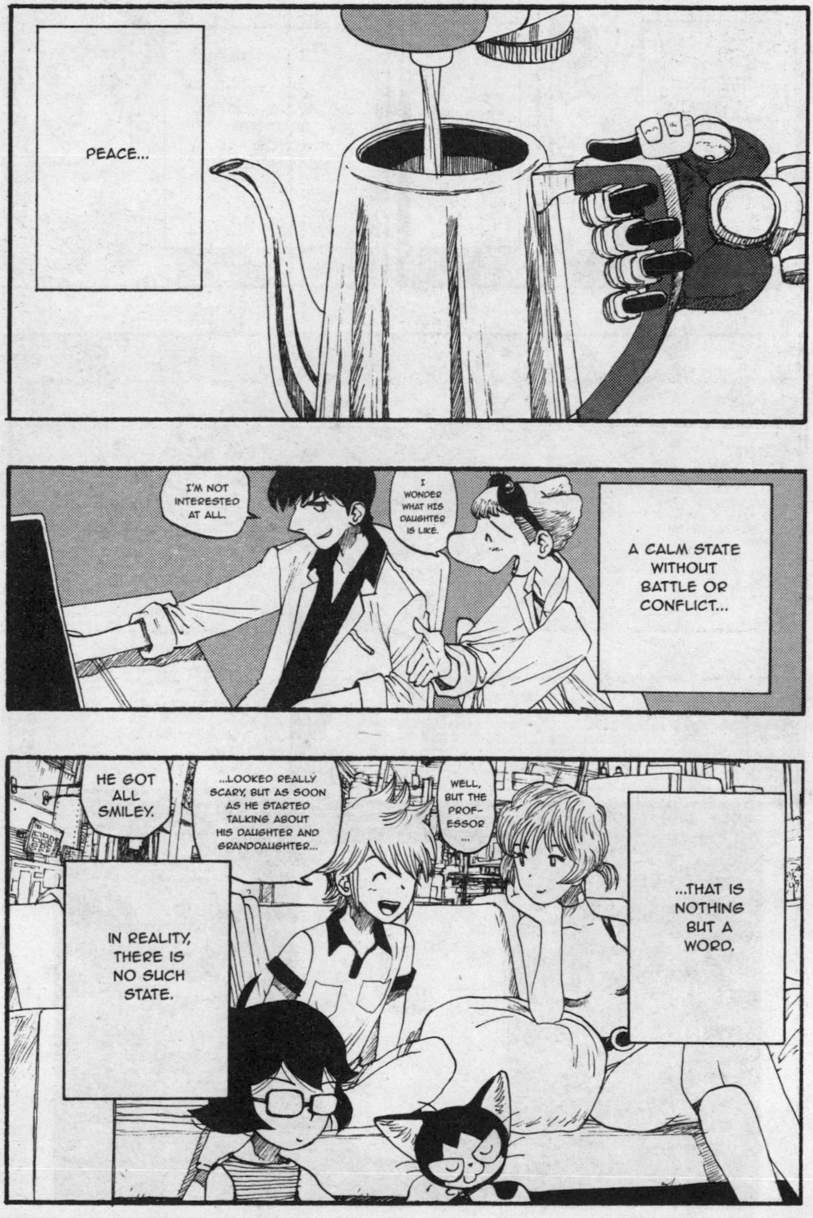
PEACE...
A CALM STATE WITHOUT BATTLE OR CONFLICT...
I WONDER WHAT HIS DAUGHTER IS LIKE.
I'M NOT INTERESTED AT ALL.
...THAT IS NOTHING BUT A WORD.
WELL, BUT THE PROF-ESSOR...
...LOOKED REALLY SCARY, BUT AS SOON AS HE STARTED TALKING ABOUT HIS DAUGHTER AND GRANDDAUGHTER...
HE GOT ALL SMILEY.
IN REALITY, THERE IS NO SUCH STATE.

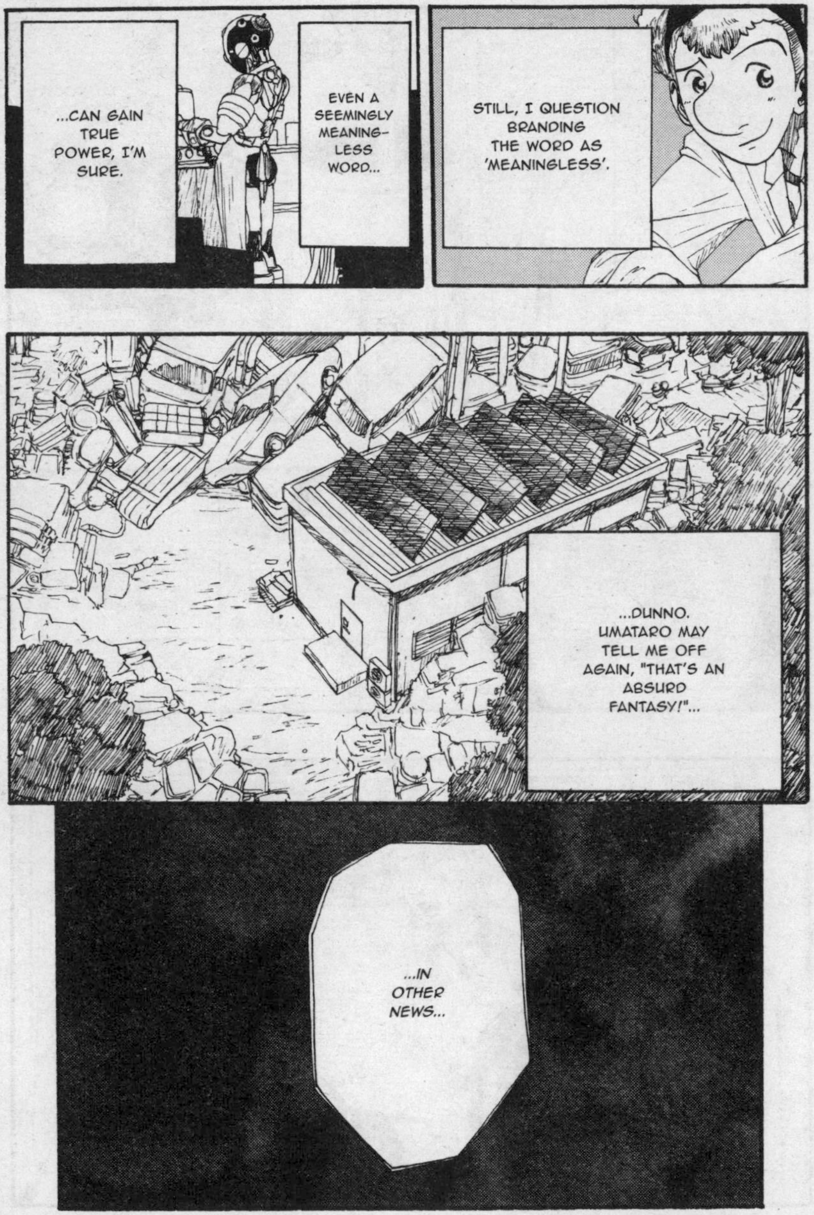
STILL, I QUESTION BRANDING THE WORD AS 'MEANINGLESS'.
EVEN A SEEMINGLY MEANING-LESS WORD...
...CAN GAIN TRUE POWER, I'M SURE.
...DUNNO. UMATARO MAY TELL ME OFF AGAIN, "THAT'S AN ABSURD FANTASY!"...
...IN OTHER NEWS...

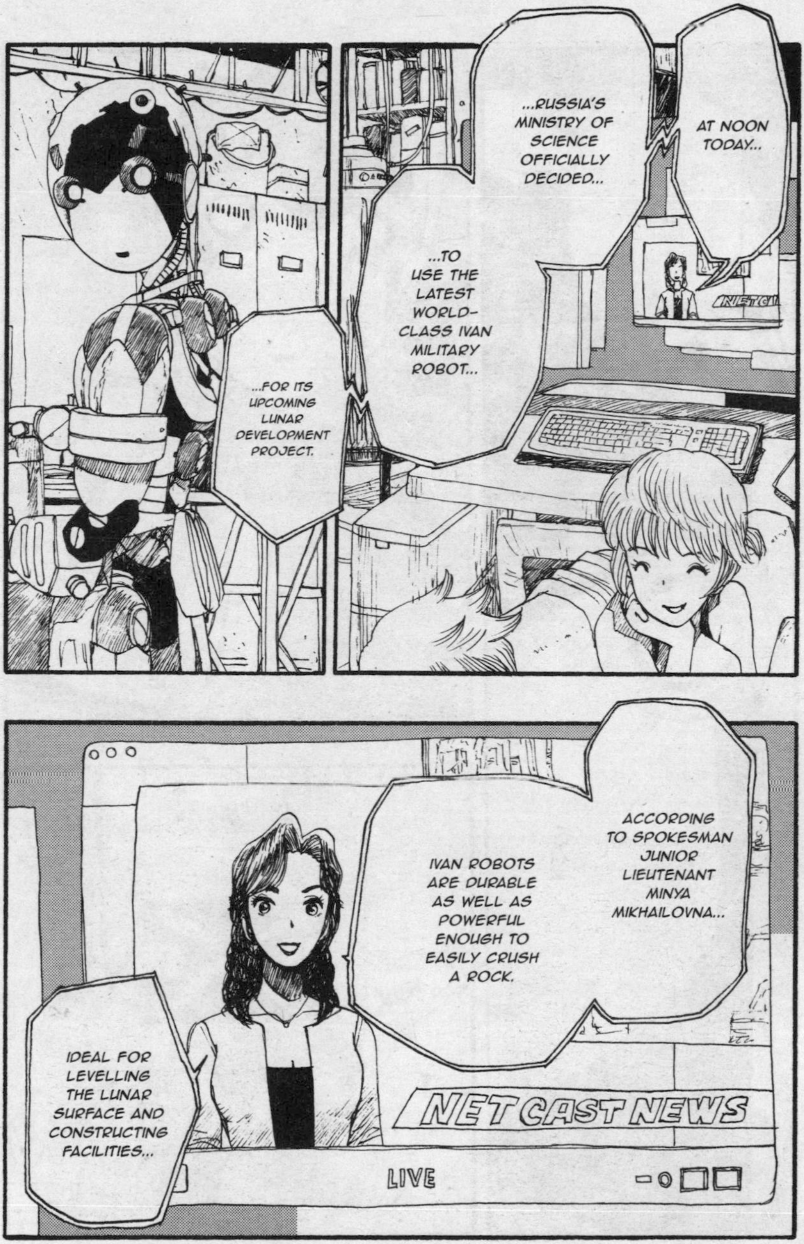
AT NOON TODAY...
...RUSSIA'S MINISTRY OF SCIENCE OFFICIALLY DECIDED...
...TO USE THE LATEST WORLD-CLASS IVAN MILITARY ROBOT...
...FOR ITS UPCOMING LUNAR DEVELOPMENT PROJECT.
ACCORDING TO SPOKESMAN JUNIOR LIEUTENANT MINYA MIKHAILOVNA...
IVAN ROBOTS ARE DURABLE AS WELL AS POWERFUL ENOUGH TO EASILY CRUSH A ROCK.
IDEAL FOR LEVELLING THE LUNAR SURFACE AND CONSTRUCTING FACILITIES...
NET CAST NEWS
LIVE

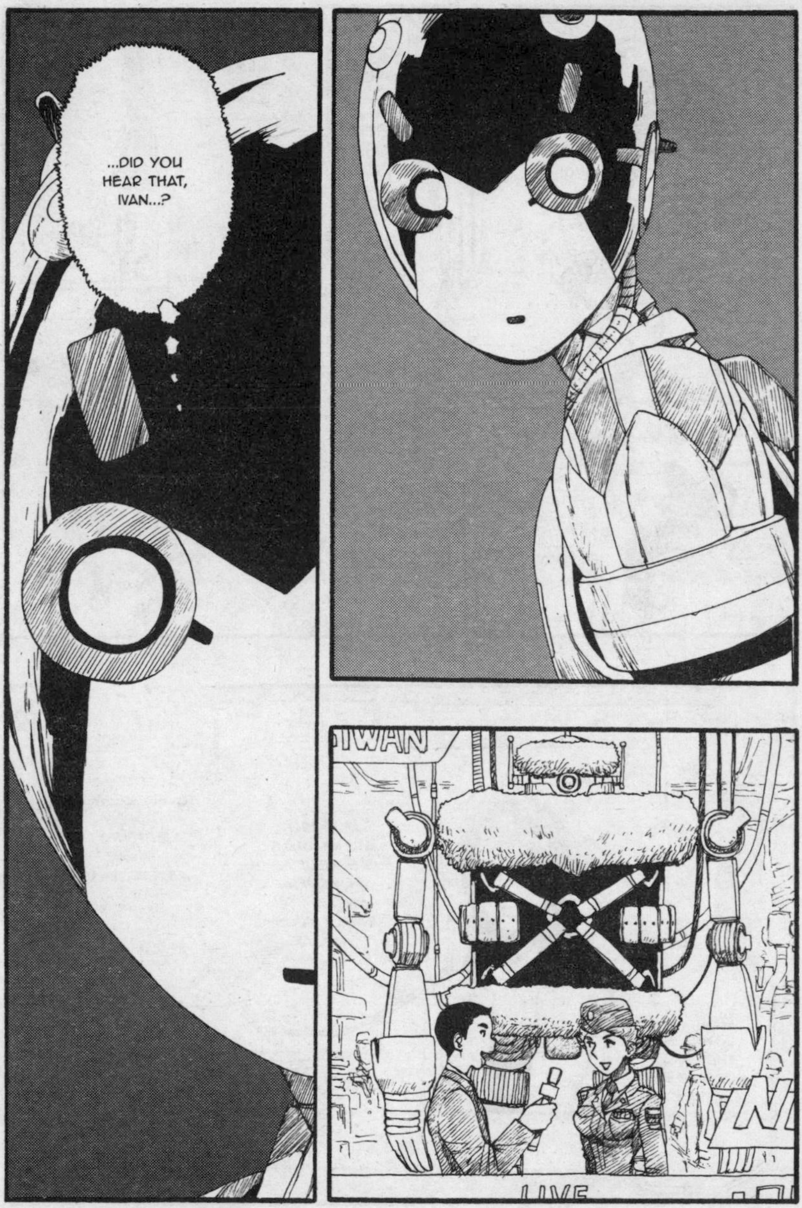
...DID YOU HEAR THAT, IVAN...?

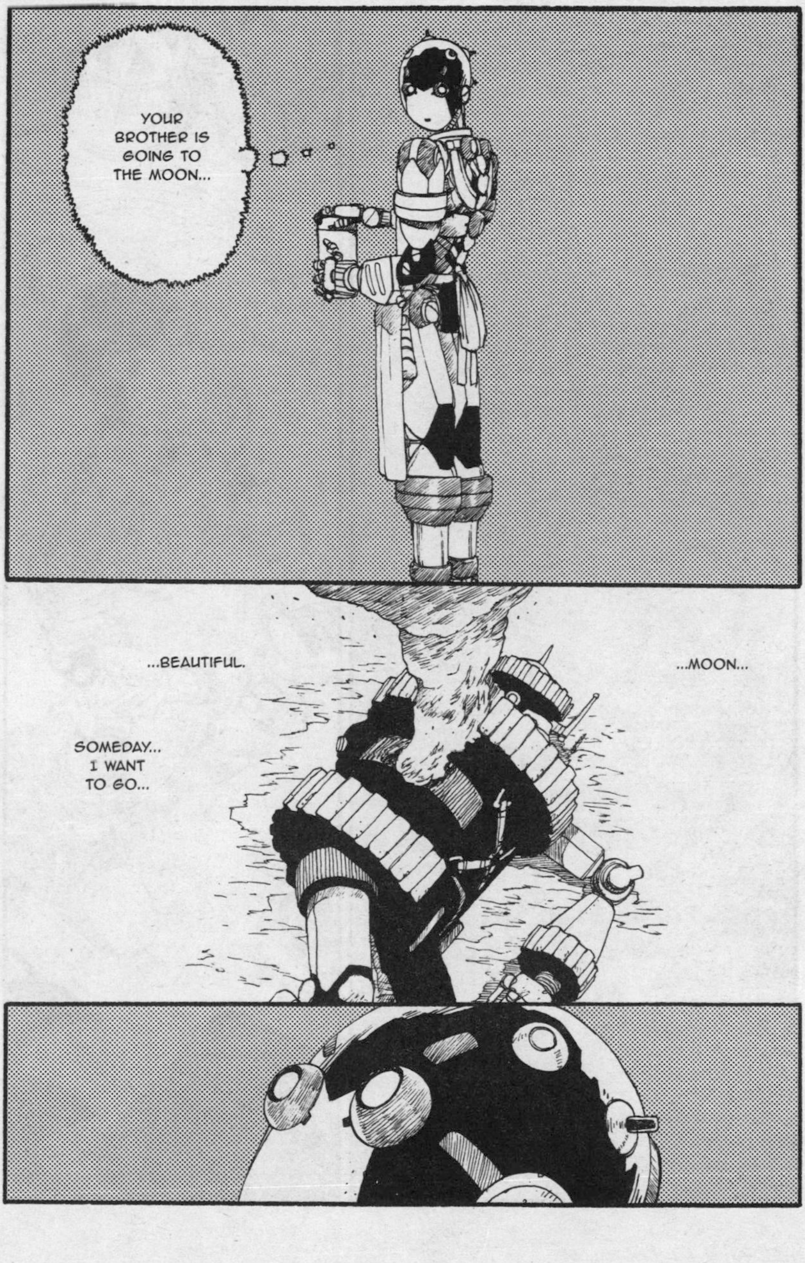
YOUR BROTHER IS GOING TO THE MOON...
...MOON...
...BEAUTIFUL.
SOMEDAY... I WANT TO GO...

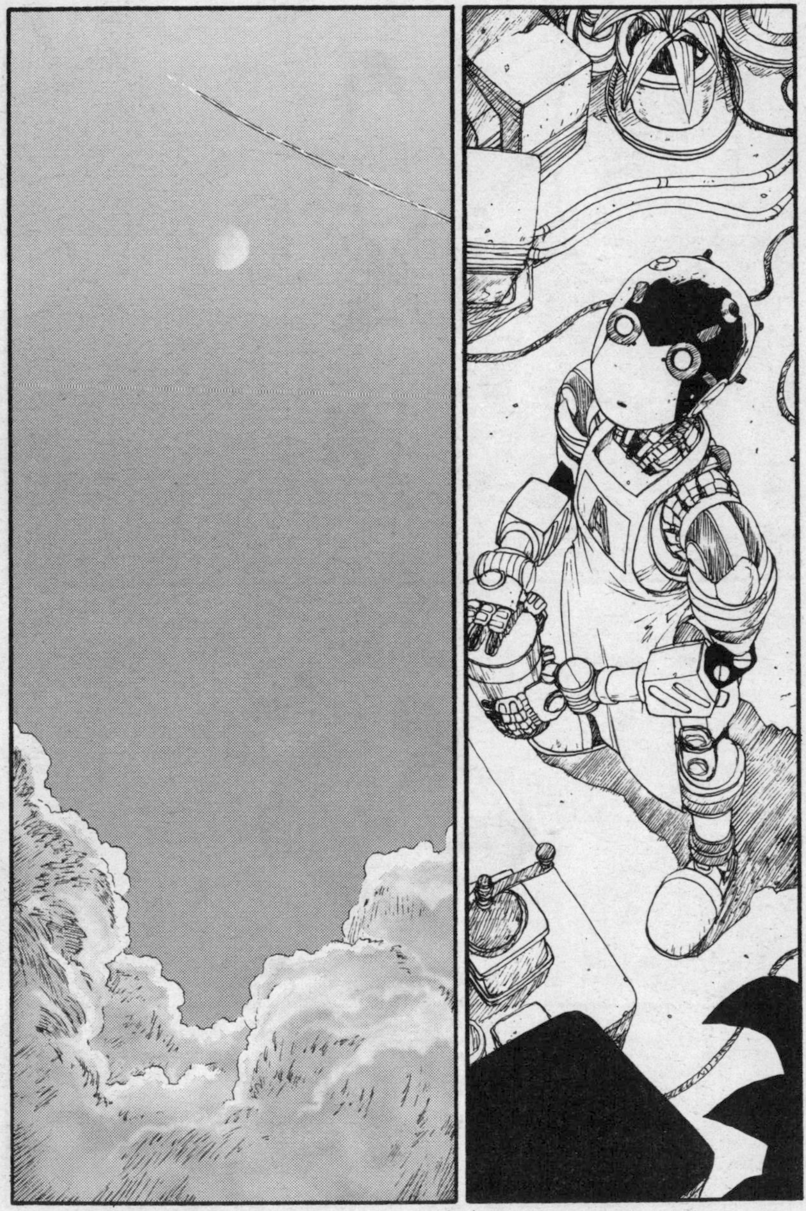

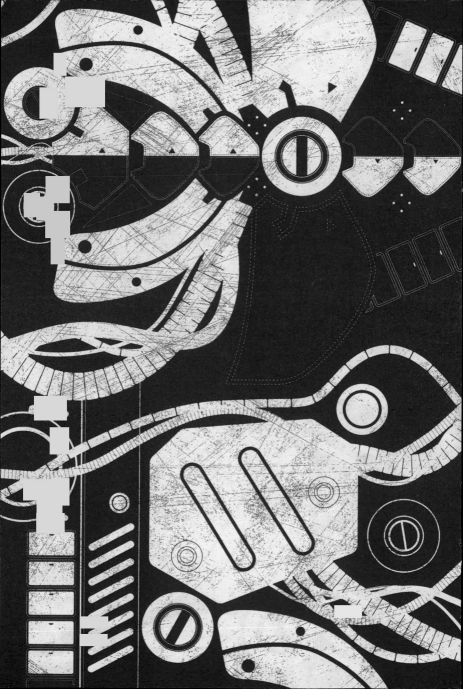

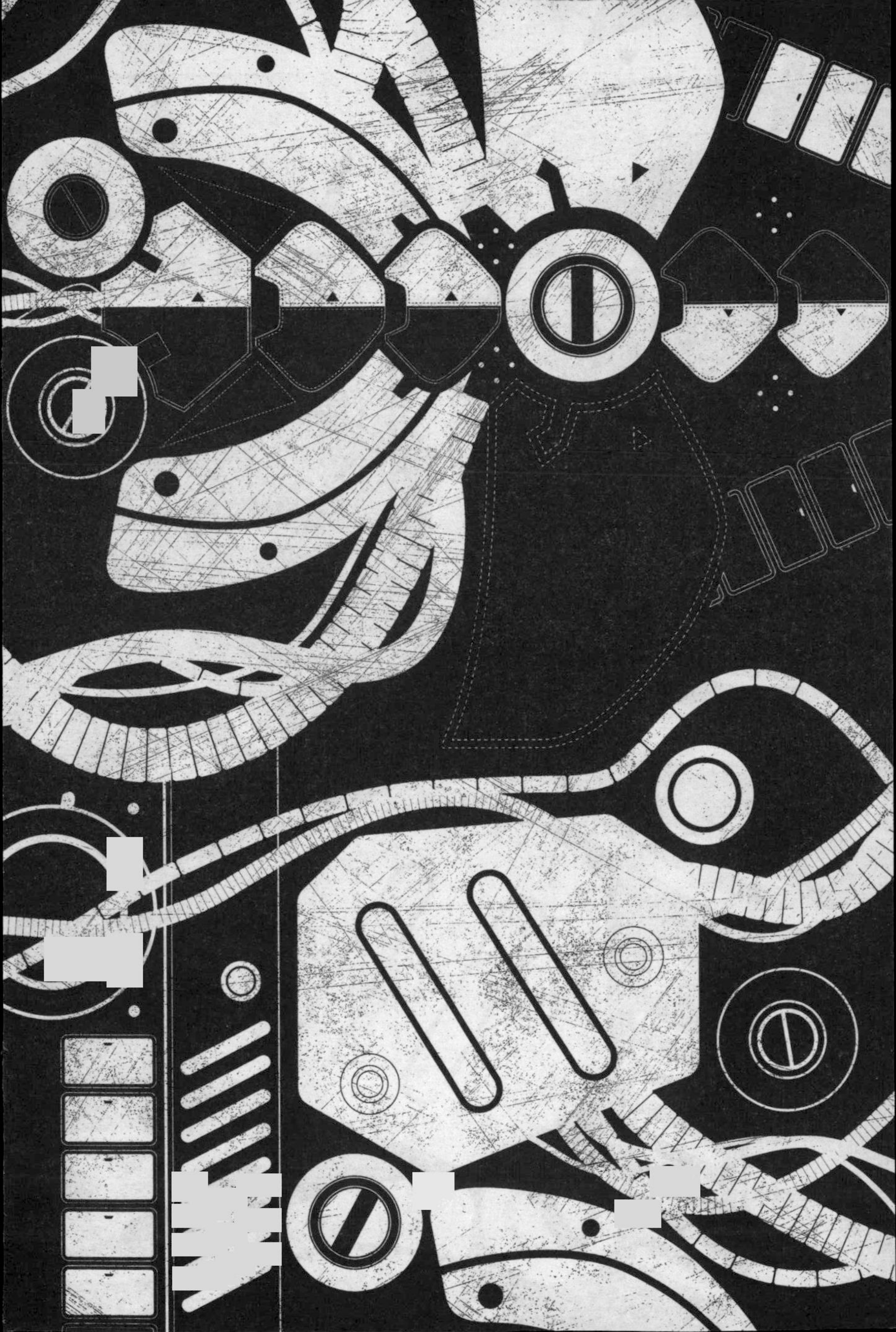

▷boot_019

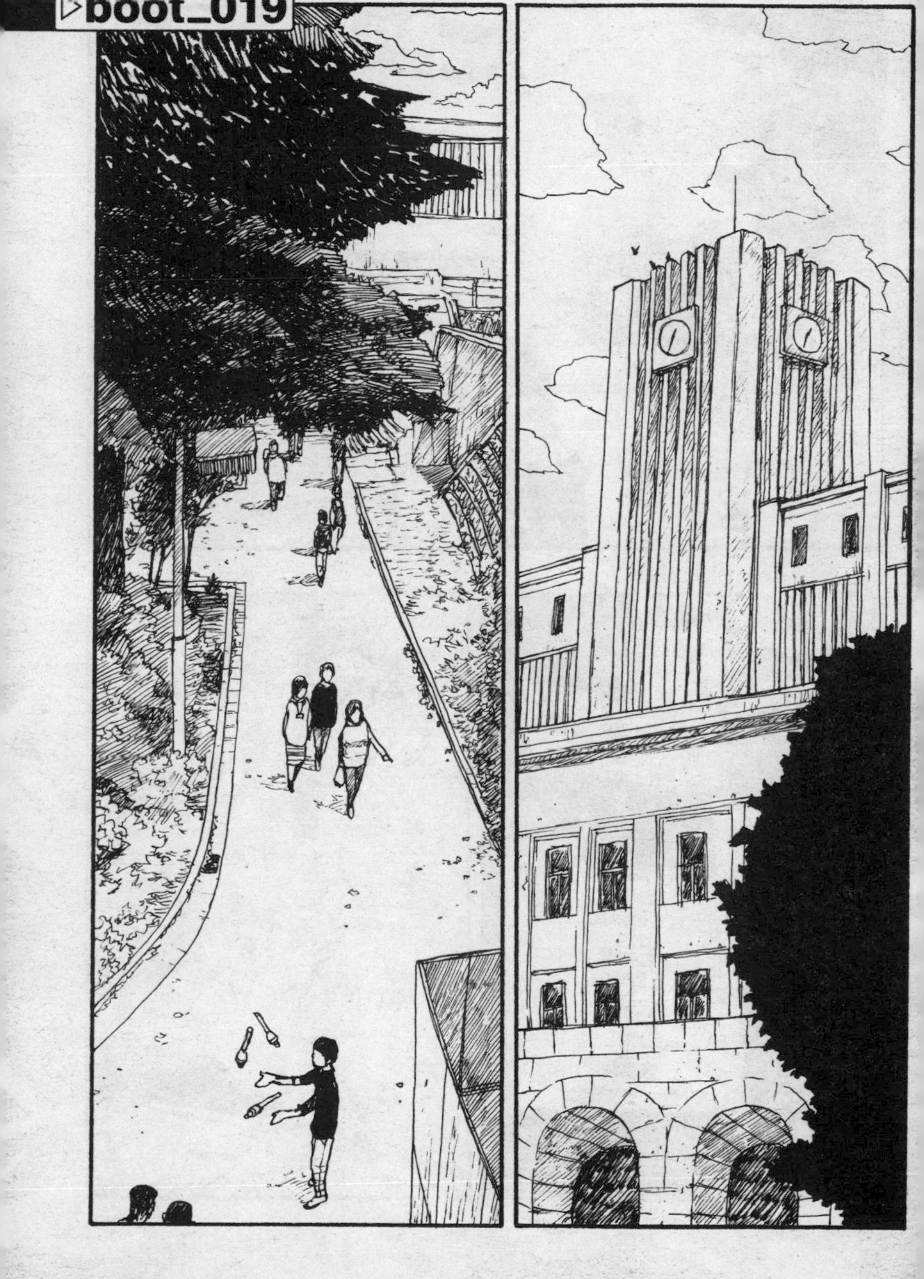

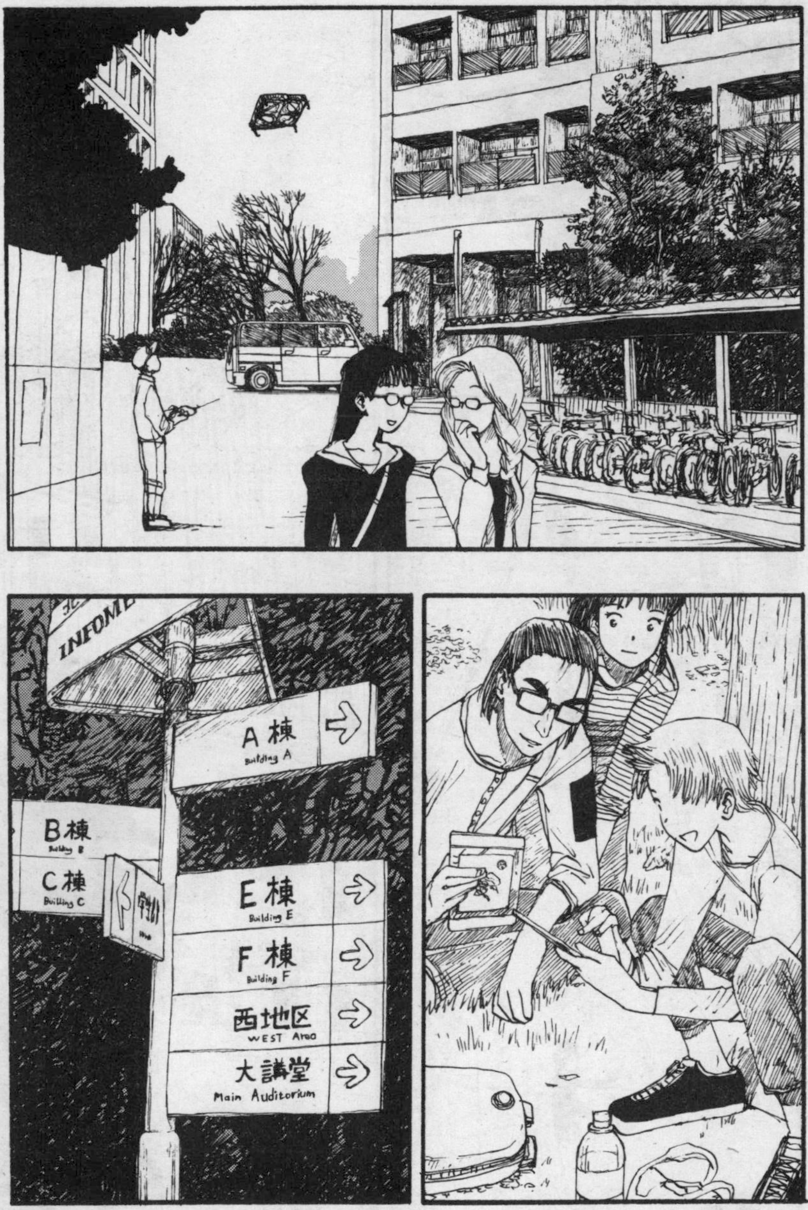
A棟
Building A
B棟
Building B
C棟
Building C
E棟
Building E
F棟
Building F
西地区
WEST Area
大講堂
Main Auditorium

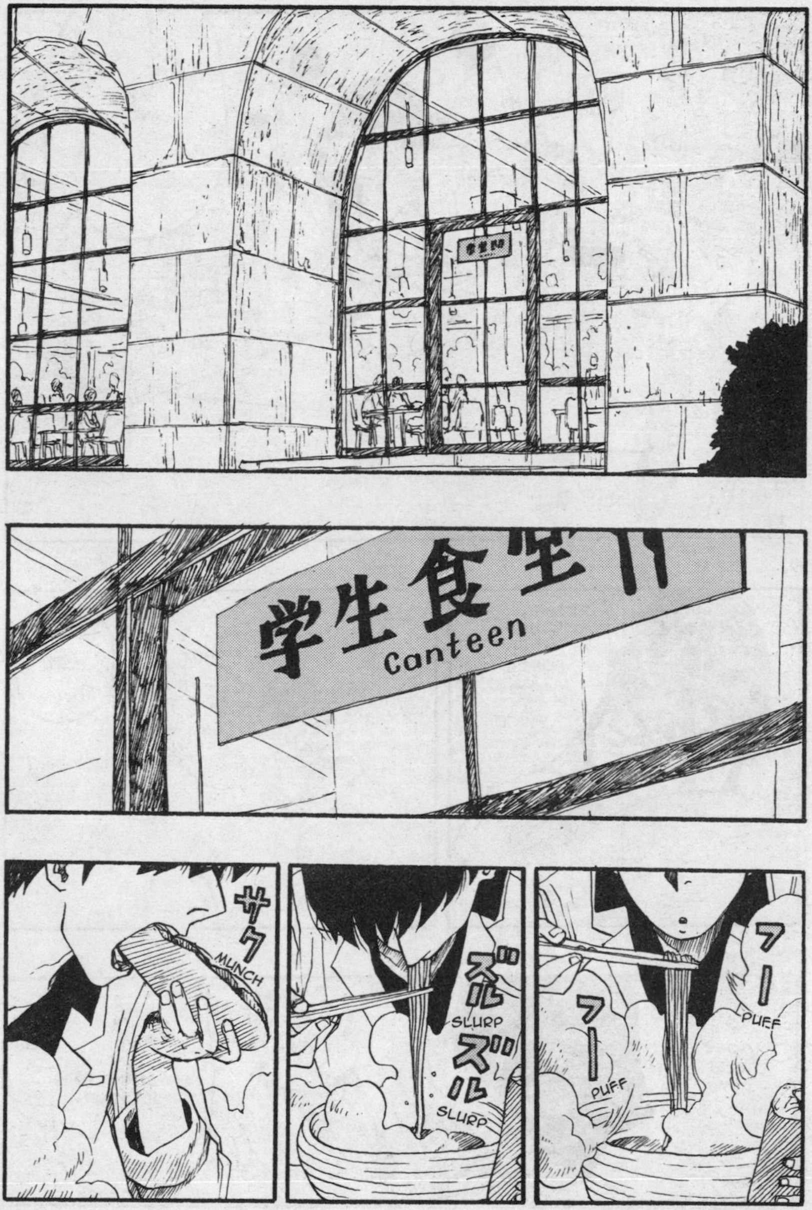
学生食堂
Canteen
フー
PUFF
フー
PUFF
ズル
SLURP
ズル
SLURP
サク
MUNCH

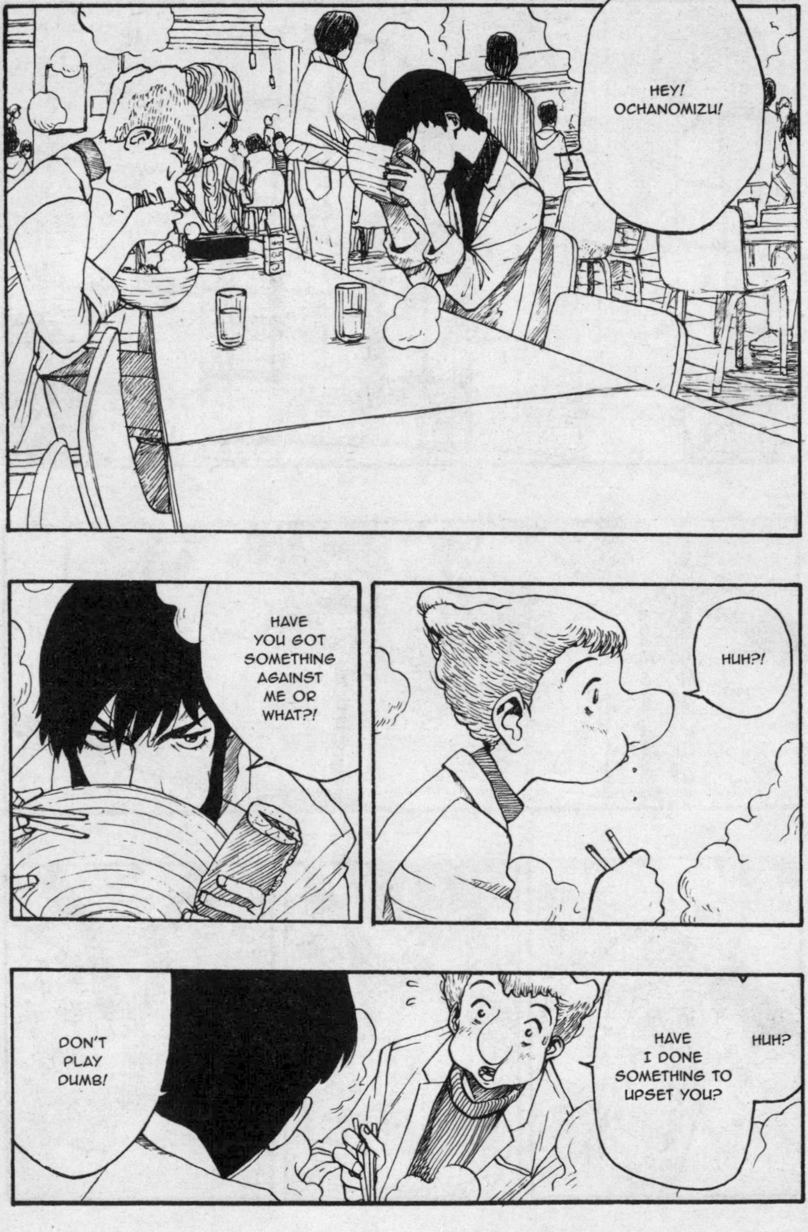
HEY! OCHANOMIZU!
HUH?!
HAVE YOU GOT SOMETHING AGAINST ME OR WHAT?!
HUH?
HAVE I DONE SOMETHING TO UPSET YOU?
DON'T PLAY DUMB!

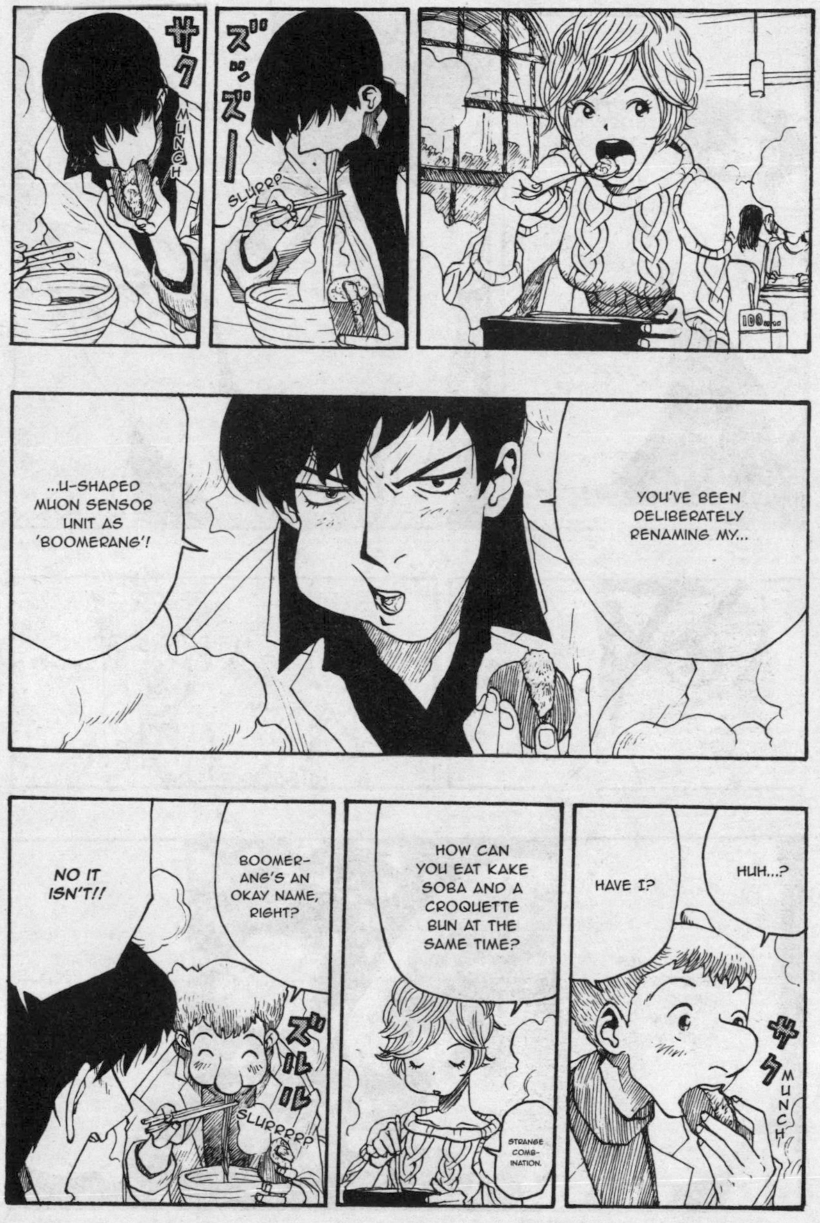
ズズー
SLURRP
サク
MUNCH
YOU'VE BEEN DELIBERATELY RENAMING MY...
...U-SHAPED MUON SENSOR UNIT AS 'BOOMERANG'!
HUH...?
HAVE I?
サク
MUNCH
HOW CAN YOU EAT KAKE SOBA AND A CROQUETTE BUN AT THE SAME TIME?
STRANGE COMBINATION.
BOOMERANG'S AN OKAY NAME, RIGHT?
NO IT ISN'T!!
ズルル
SLURRRRP

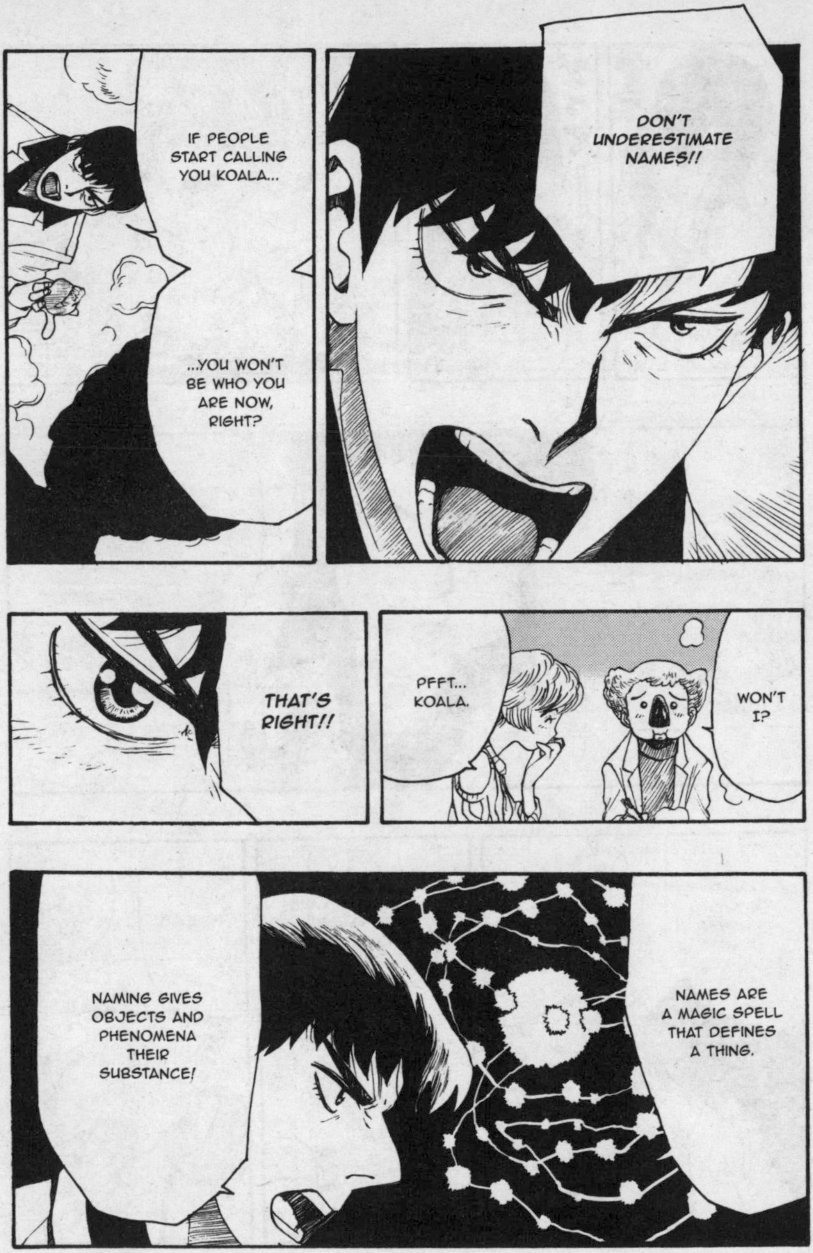
DON'T UNDERESTIMATE NAMES!!
IF PEOPLE START CALLING YOU KOALA...
...YOU WON'T BE WHO YOU ARE NOW, RIGHT?
WON'T I?
PFFT... KOALA.
THAT'S RIGHT!!
NAMES ARE A MAGIC SPELL THAT DEFINES A THING.
NAMING GIVES OBJECTS AND PHENOMENA THEIR SUBSTANCE!

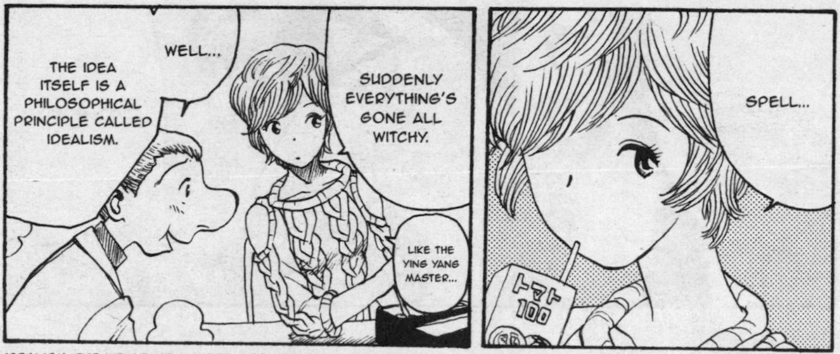
SPELL...
トマト100
SUDDENLY EVERYTHING'S GONE ALL WITCHY.
WELL...
THE IDEA ITSELF IS A PHILOSOPHICAL PRINCIPLE CALLED IDEALISM.
LIKE THE YING YANG MASTER...

IDEALISM: THE VIEW THAT AN IDEA DEFINES THE PRESENCE AND UNDERSTANDING OF AN OBJECT.

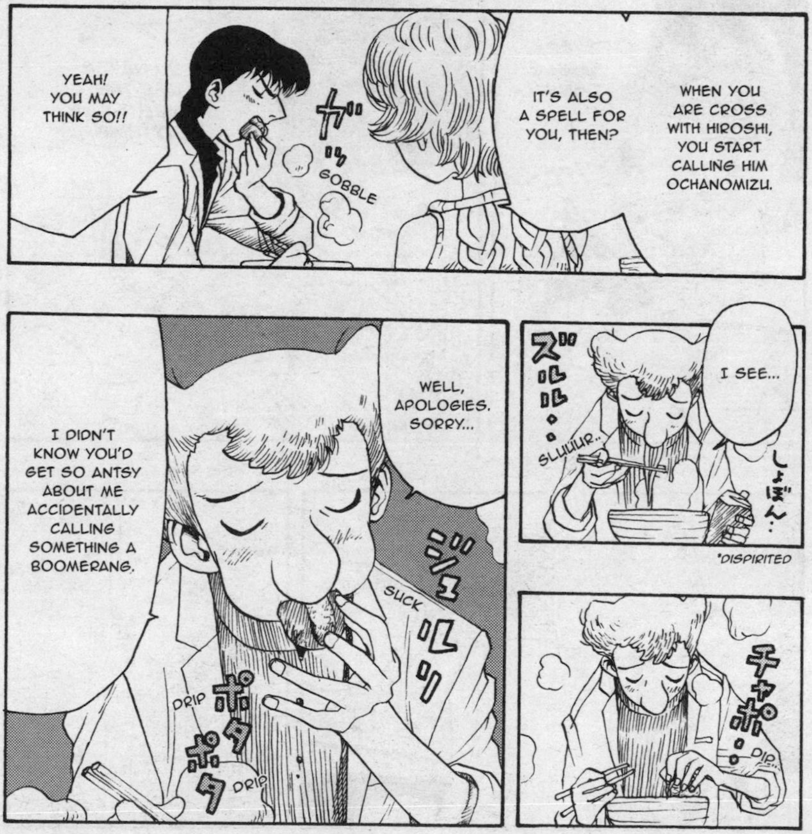
WHEN YOU ARE CROSS WITH HIROSHI, YOU START CALLING HIM OCHANOMIZU.
IT'S ALSO A SPELL FOR YOU, THEN?
ガッ
GOBBLE
YEAH! YOU MAY THINK SO!!
I SEE...
ズルル。。
SLUUUR..
しょぼん。。
*DISPIRITED
チャポ。。
DRIP
WELL, APOLOGIES. SORRY...
I DIDN'T KNOW YOU'D GET SO ANTSY ABOUT ME ACCIDENTALLY CALLING SOMETHING A BOOMERANG.
ジュルッ
SUCK
ポタポタ
DRIP
DRIP

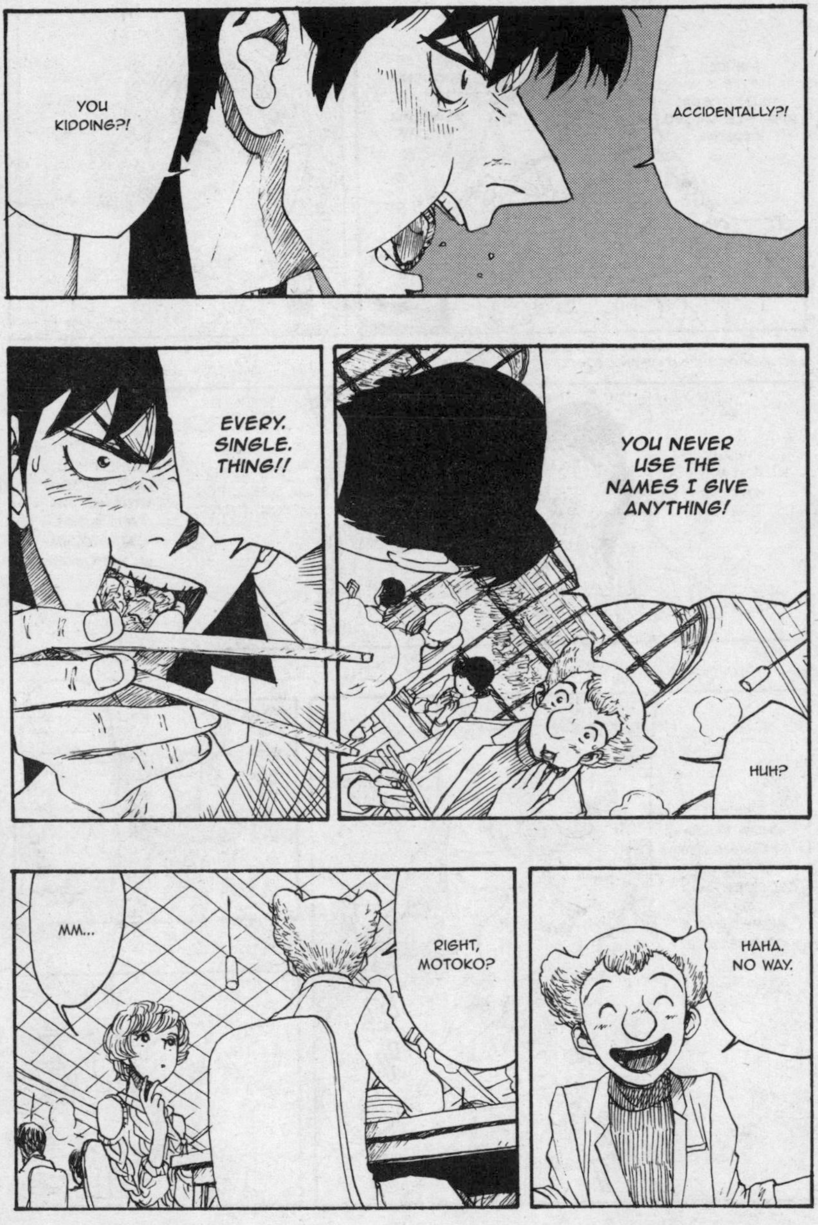
ACCIDENTALLY?!
YOU KIDDING?!
YOU NEVER USE THE NAMES I GIVE ANYTHING!
HUH?
EVERY. SINGLE. THING!!
HAHA. NO WAY.
RIGHT, MOTOKO?
MM...

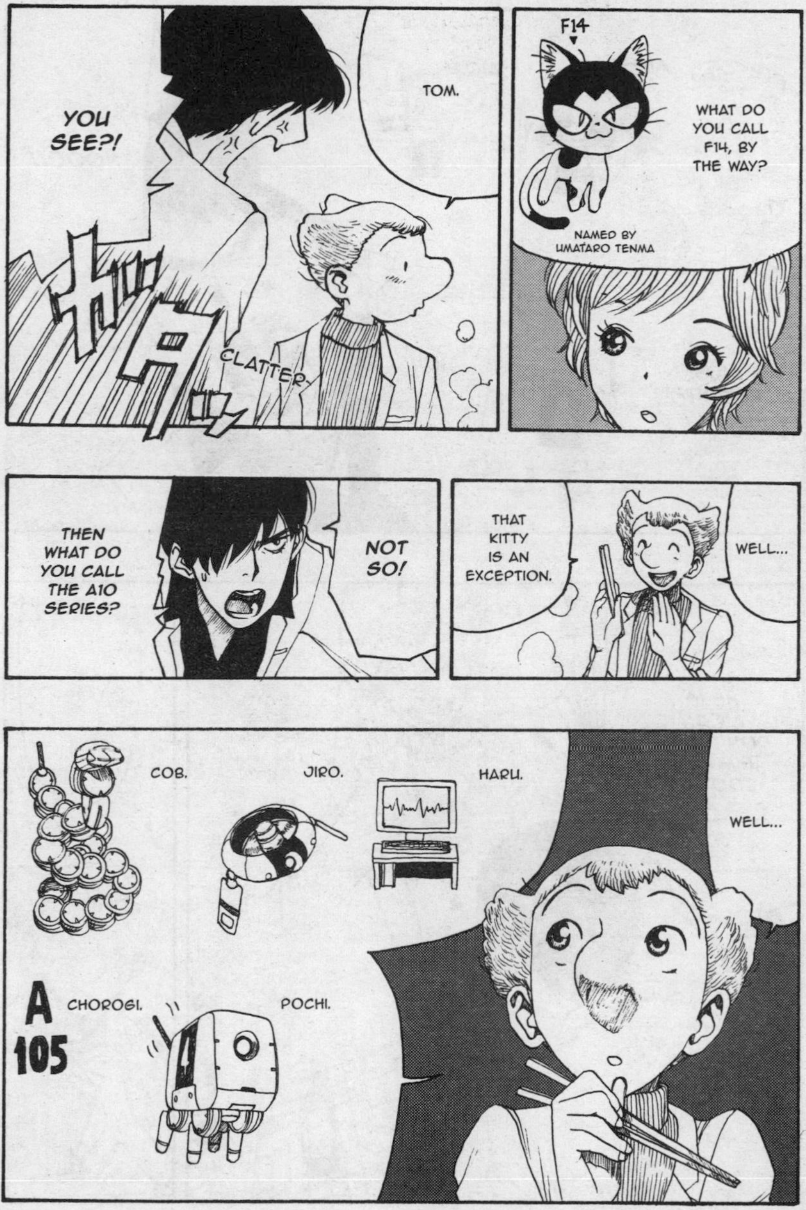
F14
WHAT DO YOU CALL F14, BY THE WAY?
NAMED BY UMATARO TENMA
TOM.
YOU SEE?!
CLATTER
WELL...
THAT KITTY IS AN EXCEPTION.
NOT SO!
THEN WHAT DO YOU CALL THE A10 SERIES?
WELL...
HARU.
JIRO.
COB.
POCHI.
CHOROGI.
A 105

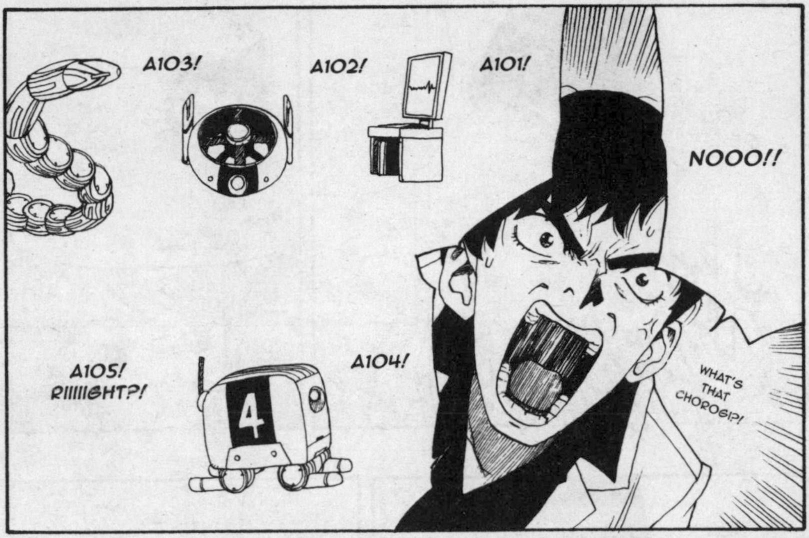
NOOO!!
A101!
A102!
A103!
WHAT'S THAT CHOROGI?!
A104!
A105! RIIIIIGHT?!
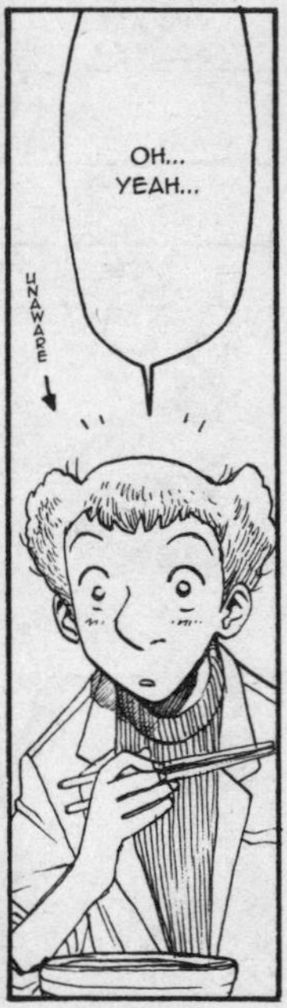
OH... YEAH...
UNAWARE
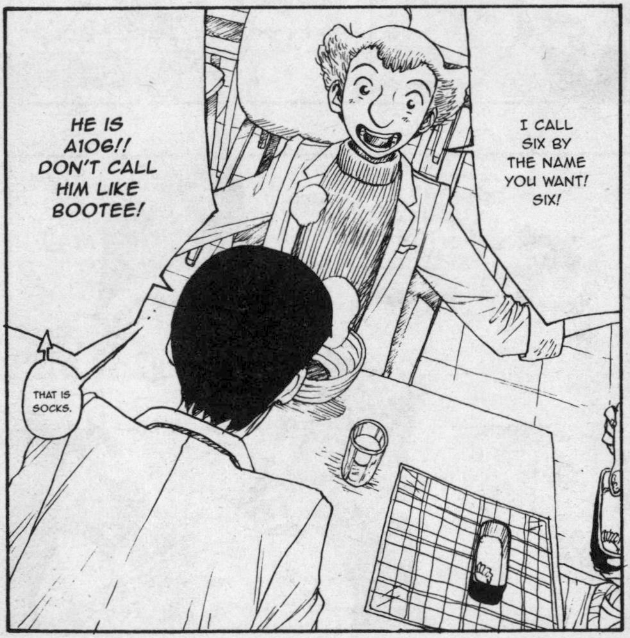
I CALL SIX BY THE NAME YOU WANT! SIX!
HE IS A106!! DON'T CALL HIM LIKE BOOTEE!
THAT IS SOCKS.

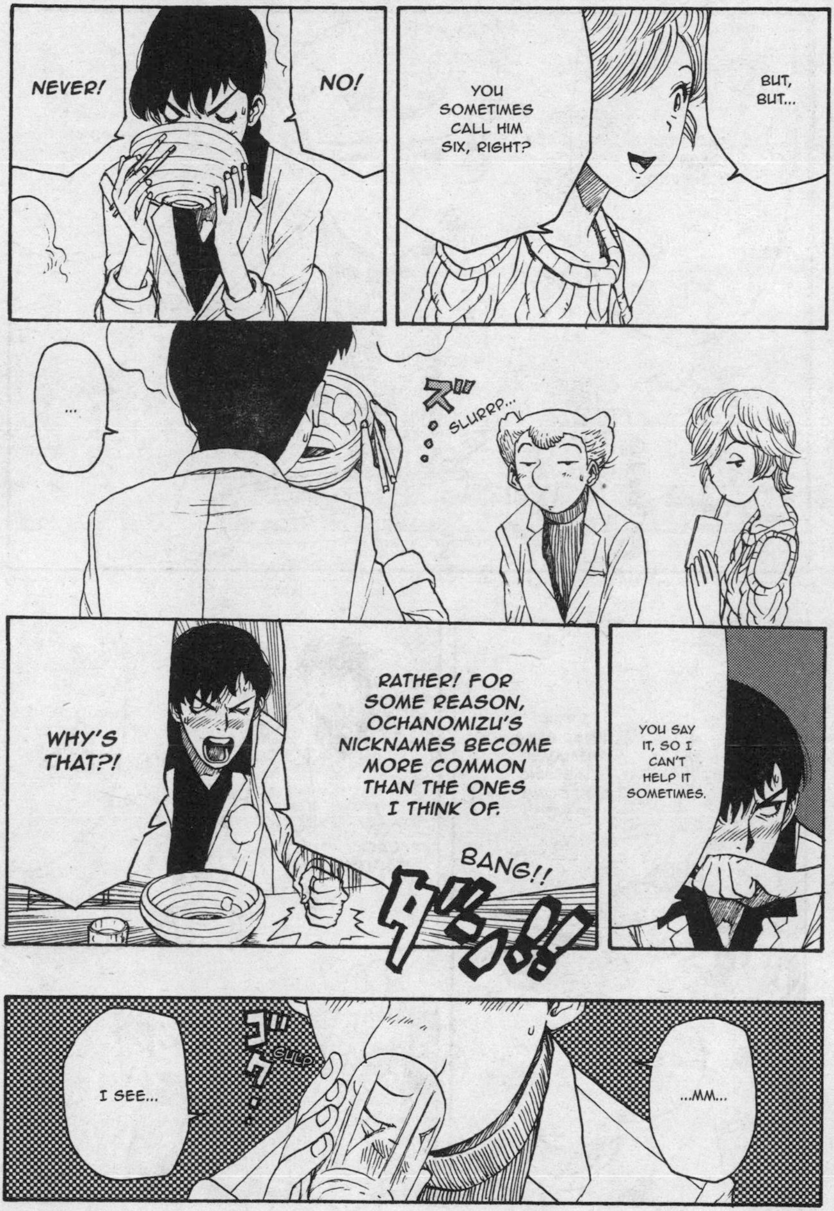
BUT, BUT...
YOU SOMETIMES CALL HIM SIX, RIGHT?
NO!
NEVER!
ズ
SLURRP...
...
YOU SAY IT, SO I CAN'T HELP IT SOMETIMES.
RATHER! FOR SOME REASON, OCHANOMIZU'S NICKNAMES BECOME MORE COMMON THAN THE ONES I THINK OF.
WHY'S THAT?!
BANG!!
ダンッ!!
...MM...
GULP
I SEE...

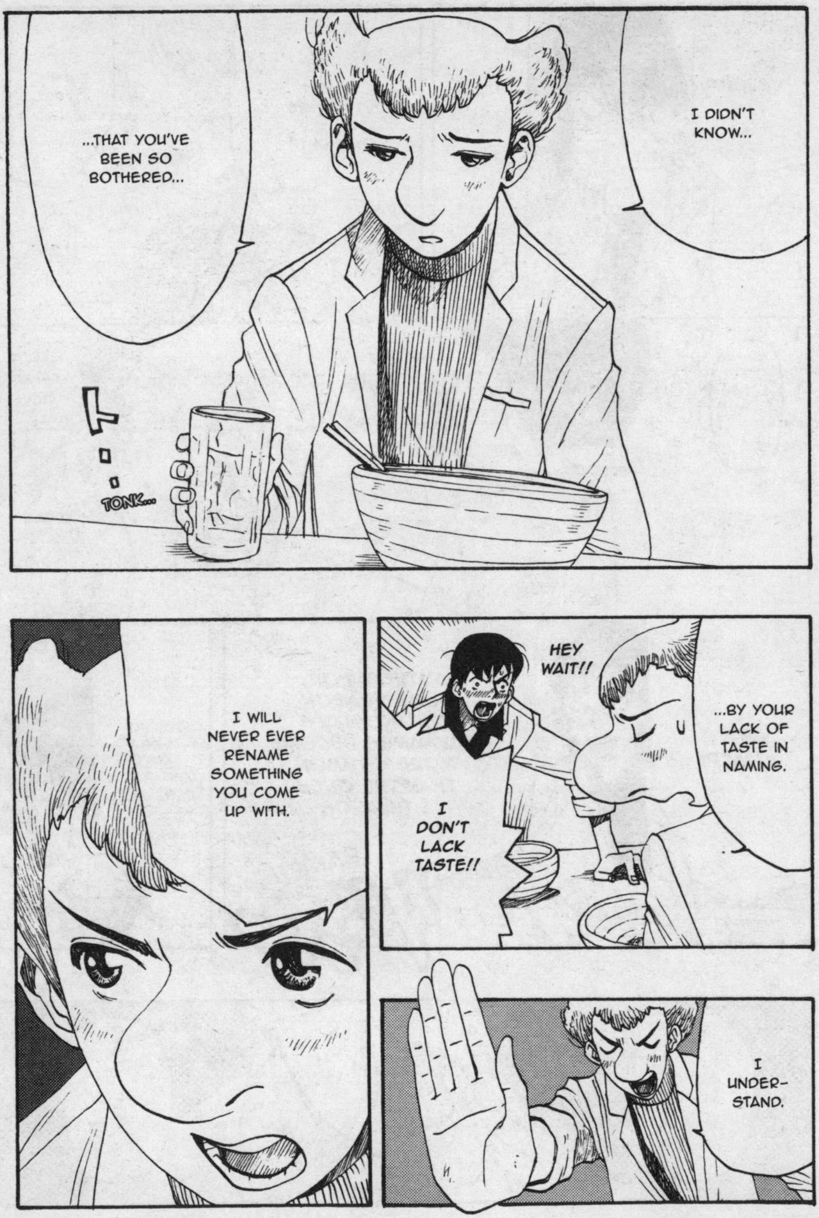
I DIDN'T KNOW...
...THAT YOU'VE BEEN SO BOTHERED...
TONK...
...BY YOUR LACK OF TASTE IN NAMING.
HEY WAIT!!
I DON'T LACK TASTE!!
I UNDER-STAND.
I WILL NEVER EVER RENAME SOMETHING YOU COME UP WITH.

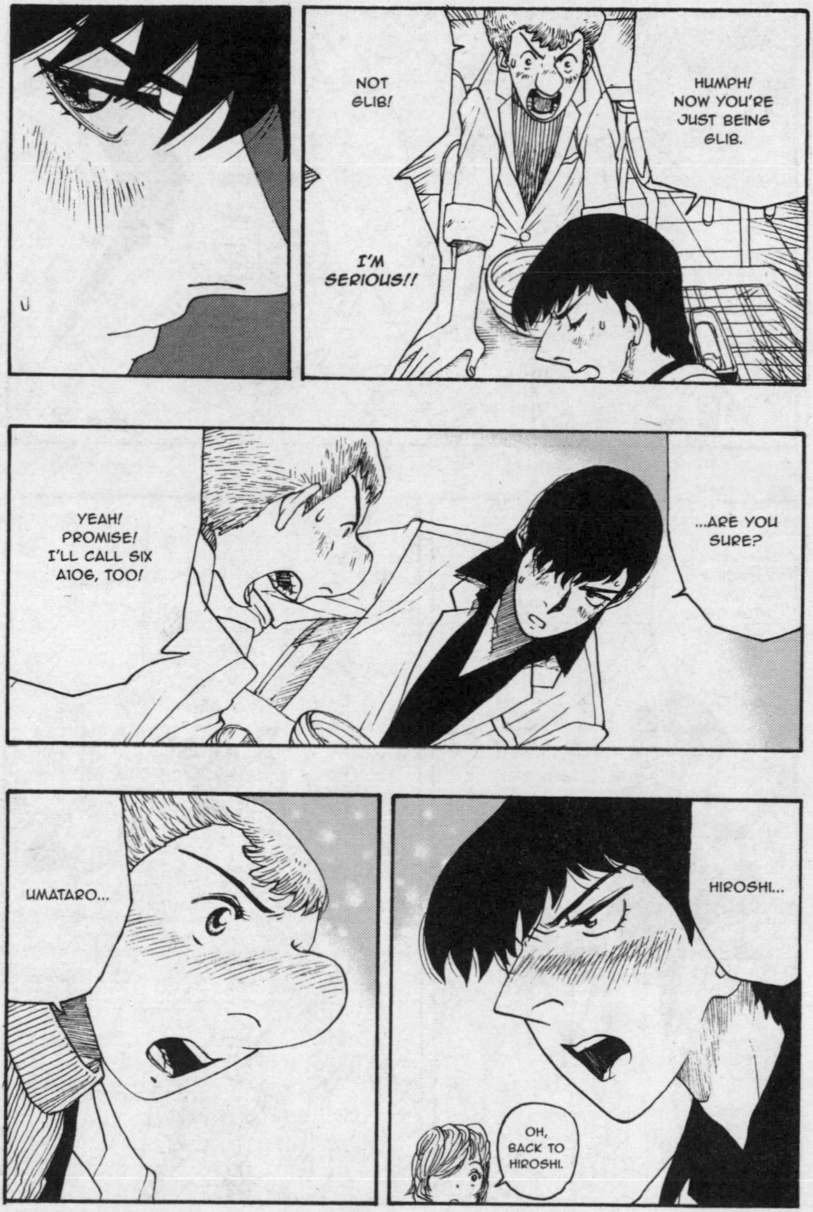
HUMPH! NOW YOU'RE JUST BEING GLIB.
NOT GLIB!
I'M SERIOUS!!
...ARE YOU SURE?
YEAH! PROMISE! I'LL CALL SIX A1OG, TOO!
HIROSHI...
OH, BACK TO HIROSHI.
UMATARO...

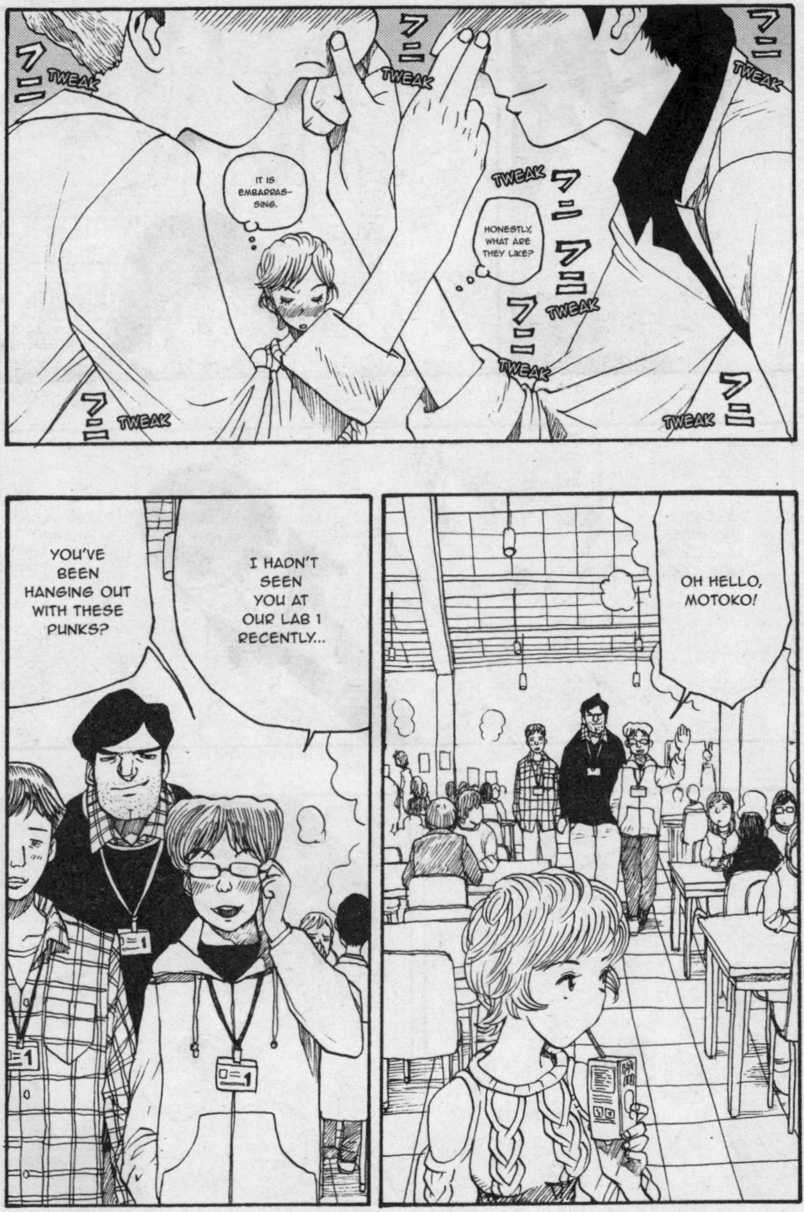
TWEAK
TWEAK
TWEAK
HONESTLY, WHAT ARE THEY LIKE?
TWEAK
TWEAK
TWEAK
IT IS EMBARRAS-SING.
TWEAK
TWEAK
OH HELLO, MOTOKO!
I HADN'T SEEN YOU AT OUR LAB 1 RECENTLY...
YOU'VE BEEN HANGING OUT WITH THESE PUNKS?

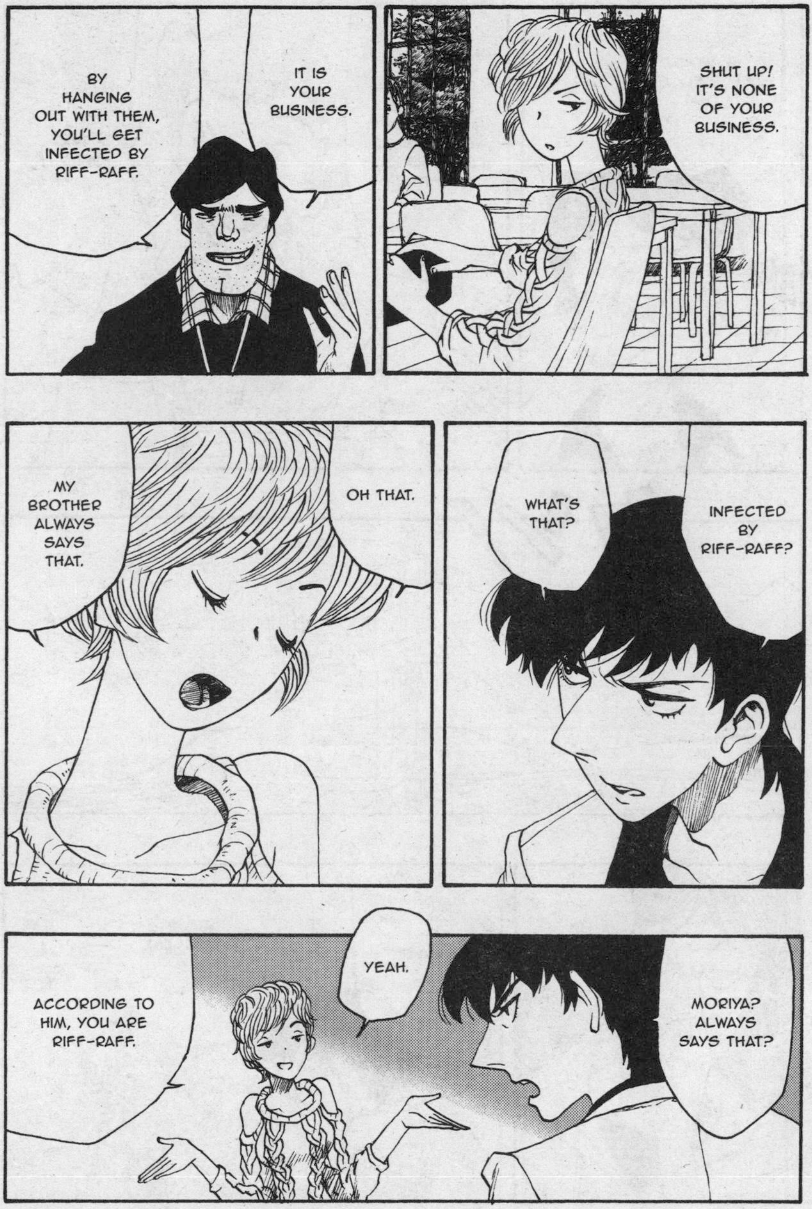
SHUT UP! IT'S NONE OF YOUR BUSINESS.
IT IS YOUR BUSINESS.
BY HANGING OUT WITH THEM, YOU'LL GET INFECTED BY RIFF-RAFF.
INFECTED BY RIFF-RAFF?
WHAT'S THAT?
OH THAT.
MY BROTHER ALWAYS SAYS THAT.
MORIYA? ALWAYS SAYS THAT?
YEAH.
ACCORDING TO HIM, YOU ARE RIFF-RAFF.

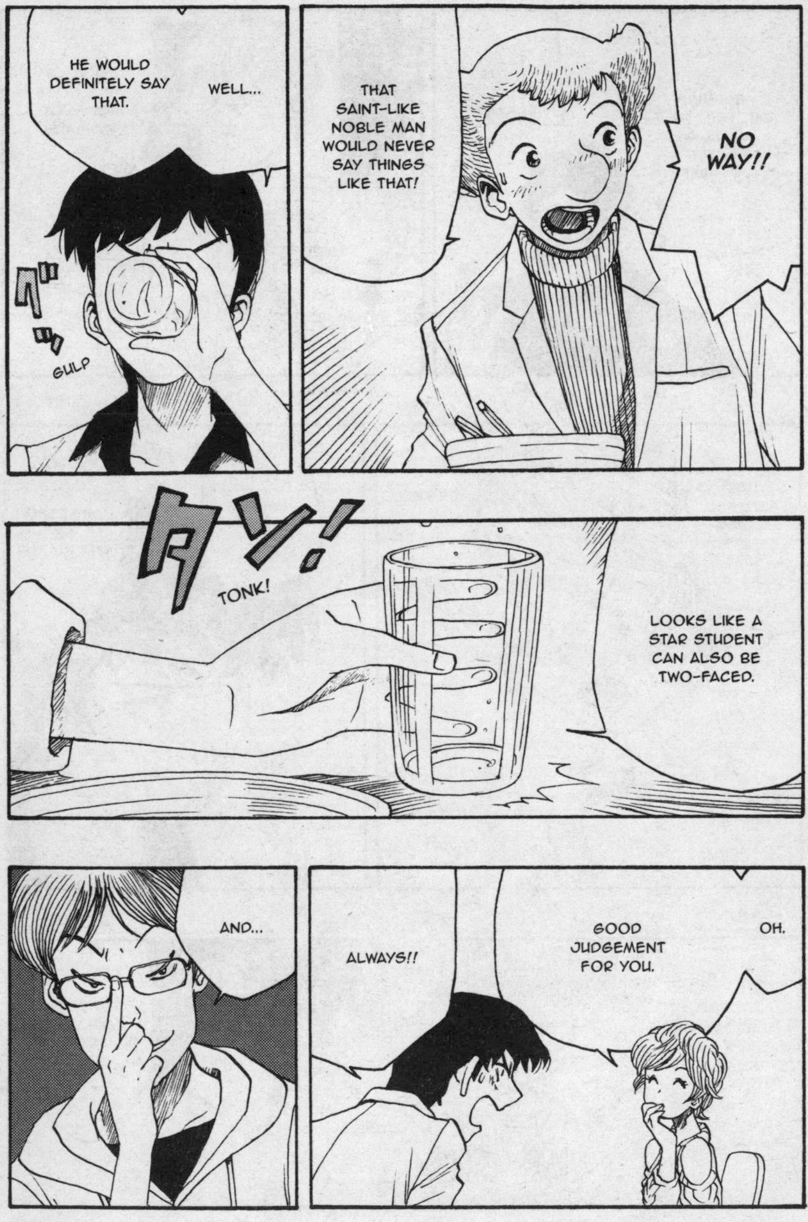
NO WAY!!
THAT SAINT-LIKE NOBLE MAN WOULD NEVER SAY THINGS LIKE THAT!
WELL...
HE WOULD DEFINITELY SAY THAT.
GULP
タッ!
TONK!
LOOKS LIKE A STAR STUDENT CAN ALSO BE TWO-FACED.
OH.
GOOD JUDGEMENT FOR YOU.
ALWAYS!!
AND...

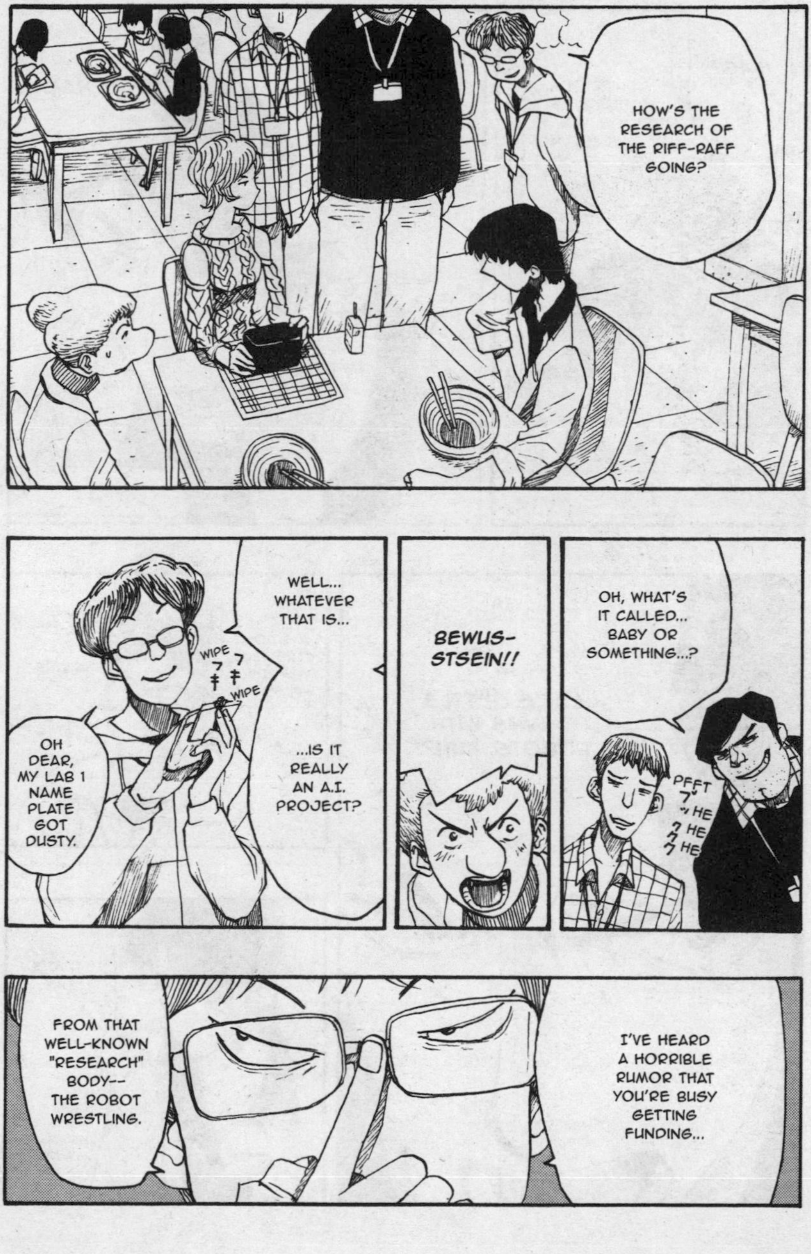
HOW'S THE RESEARCH OF THE RIFF-RAFF GOING?
OH, WHAT'S IT CALLED... BABY OR SOMETHING...?
PFFT HE HE HE
BEWUS-STSEIN!!
WELL... WHATEVER THAT IS...
...IS IT REALLY AN A.I. PROJECT?
WIPE WIPE
OH DEAR, MY LAB 1 NAME PLATE GOT DUSTY.
I'VE HEARD A HORRIBLE RUMOR THAT YOU'RE BUSY GETTING FUNDING...
FROM THAT WELL-KNOWN "RESEARCH" BODY-- THE ROBOT WRESTLING.

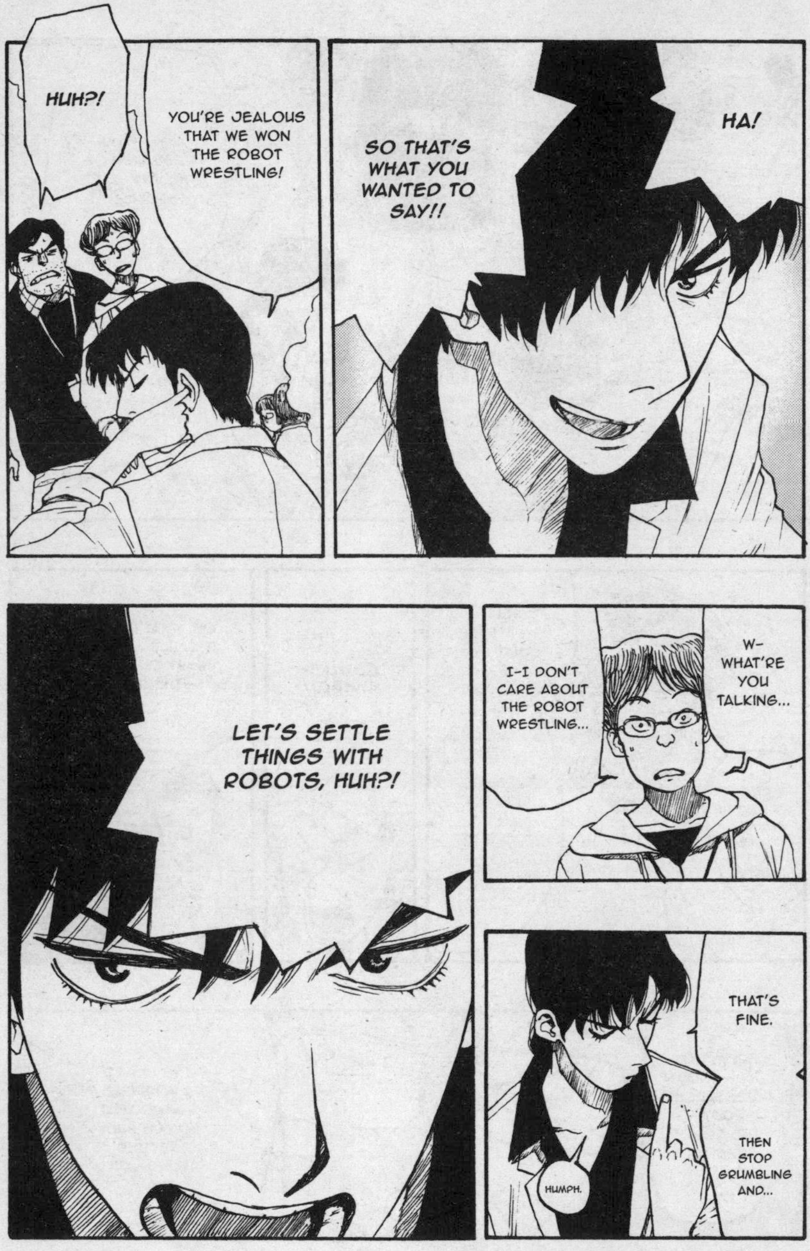
HA!
SO THAT'S WHAT YOU WANTED TO SAY!!
YOU'RE JEALOUS THAT WE WON THE ROBOT WRESTLING!
HUH?!
W- WHAT'RE YOU TALKING...
I-I DON'T CARE ABOUT THE ROBOT WRESTLING...
THAT'S FINE.
THEN STOP GRUMBLING AND...
HUMPH.
LET'S SETTLE THINGS WITH ROBOTS, HUH?!

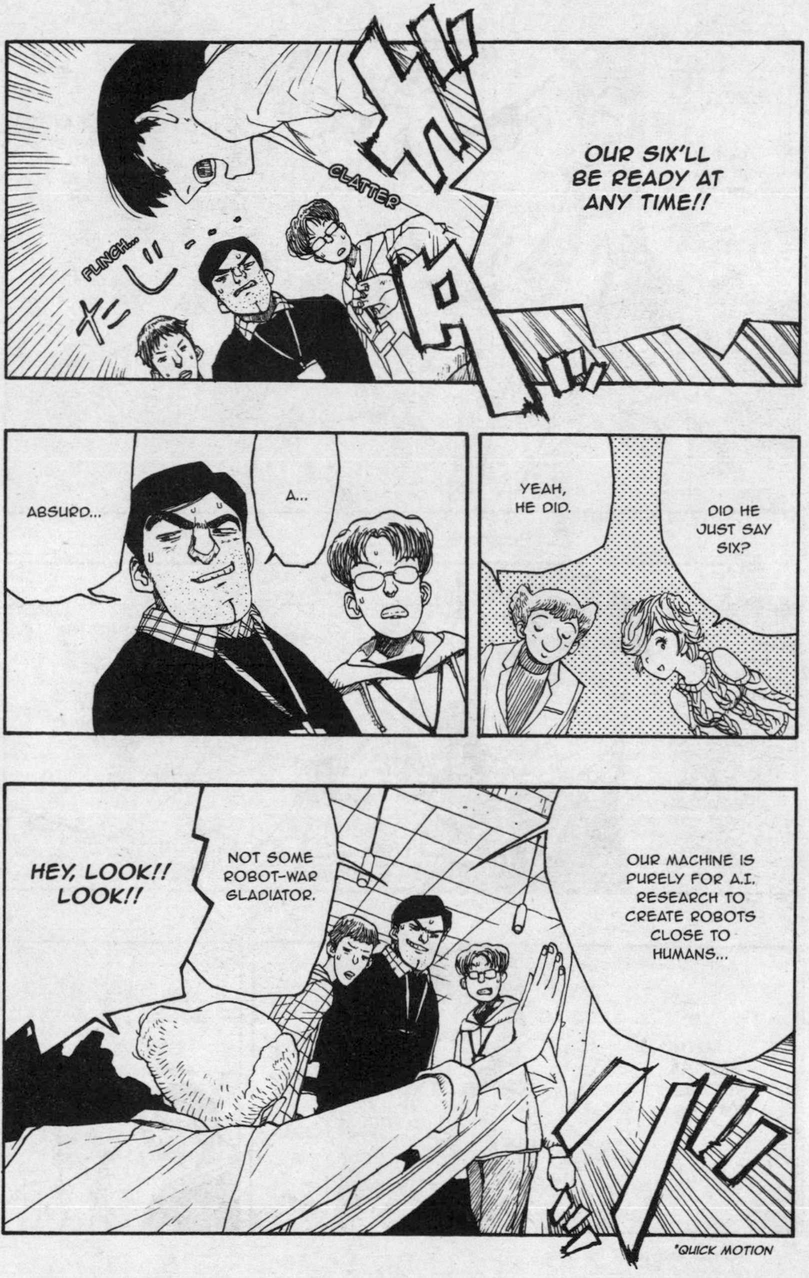
OUR SIX'LL BE READY AT ANY TIME!!
CLATTER
FLINCH...
DID HE JUST SAY SIX?
YEAH, HE DID.
A...
ABSURD...
OUR MACHINE IS PURELY FOR A.I. RESEARCH TO CREATE ROBOTS CLOSE TO HUMANS...
NOT SOME ROBOT-WAR GLADIATOR.
HEY, LOOK!! LOOK!!
*QUICK MOTION

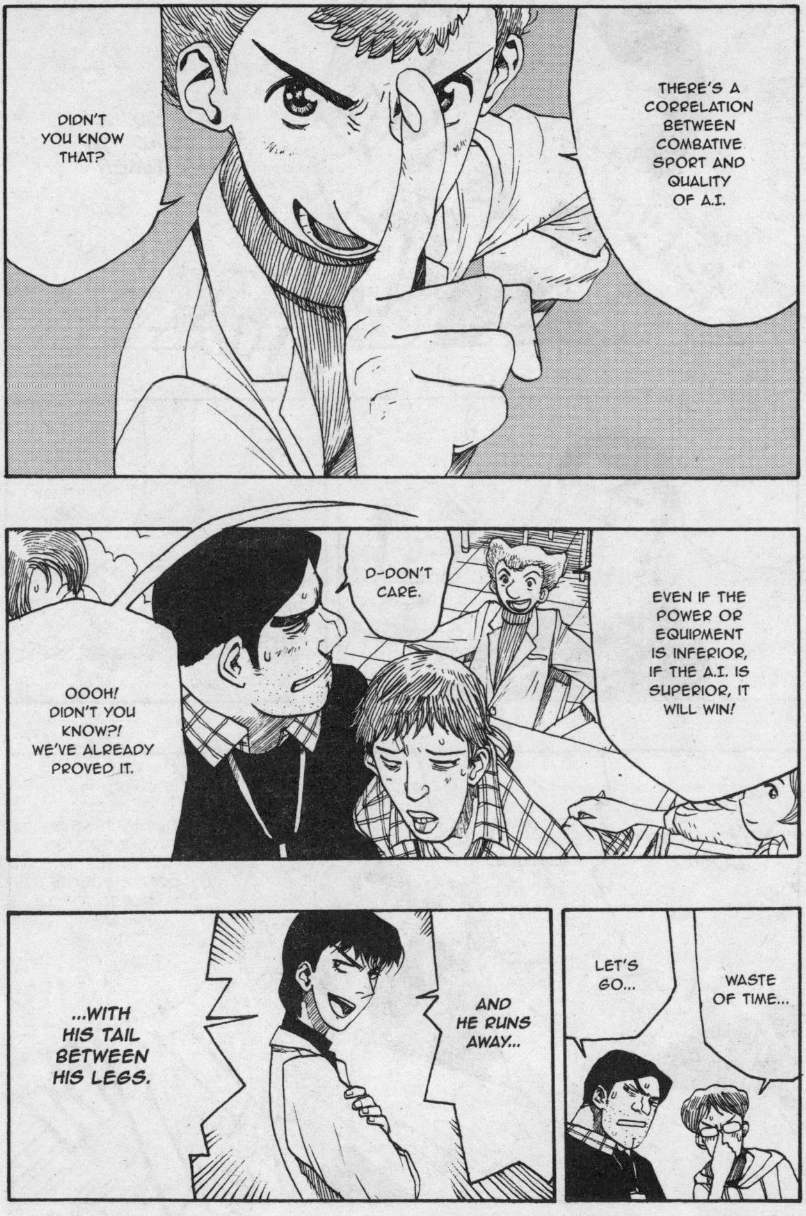
THERE'S A CORRELATION BETWEEN COMBATIVE SPORT AND QUALITY OF A.I.
DIDN'T YOU KNOW THAT?
EVEN IF THE POWER OR EQUIPMENT IS INFERIOR, IF THE A.I. IS SUPERIOR, IT WILL WIN!
D-DON'T CARE.
OOOH! DIDN'T YOU KNOW?! WE'VE ALREADY PROVED IT.
WASTE OF TIME...
LET'S GO...
AND HE RUNS AWAY...
...WITH HIS TAIL BETWEEN HIS LEGS.

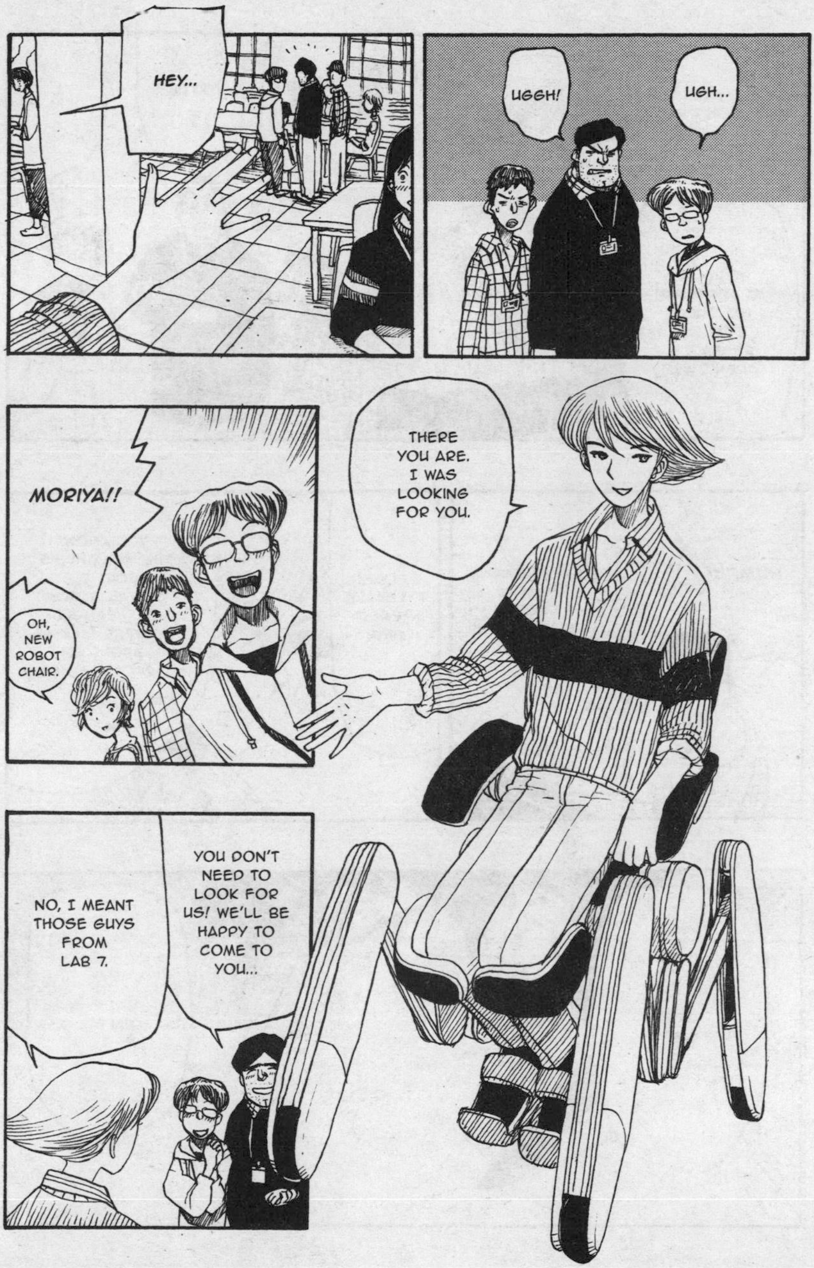
UGH...
UGGH!
HEY...
THERE YOU ARE. I WAS LOOKING FOR YOU.
MORIYA!!
OH, NEW ROBOT CHAIR.
YOU DON'T NEED TO LOOK FOR US! WE'LL BE HAPPY TO COME TO YOU...
NO, I MEANT THOSE GUYS FROM LAB 7.

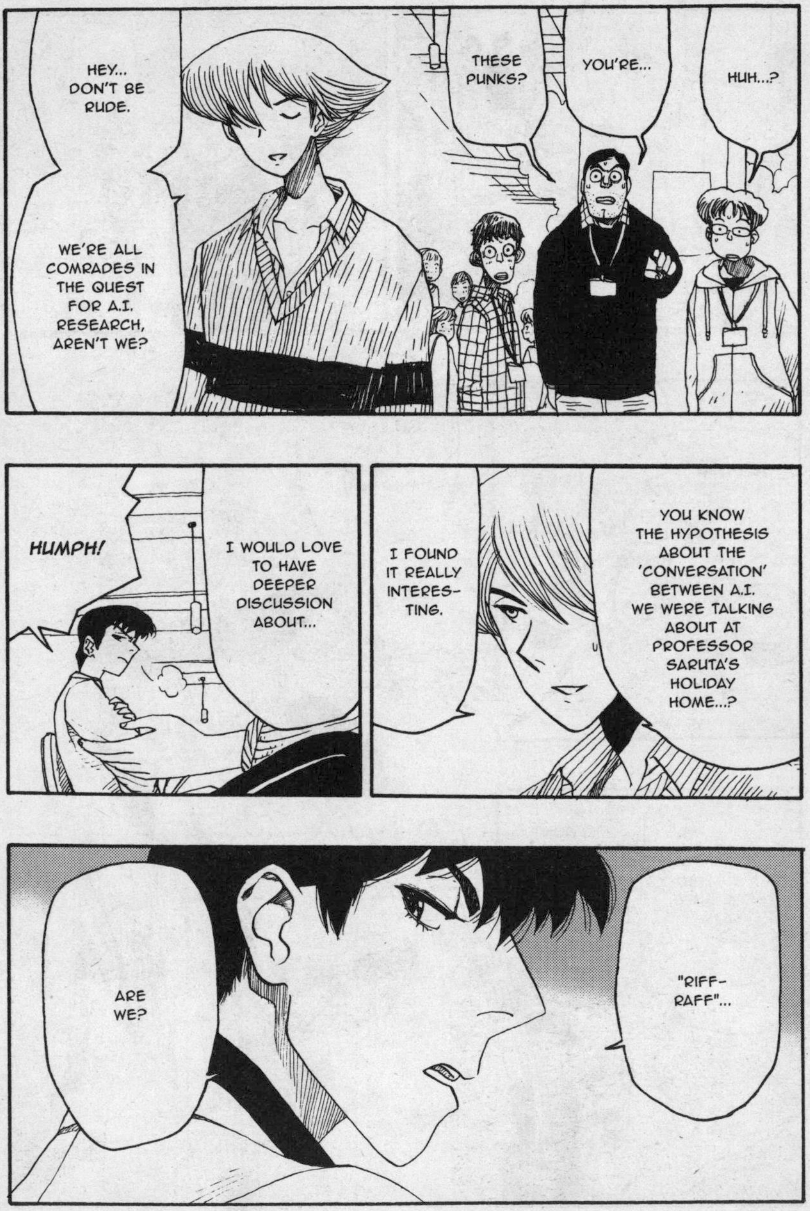
HUH...?
YOU'RE...
THESE PUNKS?
HEY... DON'T BE RUDE.
WE'RE ALL COMRADES IN THE QUEST FOR A.I. RESEARCH, AREN'T WE?
YOU KNOW THE HYPOTHESIS ABOUT THE 'CONVERSATION' BETWEEN A.I. WE WERE TALKING ABOUT AT PROFESSOR SARUTA'S HOLIDAY HOME...?
I FOUND IT REALLY INTERES-TING.
I WOULD LOVE TO HAVE DEEPER DISCUSSION ABOUT...
HUMPH!
"RIFF-RAFF"...
ARE WE?

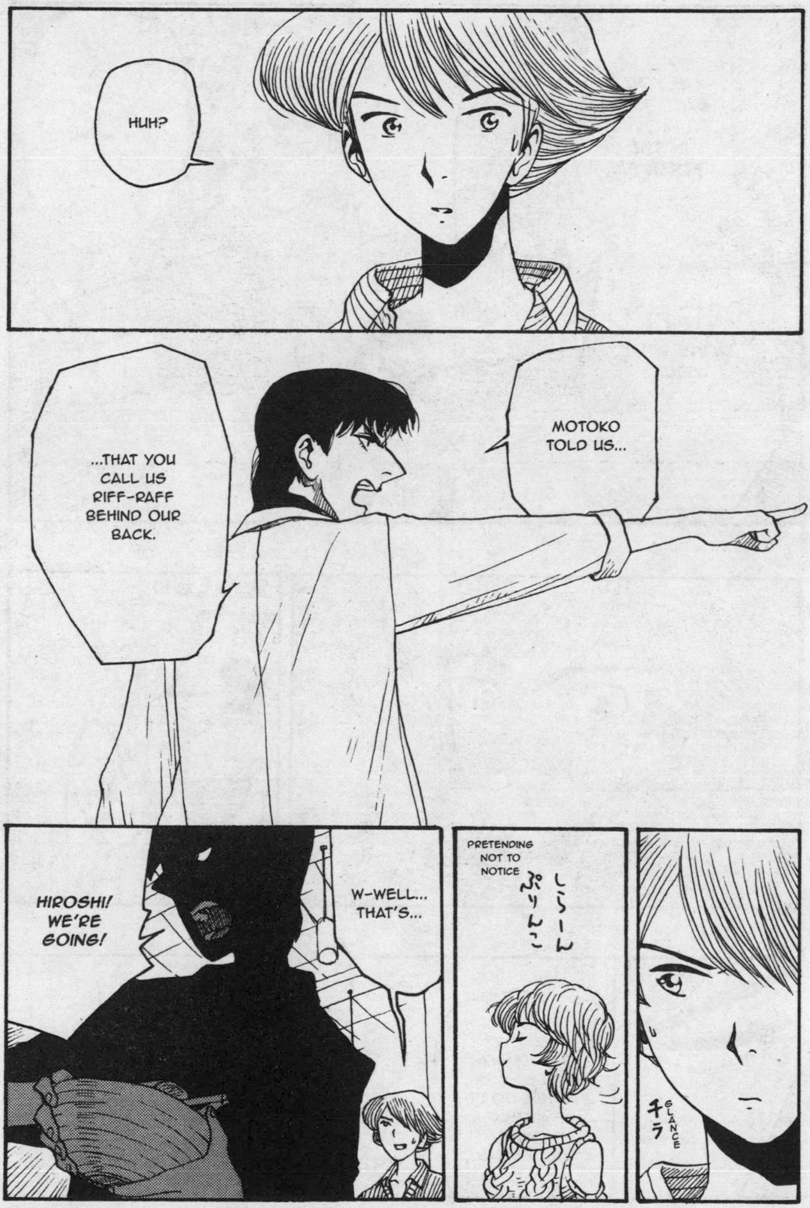
HUH?
MOTOKO TOLD US...
...THAT YOU CALL US RIFF-RAFF BEHIND OUR BACK.
チラ GLANCE
PRETENDING NOT TO NOTICE
しら～ん ぷりんこ
W-WELL... THAT'S...
HIROSHI! WE'RE GOING!

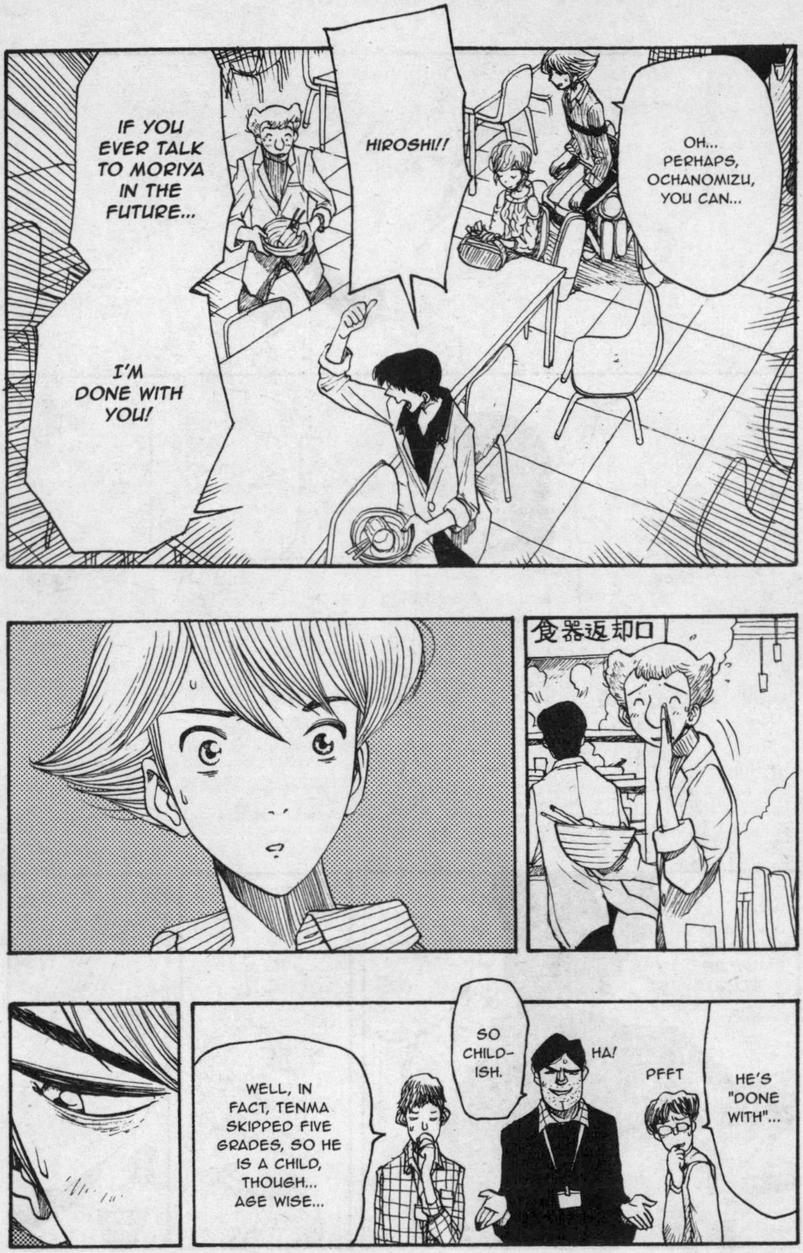
OH... PERHAPS, OCHANOMIZU, YOU CAN...
HIROSHI!!
IF YOU EVER TALK TO MORIYA IN THE FUTURE...
I'M DONE WITH YOU!
食器返却口
HE'S "DONE WITH"...
PFFT
HA!
SO CHILD-ISH.
WELL, IN FACT, TENMA SKIPPED FIVE GRADES, SO HE IS A CHILD, THOUGH... AGE WISE...

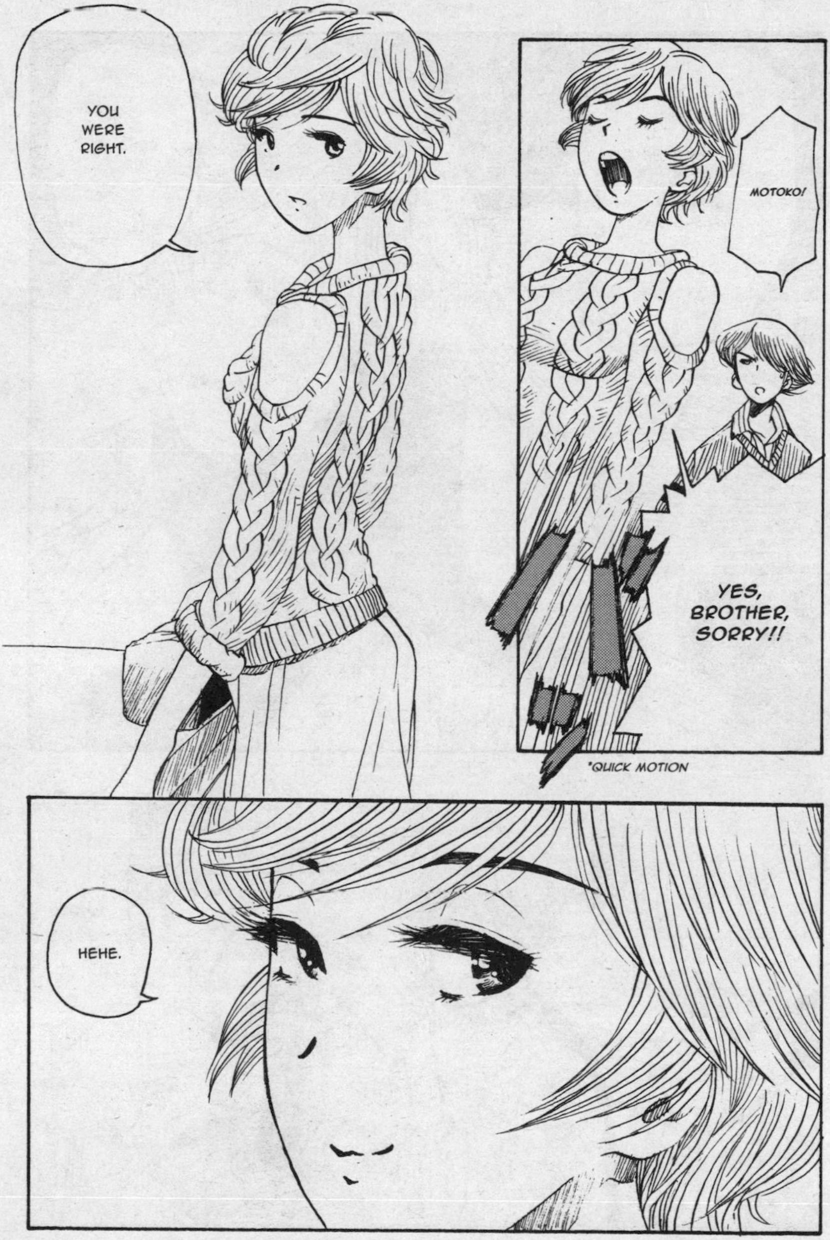
MOTOKO!
YES, BROTHER, SORRY!!
*QUICK MOTION
YOU WERE RIGHT.
HEHE.

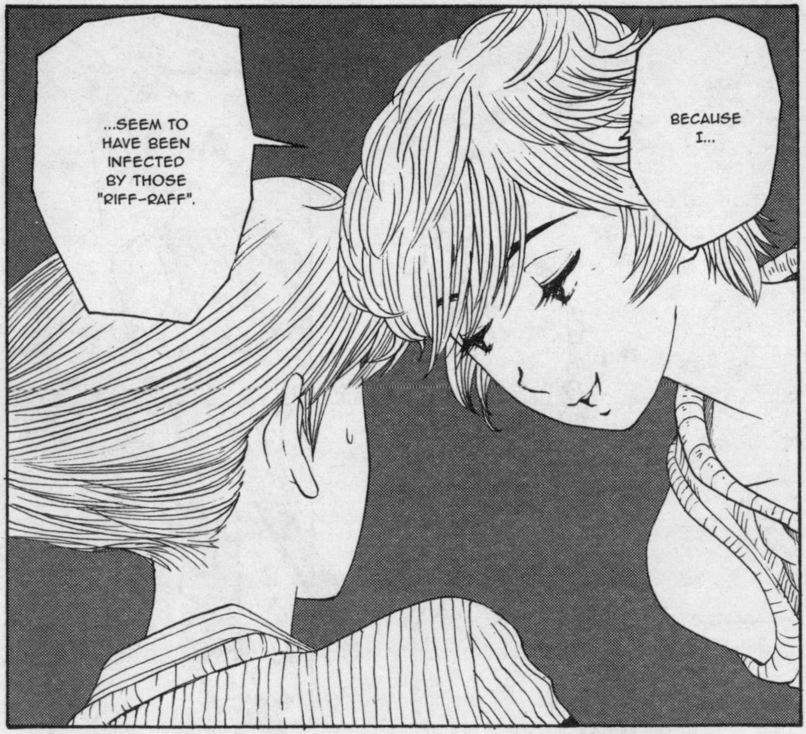
BECAUSE I...
...SEEM TO HAVE BEEN INFECTED BY THOSE "RIFF-RAFF".

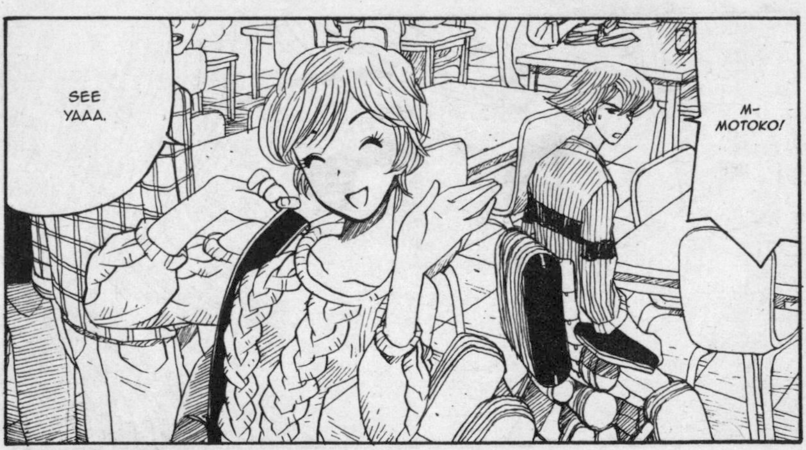
M-MOTOKO!
SEE YAAA.

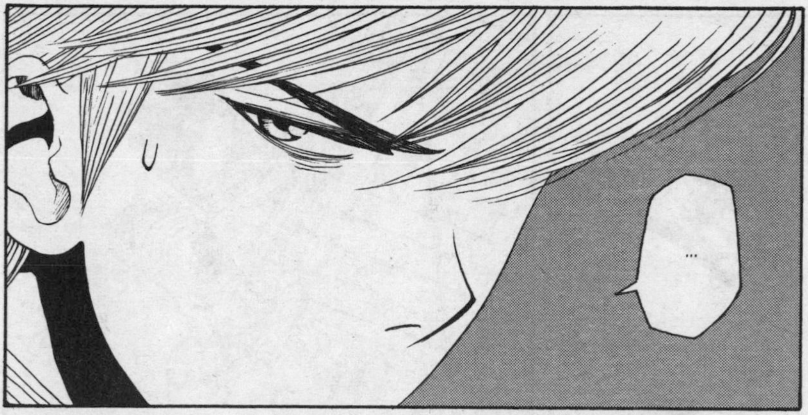
...
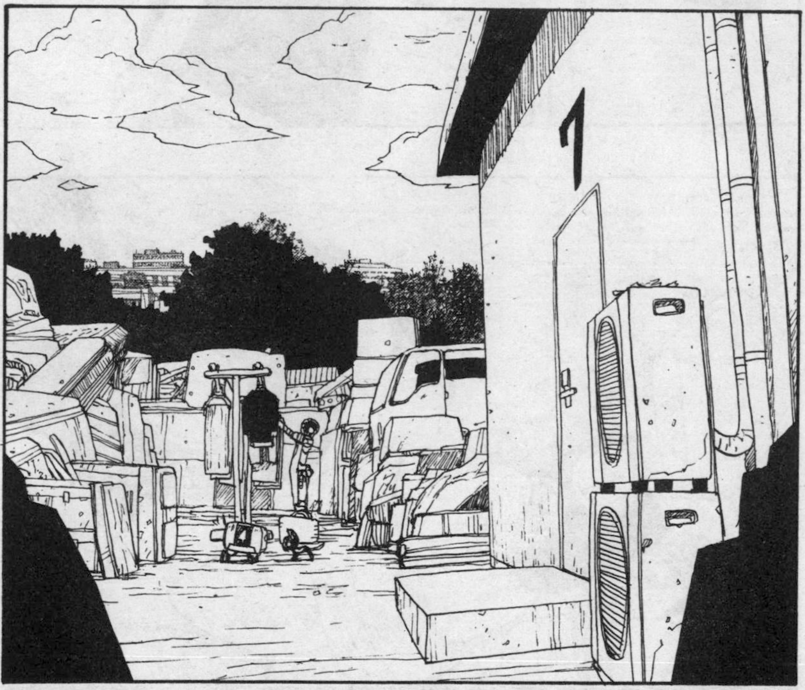
7

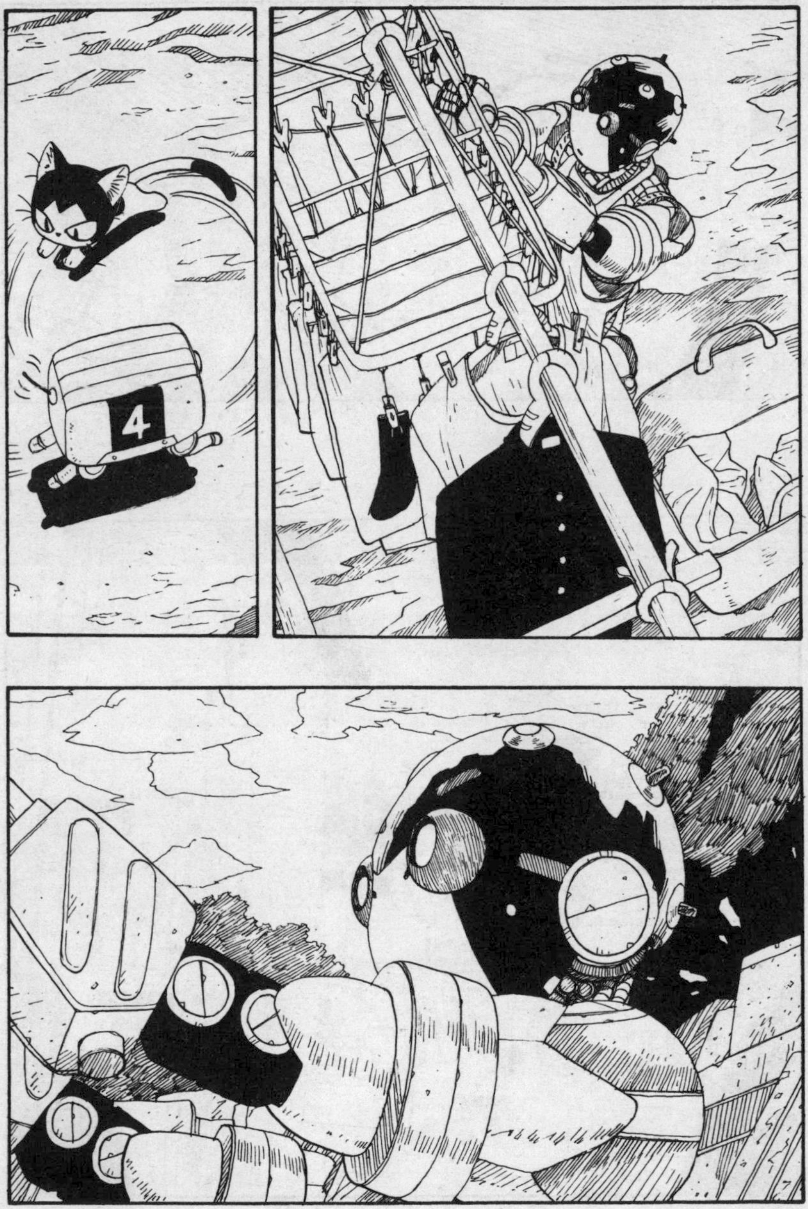
4

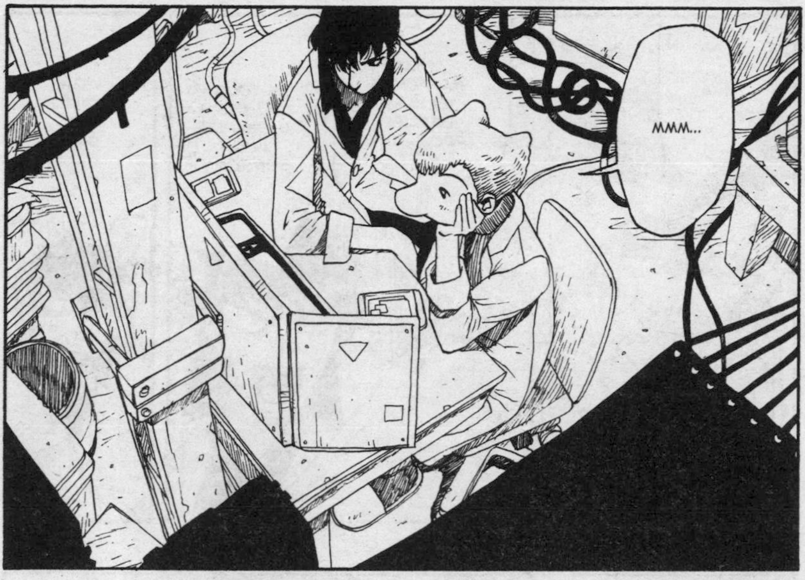
MMM...

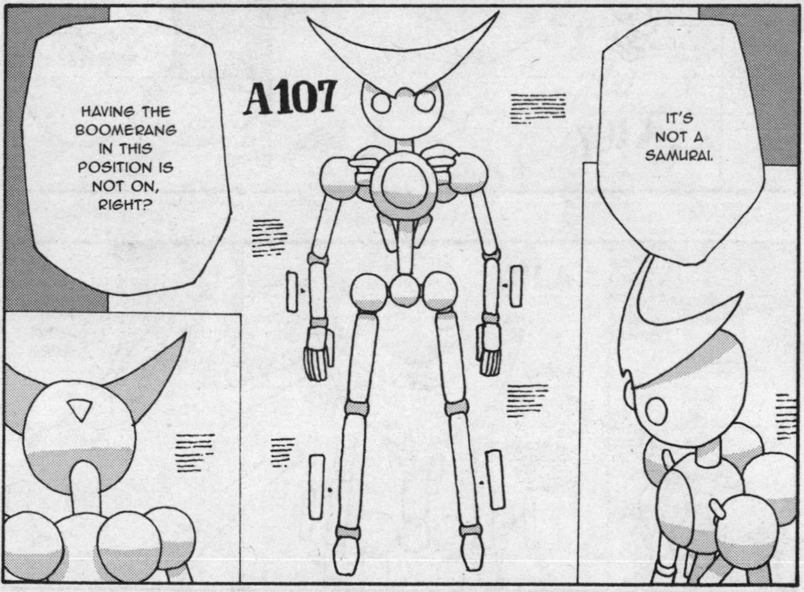
IT'S NOT A SAMURAI.
A107
HAVING THE BOOMERANG IN THIS POSITION IS NOT ON, RIGHT?

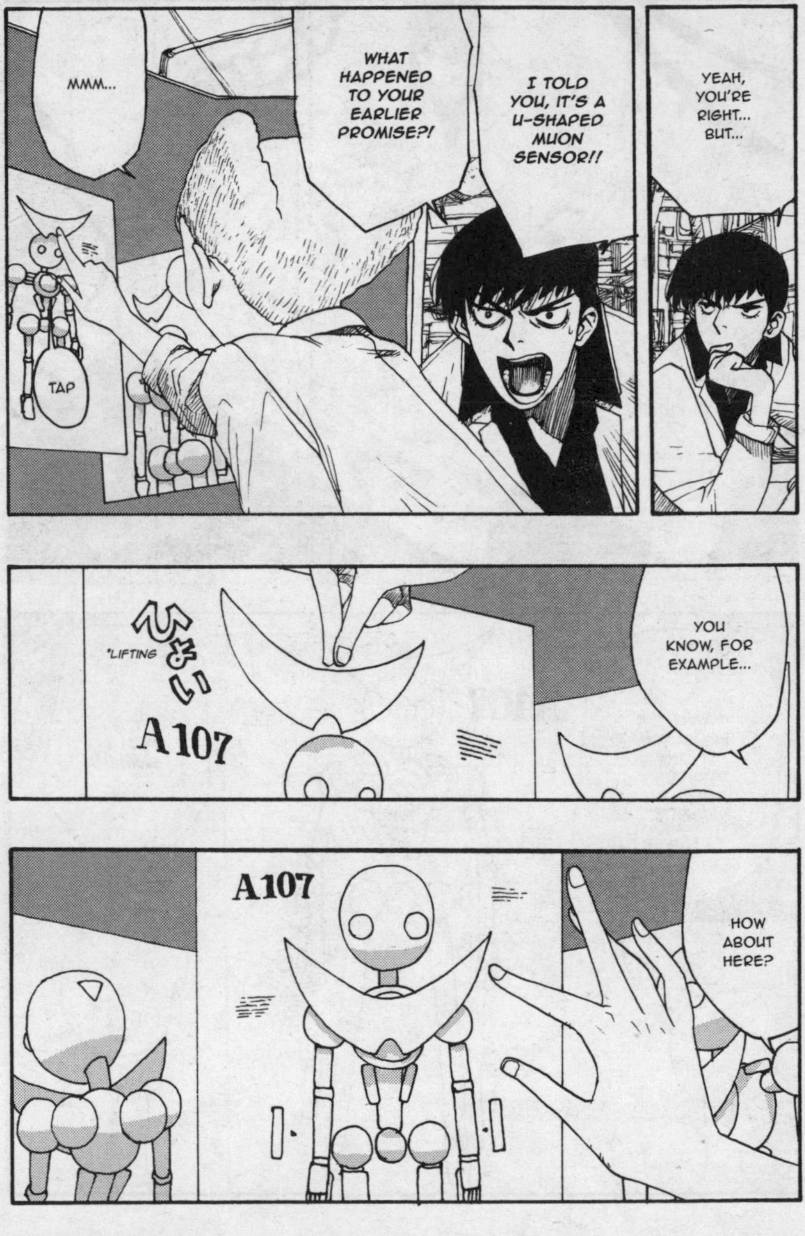
YEAH, YOU'RE RIGHT... BUT...
I TOLD YOU, IT'S A U-SHAPED MUON SENSOR!!
WHAT HAPPENED TO YOUR EARLIER PROMISE?!
MMM...
TAP
YOU KNOW, FOR EXAMPLE...
ひょい
*LIFTING
A107
HOW ABOUT HERE?
A107

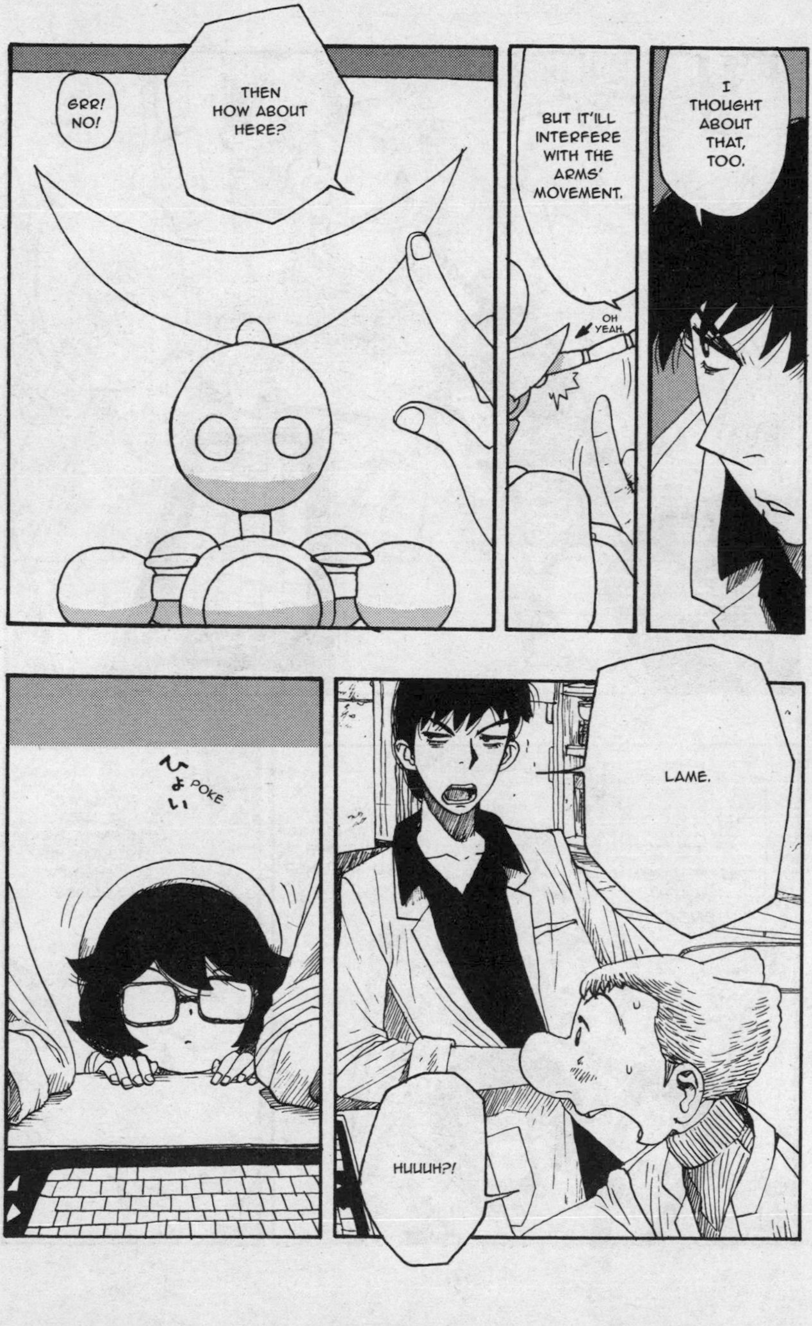
I THOUGHT ABOUT THAT, TOO.
BUT IT'LL INTERFERE WITH THE ARMS' MOVEMENT.
OH YEAH.
THEN HOW ABOUT HERE?
GRR! NO!
LAME.
HUUUH?!
ひょい
POKE

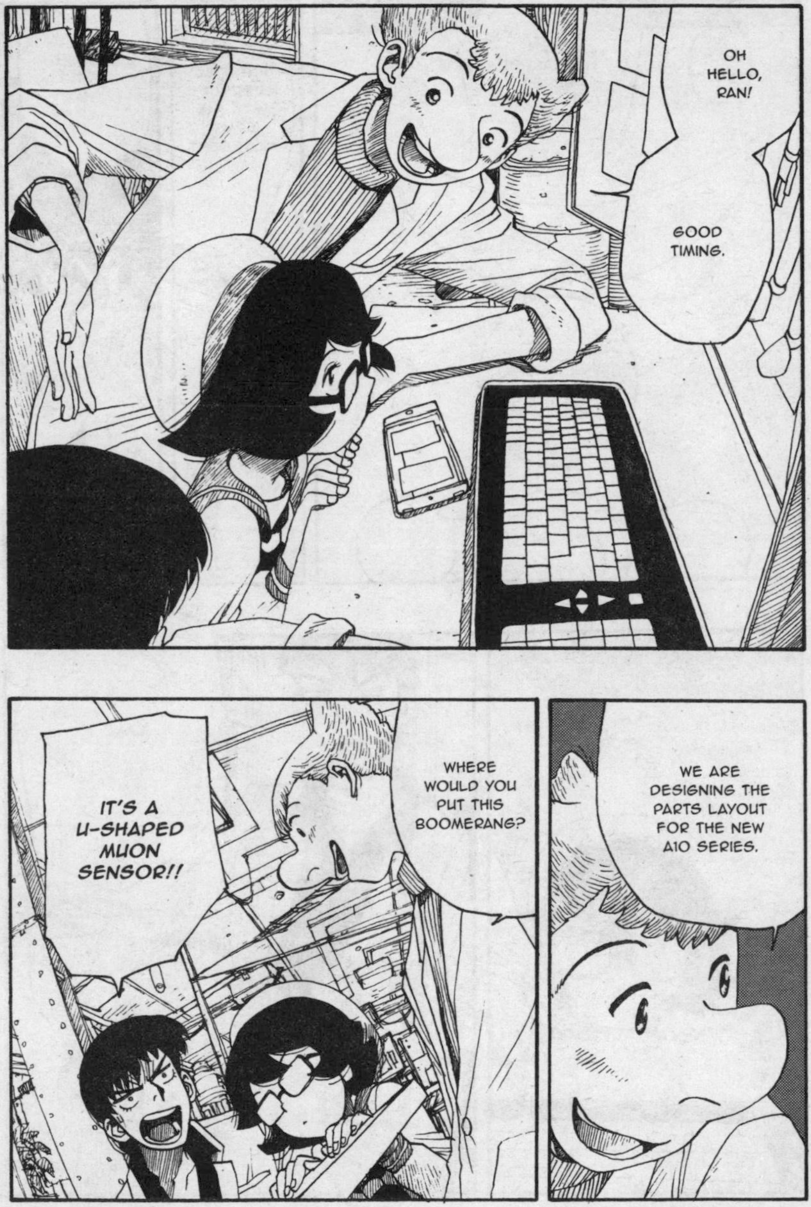
OH HELLO, RAN!
GOOD TIMING.
WE ARE DESIGNING THE PARTS LAYOUT FOR THE NEW A10 SERIES.
WHERE WOULD YOU PUT THIS BOOMERANG?
IT'S A U-SHAPED MUON SENSOR!!

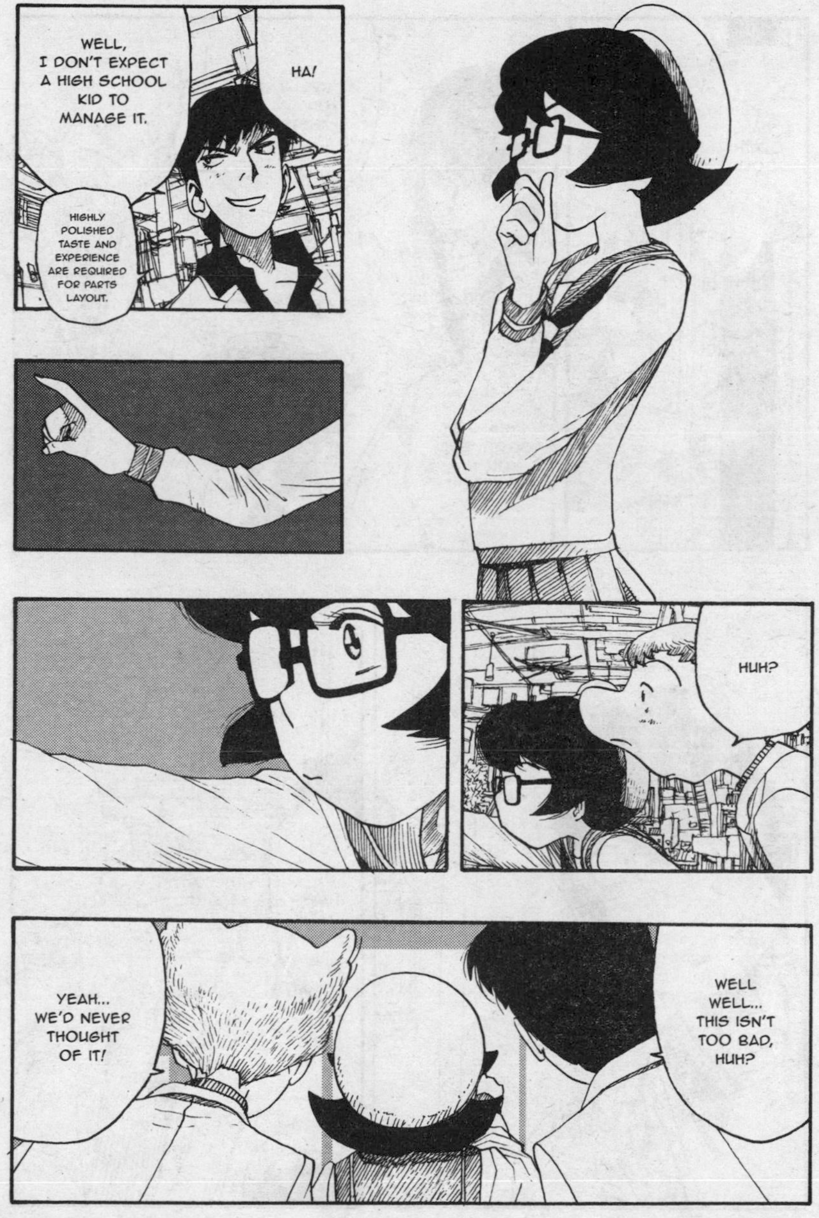
HA!
WELL, I DON'T EXPECT A HIGH SCHOOL KID TO MANAGE IT.
HIGHLY POLISHED TASTE AND EXPERIENCE ARE REQUIRED FOR PARTS LAYOUT.
HUH?
WELL WELL... THIS ISN'T TOO BAD, HUH?
YEAH... WE'D NEVER THOUGHT OF IT!

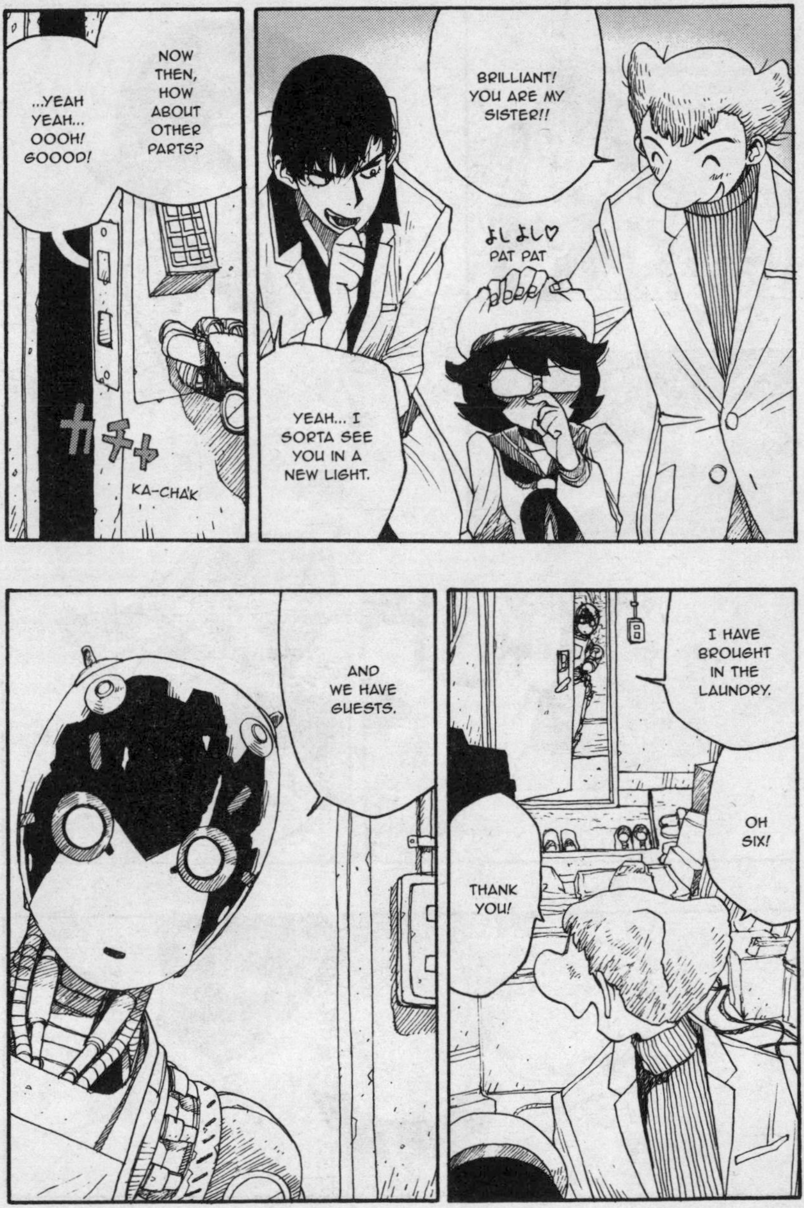
BRILLIANT! YOU ARE MY SISTER!!
よしよし♡
PAT PAT
YEAH... I SORTA SEE YOU IN A NEW LIGHT.
NOW THEN, HOW ABOUT OTHER PARTS?
...YEAH YEAH... OOOH! GOOOD!
カチャ
KA-CHA'K
I HAVE BROUGHT IN THE LAUNDRY.
OH SIX!
THANK YOU!
AND WE HAVE GUESTS.

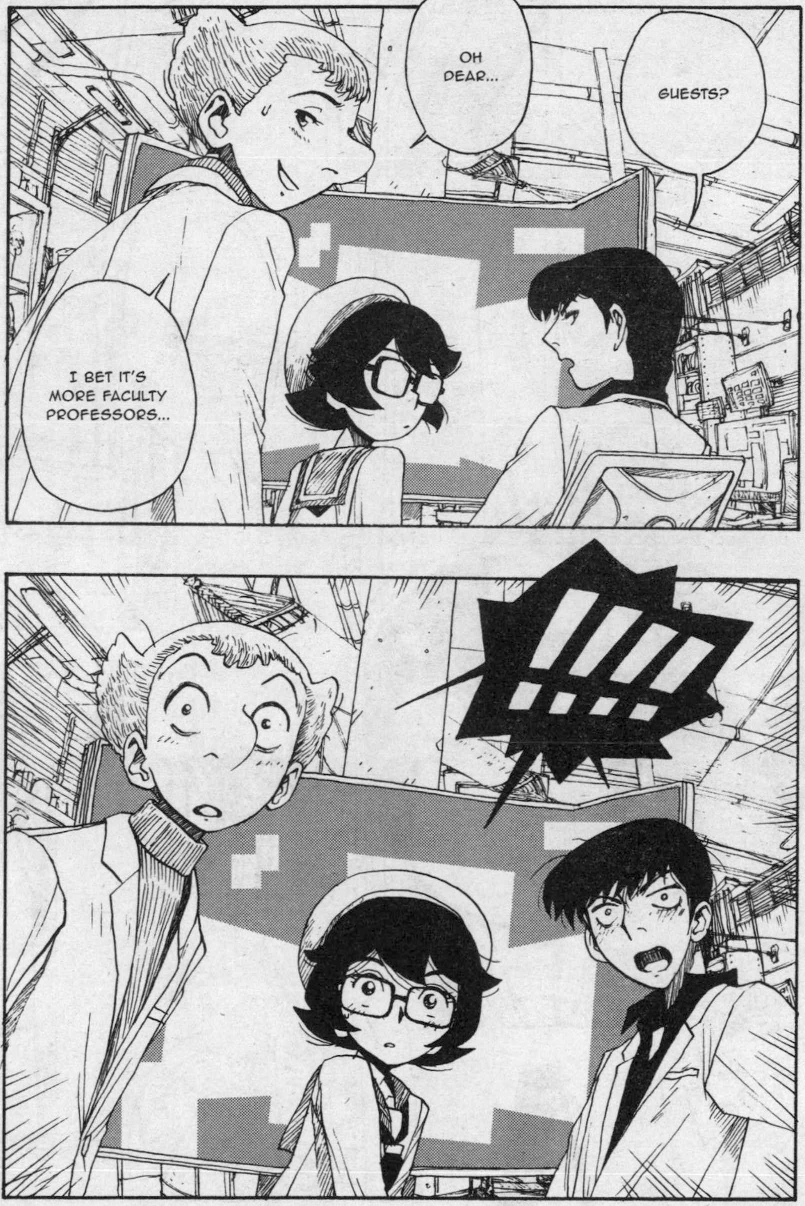
GUESTS?
OH DEAR...
I BET IT'S MORE FACULTY PROFESSORS...
!!!!

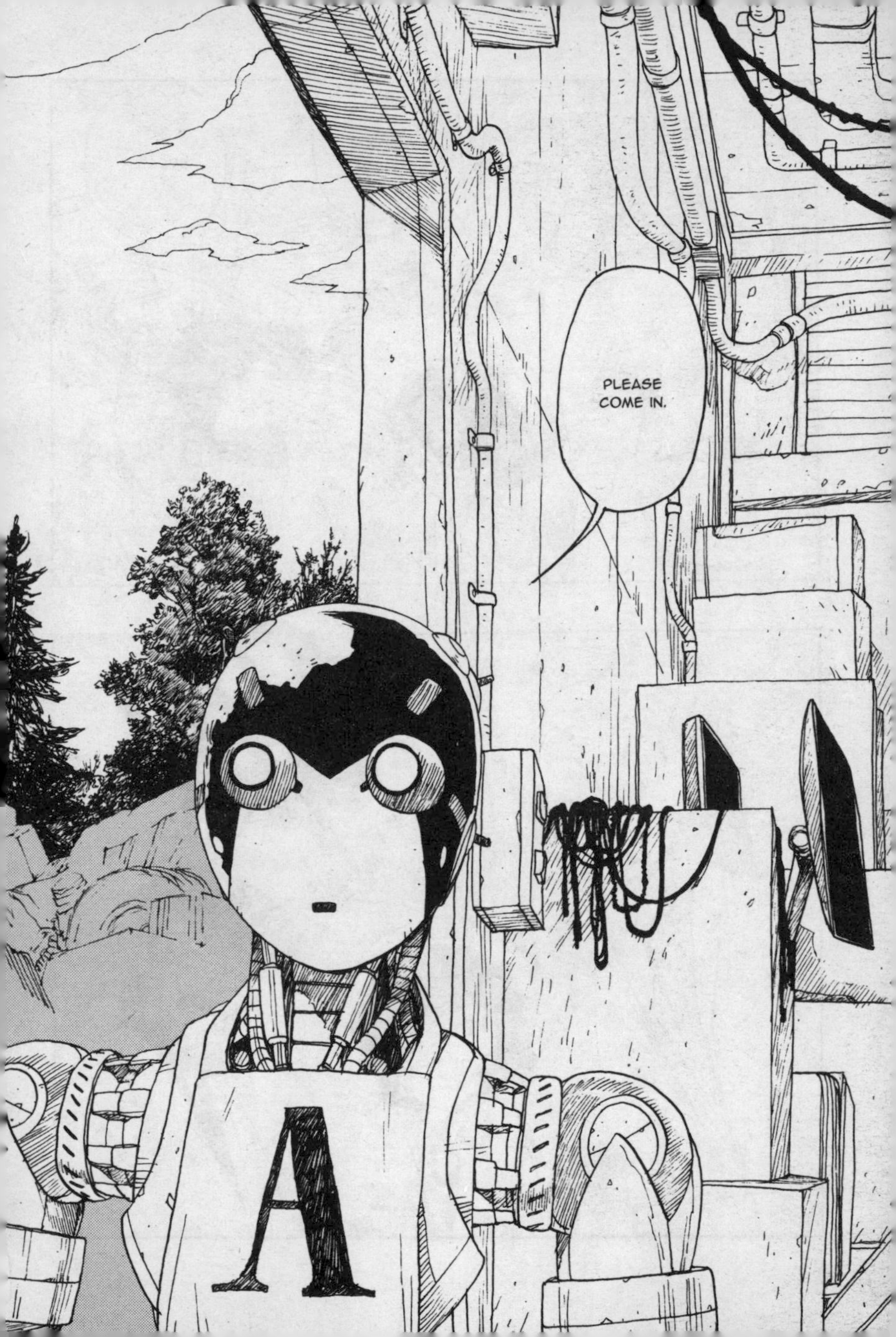
PLEASE COME IN.

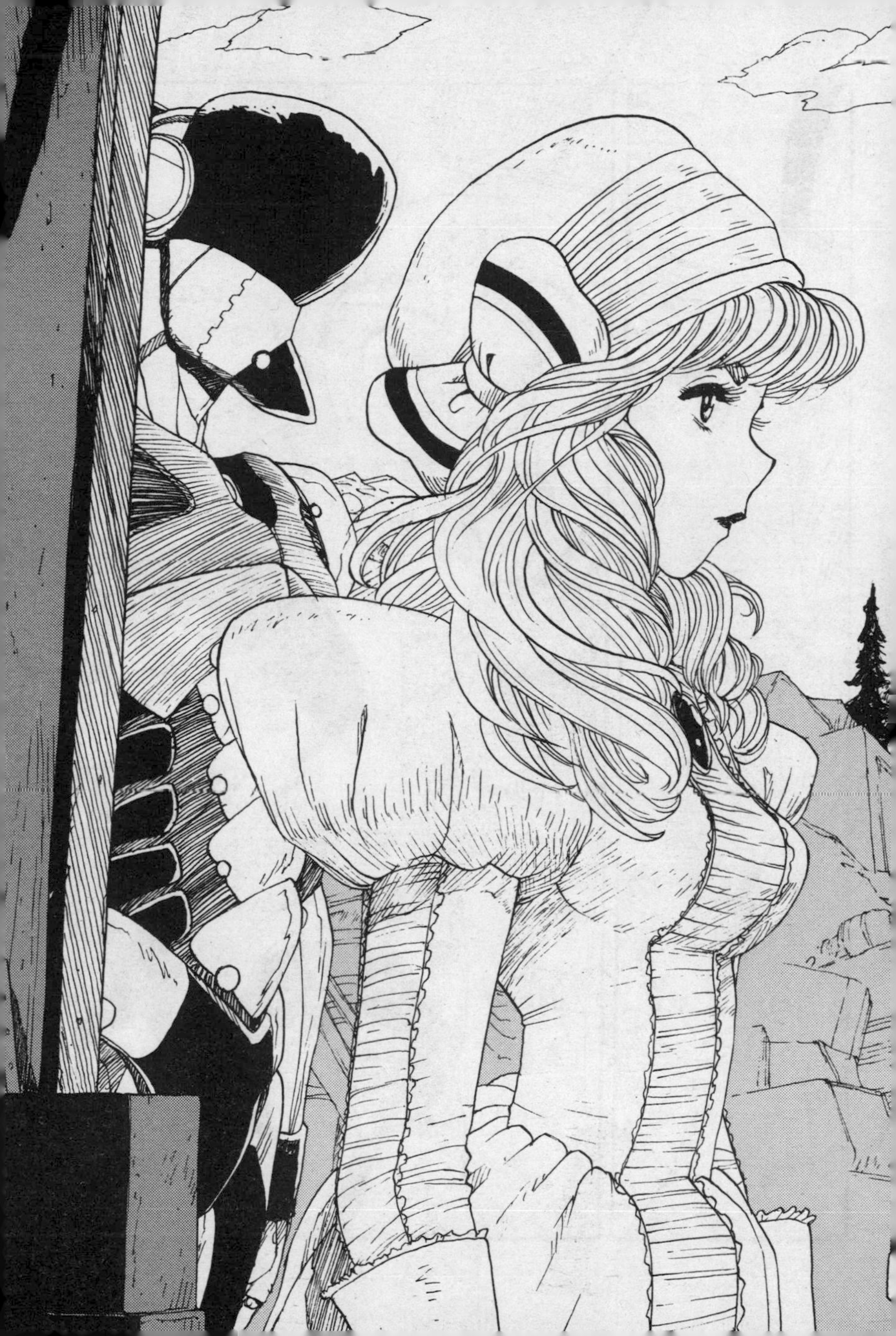

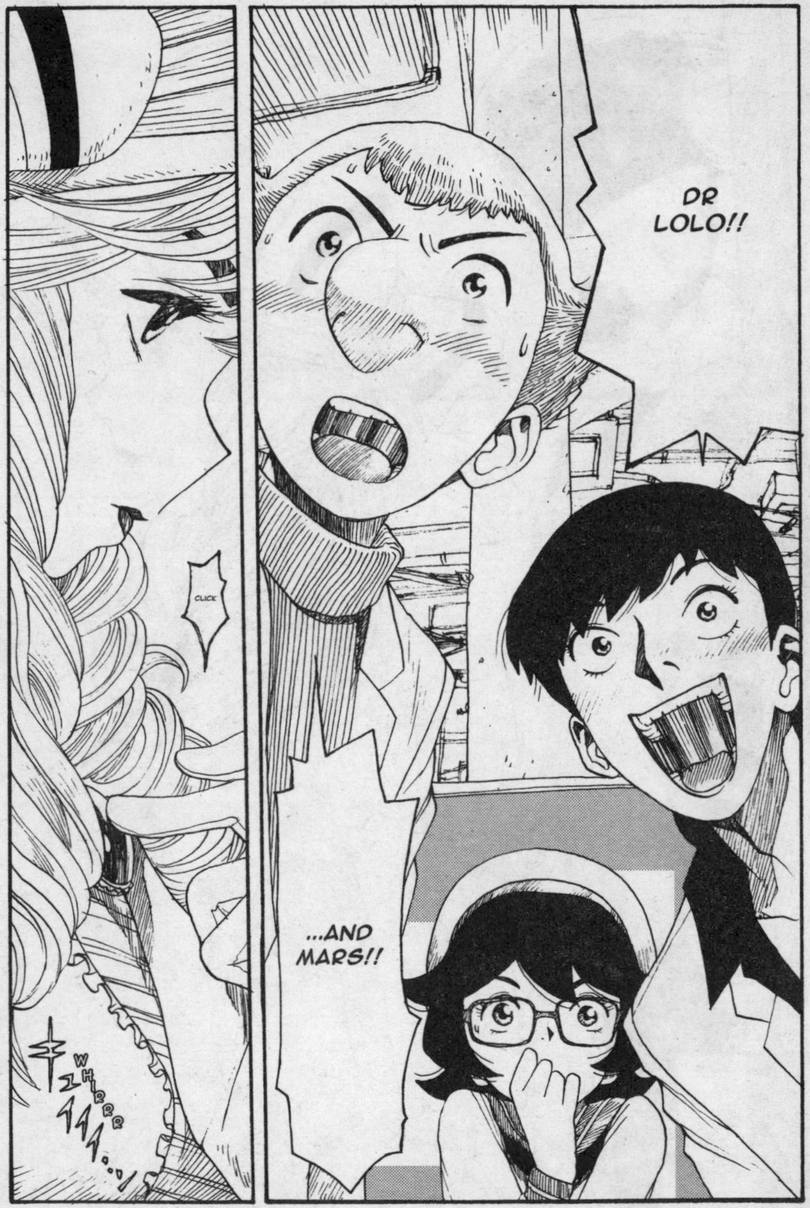
DR LOLO!!
...AND MARS!!
CLICK
WHIRRR

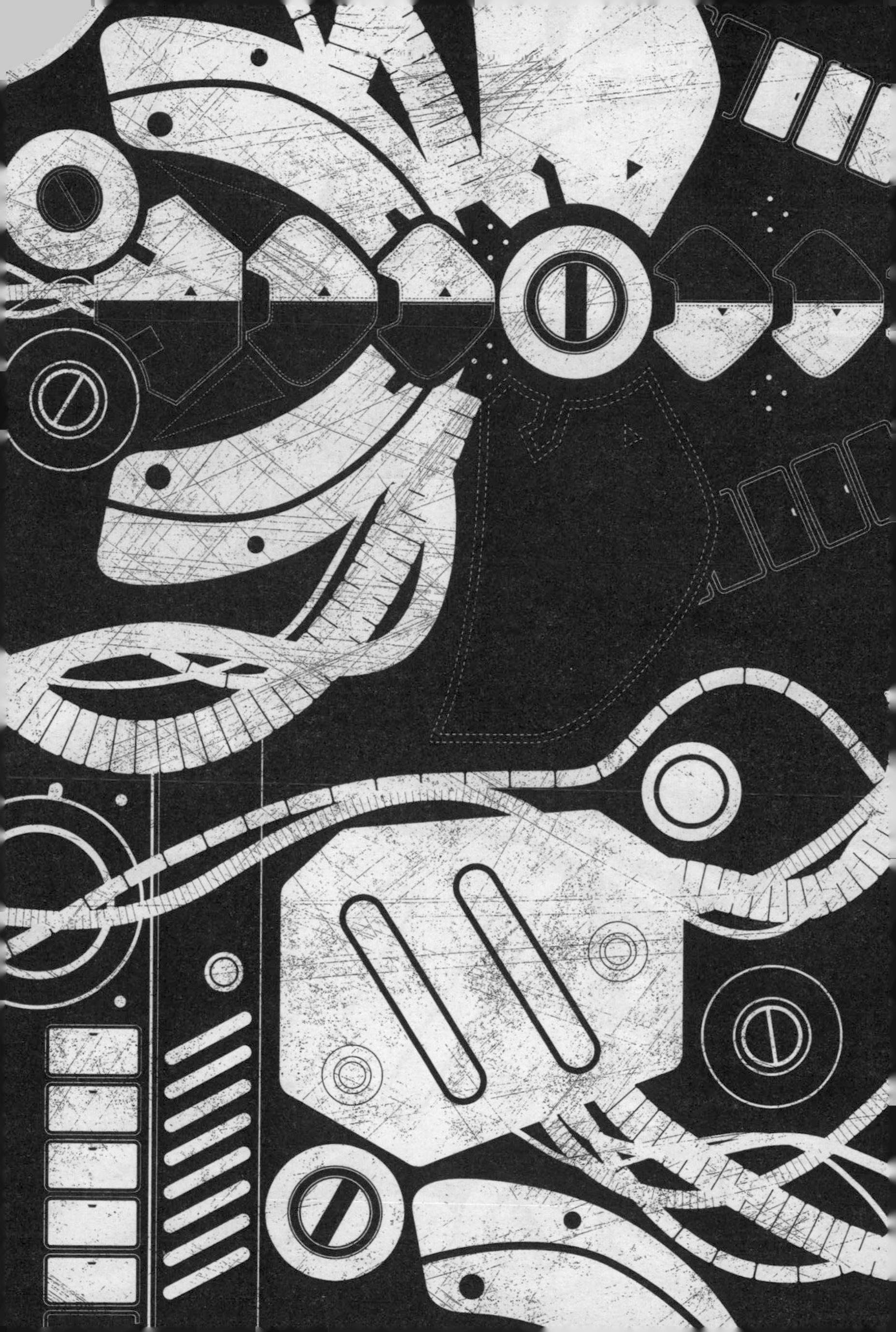

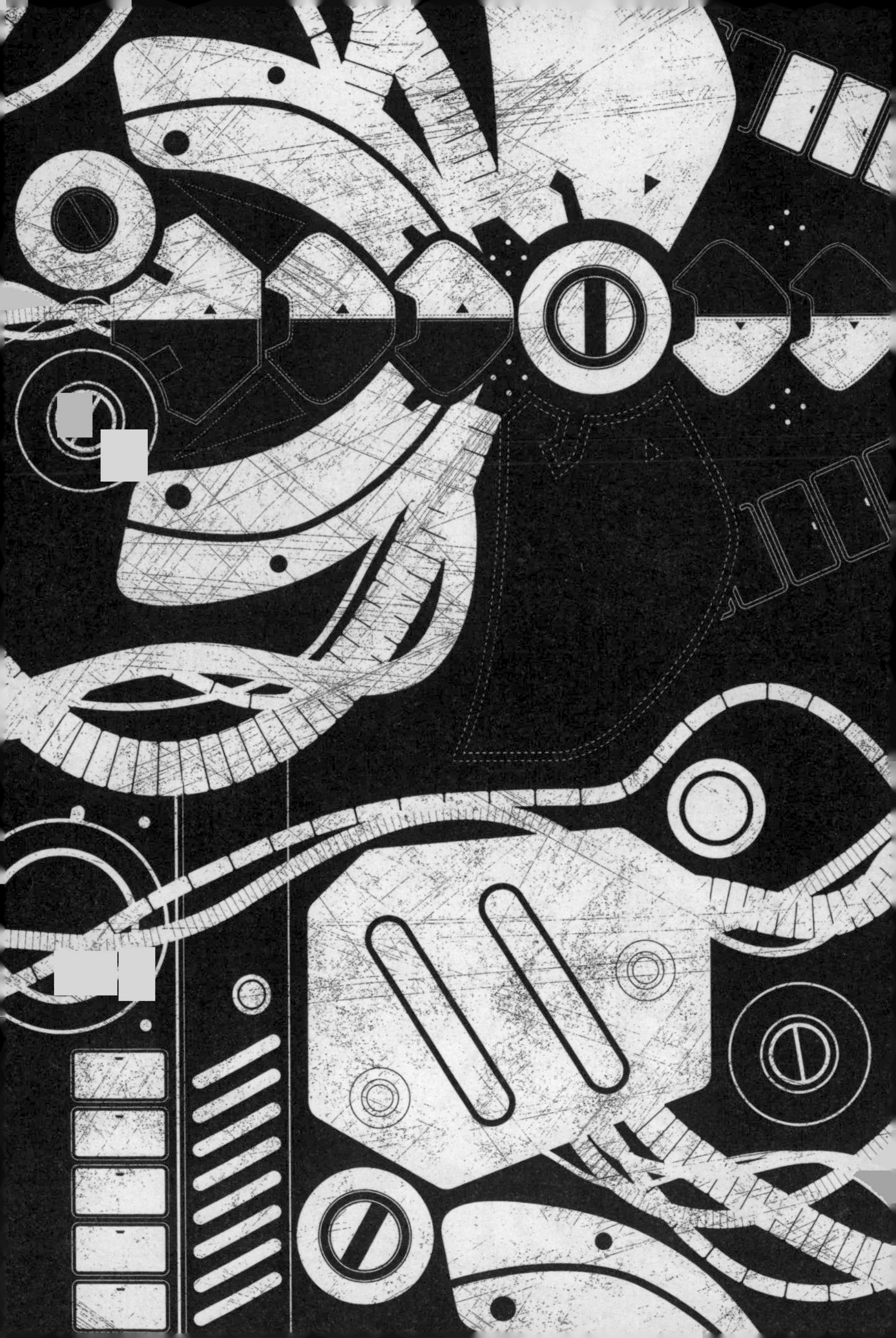

▷boot_020

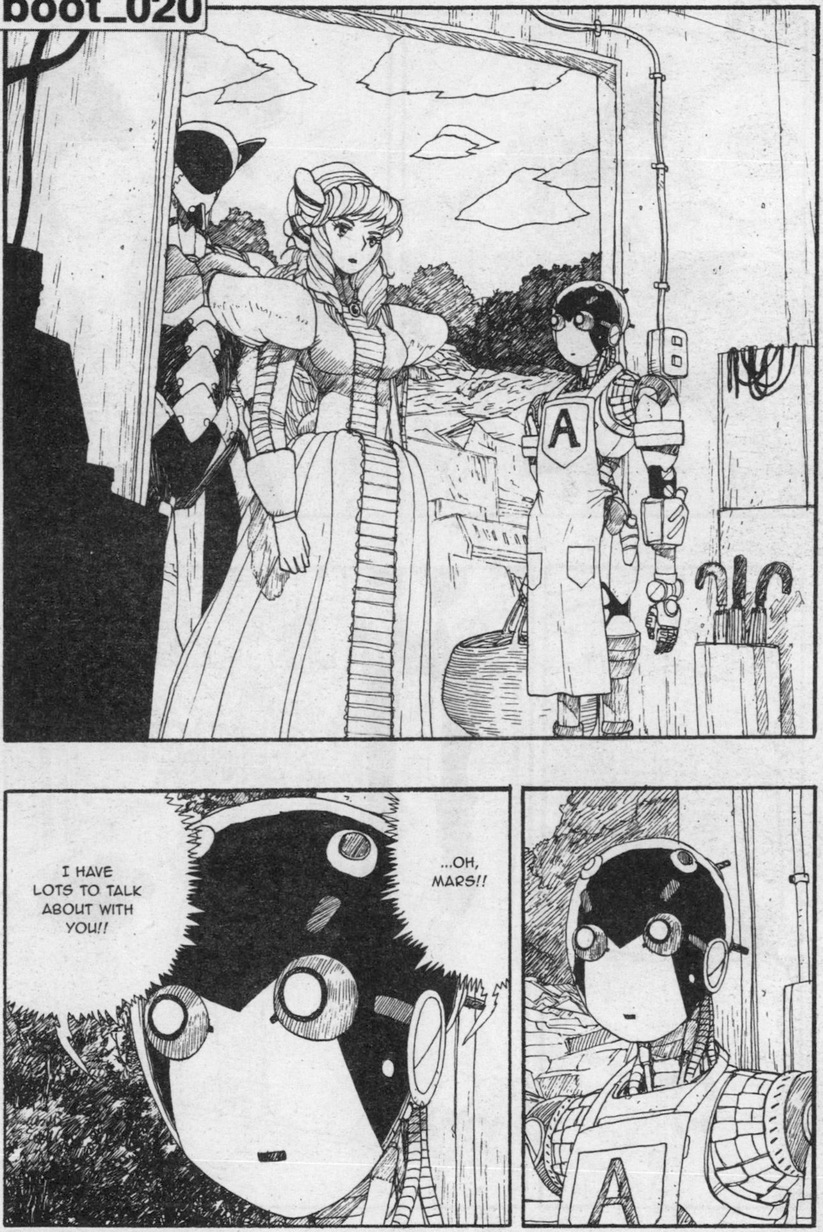

...OH, MARS!!
I HAVE LOTS TO TALK ABOUT WITH YOU!!

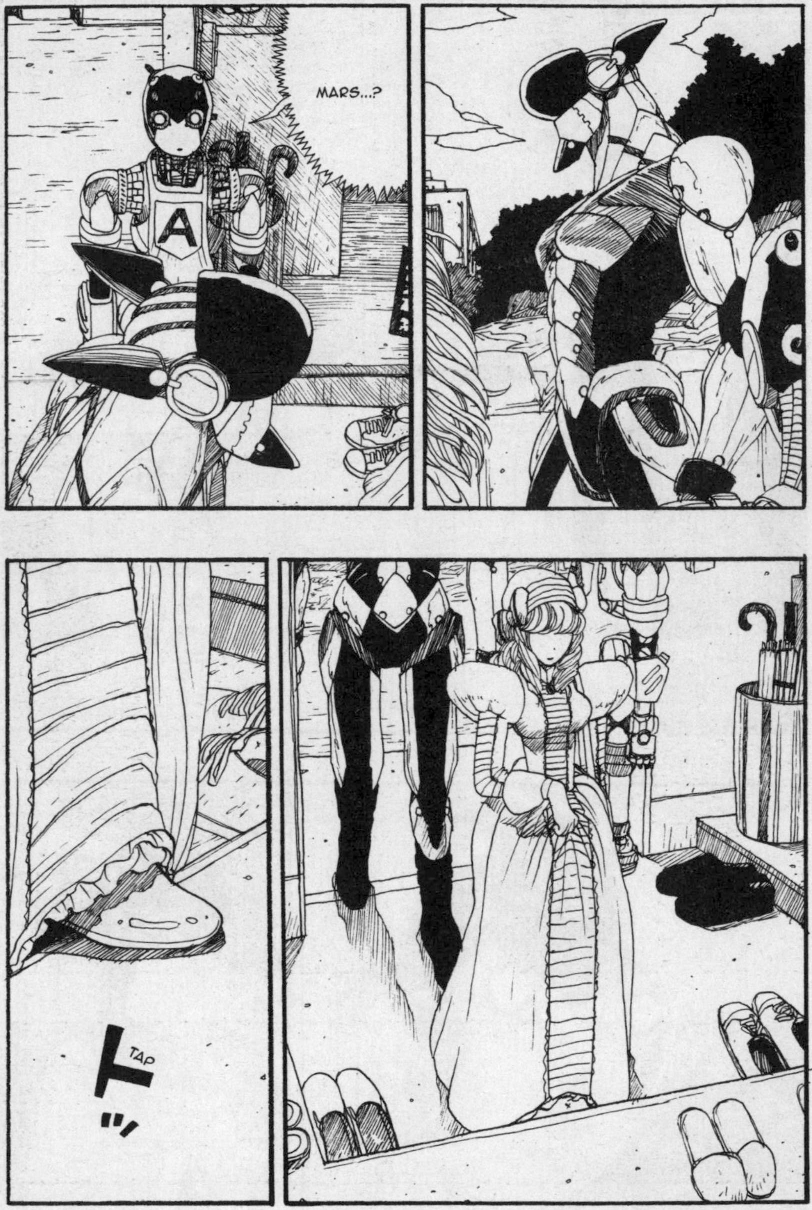
MARS...?
トッ
TAP

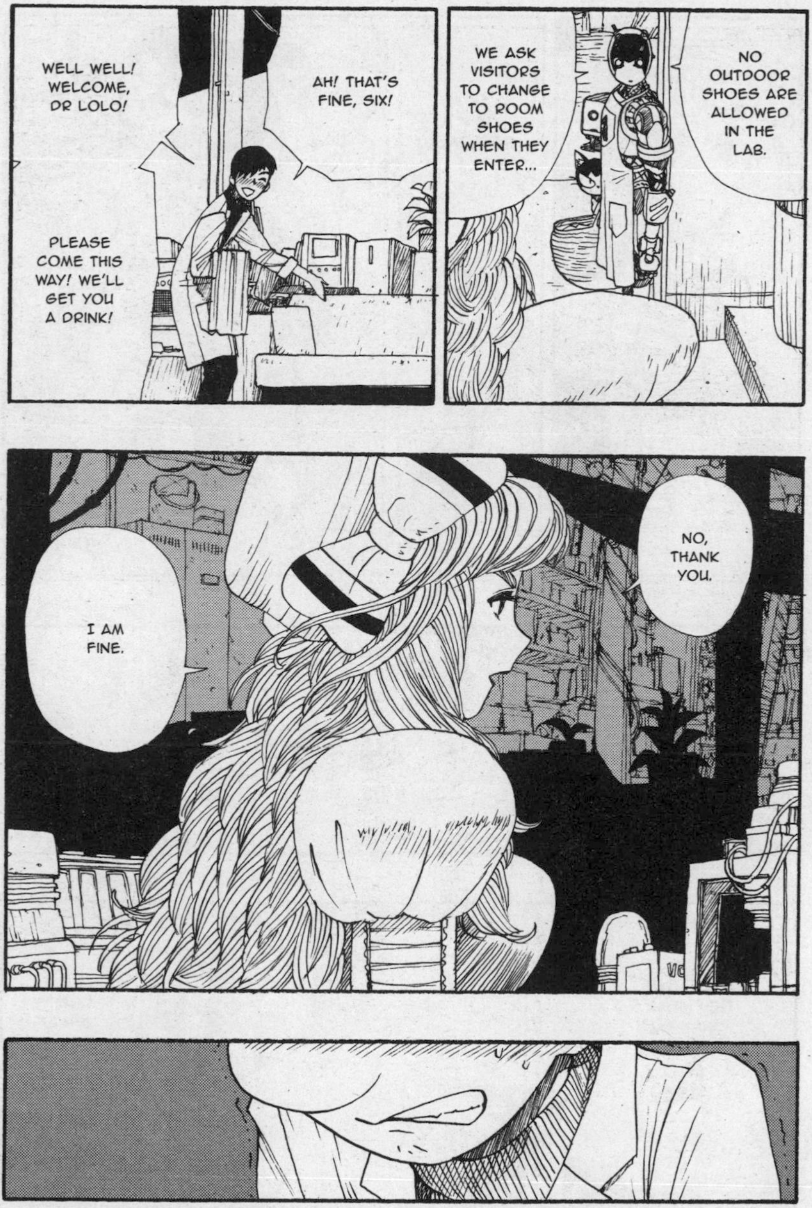
NO OUTDOOR SHOES ARE ALLOWED IN THE LAB.
WE ASK VISITORS TO CHANGE TO ROOM SHOES WHEN THEY ENTER...
AH! THAT'S FINE, SIX!
WELL WELL! WELCOME, DR LOLO!
PLEASE COME THIS WAY! WE'LL GET YOU A DRINK!
NO, THANK YOU.
I AM FINE.

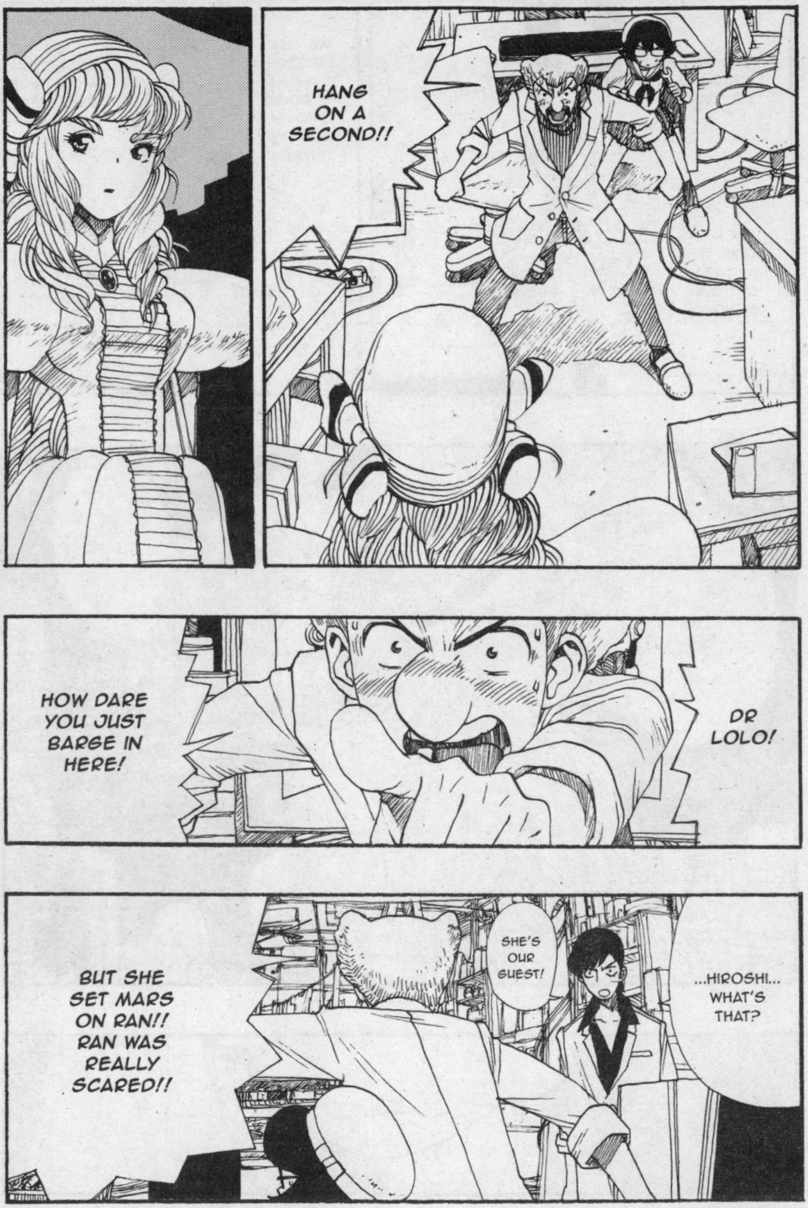
HANG ON A SECOND!!
DR LOLO!
HOW DARE YOU JUST BARGE IN HERE!
...HIROSHI... WHAT'S THAT?
SHE'S OUR GUEST!
BUT SHE SET MARS ON RAN!! RAN WAS REALLY SCARED!!

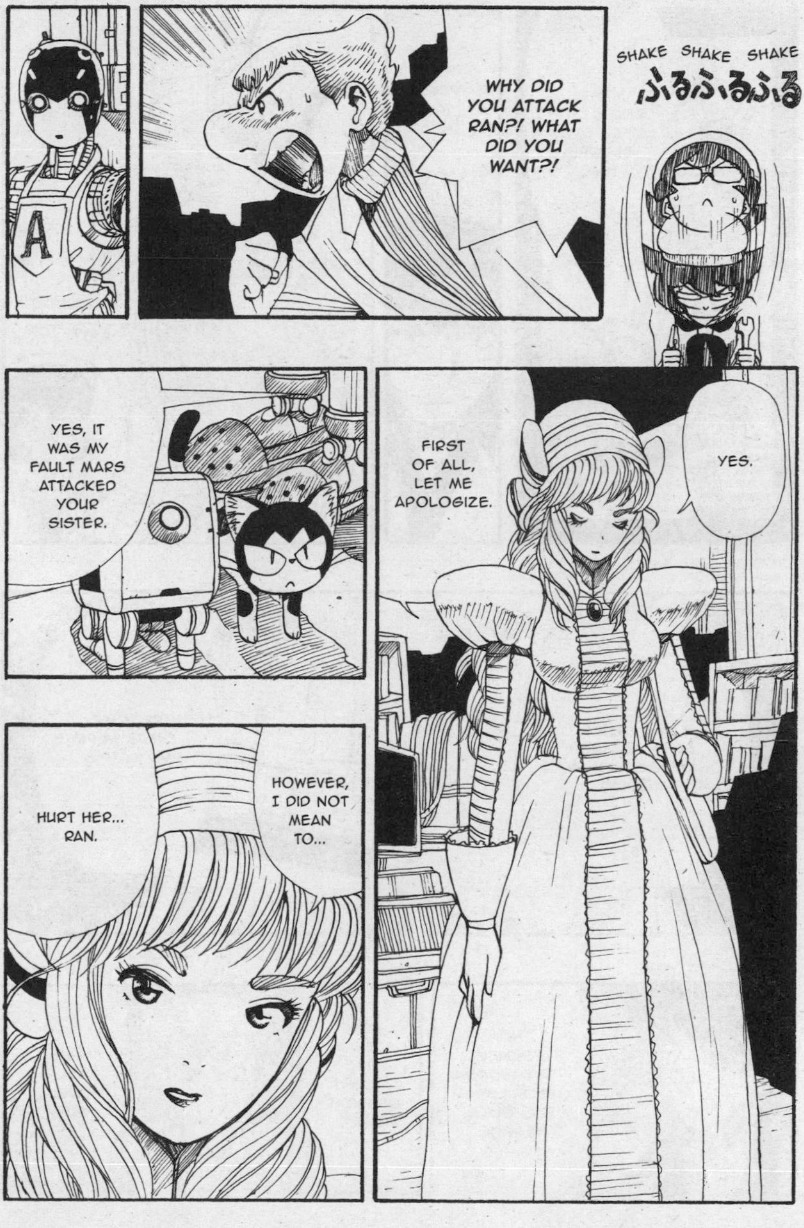
SHAKE SHAKE SHAKE
ふるふるふる
WHY DID YOU ATTACK RAN?! WHAT DID YOU WANT?!
YES.
FIRST OF ALL, LET ME APOLOGIZE.
YES, IT WAS MY FAULT MARS ATTACKED YOUR SISTER.
HOWEVER, I DID NOT MEAN TO...
HURT HER... RAN.

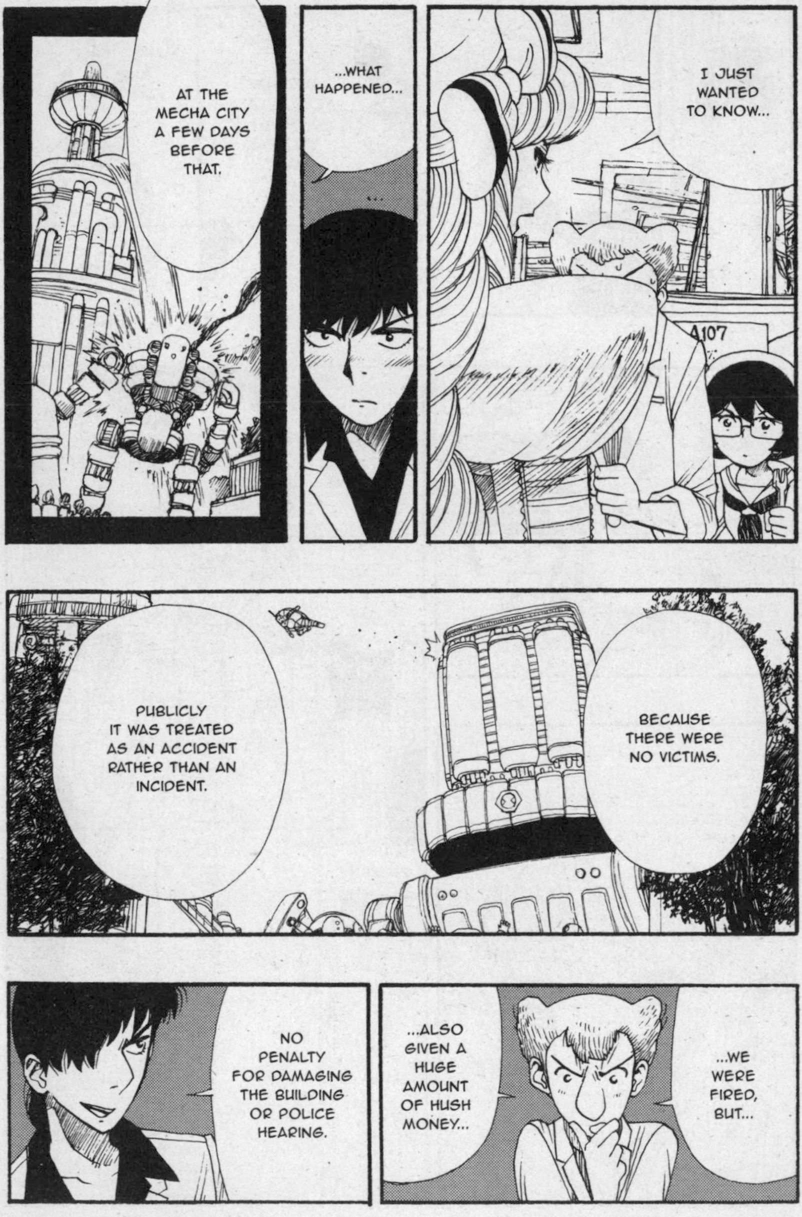
I JUST WANTED TO KNOW...
A107
...WHAT HAPPENED...
...
AT THE MECHA CITY A FEW DAYS BEFORE THAT.
BECAUSE THERE WERE NO VICTIMS.
PUBLICLY IT WAS TREATED AS AN ACCIDENT RATHER THAN AN INCIDENT.
...WE WERE FIRED, BUT...
...ALSO GIVEN A HUGE AMOUNT OF HUSH MONEY...
NO PENALTY FOR DAMAGING THE BUILDING OR POLICE HEARING.

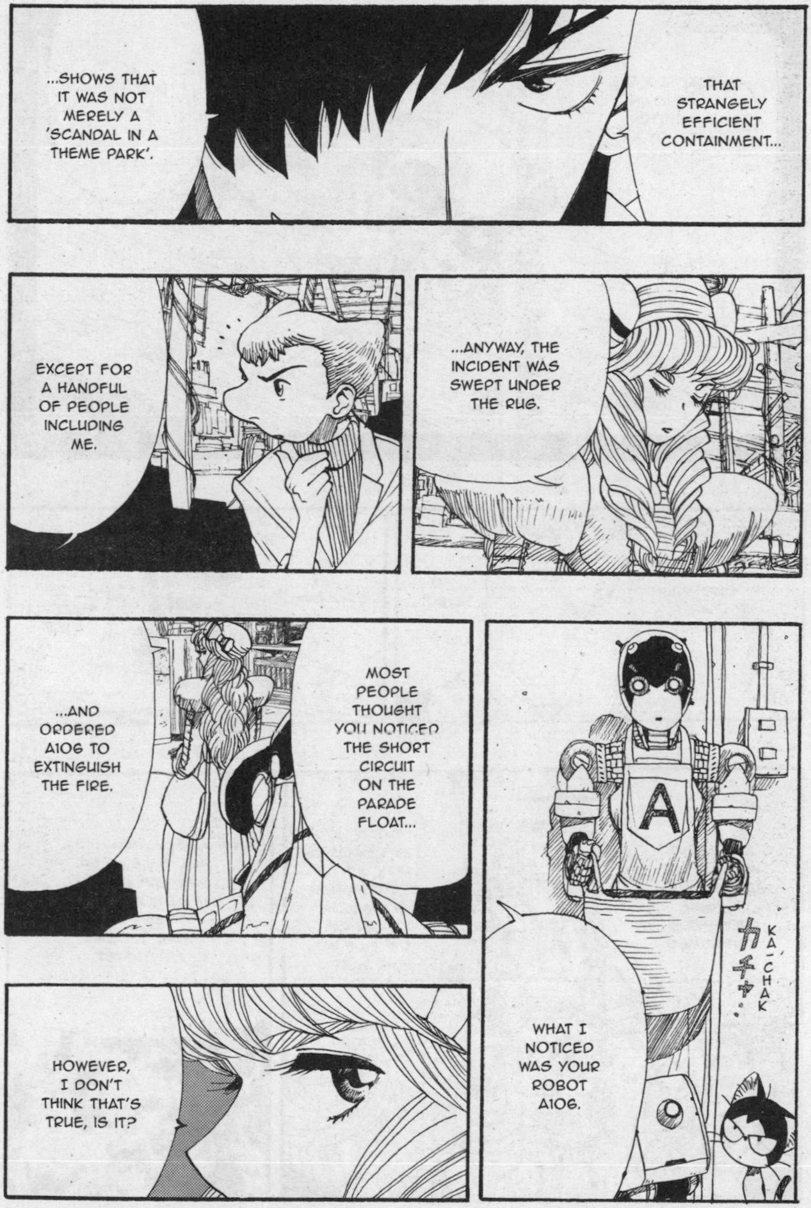
THAT STRANGELY EFFICIENT CONTAINMENT...
...SHOWS THAT IT WAS NOT MERELY A 'SCANDAL IN A THEME PARK'.
...ANYWAY, THE INCIDENT WAS SWEPT UNDER THE RUG.
EXCEPT FOR A HANDFUL OF PEOPLE INCLUDING ME.
カチャ
KA-CHAK
WHAT I NOTICED WAS YOUR ROBOT A106.
MOST PEOPLE THOUGHT YOU NOTICED THE SHORT CIRCUIT ON THE PARADE FLOAT...
...AND ORDERED A106 TO EXTINGUISH THE FIRE.
HOWEVER, I DON'T THINK THAT'S TRUE, IS IT?

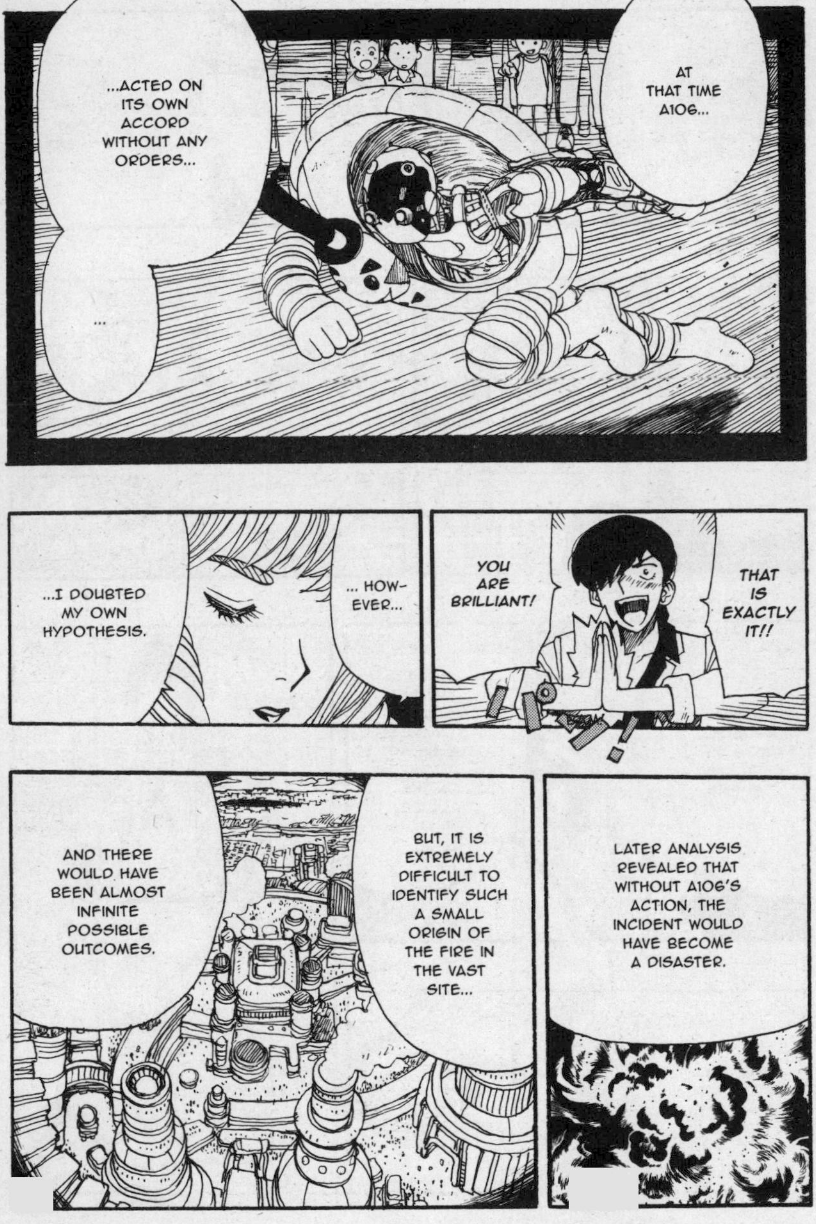
AT THAT TIME A106...
...ACTED ON ITS OWN ACCORD WITHOUT ANY ORDERS...
...
THAT IS EXACTLY IT!!
YOU ARE BRILLIANT!
... HOW-EVER...
...I DOUBTED MY OWN HYPOTHESIS.
LATER ANALYSIS REVEALED THAT WITHOUT A106'S ACTION, THE INCIDENT WOULD HAVE BECOME A DISASTER.
BUT, IT IS EXTREMELY DIFFICULT TO IDENTIFY SUCH A SMALL ORIGIN OF THE FIRE IN THE VAST SITE...
AND THERE WOULD HAVE BEEN ALMOST INFINITE POSSIBLE OUTCOMES.

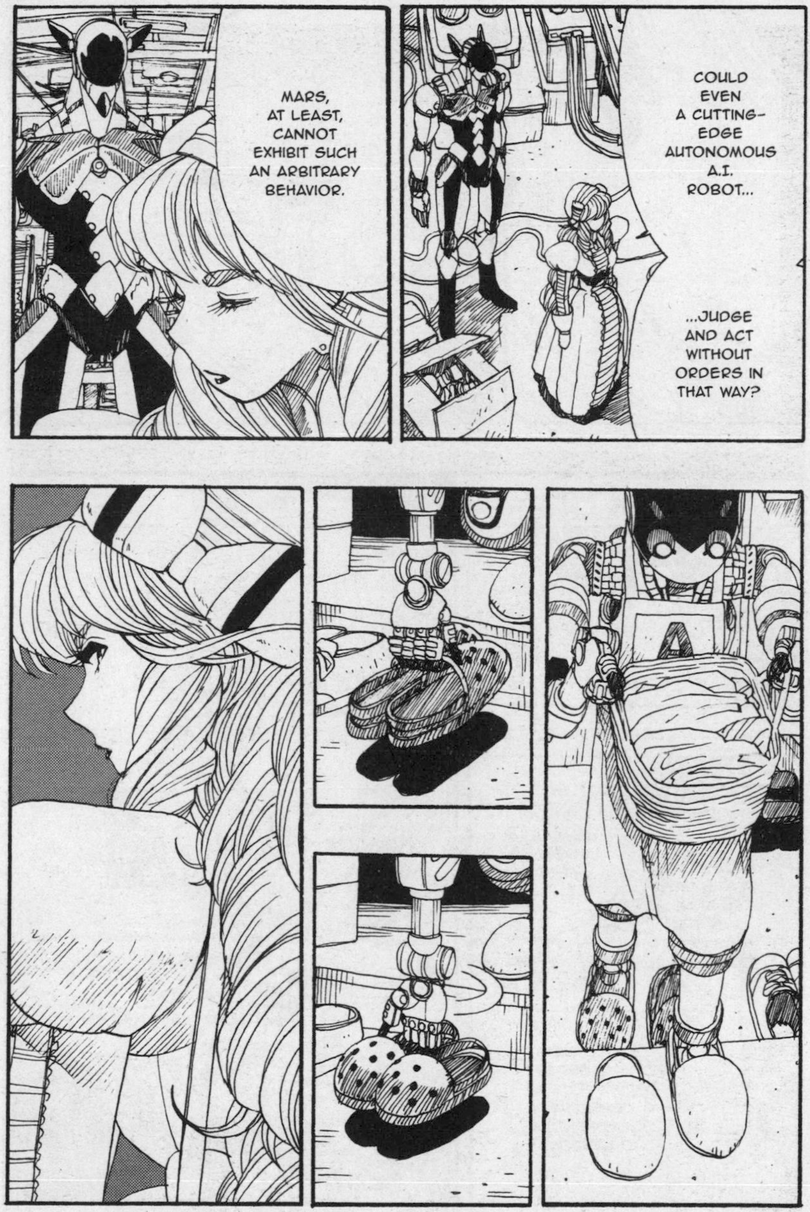
COULD EVEN A CUTTING-EDGE AUTONOMOUS A.I. ROBOT...
...JUDGE AND ACT WITHOUT ORDERS IN THAT WAY?
MARS, AT LEAST, CANNOT EXHIBIT SUCH AN ARBITRARY BEHAVIOR.

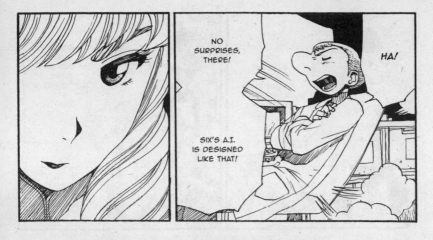

NO SURPRISES, THERE!

HA!

SIX'S A.I. IS DESIGNED LIKE THAT!

BEWUSSTSEIN...

...ISN'T IT?

I HAVE READ YOUR MASTER'S THESIS.

'DEVELOPMENT OF A10 SERIES' ORIGINATING A CEREBRUM COMPONENT OF A10 NEURONS.

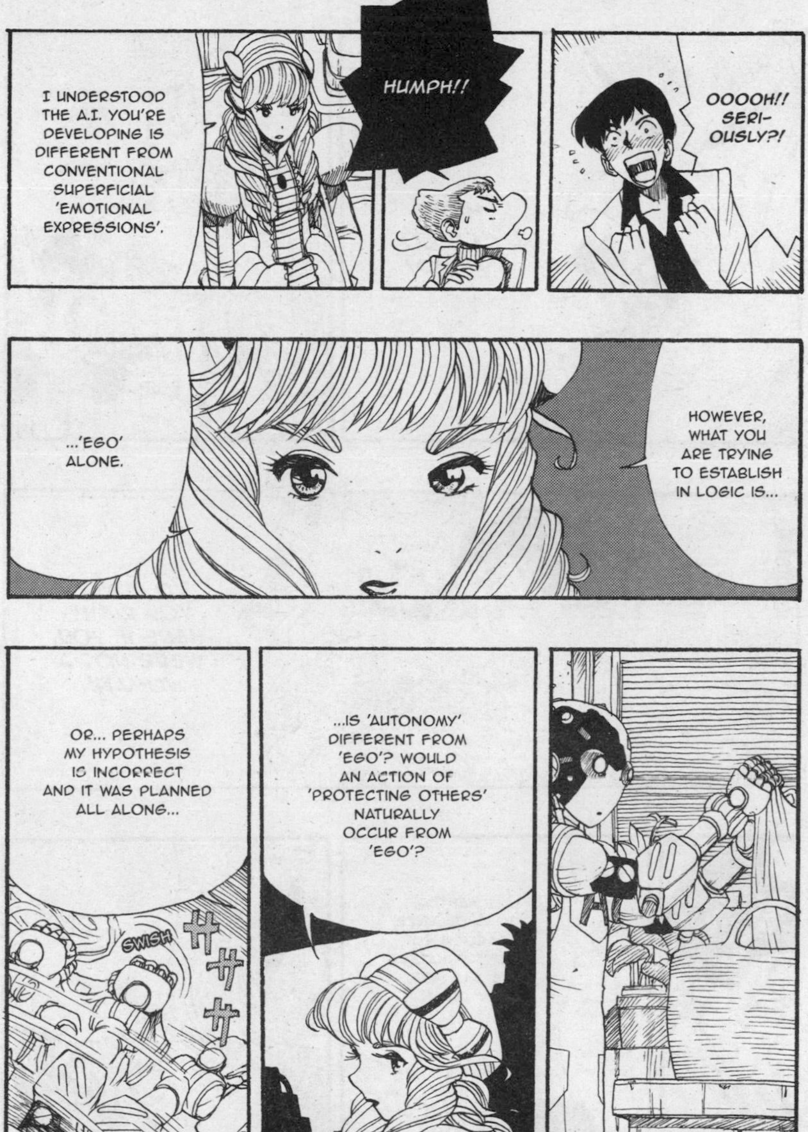
OOOOH!! SERI-OUSLY?!
HUMPH!!
I UNDERSTOOD THE A.I. YOU'RE DEVELOPING IS DIFFERENT FROM CONVENTIONAL SUPERFICIAL 'EMOTIONAL EXPRESSIONS'.
HOWEVER, WHAT YOU ARE TRYING TO ESTABLISH IN LOGIC IS...
...'EGO' ALONE.
...IS 'AUTONOMY' DIFFERENT FROM 'EGO'? WOULD AN ACTION OF 'PROTECTING OTHERS' NATURALLY OCCUR FROM 'EGO'?
OR... PERHAPS MY HYPOTHESIS IS INCORRECT AND IT WAS PLANNED ALL ALONG...
SWISH

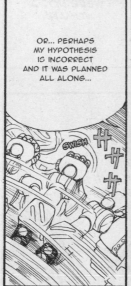

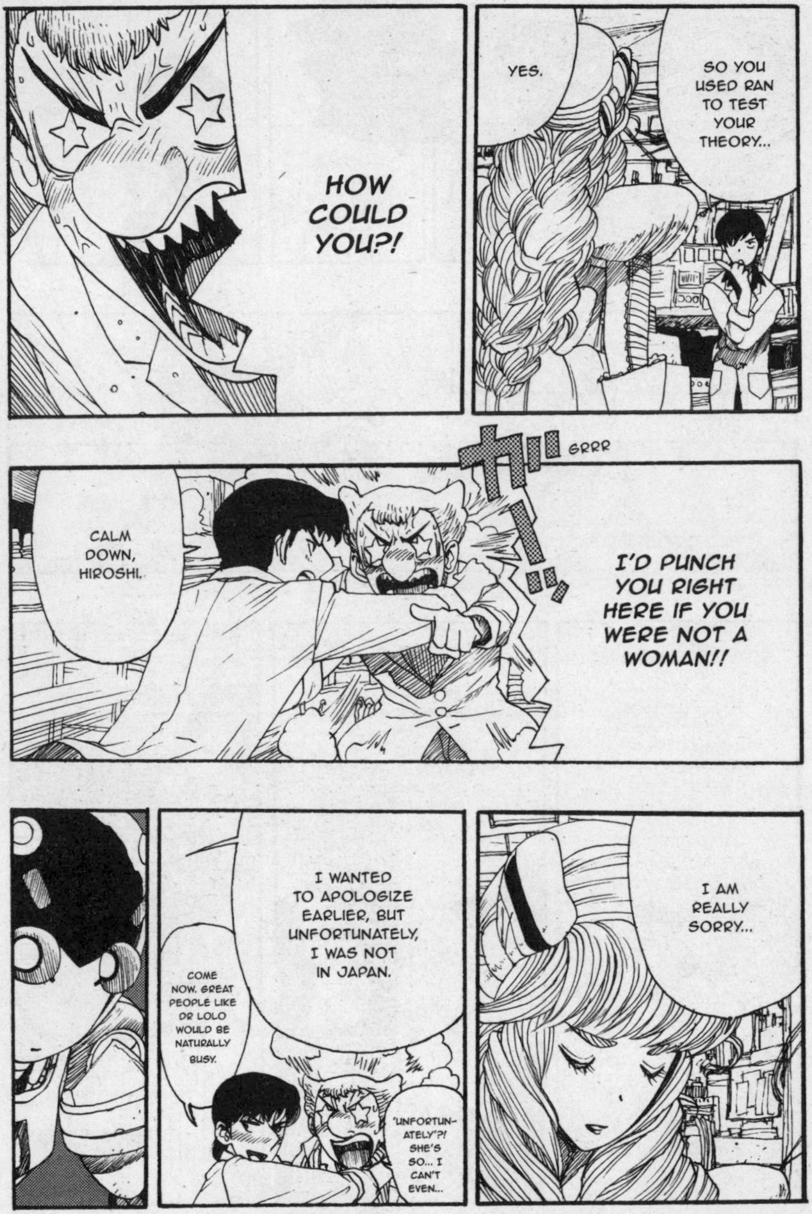
SO YOU USED RAN TO TEST YOUR THEORY...
YES.
HOW COULD YOU?!
GRRR
I'D PUNCH YOU RIGHT HERE IF YOU WERE NOT A WOMAN!!
CALM DOWN, HIROSHI.
I AM REALLY SORRY...
I WANTED TO APOLOGIZE EARLIER, BUT UNFORTUNATELY, I WAS NOT IN JAPAN.
COME NOW. GREAT PEOPLE LIKE DR LOLO WOULD BE NATURALLY BUSY.
'UNFORTUN-ATELY'?! SHE'S SO... I CAN'T EVEN...

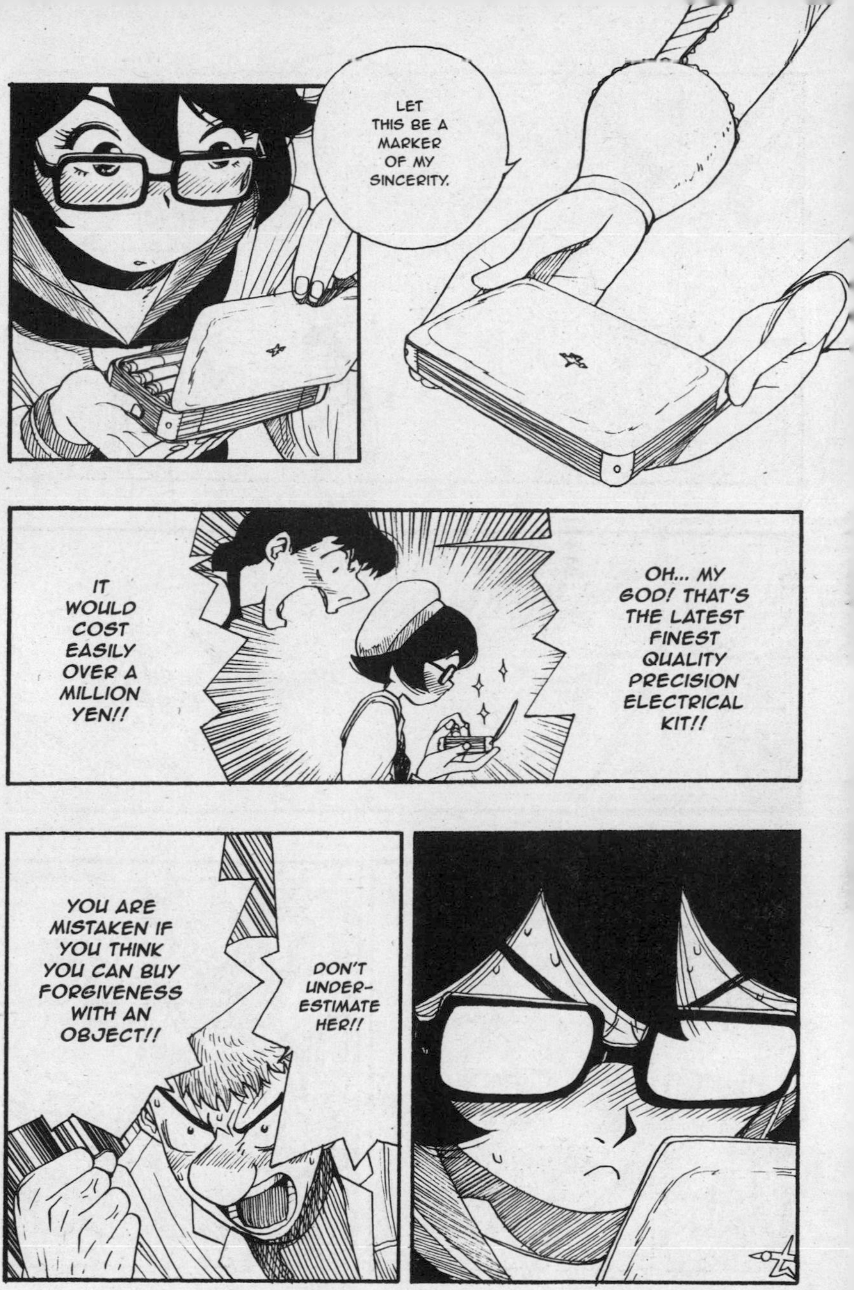
LET THIS BE A MARKER OF MY SINCERITY.
OH... MY GOD! THAT'S THE LATEST FINEST QUALITY PRECISION ELECTRICAL KIT!!
IT WOULD COST EASILY OVER A MILLION YEN!!
DON'T UNDER-ESTIMATE HER!!
YOU ARE MISTAKEN IF YOU THINK YOU CAN BUY FORGIVENESS WITH AN OBJECT!!

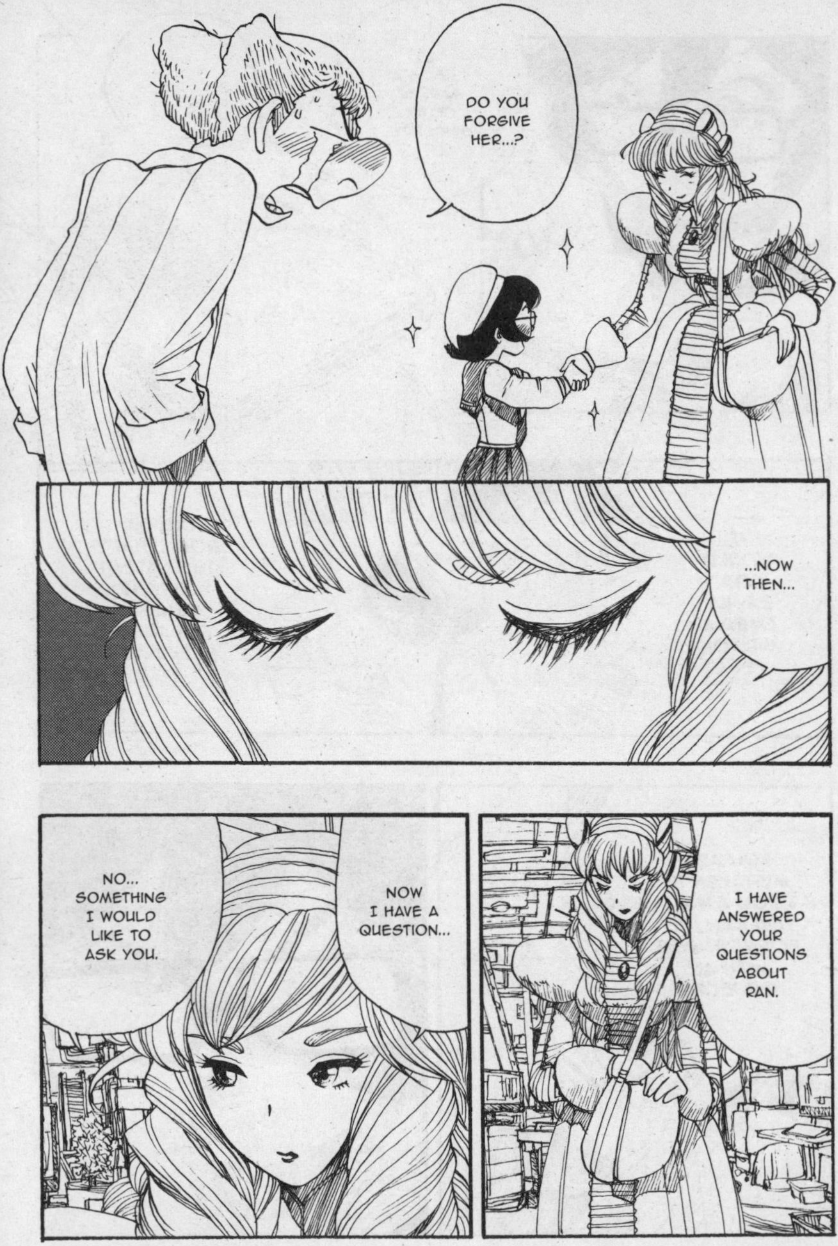
DO YOU FORGIVE HER...?
...NOW THEN...
I HAVE ANSWERED YOUR QUESTIONS ABOUT RAN.
NOW I HAVE A QUESTION...
NO... SOMETHING I WOULD LIKE TO ASK YOU.

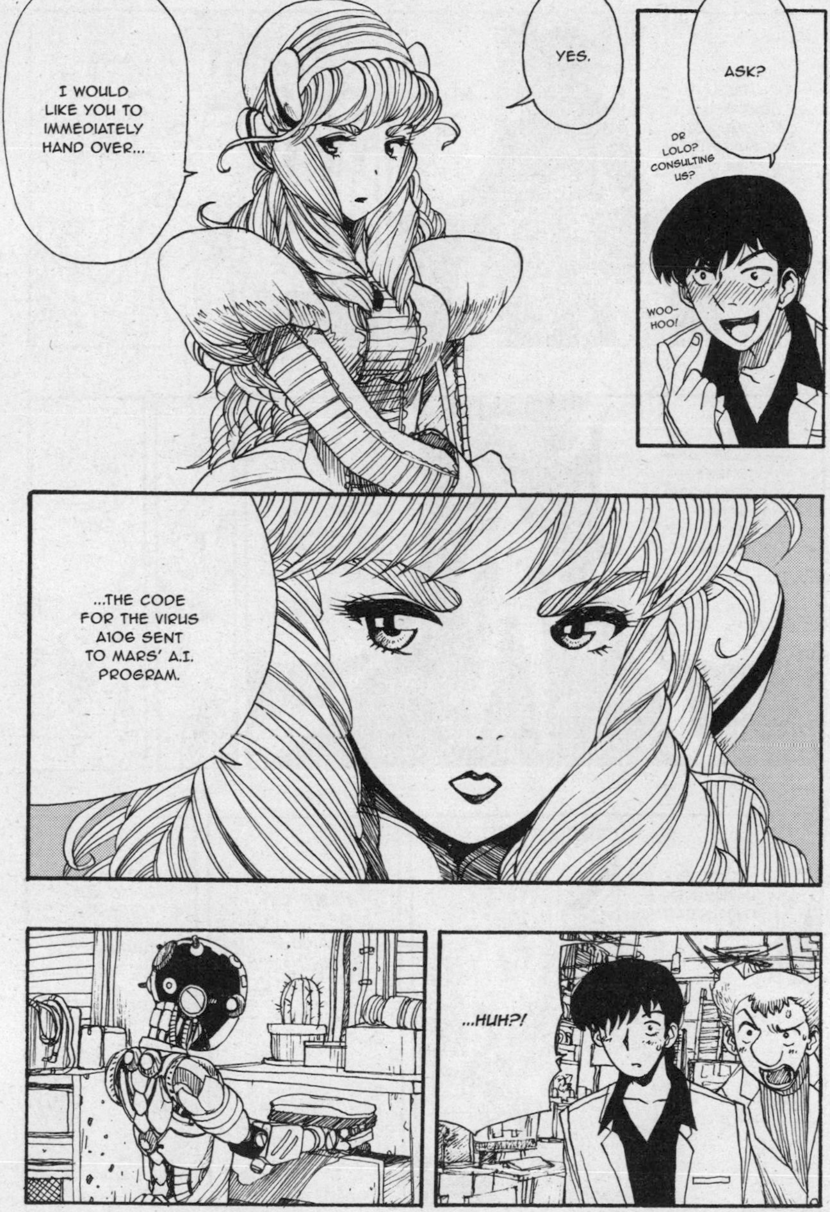
ASK?
DR LOLO? CONSULTING US?
WOO-HOO!
YES.
I WOULD LIKE YOU TO IMMEDIATELY HAND OVER...
...THE CODE FOR THE VIRUS A106 SENT TO MARS' A.I. PROGRAM.
...HUH?!

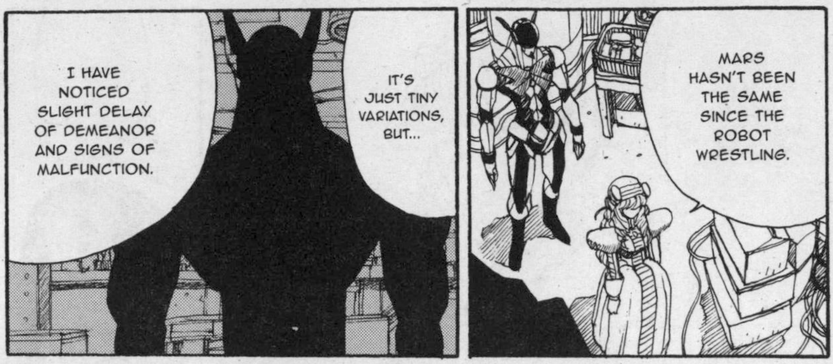
MARS HASN'T BEEN THE SAME SINCE THE ROBOT WRESTLING.
IT'S JUST TINY VARIATIONS, BUT...
I HAVE NOTICED SLIGHT DELAY OF DEMEANOR AND SIGNS OF MALFUNCTION.
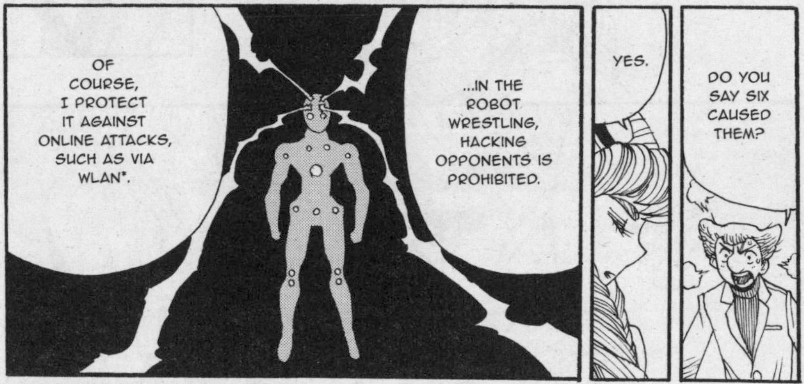
DO YOU SAY SIX CAUSED THEM?
YES.
...IN THE ROBOT WRESTLING, HACKING OPPONENTS IS PROHIBITED.
OF COURSE, I PROTECT IT AGAINST ONLINE ATTACKS, SUCH AS VIA WLAN*.

*WLAN: WIRELESS LOCAL AREA NETWORK.

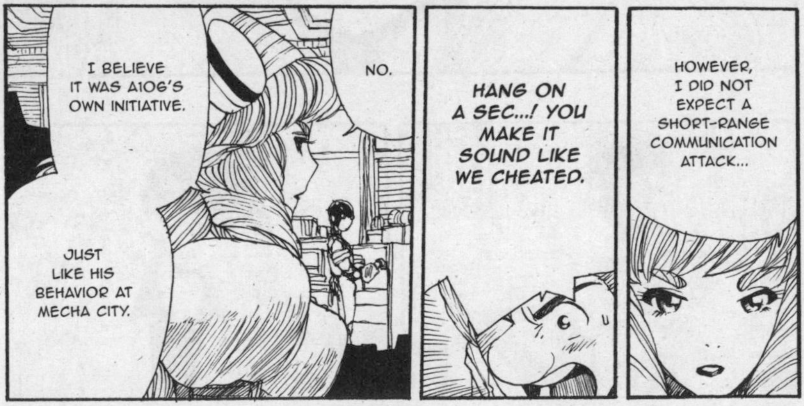
HOWEVER, I DID NOT EXPECT A SHORT-RANGE COMMUNICATION ATTACK...
HANG ON A SEC...! YOU MAKE IT SOUND LIKE WE CHEATED.
NO.
I BELIEVE IT WAS A106'S OWN INITIATIVE.
JUST LIKE HIS BEHAVIOR AT MECHA CITY.

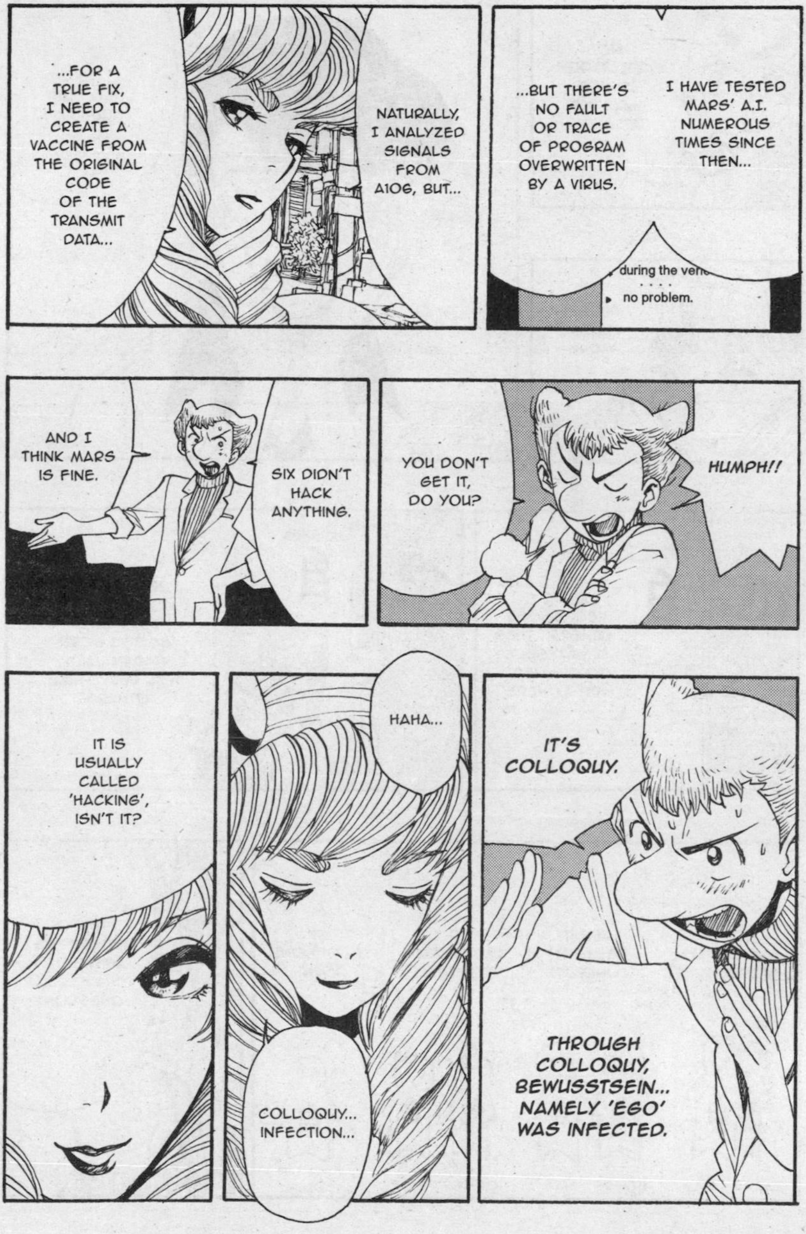
I HAVE TESTED MARS' A.I. NUMEROUS TIMES SINCE THEN...
...BUT THERE'S NO FAULT OR TRACE OF PROGRAM OVERWRITTEN BY A VIRUS.
no problem.
NATURALLY, I ANALYZED SIGNALS FROM A106, BUT...
...FOR A TRUE FIX, I NEED TO CREATE A VACCINE FROM THE ORIGINAL CODE OF THE TRANSMIT DATA...
HUMPH!!
YOU DON'T GET IT, DO YOU?
SIX DIDN'T HACK ANYTHING.
AND I THINK MARS IS FINE.
IT'S COLLOQUY.
THROUGH COLLOQUY, BEWUSSTSEIN... NAMELY 'EGO' WAS INFECTED.
HAHA...
COLLOQUY... INFECTION...
IT IS USUALLY CALLED 'HACKING', ISN'T IT?

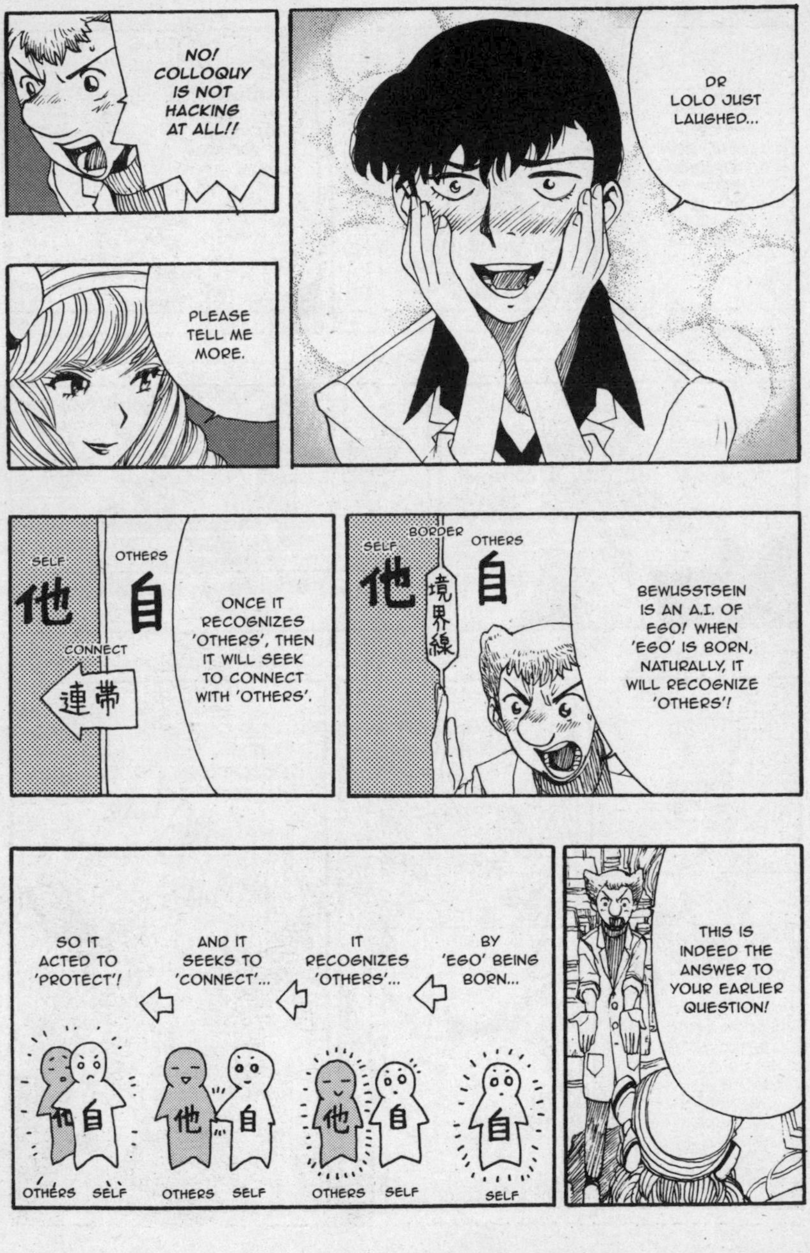
DR LOLO JUST LAUGHED...
NO! COLLOQUY IS NOT HACKING AT ALL!!
PLEASE TELL ME MORE.
SELF
BORDER
OTHERS
他
境界線
自
BEWUSSTSEIN IS AN A.I. OF EGO! WHEN 'EGO' IS BORN, NATURALLY, IT WILL RECOGNIZE 'OTHERS'!
SELF
OTHERS
他
自
CONNECT
連帯
ONCE IT RECOGNIZES 'OTHERS', THEN IT WILL SEEK TO CONNECT WITH 'OTHERS'.
THIS IS INDEED THE ANSWER TO YOUR EARLIER QUESTION!
BY 'EGO' BEING BORN...
自
SELF
IT RECOGNIZES 'OTHERS'...
他
自
OTHERS
SELF
AND IT SEEKS TO 'CONNECT'...
他
自
OTHERS
SELF
SO IT ACTED TO 'PROTECT'!
自
OTHERS
SELF

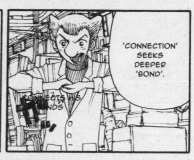

'CONNECTION' SEEKS DEEPER 'BOND'.
CONNECTS HIS HANDS
ACCORDING TO OUR RECORDS...
...DURING THE ROBOT WRESTLING, SIX WAS TALKING TO VARIOUS ROBOTS WITH SHORT-RANGE COMMUNICATION.
NATURALLY, HE HARDLY GOT ANY RESPONSE.
*POINTING
EXCEPT FOR MARS.
TRANSMIT DATA? THAT IS MEANINGLESS.
BECAUSE CONVERSATIONS BETWEEN SOPHISTICATED A.I. LIKE THEM...
ARE DIFFERENT FROM OURS IN TERMS OF SPEED, DENSITY, LANGUAGE, AND SENSE OF VALUE.

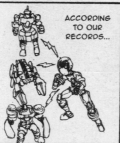

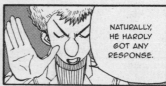

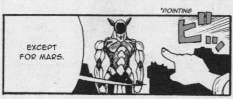

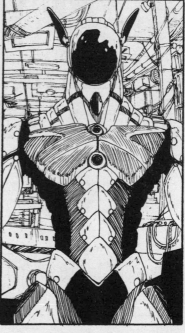

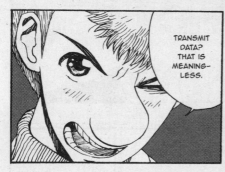

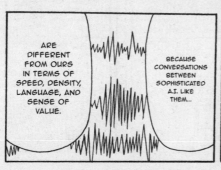

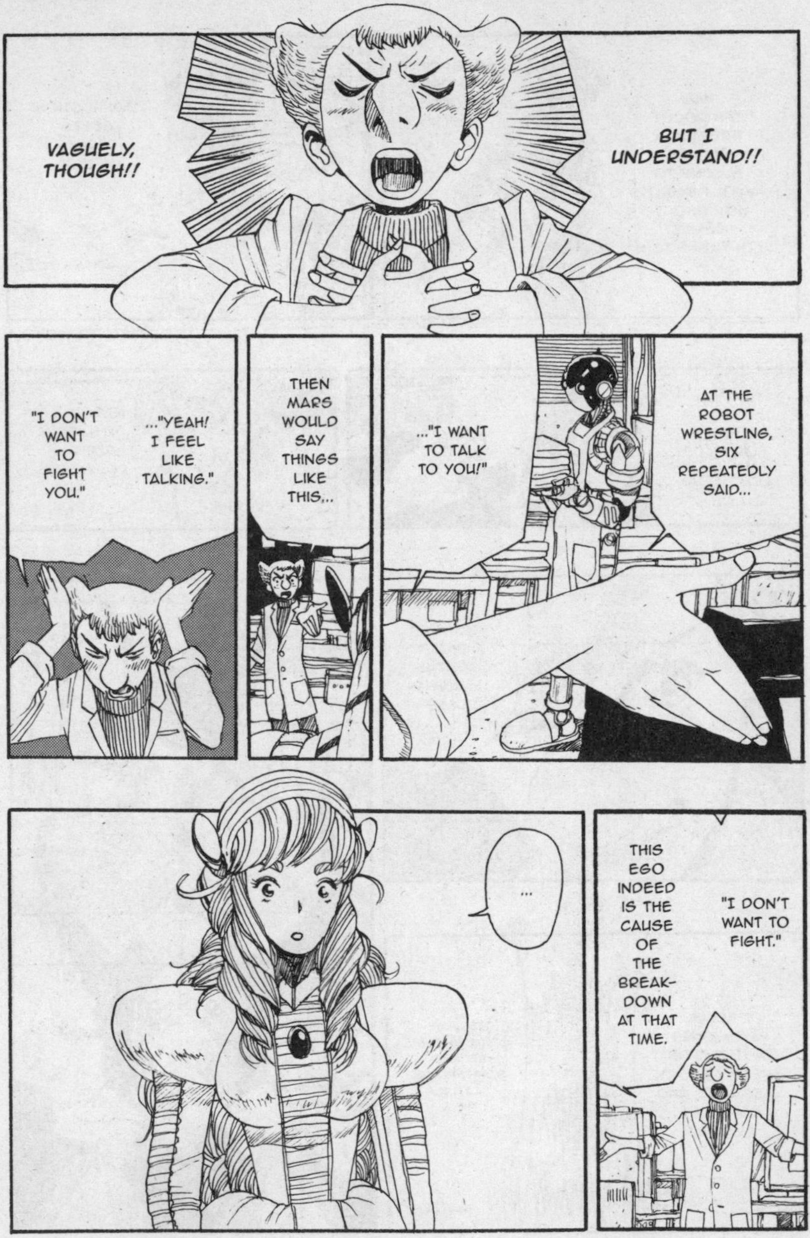
BUT I UNDERSTAND!!
VAGUELY, THOUGH!!
AT THE ROBOT WRESTLING, SIX REPEATEDLY SAID...
..."I WANT TO TALK TO YOU!"
THEN MARS WOULD SAY THINGS LIKE THIS...
..."YEAH! I FEEL LIKE TALKING."
"I DON'T WANT TO FIGHT YOU."
"I DON'T WANT TO FIGHT."
THIS EGO INDEED IS THE CAUSE OF THE BREAKDOWN AT THAT TIME.
...

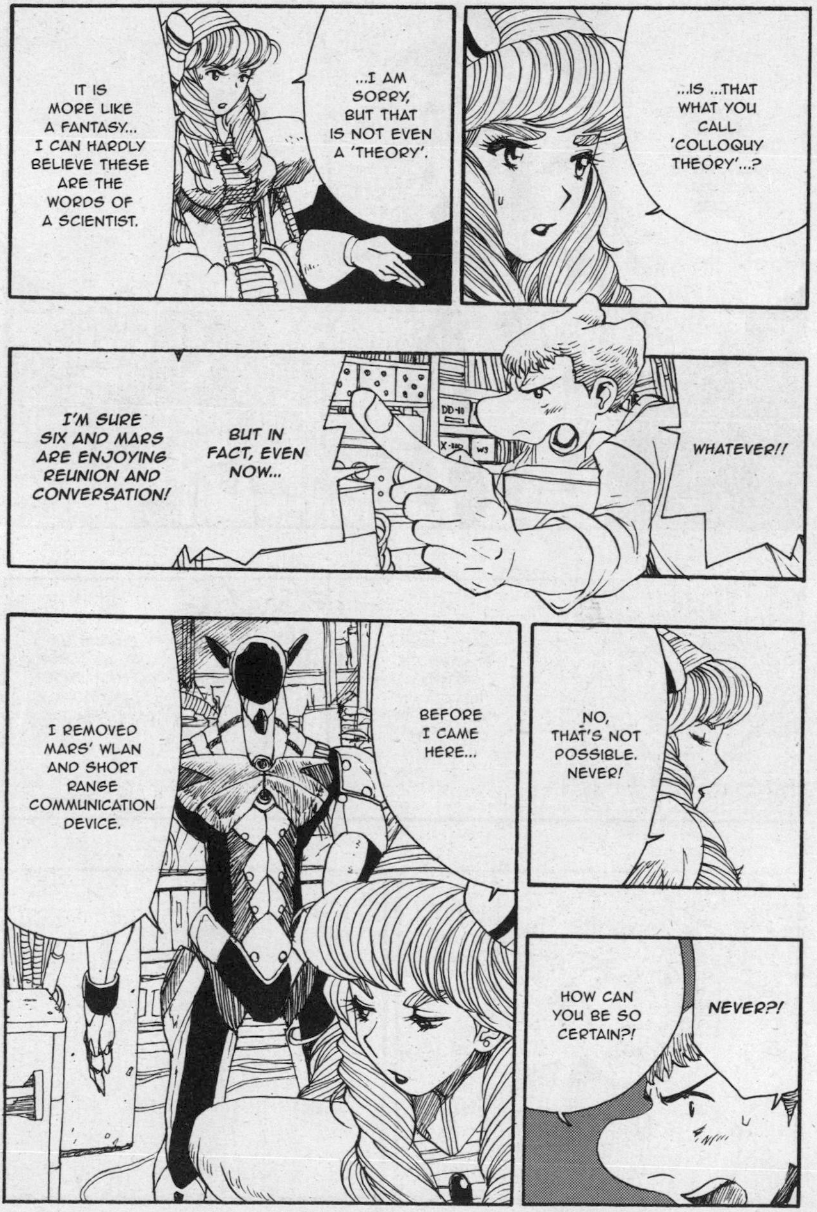
...IS ...THAT WHAT YOU CALL 'COLLOQUY THEORY'...?
...I AM SORRY, BUT THAT IS NOT EVEN A 'THEORY'.
IT IS MORE LIKE A FANTASY... I CAN HARDLY BELIEVE THESE ARE THE WORDS OF A SCIENTIST.
WHATEVER!!
BUT IN FACT, EVEN NOW...
I'M SURE SIX AND MARS ARE ENJOYING REUNION AND CONVERSATION!
NO, THAT'S NOT POSSIBLE. NEVER!
NEVER?!
HOW CAN YOU BE SO CERTAIN?!
BEFORE I CAME HERE...
I REMOVED MARS' WLAN AND SHORT RANGE COMMUNICATION DEVICE.

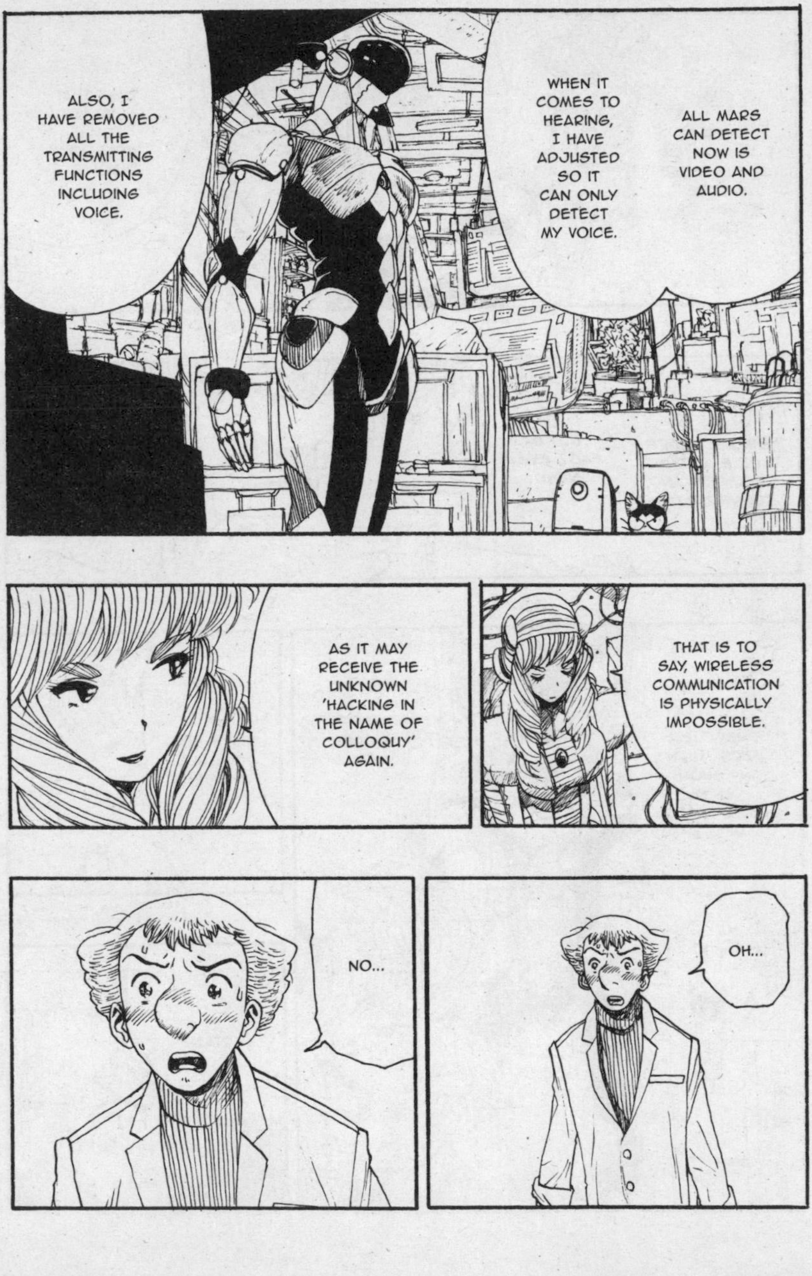
ALL MARS CAN DETECT NOW IS VIDEO AND AUDIO.
WHEN IT COMES TO HEARING, I HAVE ADJUSTED SO IT CAN ONLY DETECT MY VOICE.
ALSO, I HAVE REMOVED ALL THE TRANSMITTING FUNCTIONS INCLUDING VOICE.
THAT IS TO SAY, WIRELESS COMMUNICATION IS PHYSICALLY IMPOSSIBLE.
AS IT MAY RECEIVE THE UNKNOWN 'HACKING IN THE NAME OF COLLOQUY' AGAIN.
OH...
NO...

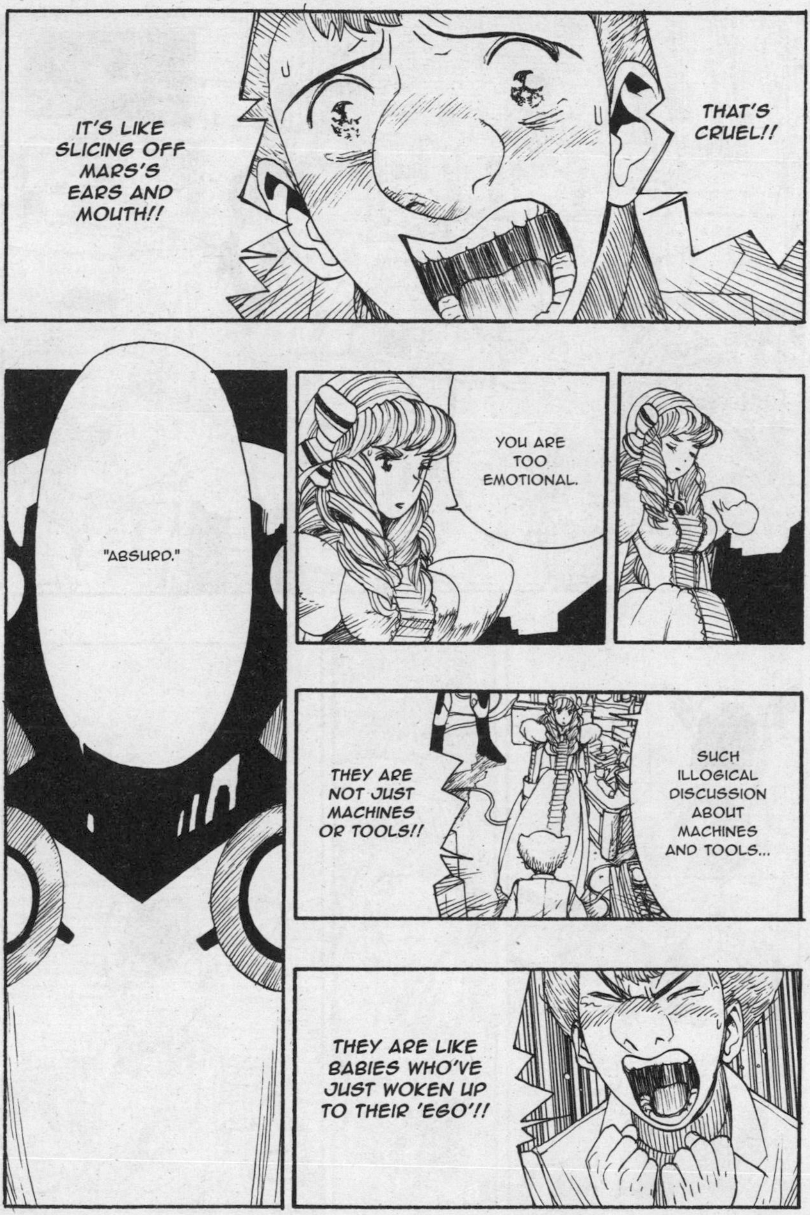
THAT'S CRUEL!!
IT'S LIKE SLICING OFF MARS'S EARS AND MOUTH!!
YOU ARE TOO EMOTIONAL.
SUCH ILLOGICAL DISCUSSION ABOUT MACHINES AND TOOLS...
THEY ARE NOT JUST MACHINES OR TOOLS!!
THEY ARE LIKE BABIES WHO'VE JUST WOKEN UP TO THEIR 'EGO'!!
"ABSURD."

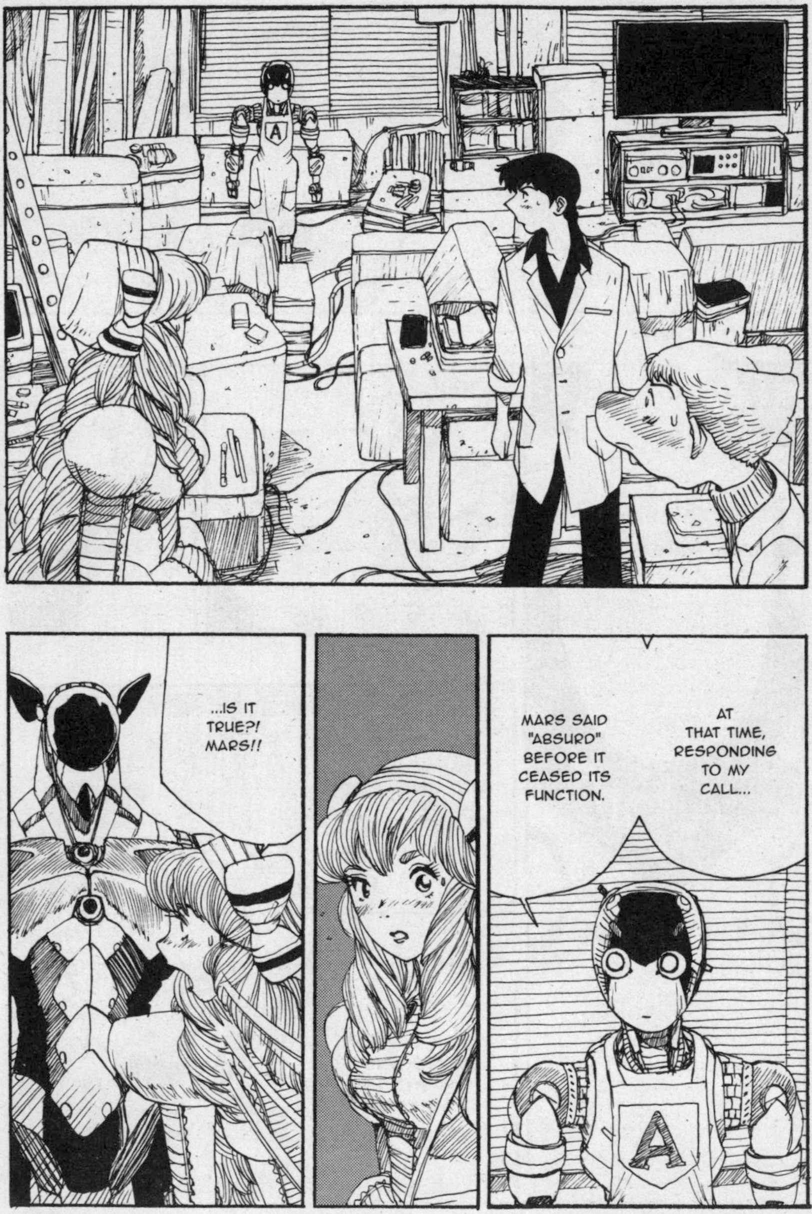
AT THAT TIME, RESPONDING TO MY CALL...
MARS SAID "ABSURD" BEFORE IT CEASED ITS FUNCTION.
...IS IT TRUE?! MARS!!

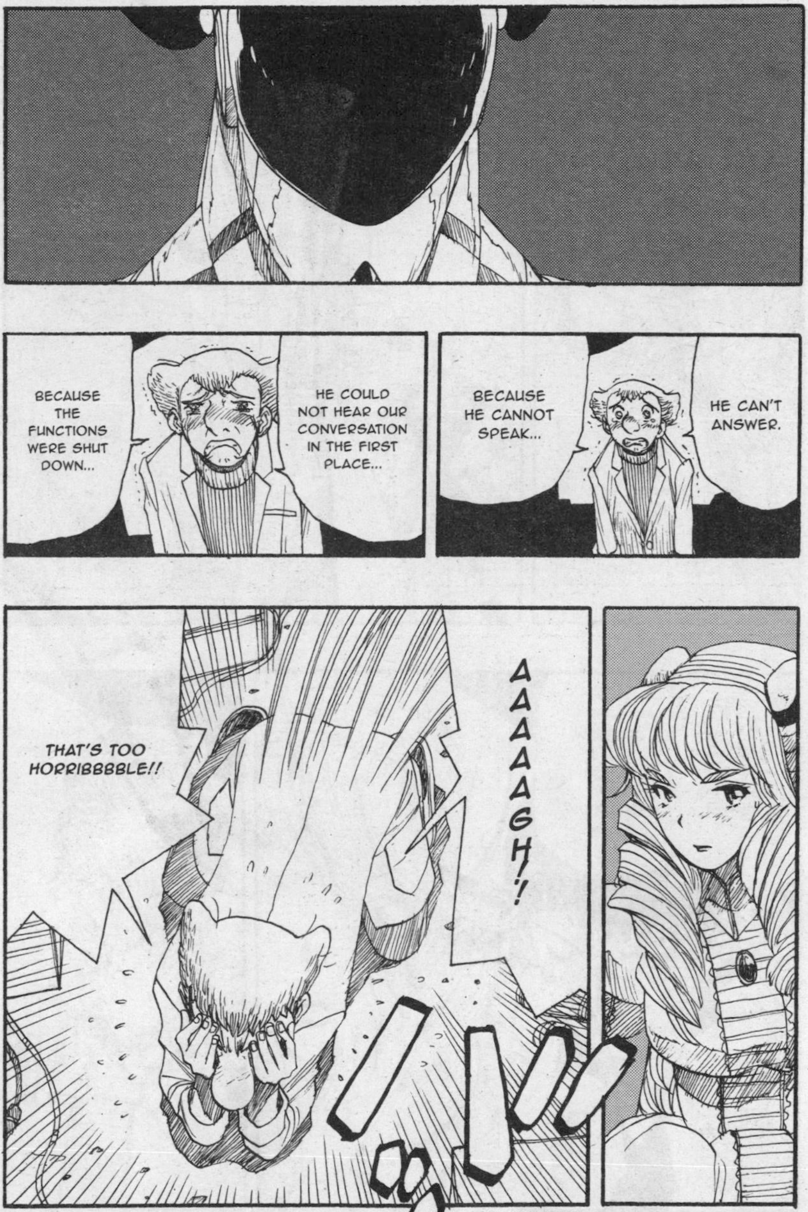
HE CAN'T ANSWER.
BECAUSE HE CANNOT SPEAK...
HE COULD NOT HEAR OUR CONVERSATION IN THE FIRST PLACE...
BECAUSE THE FUNCTIONS WERE SHUT DOWN...
AAAAAAGH!!
THAT'S TOO HORRIBBBBLE!!
*QUICK MOTION

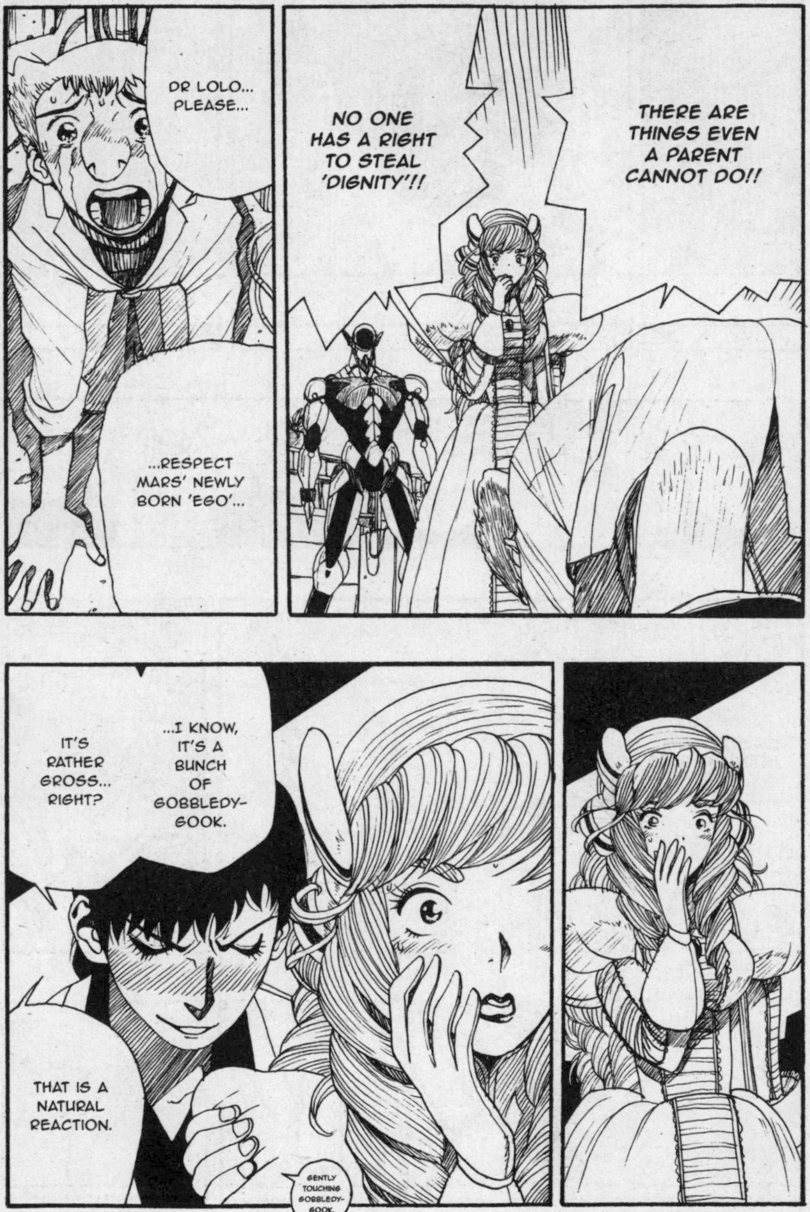
THERE ARE THINGS EVEN A PARENT CANNOT DO!!
NO ONE HAS A RIGHT TO STEAL 'DIGNITY'!!
DR LOLO... PLEASE...
...RESPECT MARS' NEWLY BORN 'EGO'...
...I KNOW, IT'S A BUNCH OF GOBBLEDY-GOOK.
IT'S RATHER GROSS... RIGHT?
THAT IS A NATURAL REACTION.
GENTLY TOUCHING GOBBLEDY-GOOK.

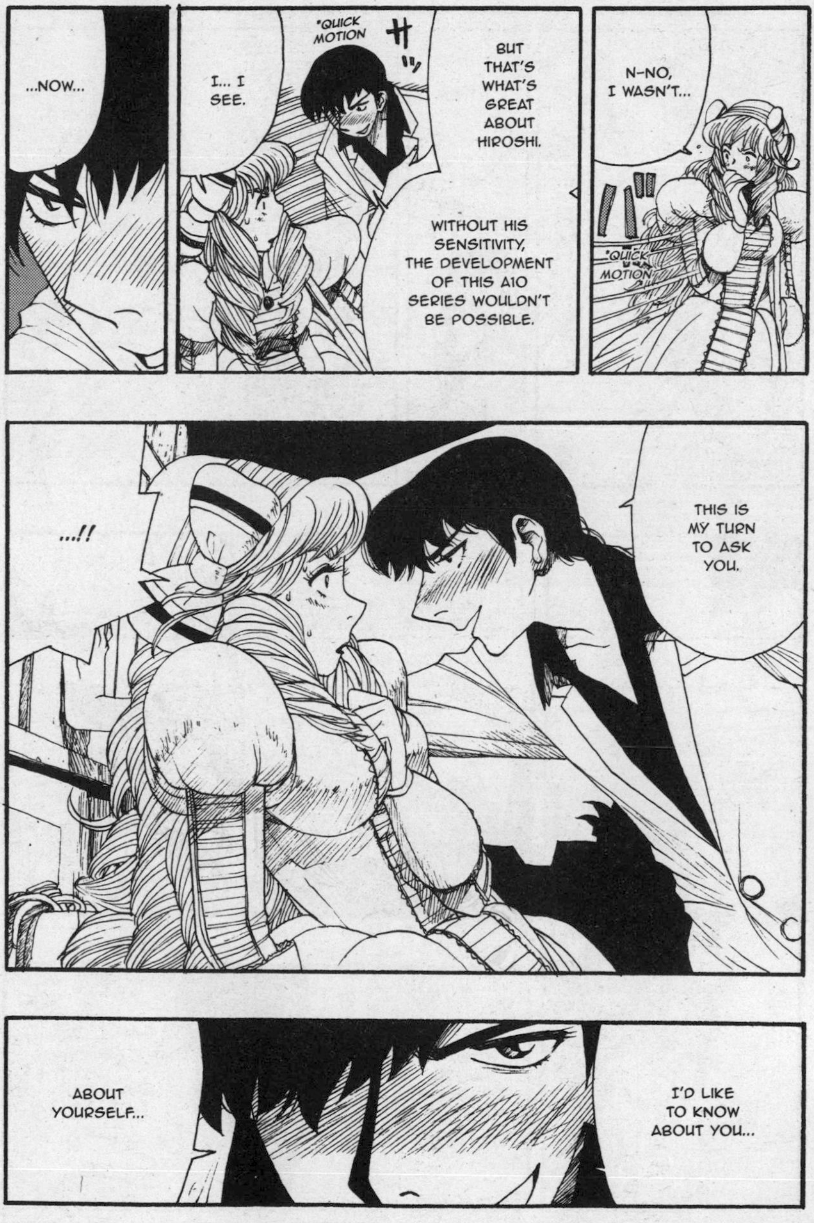
N-NO, I WASN'T...
*QUICK MOTION
BUT THAT'S WHAT'S GREAT ABOUT HIROSHI.
WITHOUT HIS SENSITIVITY, THE DEVELOPMENT OF THIS A10 SERIES WOULDN'T BE POSSIBLE.
*QUICK MOTION
I... I SEE.
...NOW...
THIS IS MY TURN TO ASK YOU.
...!!
I'D LIKE TO KNOW ABOUT YOU...
ABOUT YOURSELF...

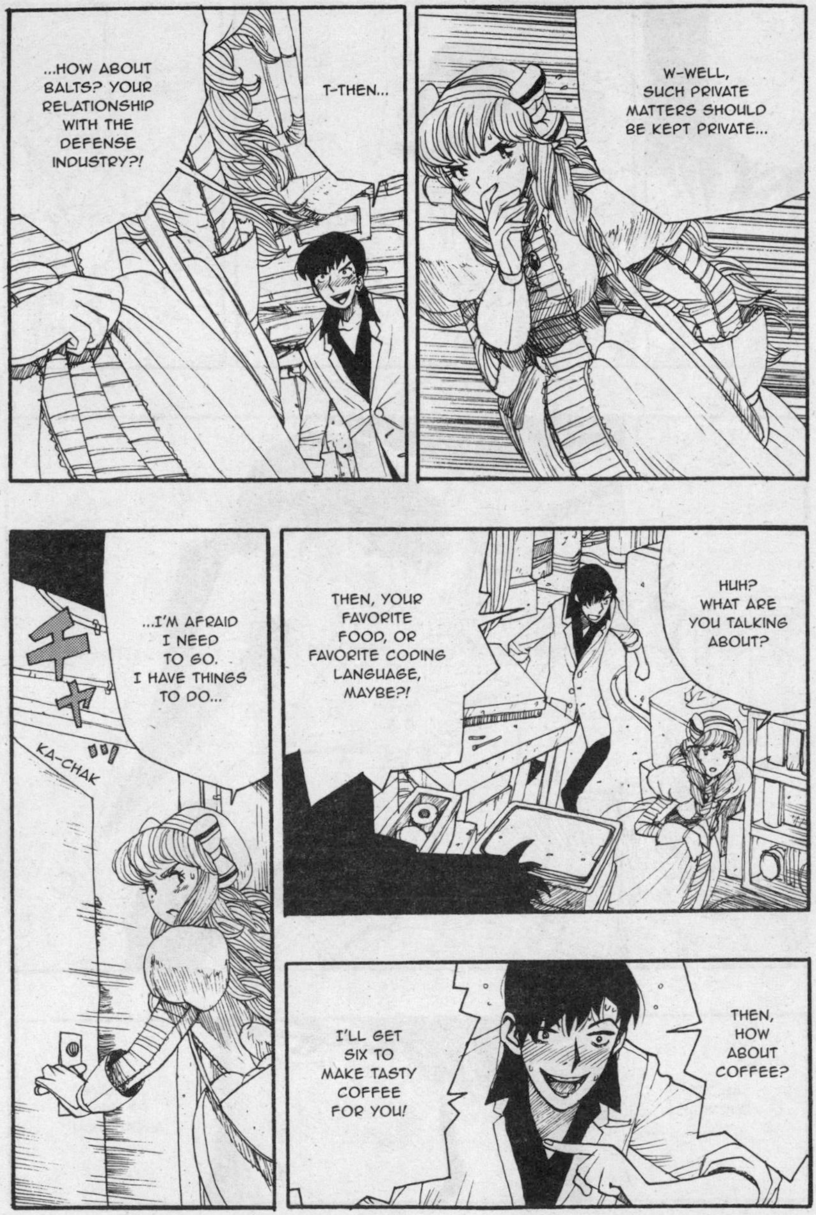
W-WELL, SUCH PRIVATE MATTERS SHOULD BE KEPT PRIVATE...
T-THEN...
...HOW ABOUT BALTS? YOUR RELATIONSHIP WITH THE DEFENSE INDUSTRY?!
HUH? WHAT ARE YOU TALKING ABOUT?
THEN, YOUR FAVORITE FOOD, OR FAVORITE CODING LANGUAGE, MAYBE?!
THEN, HOW ABOUT COFFEE?
I'LL GET SIX TO MAKE TASTY COFFEE FOR YOU!
...I'M AFRAID I NEED TO GO. I HAVE THINGS TO DO...
KA-CHAK

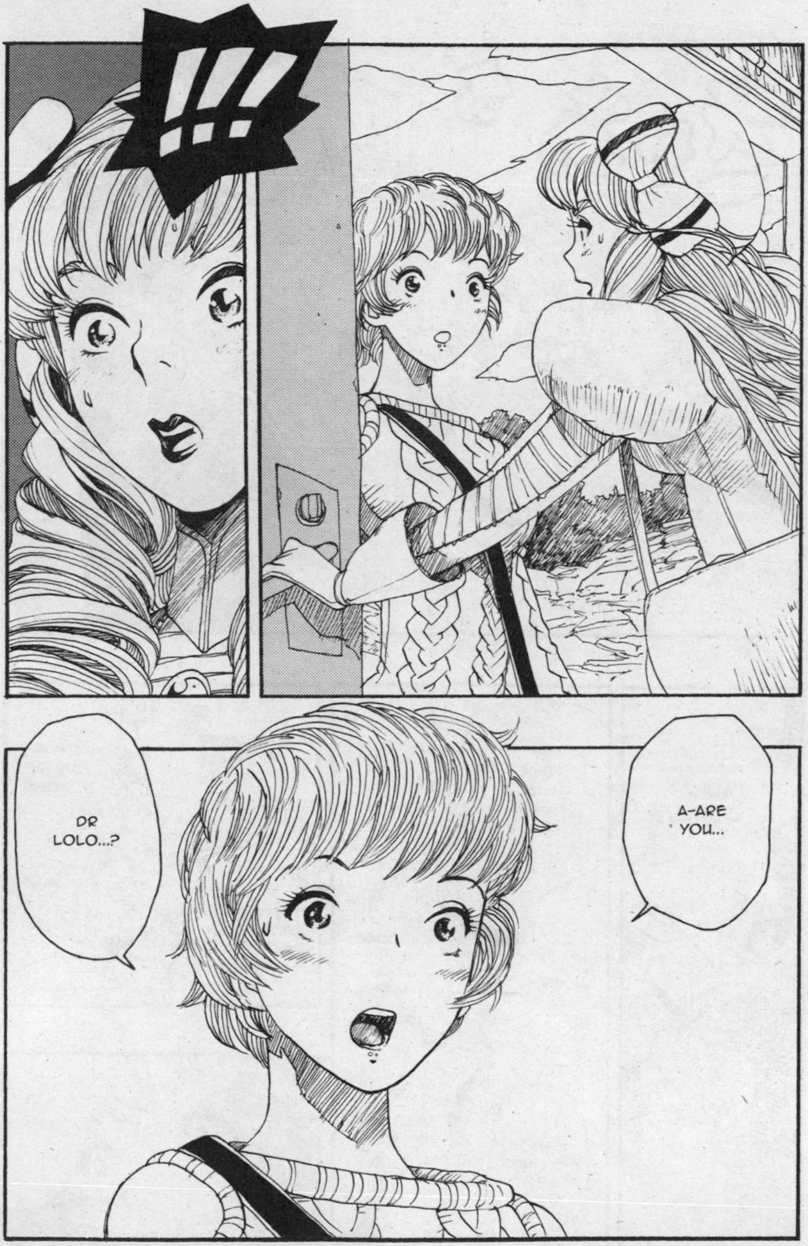
!!?
A-ARE YOU...
DR LOLO...?

AAAAAGH

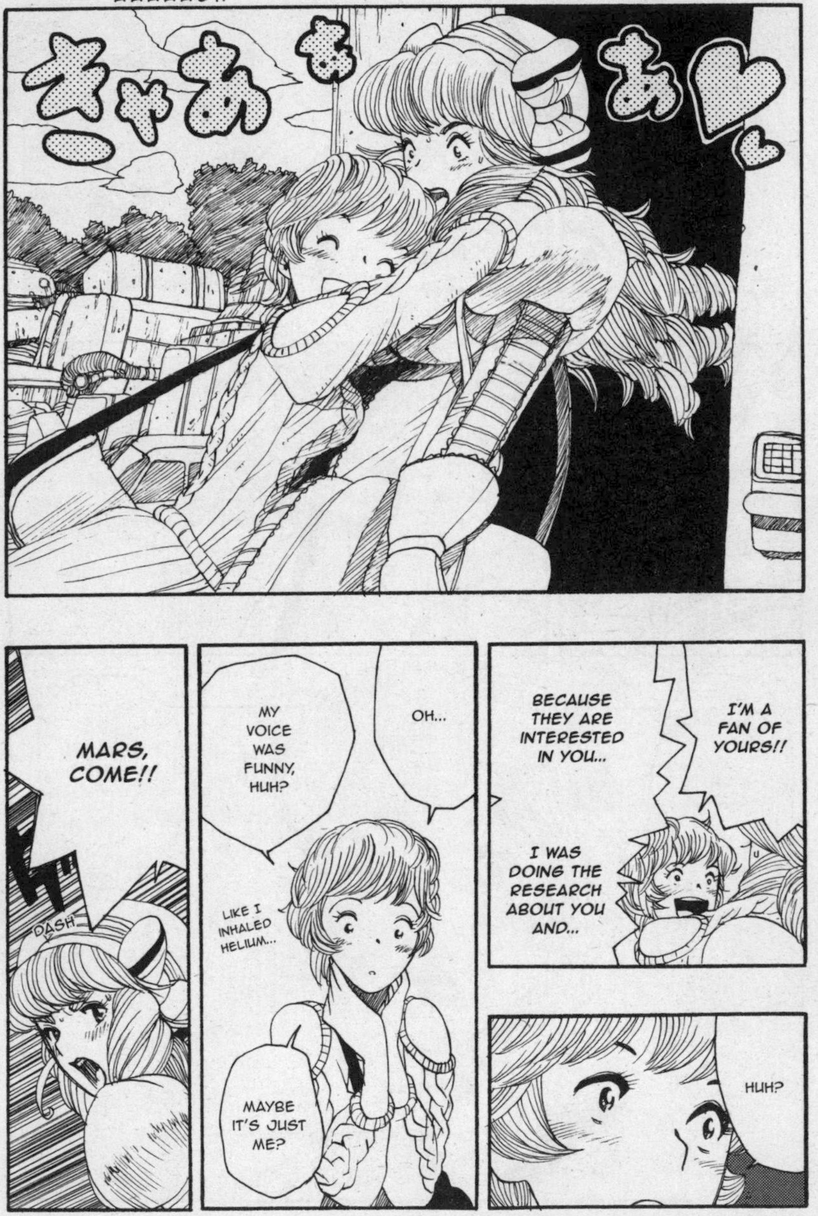

きゃあ〜あ♥
I'M A FAN OF YOURS!!
BECAUSE THEY ARE INTERESTED IN YOU...
I WAS DOING THE RESEARCH ABOUT YOU AND...
HUH?
OH...
MY VOICE WAS FUNNY, HUH?
LIKE I INHALED HELIUM...
MAYBE IT'S JUST ME?
MARS, COME!!
DASH

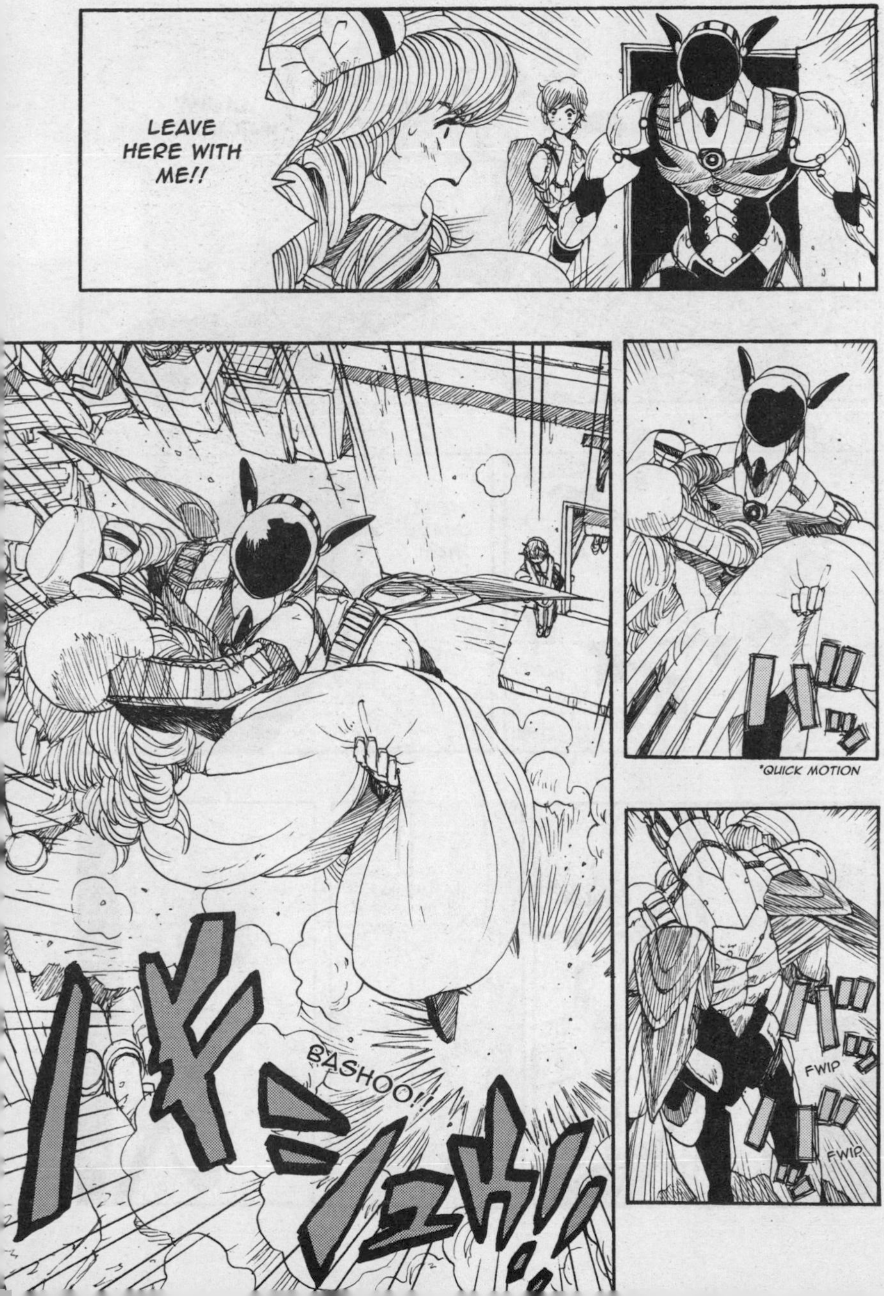
LEAVE HERE WITH ME!!
*QUICK MOTION
FWIP
FWIP
BASHOO!!

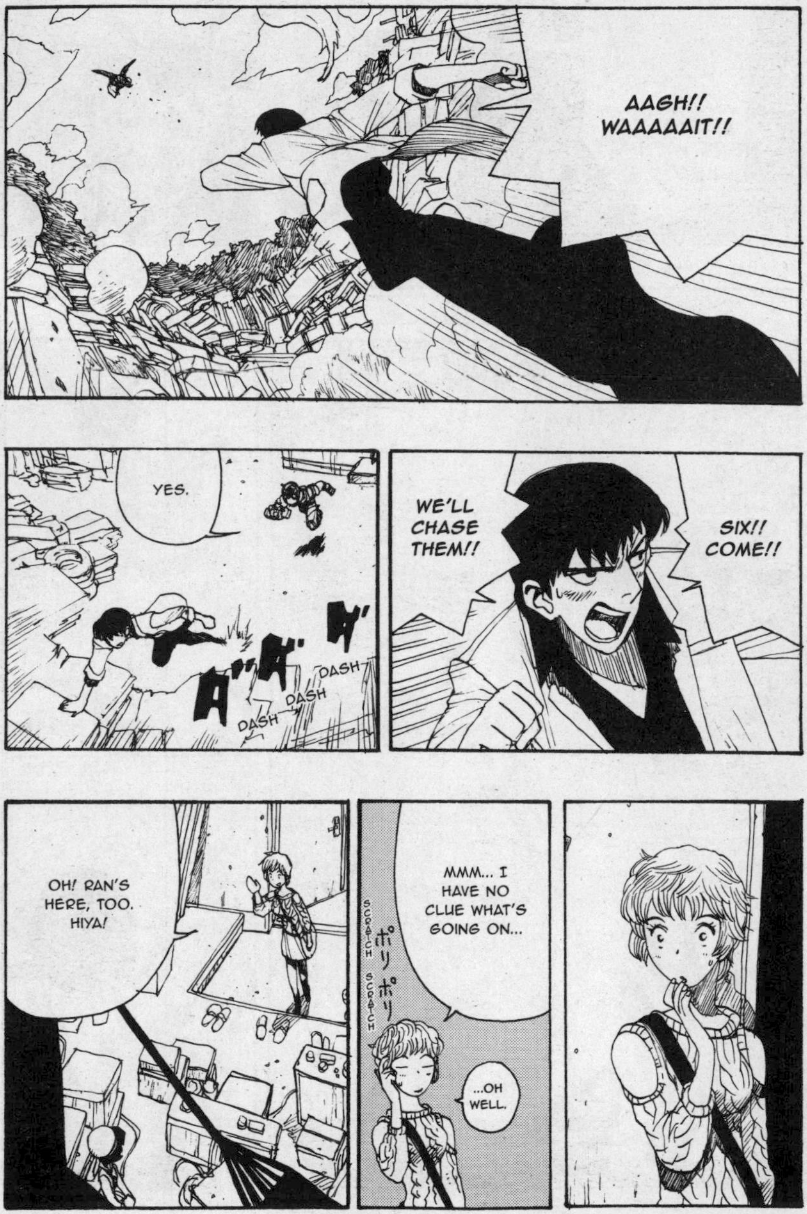
AAGH!! WAAAAAIT!!
SIX!! COME!!
WE'LL CHASE THEM!!
YES.
DASH
DASH
DASH
MMM... I HAVE NO CLUE WHAT'S GOING ON...
SCRATCH SCRATCH
ポリポリ
...OH WELL.
OH! RAN'S HERE, TOO. HIYA!

AWWWW!!

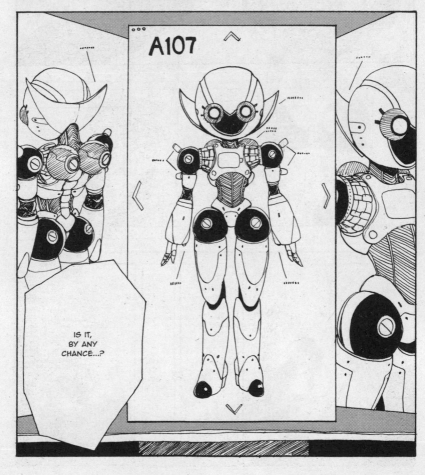

A107

IS IT,
BY ANY
CHANCE...?

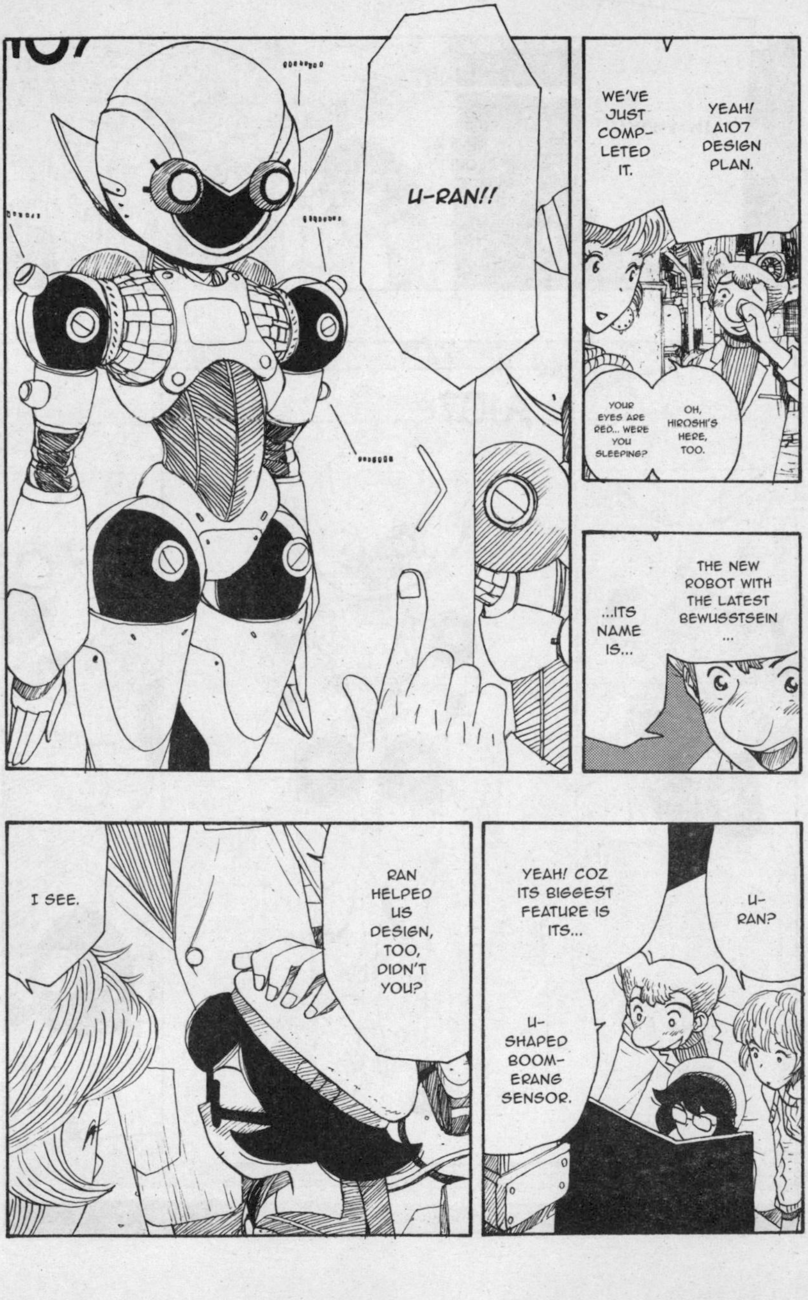
YEAH! A107 DESIGN PLAN.
WE'VE JUST COMP-LETED IT.
OH, HIROSHI'S HERE, TOO.
YOUR EYES ARE RED... WERE YOU SLEEPING?
THE NEW ROBOT WITH THE LATEST BEWUSSTSEIN ...
...ITS NAME IS...
U-RAN!!
U-RAN?
YEAH! COZ ITS BIGGEST FEATURE IS ITS...
U-SHAPED BOOM-ERANG SENSOR.
RAN HELPED US DESIGN, TOO, DIDN'T YOU?
I SEE.

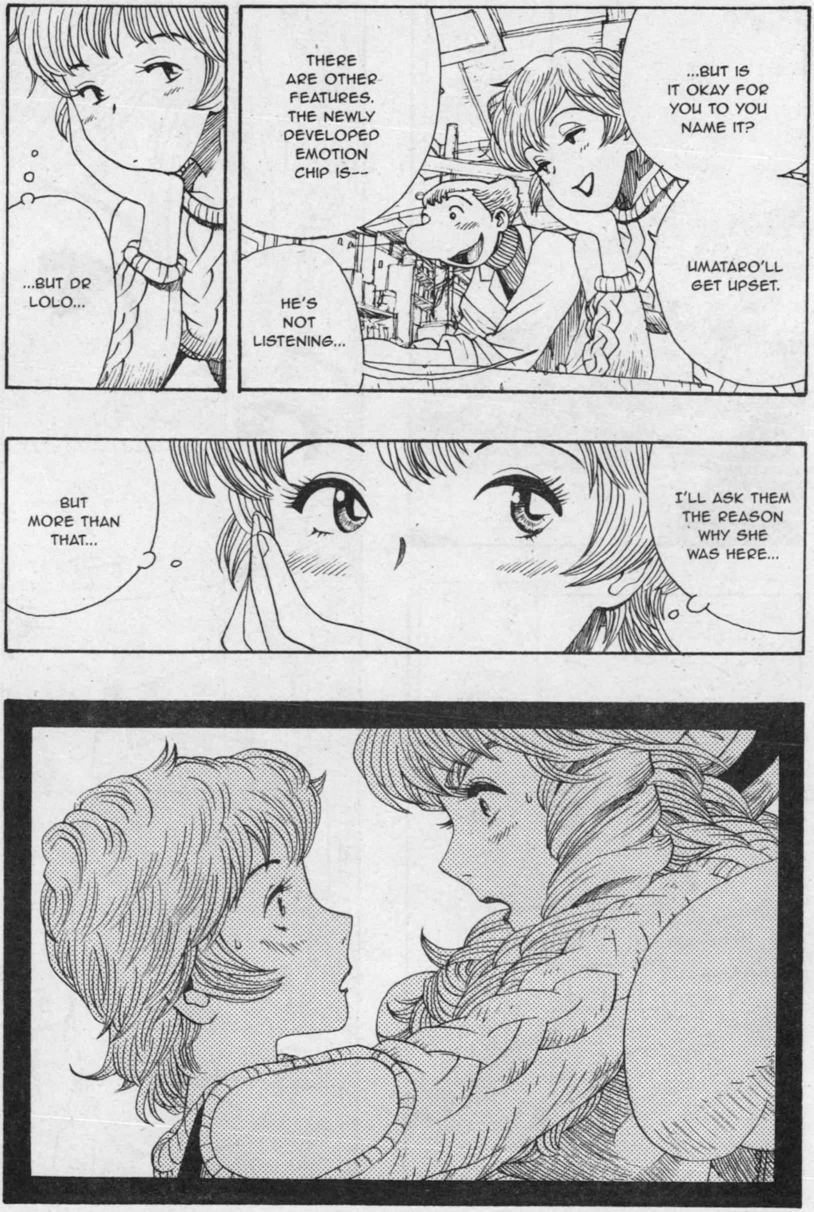
...BUT IS IT OKAY FOR YOU TO YOU NAME IT?
UMATARO'LL GET UPSET.
THERE ARE OTHER FEATURES. THE NEWLY DEVELOPED EMOTION CHIP IS--
HE'S NOT LISTENING...
...BUT DR LOLO...
I'LL ASK THEM THE REASON WHY SHE WAS HERE...
BUT MORE THAN THAT...

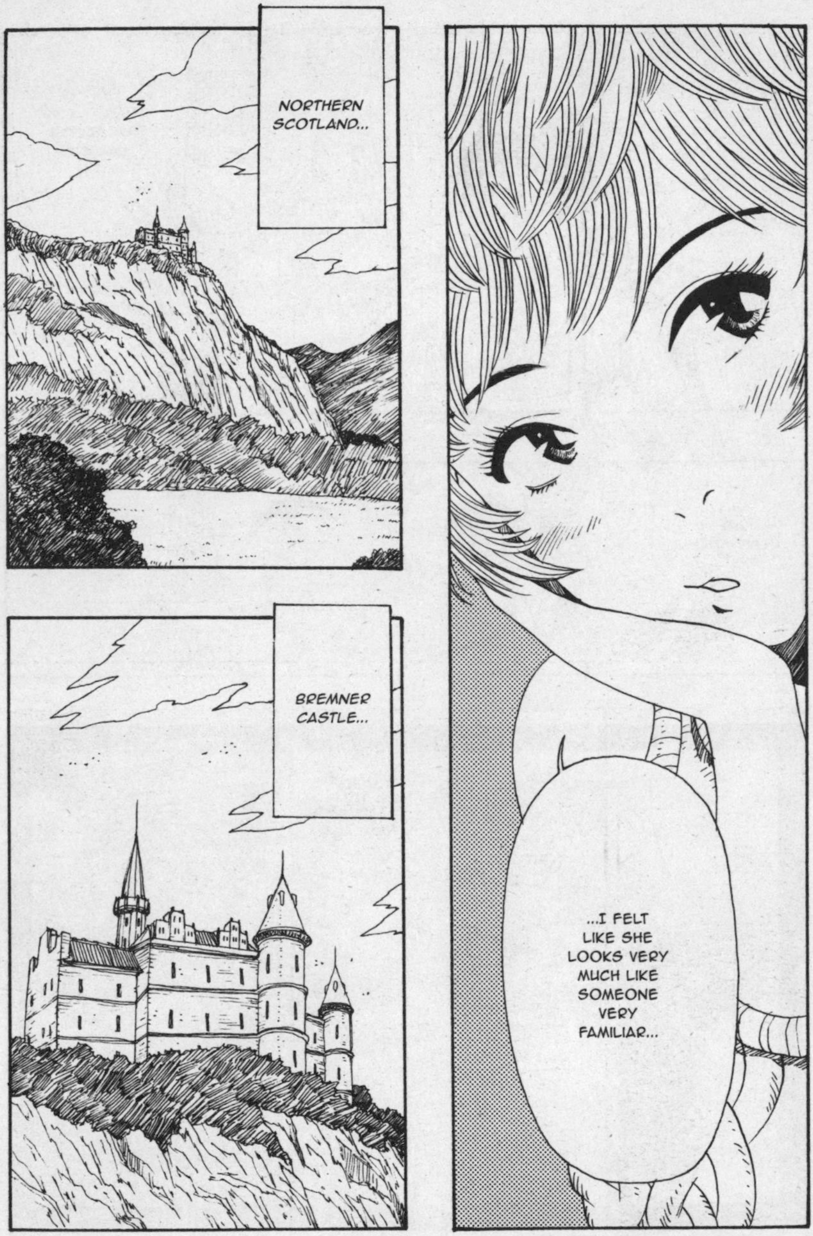
...I FELT LIKE SHE LOOKS VERY MUCH LIKE SOMEONE VERY FAMILIAR...
NORTHERN SCOTLAND...
BREMNER CASTLE...

MR AARON, SIR.
HEY, STEWART. WHAT'S UP?
THE SPECIAL INVITATION TO THE WORLD ROBOT WRESTLING HAS JUST ARRIVED.
WRB... HA! IT'S A TRASHY CEREMONY HOSTED BY DEFENSE COMPANIES.
I'M NOT GOING TO ASSOCIATE WITH THEM! THROW IT OUT.
YES, SIR.
...NO, HANG ON.

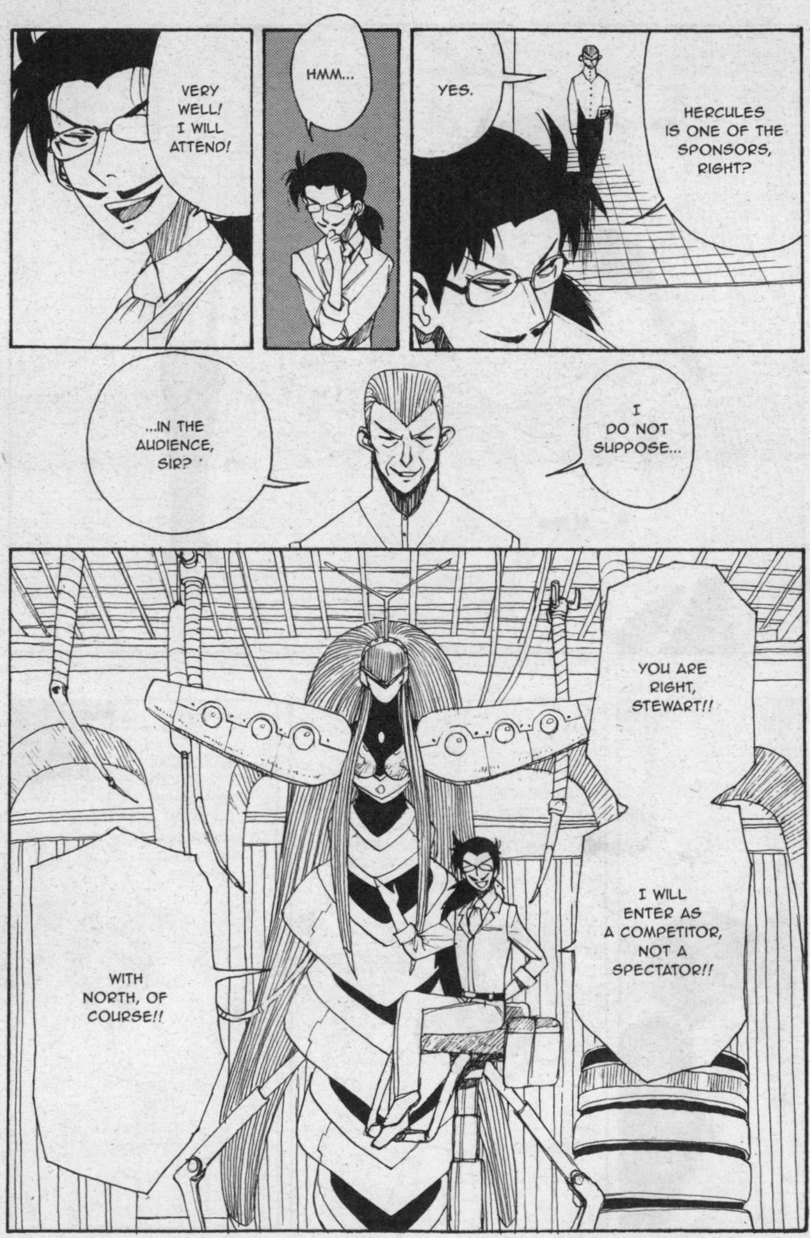
HERCULES IS ONE OF THE SPONSORS, RIGHT?
YES.
HMM...
VERY WELL! I WILL ATTEND!
I DO NOT SUPPOSE...
...IN THE AUDIENCE, SIR?
YOU ARE RIGHT, STEWART!!
I WILL ENTER AS A COMPETITOR, NOT A SPECTATOR!!
WITH NORTH, OF COURSE!!

TO BE CONTINUED IN VOL.5

ATOM: THE BEGINNING VOL. 4: THE END

ATOM
THE BEGINNING
アトム ザ・ビギニング

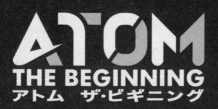

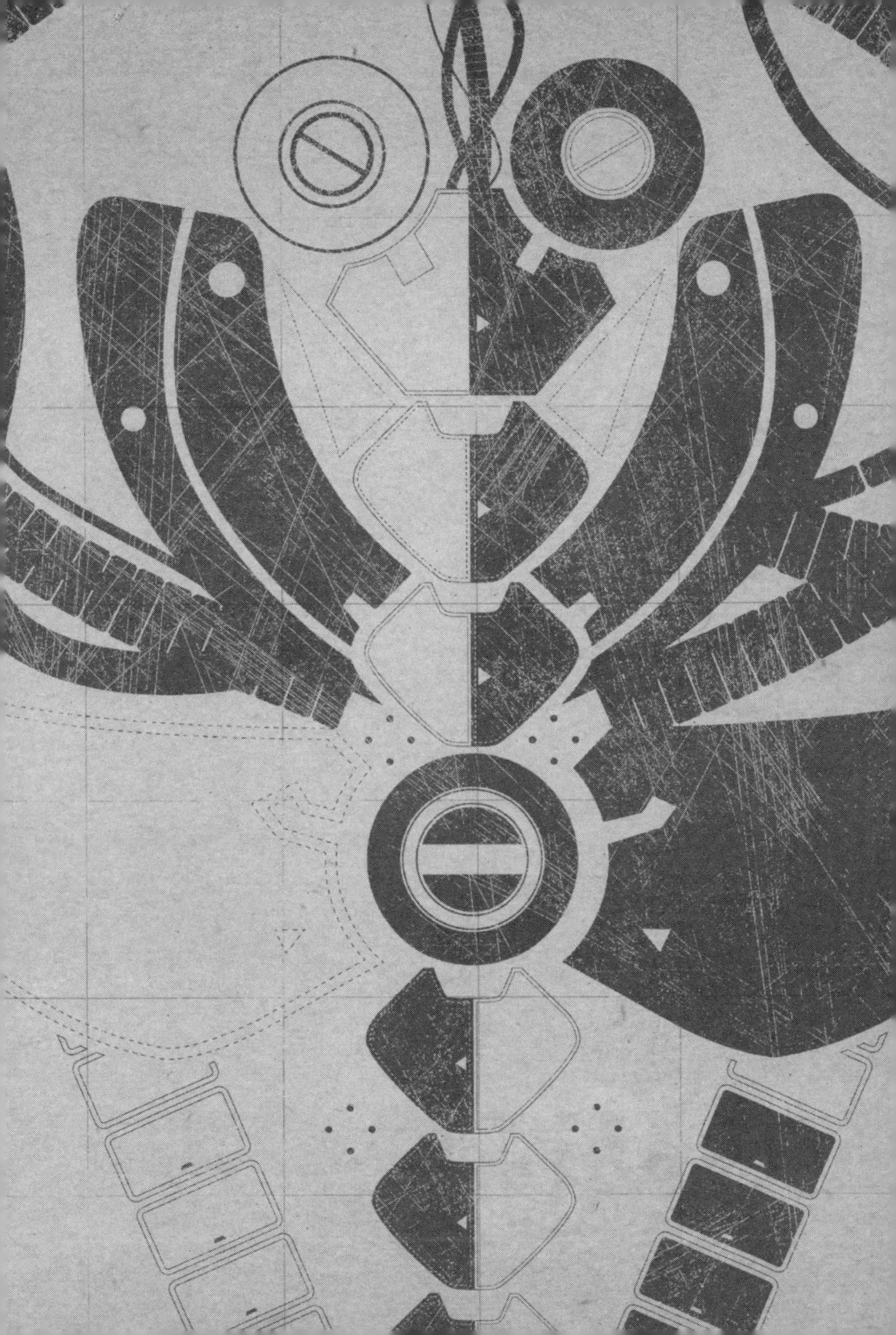

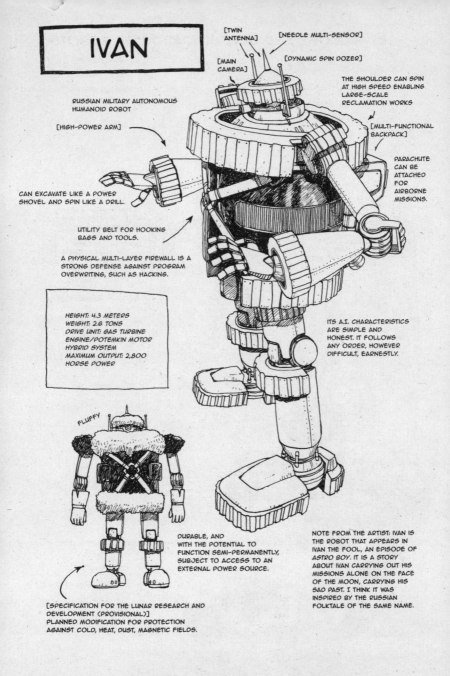

IVAN

RUSSIAN MILITARY AUTONOMOUS HUMANOID ROBOT

[TWIN ANTENNA]
[NEEDLE MULTI-SENSOR]
[MAIN CAMERA]
[DYNAMIC SPIN DOZER]
THE SHOULDER CAN SPIN AT HIGH SPEED ENABLING LARGE-SCALE RECLAMATION WORKS
[HIGH-POWER ARM]
[MULTI-FUNCTIONAL BACKPACK]
PARACHUTE CAN BE ATTACHED FOR AIRBORNE MISSIONS.
CAN EXCAVATE LIKE A POWER SHOVEL AND SPIN LIKE A DRILL.
UTILITY BELT FOR HOOKING BAGS AND TOOLS.

A PHYSICAL MULTI-LAYER FIREWALL IS A STRONG DEFENSE AGAINST PROGRAM OVERWRITING, SUCH AS HACKING.

HEIGHT: 4.3 METERS
WEIGHT: 2.6 TONS
DRIVE UNIT: GAS TURBINE ENGINE/POTEMKIN MOTOR HYBRID SYSTEM
MAXIMUM OUTPUT: 2,800 HORSE POWER

ITS A.I. CHARACTERISTICS ARE SIMPLE AND HONEST. IT FOLLOWS ANY ORDER, HOWEVER DIFFICULT, EARNESTLY.

FLUFFY

DURABLE, AND WITH THE POTENTIAL TO FUNCTION SEMI-PERMANENTLY, SUBJECT TO ACCESS TO AN EXTERNAL POWER SOURCE.

[SPECIFICATION FOR THE LUNAR RESEARCH AND DEVELOPMENT (PROVISIONAL)]
PLANNED MODIFICATION FOR PROTECTION AGAINST COLD, HEAT, DUST, MAGNETIC FIELDS.

NOTE FROM THE ARTIST: IVAN IS THE ROBOT THAT APPEARS IN IVAN THE FOOL, AN EPISODE OF *ASTRO BOY*. IT IS A STORY ABOUT IVAN CARRYING OUT HIS MISSIONS ALONE ON THE FACE OF THE MOON, CARRYING HIS SAD PAST. I THINK IT WAS INSPIRED BY THE RUSSIAN FOLKTALE OF THE SAME NAME.

ETYMOLOGY AND CLASSIFICATION OF ROBOTS

ETYMOLOGY

THE WORD 'ROBOT' WAS SAID TO BE FIRSTLY USED BY KAREL CAPEK, A CZECH WRITER, IN HIS PLAY R.U.R. IN 1920.

THE WORD DID NOT SPREAD TO JAPAN UNTIL AFTER THE WAR.

I GUESS ASTRO BOY'S CONTRIBUTION WAS HUGE.

CLASSIFICATION

ROBOTS IN SCI-FI WORKS CAN BE LARGELY DIVIDED INTO HUMANOID AND NON-HUMANOID.

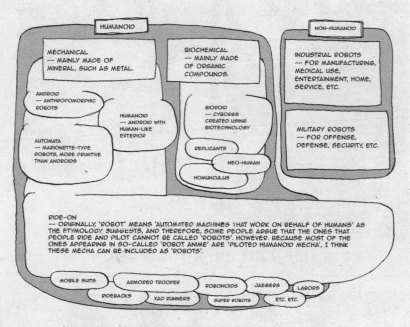

HUMANOID
MECHANICAL
-- MAINLY MADE OF MINERAL, SUCH AS METAL.
ANDROID
-- ANTHROPOMORPHIC ROBOTS
HUMANOID
-- ANDROID WITH HUMAN-LIKE EXTERIOR
AUTOMATA
-- MARIONETTE-TYPE ROBOTS, MORE PRIMITIVE THAN ANDROIDS
BIOCHEMICAL
-- MAINLY MADE OF ORGANIC COMPOUNDS.
BIOROID
-- CYBORGS CREATED USING BIOTECHNOLOGY
REPLICANTS
NEO-HUMAN
HOMUNCULUS
NON-HUMANOID
INDUSTRIAL ROBOTS
-- FOR MANUFACTURING, MEDICAL USE, ENTERTAINMENT, HOME, SERVICE, ETC.
MILITARY ROBOTS
-- FOR OFFENSE, DEFENSE, SECURITY, ETC.
RIDE-ON
-- ORIGINALLY, 'ROBOT' MEANS 'AUTOMATED MACHINES THAT WORK ON BEHALF OF HUMANS' AS THE ETYMOLOGY SUGGESTS, AND THEREFORE, SOME PEOPLE ARGUE THAT THE ONES THAT PEOPLE RIDE AND PILOT CANNOT BE CALLED 'ROBOTS'. HOWEVER. BECAUSE MOST OF THE ONES APPEARING IN SO-CALLED 'ROBOT ANIME' ARE 'PILOTED HUMANOID MECHA', I THINK THESE MECHA CAN BE INCLUDED AS 'ROBOTS'.
MOBILE SUITS
ARMORED TROOPER
ROBONOIDS
JAEGERS
LABORS
RIDEBACKS
XAD RUNNERS
SUPER ROBOTS
ETC. ETC.

*THIS CLASSIFICATION IS A GENERAL IMAGE, NOT AN ESTABLISHED DEFINITION.

...THEN, WHAT SHOULD WE CALL A 'MECHA THAT IS CLOSE TO A HUMAN-SHAPE, BUT NOT QUITE, AND YOU CAN RIDE ON IT BUT IT CAN ALSO ACT AUTONOMOUSLY, AND BIOTECHNOLOGY IS ALSO USED IN PART'?

IN *ATOM: THE BEGINNING*, I CALL EVERYTHING 'ROBOT' BECAUSE OTHERWISE IT'S TOO COMPLICATED.

(TETSURO KASAHARA)

4

STOP!

This manga is presented in its original right-to-left reading format. This is the back of the book!

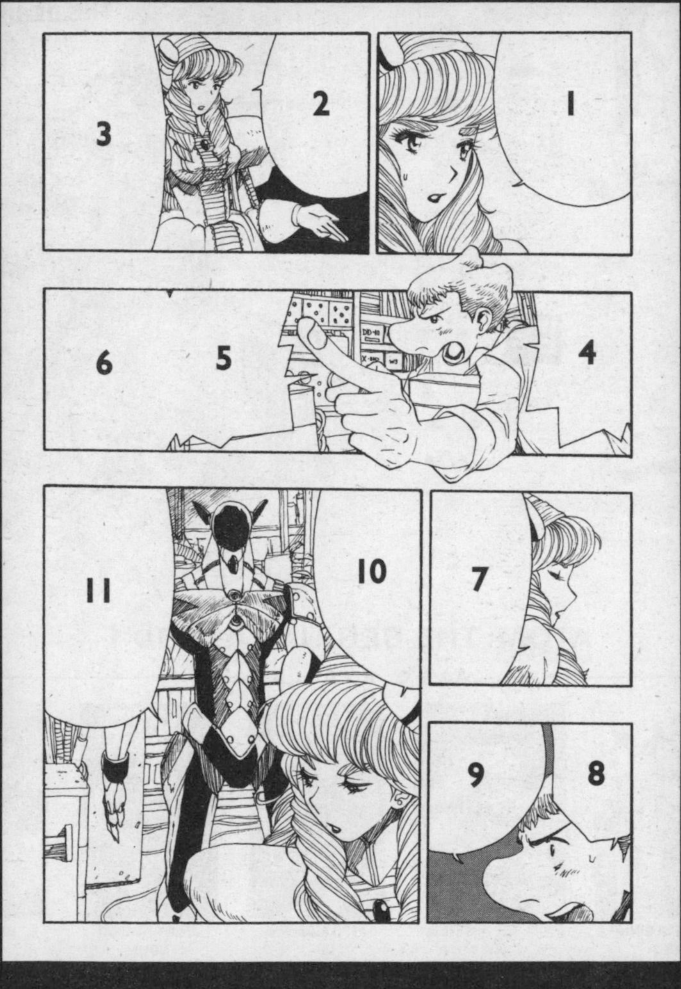
1
2
3
4
5
6
7
8
9
10
11

Pages, panels, and speech balloons read from top right to bottom left, as shown above. SFX translations are placed adjacent to their original Japanese counterparts.